W9-DCL-382

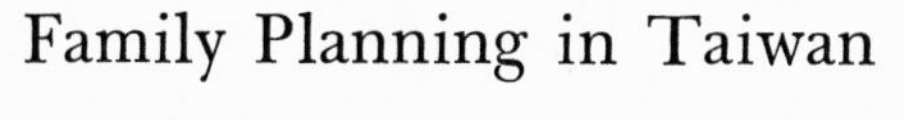

Family Planning in Taiwan

Family Planning in Taiwan

AN EXPERIMENT IN SOCIAL CHANGE

By Ronald Freedman and

John Y. Takeshita

WITH CONTRIBUTIONS BY

L. P. Chow – A. Hermalin

A. K. Jain – C. H. Lee – J. A. Palmore

R. G. Potter, Jr. – T. H. Sun

PRINCETON UNIVERSITY PRESS

PRINCETON, NEW JERSEY

1969

L.C. Card: 68-56309
S.B.N. 691-09345-8

This book has been composed in Baskerville type

Printed in the United States of America
by Princeton University Press
Princeton, New Jersey

Preface

This book is a record of the responses and actions of the young Chinese couples of Taichung. It is based on the work of Chinese health workers and officials who offered family planning services to the couples and cooperated in a program to measure and evaluate the results. Our first and greatest debt is to all these Chinese citizens and leaders of Taiwan, part of whose life and work is described in this book. The list of those to whom we are indebted is so long that we can mention only a few. Dr. S. C. Hsu, chief of the Rural Health Division of the Joint Commission on Rural Reconstruction, has been an inspiring leader of population work in Taiwan from its beginnings. The cooperative relationships with the Taiwan Population Studies Center were made possible by two successive health commissioners, Dr. C. H. Yen and Dr. T. C. Hsu. Dr. J. Y. Peng was Associate Director of the Taiwan Population Studies Center in its earliest days and directed the Taichung action program described in Chapter VI. He was succeeded by Dr. L. P. Chow, Deputy Health Commissioner of Taiwan, whose help and scholarly collaboration extended to coauthorship of several chapters in this volume. Other Chinese who have been especially helpful include: Mr. T. H. Sun, Mr. H. C. Chen, Mr. P.K.C. Liu, Miss Laura Pan Lu, and Mrs. Tessie Huang. We regret that the many others who helped in many ways over the years are too numerous to list.

The Population Council has provided both financial support and technical advice for the work in Taiwan from the beginning. We are indebted especially to Dr. Bernard Berelson for his contribution in sketching the initial design of the Taichung study and his continuing interest in that work. In Taiwan we have been sustained by the wit and wisdom of S. M. Keeny, the Population Council representative, and by assistance from Mr. George Cernada and Mr. Robert Gillespie of the Council staff there.

Our work has also received financial support through grants from the Ford Foundation and the National Institute of Child Health and Development. In addition to those listed as coauthors of chapters in this book, many people at the University of Michigan have assisted and advised on Taiwan projects since we began our work in 1962. While we can do no more than list their names, we are aware of our debt to Beverly Beers, Christine Chang, Vivian Choi, Solomon Chu,

Michael Coble, Mary Coombs, Julia Ann Ericksen, Kay Grossman, Charles Kinderman, P. Mohapatra, Mary Oh, Sylvia Pedraza, Mary Scott, Mary Speare, K. Srikantan, E. Tedesco, Betty Ullman, and Susan Woodburne. We are grateful for the very helpful editorial assistance given to us by Linda Peterson of the Princeton University Press.

The Demography Department of the University of California at Berkeley generously provided office space and other facilities for the work of Dr. Freedman during the period from April to August of 1967.

As is usual, we absolve all of our coworkers from guilt for errors and accept the responsibility for the bad and some fraction of the good in the pages that follow.

R. Freedman
J. Y. Takeshita

Contents

Contents

List of Tables

List of Figures

PART 1. INTRODUCTION

I. The Problem

This is not another abstract tract on the population problem. It is the story of a large-scale effort to do something about the problem in Taiwan. That a "population problem" exists in many countries, and for the world as a whole, is now widely accepted in principle by an increasing number of the world's statesmen and intellectuals. We have moved on to another stage which requires detailed studies of what is done, how, and when. The rhetoric of general policy is still relevant, but action to implement the policy requires a step-by-step analysis of a complex problem in a variety of cultural settings.

An experiment to bring family planning to the people of the major city of Taichung was begun by the Taiwan Provincial Health Department in 1963. At that time this was the largest intensive program for family planning ever carried out for a sizable population in a limited geographical area.[1] The initial success of the Taichung program during its first year led to the extension of the family planning program to the whole island of Taiwan. In several ways Taiwan's program has become a model for those in other countries. As of 1967, when this is being written, there have been many other programs and studies,[2] but Taichung still remains one of the few involving an intensive effort in a significant population unit, with data that permit careful analysis of what happened. The work in Taiwan and Taichung is still widely followed, because it has a longer history than most other programs, with enough documentation to make it possible to analyze both the achievements and the failures in specific terms.

Such experience is valuable, because there are few precedents to guide the increasing number of national family planning programs. The historic fertility declines in the already developed countries were

1 The programs begun earlier in India involved more money and personnel, but these were rather thinly and unevenly dispersed over India's vastly larger area and population.

2 For a review of national programs, see B. Berelson et al., eds., *Family Planning and Population*, Chicago: University of Chicago Press, 1965; *Studies in Family Planning* (a periodical publication of the Population Council, 245 Park Ave., New York); and B. Berelson, "National Family Planning Programs: Where We Stand," *Fertility and Family Planning: A World View*, Ann Arbor: University of Michigan Press, 1969.

not the result of a deliberately organized social effort.[3] The birth rate declines usually followed only after a rather long period of social and economic development which radically altered the traditional role of families in the society and of children in the family. Large numbers of children became less important for gaining and keeping the good things of life, while rising levels of aspiration for each child provided additional motivation for family limitation. Along with social and economic development came large declines in mortality, which further reduced the number of babies needed if the desired number of children were to survive. During the process of development and mortality decline there was considerable population growth in the Western countries, because the decline of the death rate preceded the birth rate decline, usually by 50 years and sometimes by even more. For most countries the decline in the death rate was rather gradual. This sequence of events, producing changes from initially high mortality and fertility to low mortality and fertility, is known as the demographic transition.

Many developing countries are adopting family planning programs precisely because they want to shorten this period of demographic transition. They are unwilling to wait for social and economic development to produce lower birth rates, as it did in the West. First of all, the planners in the developing countries fear that a delay of even forty years between present rapid mortality decline and a later birth rate decline will produce a rate of population growth so high that it will jeopardize their development plans. The death rates of the developing countries have been falling much more quickly and to lower levels than was the case in the earlier histories of the developed countries. This means that rates of population growth have increased rapidly to levels never reached in the West. For example, in Taiwan the death rate fell from about fourteen to five per thousand between 1948 and 1962. Since fertility rates remained high, the annual rate of population growth reached 3.5 per cent in the years betweeen 1951 and 1956. In this respect, Taiwan is not unique. Quite a few developing countries have reached annual growth rates of more than 3 per cent. Even the 2 per cent growth rate already attained by a country like India is quite high in historic terms. The 3.5 per cent growth rate would

[3] For a general discussion of the fertility declines in the West, see R. Freedman, "The Sociology of Human Fertility," *Current Sociology*, Vols. X-XI; and D. V. Glass and D.E.C. Eversley, eds., *Population in History*, Chicago: Aldine Press, 1965.

mean a doubling of the population in only twenty years, if continued that long. Even a 2 per cent growth rate means doubling of the population in thirty-five years. In India a doubling of the population means the addition of 500,000,000 people.

During the period of demographic transition in the West, many families faced new and serious problems as they tried to stretch their meager resources to accommodate the increasing numbers of children surviving. For millennia, high death rates for children had meant that many babies had to be born if a moderate number were to survive. Now an increasing number of women were finding that by the time they reached the age of thirty or so, they had alive all the children they wanted or more. The number of surviving children in many families was too large for housing and various social arrangements worked out over a long period of time on the implicit assumption that many children would die. Faced with the terrible living conditions of the early modern city and the rising aspirations concerning education and living standards, an increasing number of couples began to experiment with ways to solve this problem. Apparently, there was considerable use of illegal induced abortion under very primitive medical conditions.[4] Various methods of contraception, and especially coitus interruptus, were used by increasing numbers of couples to limit family growth, although these methods were often ineffective.[5] Nevertheless, the cumulative result was to produce a declining birth rate, even though families still had more children than they wanted despite their practice of birth control.

The poverty, illness, and suffering which was the fate of millions of families in the period of demographic transition in the West may have been as great as that which characterizes many developing countries today. There is, however, less tolerance today for such conditions, either in the developing societies or in the larger arena of world opinion. The "revolution of rising expectations" is based largely on the increasing awareness everywhere that primordially low levels of living have been left behind for most people in the developed societies.

[4] K. Davis, "The Theory of Change and Response in Modern Demographic History," *Population Index*, 29, No. 4, October 1963, 345-66.

[5] For example, see H. Bergues et al., *La prévention des naissances dans la famille*, Institut national d'études démographiques, Cahiers de Travaux et Documents, 35, Paris: Presses Universitaires de France, 1959; also E. Lewis-Fanning, *Report on an Inquiry into Family Limitation During the Past Fifty Years*, Papers of the Royal Commission on Population, Vol. 1, London: H.M. Stationery Office, 1949.

There is an increasing awareness both among the elites and the masses that higher standards of life can be attained by changing technological, demographic, and social conditions. There is great reluctance to wait for long-run developments to solve social and demographic problems. Besides, there is some doubt whether this would be a viable policy even if it were acceptable. It is possible that high rates of population growth, if continued for even twenty-five years in some societies, might so seriously impede development as to prevent entirely the ascent to higher levels of economic growth and living sought everywhere.

There are some reasons for believing that the slow demographic transition of the West need not be repeated in the newly developing nations. In the first place, the rapidity of the mortality decline which has speeded up the first part of the historic demographic change may also contribute to a more rapid decline in fertility. Secondly, the awareness of the demographic and social history of the West in itself provides a basis for hope, since both the leadership and increasing numbers of the people can base higher levels of aspiration on what has already happened elsewhere.

New forms of contraception provide a third reason for believing that Western demographic history may not provide suitable precedents for the developing countries. In particular, the intrauterine contraceptive device (henceforth designated as IUD) and the contraceptive pill[6] both differ radically from earlier forms of contraception. Neither the IUD nor the pill has any immediate connection with the sex act, and so do not require rational action in a moment of passion. Both methods, and especially the pill when properly used, are highly effective in preventing pregnancy. The IUD requires no continuing supplies, action, or remembering. These characteristics of the new contraceptives may mean that they can be used effectively by couples who are not highly motivated or, at least, by couples whose level of sophistication is not very high. All of the new national family planning programs are now using one or both of these new contraceptives.[7] The

[6] For discussion of the characteristics of various types of contraceptives, see Berelson et al., *op.cit.*, Part 3.

[7] By 1966 the IUD was the principal method being used in the programs of Taiwan, Korea, India, Pakistan, Tunisia, Turkey, and Hong Kong. The contraceptive pill was also being introduced on a small scale in all of these places. It was the principal method in the new Singapore government program. The Malaysian program begun in 1967 is expected to rely mainly on the pill, with secondary emphasis on the IUD.

population of Taichung was one of the first to which the IUD was made available on a mass scale. Whether this new contraceptive makes a distinctive difference is one of the points at issue in the Taichung study.

A fourth departure from the precedents of earlier demographic history is the development of the kinds of large-scale family planning programs which this book describes. Many countries are now experimenting with such programs.

Despite the new elements in the situation, most observers agree that some minimal changes in mortality and in social and economic levels are probably needed to stimulate more extensive practice of birth control and a declining birth rate. Organized family planning programs are no substitute for general social and economic development. However, there is little knowledge of how much change, and in what, is needed to initiate or accelerate a birth rate decline.[8]

There has been a reasonable doubt in many minds as to whether any planned intervention for family planning alone can modify on a mass scale the reproductive behavior and attitudes which are at once so personal and so involved in the important familial institutions. In India, for example, family planning programs had already been underway for years[9] with little visible success when the Taiwan efforts first began. Indian development levels were still low enough and mortality levels still high enough to justify the fears of villagers that having only a few children might mean that none would survive. Was the failure of the early Indian effort due to the inadequacies of the program, to the low development level, or to both? In retrospect, it is easy to point to serious deficiencies in the scale and content of the early Indian program, but it is not possible to say definitely that even an all-out effort using the best available methods would have been successful under Indian social conditions of that time.

Even when there is agreement that some development is a prerequisite, there may be disagreement on whether or not such develop-

[8] How current fertility rates are related to large numbers of development measures is discussed in United Nations, *Population Bulletin*, No. 7, 1963, but this cross-sectional view provides no data on the relationship between changes in development levels and changes in fertility.

[9] The Indian national program was reorganized completely and the scale of the effort greatly increased in the period from 1964 to 1966, but it is too early to evaluate the results.

ment has already occurred.[10] We believe that it is unlikely that family planning programs will have much effect without at least some simultaneous social and economic progress which will decrease dependence on family ties and on numerous progeny.

The most difficult objective for a family planning program is to initiate a fertility decline. It is probably much easier to accelerate a fertility decline that is already underway, because such declines to date have occurred only where there is significant development already, and because the beginning of fertility change in itself indicates a readiness for family planning in some part of the population.

The program in Taiwan and Taichung had this easier task. Following a very rapid mortality decline and considerable social and economic development, the birth rates of Taichung and Taiwan had been declining for a number of years before the establishment of any significant organized effort. In Taichung it was possible to study first of all the factors associated with family limitation and with the birth rate decline which had taken place before the organized program began. The second and principal purpose of the study was to see how these preexisting levels of contraceptive use were affected by the intervention of the family planning program.

Since 1963 we have been receiving the first presumptive evidence from Taiwan, Korea, and several other places in Asia that planned programs can make a difference in reproductive behavior.[11] There has been a significant increase in family planning, and probably also a decrease in the birth rate in several countries. All of these, including Taiwan, have rates and levels of development which place them far above the average for Asia. Therefore, what has happened in these few small countries may not be relevant to some of the larger and less developed countries. Even for the "successful" countries it is important

[10] Donald Bogue presents the viewpoint that the desired minimum change has already occurred in "The Demographic Breakthrough: From Projection to Control," *Population Index*, 30, No. 4, October 1964, 449-53.

[11] The 10 per cent decline in Hong Kong's birth rate between 1965 and 1966 appears to be a result in large part of the IUD program of the Hong Kong Family Planning Association in the period from 1964 to April 1966. The Singapore birth rate decline probably results partly from the significant program of the Singapore Family Planning Association and, in the case of the larger decline more recently, from the new government program. For the data on Taiwan and Korea, see S. M. Keeny, "Korea and Taiwan: The Score for 1966," *Studies in Family Planning*, No. 19, May 1967, 1-7, and R. Freedman, "Taiwan: Births Averted by the IUD Program," *Studies in Family Planning*, No. 20, June 1967, 7-8.

not to attribute to the family planning program changes in behavior which might have occurred anyway as a result of other social changes already underway.

After all these reservations are expressed, it remains important to know that, at least under the favorable conditions found in a place like Taiwan, the changes already underway can be accelerated by planned intervention—or at least that the desired decline and the intervention seem to coincide. After all, it was possible that none of the desired changes would occur.

Whether the experiences of Taiwan can be generalized to apply to other, less favored places is a larger question which requires additional detailed studies in countries varying in culture and in the level of social development. It seems likely that some parts of the Taiwan experience will be applicable elsewhere, at least as far as the methods of evaluation and some of the relationships between social conditions and fertility are concerned.

The possibility that some part of the Taiwan experience may have some general relevance is enhanced if the complexity of the program and the problem are appreciated. Sometimes the prevailing image is that once traditional taboos and policy restrictions are removed, it is a simple matter to bring contraception to couples who are waiting on the doorstep to receive the information and the service they want. Some potential clients are like that. However, even where a large number of couples are under such pressures that they want no more children, many of them need help to define both the nature of their problem and the possible solutions. Even when they come forward to accept information and services they may not use contraception regularly or effectively, because their desired goal of limiting family growth must contend with conflicting traditional values or with fears about the consequences of new behavior. Some of the couples are more ready than others because they have already experimented with some method of restricting family growth. The approach and the result will depend also on the stage of family growth already reached, the literacy of the couples, whether they live in an extended family with their parents, and a host of other factors. It cannot be taken for granted that those who accept family planning from the program will continue with it indefinitely. We know that large numbers do not. It then becomes important to know how many couples continue to use contraception for various periods of time, what affects the rate of termination of use, and what is done about family limitation by those who discontinue. The final questions in every case are what happens to the fertility both of those who continue in the program and of those who discontinue and how this compares with their previous fertility and with that of the couples never in the program at all.

This partial list of the things to be observed in the Taichung program does not mean that more research on all of them is needed before a program of action is begun. Many of the important studies can only be done if the program does proceed on the basis of the best available information. The overall success or failure of the Taichung program may not tell us whether a similar effort will succeed or fail under very different conditions. However, some parts of the detailed experience recorded in this early study are likely to serve as guideposts, if only as warnings against dead-end roads.

THE QUESTIONS TO BE ANSWERED

The Taichung study data provide some partial answers to the following questions:

1. *What were the existing patterns of fertility and family planning before the organized program began?*

a. How many children were wanted and how many were being born; what was the contrast between ideal and reality?
b. What methods of birth control were already in use to reconcile ideal and reality?
c. How did the level of modernization of the couples affect how many children they had and when they had them, how many children they wanted, and what they did to realize this ideal?

2. *How effective was the experimental family planning program?*

a. Was the intensive mass program successful in increasing the numbers practicing contraception, without major political repercussions?
b. How were the results affected by such features of the program as: the new IUD and other traditional contraceptives?—personal visits to wife alone or to both husband and wife?—group meetings of greater or less effectiveness?—varying density and spacing of these different "treatments"?

Some important specific questions to which the experiment was pertinent were:

Can visits to the wife alone accomplish as much as the more expensive visits to both husband and wife?—Can diffusion by word of mouth from an intensive direct approach in a number of well-spaced neighborhoods inform and influence large numbers of people in other neighborhoods?—Does interest in a new method like the IUD diffuse more rapidly than that in traditional methods?

c. How did the social and demographic characteristics of the couples affect the incidence and timing of contraception? Did the program successfully reach significant numbers of the poorer and less educated couples?

d. Did the stated intentions of the couples about adopting family planning indicate a real commitment which was reflected in their later actions?

e. Are acceptance rates affected by informal communications with friends, relatives, and neighbors and by the perception that such informal associates are practicing contraception?

3. *What happens after acceptance?*

a. What determines, for example, how long an IUD is kept in place and why its use is terminated?

b. Once a termination occurs, what is the probability that birth control will be continued by other methods; that is, what is the history of the user rather than of the device?

c. How many births are averted or prevented by entry into the program—either by use of the initial device accepted or by something that is adopted afterwards?

Our answers to these important questions are often inadequate, and some important questions are not answered at all. In retrospect, this is partly a result of our own errors, omissions, and lack of insight. Many of the questions now known to be important were not recognized as problems in Taiwan or elsewhere in 1962. But the limitations of the study also result partly from the unforeseen rapid enlargement of the scale of the Taichung study and the exigencies of a rapidly developing action program which strained the limited personnel resources. This necessitated curtailing or abandoning some desirable research activities. Therefore, this volume does not contain the optimal closely integrated and logical sequence of evidence and investigation. However, since we know of no other analysis that approaches more closely the desired definitive treatment, we present what we have as a partial guide for better studies in Taiwan and elsewhere. A brief history of how the Taichung study developed may indicate some of the sources of its limitations.

A CAPSULE HISTORY OF THE TAICHUNG STUDY

Even before the Taichung study began there were organized family planning activities in Taiwan, including some research.[12] From 1954 to 1959 the China Family Planning Association, a small voluntary agency, carried on a small program based on the traditional contraceptives available then. Like the efforts of most private family planning groups of that period, this activity was probably more important in increasing awareness of the possibility of family planning than for the direct services it rendered.

From 1959 to 1962 the Taiwan Provincial Maternal and Child Health Institute included as part of its health activities what was euphemistically named the Pre-Pregnancy Health Program (PPH). The necessity for a euphemism is an indication of the official climate of opinion at that time. The PPH program, based on traditional contraceptives and door-to-door visits by a single family planning worker in each township, eventually reached into about 100 of the 361 townships in Taiwan. It is estimated that nearly 44,000 women received contraceptive information and supplies in this program. Undoubtedly it further increased the level of awareness about contraception and its legitimacy. It served as the training ground for many of the important workers in the subsequent large-scale efforts.

By 1961 several key Chinese health officials, and especially Dr. S. C. Hsu of the Joint Commission for Rural Reconstruction, felt that a larger effort was desirable and feasible. Support was obtained from the Population Council for pilot projects that would test both a more intensive field program and the acceptability of the new IUD. Arrangements were made for the University of Michigan Population Studies

[12] The following are illustrative of the research during this early period: S. C. Hsu, L. P. Chow, and T. K. Shu Kan, "Field Study on the Effectiveness of Various Contraceptive Methods in Taiwan," *The Taiwan Public Health Journal*, 1, No. 2, June 1961, 64-75; and J. Y. Peng, "Some Observations on the Use of Intra-Uterine Contraceptive Rings in Taiwan (China)," *Proceedings of the New York Conference on Intra-Uterine Contraceptive Devices*, April 30-May 1, 1962, pp. 49-52.

Center to provide consultation for the Taiwan Population Studies Center, created in 1962 in association with the Taiwan Provincial Health Department to conduct the necessary research.[13]

In 1962 no one proposed an effort large enough to cover a large city like Taichung. The initial plans were for intensive pilot programs in one or two sections of the city, and perhaps also in a few village areas scattered over the island. A sample survey covering the city of Taichung was planned to measure knowledge, attitudes, and practice, but initially this was not seen as the bench mark for a city-wide program. It was intended to provide research findings that could be used in general educational and informational programs. The public relations aspects of such a study were considered important.

Taichung, with a population of about 325,000, was selected as the site of the first project for several reasons. It was large enough to accommodate studies on several levels, it was the home base of the health personnel who would conduct the studies, and it was far enough from Taipei to escape some of the political problems that might be expected in that international center.

There was an imaginative escalation of the planned programs only after the rather unexpected success of small-scale pilot action projects and pre-test surveys late in 1961 and early in 1962. In small trials the IUD was found to be highly acceptable both to the medical staff and to the population being served. Small pilot surveys found that the overwhelming majority of both husbands and wives approved of family planning and wanted to learn more about it. A large number of couples wanted no more children. Many were already trying to practice birth control, but the methods were often ineffective, harmful,

[13] The staff of the Taiwan Population Studies Center has been almost entirely Chinese from the very beginning. During the years 1962-64, Dr. John Y. Takeshita and Dr. R. Freedman of the University of Michigan were actively involved in planning the research, with Dr. Takeshita a continuous resident as Associate Director of the Taiwan Center. At this time Dr. J. Y. Peng was the Associate Director actively in charge of the Taiwan program. By July 1964 the Taiwan Population Studies Center was completely under Chinese direction, with Dr. L. P. Chow assuming the role of the Associate Director and Dr. T. C. Hsu, the Health Commissioner, as Director. Since 1964 the Michigan Center has provided research consultation. A very significant continuing role has been played throughout these years by Dr. S. C. Hsu of the Joint Commission on Rural Reconstruction, who helped to found and to arrange continuing support of the Taiwan Center and the various action programs. Dr. Bernard Berelson of the Population Council was closely involved in consultation about the design of the Taichung study.

and too late. The obvious popular interest and demand, as well as the fact that no significant technical or political problems developed in these pilot phases, were the basis for increasing significantly the scale of the program. Only in July 1962 was the decision made to project the pilot study on a much wider area, to cover all of Taichung and to use a large experimental design which might test a number of important questions. This is the experiment described in detail in Chapter VI.

The intensive city-wide sample survey was now seen for the first time as a bench mark for the city-wide program, to provide the information about fertility and family planning before the experiment.[14] This intensive pre-program survey is the basis for the analysis in Chapters II through V of the situation as it existed before the experiment.

At the same time, plans were made for a less intensive Household Survey with a larger sample, as an integral part of the action program. One part of the design of the experiment involved visits to every household with a married woman of childbearing years (under 40) in the 854 neighborhoods receiving the intensive program, which came to be called the "Everything" treatment because all the households in these neighborhoods received all the stimuli of the program.[15] The more than 11,000 women visited in this way were interviewed briefly about a few salient background facts and about whether they intended to accept contraception in the program. Since the 854 "Everything" neighborhoods were a probability sample of all the 2,389 neighborhoods in the city, the 11,000 women interviewed were a good sample of all the women in the city so far as their background characteristics were concerned. They were not necessarily representative in their intentions and their acceptance of the program, since these were affected by the more intensive program in their neighborhoods.

Another set of data was provided by the records kept at the clinics when women came there for the services offered. Apart from medical histories, the data included answers to the Household Survey questions obtained from all acceptors at the clinics who lived outside of the "Everything" neighborhoods.

Still another investigation, known as the Medical Follow-Up, was designed to collect data periodically from all women who had an IUD insertion in the program clinics. The principal purpose was to check

[14] For details about the methodology of the studies see Appendix I-3.

[15] See Chap. VI for the details of the experiment.

on whether medical complications developed, but of equal importance was the data collected on how long the IUD was retained, on reasons for termination, on complaints and other problems, and on fertility and family planning practice after termination.

Finally, plans were also made to collect data from the population register on the characteristics and fertility of the couples living in each of the 2,389 neighborhoods.

Understandably, the sizable increase in the scale and the complexity of both the program and research efforts put a considerable strain on the small number of experienced professional personnel with pertinent experience. They had to recruit inexperienced personnel and train them on short notice. Not everything went according to plan. Changes required as the program developed sometimes threw askew plans developed on plausible assumptions which, in retrospect, turned out to be incorrect.

The program was planned to begin early in 1963 and to run for about nine months, with intensive surveys immediately preceding and following the action effort. The pre-program Intensive Survey was carried out from October 1962 through January 1963. The intensive action effort ran from about February through September 1963. The post-program Intensive Survey was conducted during the last three months of 1963.

The success of the action program was so evident from preliminary running counts of results that a decision was made before the action phase of the experiment was completed to begin expanding the program to an island-wide basis by early 1964. While this island-wide effort added new areas only gradually, it necessarily resulted in the shifting of most of the personnel and resources concentrated in Taichung to the larger task. This also meant that other large cities and the rest of Taiwan quickly lost their value as controls for the Taichung effort, since the experimental stimuli were diffused rather quickly to other places in ways that were impossible to sort out.

Considering the rapid rise of the program level first in Taichung and then in Taiwan, the local personnel did remarkably well in keeping reasonably close to the initial program and research designs. However, there were significant shortcomings, which will be described in connection with the relevant analyses. We illustrate here with a few examples:

1. Some analyses required the matching of clinic and interview records for those couples who were acceptors and who were also included in one of the interview samples. This was successfully done in most cases, but the match could not be made if the women moved out of the neighborhoods in which they were living when interviewed.
2. After the intensive post-program interview only those women who had an IUD inserted were followed up. This means that no data are available on the contraceptive practices of the rest of the population after the 1963 post-program Intensive Survey. At that time most birth control practice was still outside the official program. We do not know precisely how this was changed after 1963.
3. While those aspects of the Medical Follow-Up done in the clinic were carefully supervised, the field interviews for this part of the study were not supervised initially by the experienced staff of the Taiwan Population Studies Center. The result was that the information available from the field interviews was rather limited, especially for those who did not return to the clinic because they had stopped using the IUD. In part this is the wisdom of hindsight, since the relatively high level of terminations of IUD use was not anticipated at the beginning, and the significance of detailed IUD follow-up studies was appreciated only in 1965-67.

These shortcomings are illustrative of problems that we see in retrospect. Some of them could have been avoided with greater wisdom. Some were almost inevitable, given the requirements of a large-scale program on a sensitive problem with changing requirements and personnel and few precedents. Despite these deficiencies, the data provide an unusually detailed picture of the correlates and consequences of a family planning program.

TAIWAN'S POSTWAR DEVELOPMENT: BACKGROUND FOR POPULATION CHANGE

Since World War II Taiwan has had the kind of rapid social and economic development generally regarded as favorable to, if not necessary for, fertility decline. After an initial period of postwar dislocation extending to about 1952, favorable development trends began in many aspects of the society, slowly at first and then with considerable acceleration in the recent years, when fertility, too, began to decline. The result is that by almost any measure of social and economic development, Taiwan ranks far above the average level for Asian countries. While we do not know just what rate or level of development is necessary or optimal for fertility decline, Taiwan is clearly in a relatively favorable position whether with respect to the rate of change or the levels attained.

The postwar economic progress of Taiwan is very impressive. According to an exhaustive review of the situation by Jacoby, between 1951 and 1965 Taiwan "maintained a higher rate of economic growth than any other country in East Asia except Japan. . . . Despite one of the highest rates of population growth in the world, Taiwan's per capita Gross National Product increased at the astonishing annual compound interest rate of 4.2 per cent a year, exceeding that of any other Asian country except Japan. By 1965 the level of living in Taiwan was characteristic of a semi-advanced country. This impressive result was achieved despite an average growth of population of 3.3. per cent a year."[16]

This is not the place for a detailed review of Taiwan's economic development. Data on various aspects of economic and social change are presented in Table I-1. We will only list here in a summary way some of the important indicators of this economic change. There was a large increase in:

Gross National Product per capita
Industrial production, especially in the private sector
Agricultural production, total and per capita
Capital formation
Investment and savings
Production of electric power
Percentage of the GNP derived from non-agricultural sources

In 1965 the United States government discontinued its economic aid program in Taiwan, because both the United States and the Chinese governments believed that Taiwan had reached the point at which it could maintain economic growth on its own. According to Jacoby, "The fruits of this economic progress were widely diffused throughout Taiwan. . . . Output and productivity rose steadily in nearly all branches of agriculture and industry. . . . Progress was general . . . in the country and the cities. . . . All economic groups—farmers,

[16] N. Jacoby, *U.S. Aid to Taiwan*, New York: Frederick Praeger, 1966, p. 85.

Table I-1. Indicators of Economic and Social Development for Taiwan, 1952-1964[a]

Indicators	1952	1956	1960	1964
Economic indicators				
Gross National Product (GNP) index[b]	100	135	178	239
Agricultural production index	100	127	154	197
Total industrial production index	100	155	245	422
Private industrial production index	100	187	316	582
Capital formation index	100	142	234	302
Electric power production index	100	158	255	419
Production of electrical equipment and appliances	100	453	996	2343
Per cent of GNP derived from industry	--	36	43	55
Per cent of male labor force over 11 in non-agricultural occupations	44	45	49	50
Education indicators				
Per cent of population 11 and over who completed primary school:				
males	53	55	62	67
females	28	31	38	45
Communication and transportation indicators				
Daily newspaper circulation per 1000	28	40	55	70
Radios per 1000 families	34	105	350	555
Postings of domestic letters per capita	7	17	33	32
Long distance calls per capita	0.6	0.9	1.3	1.7
Daily intercity bus and train trips per 1000 population	55	87	107	103
Health indicators				
Death rates per 1000	10	8	7	6
Life expectancy for males	51	59	61	64
Population per doctor	1610	1537	1553	1520

[a] The sources for the data in this table and some discussion of them are in Appendix I-1.

[b] Base for all index numbers is 1952.

villagers, industrial workers, professional personnel, civil servants and business enterpriser—benefitted from marked increases in levels of living. Taiwan did not exhibit evidence of the economic and social dualism found in many developing countries. There was no division of the economy into a capital-poor, technically primitive, landlord-ridden, rural sector and a progressive and prosperous urban sector. . . . One fact is indisputable. Compared with most semi-developed countries,

Taiwan was freer of abysmal disparities in scale of living between rich and poor at the end of the aid period, as well as at the beginning."[17]

One of the most important means of diffusing widely the influence and benefits of the development effort was a successful land reform program, which changed the proportion of farm families who were tenants from 41 in 1947 to 13 in 1963.

Apart from these economic changes, there have been other significant social changes which may be especially important for family life and fertility. The educational level is rising rapidly for both men and women. The proportion of women 12 or older with at least a primary school education increased from 28 to 45 per cent between 1952 and 1965. Since these figures include all the older women who passed the schoolgoing ages before the war, they do not reflect adequately recent changes. The rise in the educational level for women of childbearing years is indicated by the following comparison of the percentage distribution by education of women 20-24 and 45-49 in 1965:

	20–24	*45–49*
Less than primary school graduation	34	75
Primary school graduation	47	18
Junior high school graduation	10	3
Senior high school graduation	9	4
Total	100%	100%

Increases in communication and interaction with people outside of the local family and community are probably one of the most important signs of modernization. The traditional society tends to be local and immobile, but Taiwan has been moving toward larger areas and populations in interaction. Some indications of this are rapid increases in:

The circulation of newspapers
(from 28 per 1,000 population in 1952 to 70 in 1965)

Long-distance telephone calls
(from 0.9 per capita in 1952 to 1.9 in 1965)

Written communications by mail
(from 7 per capita in 1952 to 30 in 1965)

[17] *Ibid.*, p. 101-2.

Intercity travel by bus and train
(from 55 daily trips per 1,000 in 1952 to 103 in 1964)
Ownership of radios
(from 34 per 1,000 families in 1952 to 555 in 1964)
Number of motor vehicles (including motor cycles)
(from 7 per 1,000 families in 1951 to 45 in 1963)
Number of bicycles
(from 344 per 1,000 families in 1952 to 908 in 1963)

Changes in the field of health are also particularly important, because reductions in child mortality decrease the number of children that must be born if the desired number are to survive. Following the eradication of malaria and the reduction of some other serious health risks,[18] the death rate in Taiwan fell from 14 to 6 between 1948 and 1965. Life expectancy increased from about 51 in 1952 to 64 in 1964. Even in 1952 the supply of medical personnel was relatively good by Asian standards, and the situation has improved since then. While such mortality declines and health gains do not necessarily enter into a conscious calculus of family planning, a large proportion of Taiwanese women have indicated on surveys that they know that their children have a much higher chance of surviving to adulthood than the children of the previous generation.

Taiwan's progress on this broad array of development measures has brought it to a level far above the average for Asia. If we exclude Japan as already developed, and Singapore and Hong Kong as unique city-states, Taiwan ranks very high among Asian countries when judged by the variety of measures assembled in Table I-2. By every criterion considered, it is above the average for ten Asian countries. Even before the recent spurt in its economic growth, Taiwan ranked first or second on three of the six measures, and above average on the other three. If a high rate or level of development is conducive to changes in fertility and family planning practice, Taiwan appears to be ready.

[18] For a brief history of health developments in Taiwan, see C. H. Yen, "A Forty-Year Review of Programs in Public Health in Taiwan, China," a paper presented at the 10th Pacific Science Congress in Hawaii, August 1961, 18 pp., and T. C. Hsu, "Ten Year Health Plan for Taiwan," *Journal of the Formosan Medical Association,* 64, No. 4, April 1965, 183-211.

Table I-2. Indicators of Social and Economic Development, Taiwan, Other Asian Countries, and the United States, (1960-1964)[a].

Countries	Gross National Product per capita (U.S. dollars) (1963)	Percentage economically active in agriculture (both sexes)	Circulation of daily newspapers per 1000 population	Percentage of females over 15 literate	Domestic letters posted per capita annually	Number of inhabitants per doctor
Developing countries						
Taiwan	187	54 (1964)	64 (1963)	50 (1964)	32 (1963)	1520 (1963)
Average of 10 Asian countries	154	70	27	38	12	5863[c]
Average of 4 small Asian countries with U.S. aid[b]	193	63	32	51	7	4867
Burma	72	*	9 (1962)	*	2 (1964)	9300 (1963)
Ceylon	145	*	35 (1964)	53 (1954)	35 (1964)	4600 (1962)
India	92	73 (1961)	12 (1964)	13 (1961)	13 (1964)	5800 (1962)
Indonesia	95	68 (1961)	*	30 (1961)	2 (1964)	41,000 (1962)
Korea (South)	145	57 (1964)	56 (1963)	58 (1960)	9 (1964)	3000 (1962)
Malaysia	275	*	57 (1964)	*	22 (1964)	6500 (1961)
Pakistan	93	75 (1961)	5 (1962)	7 (1961)	6 (1964)	7000 (1963)
Philippines	251	57 (1962)	17 (1963)	70 (1960)	*	1700 (1963)
Thailand	115	82 (1960)	12 (1964)	56 (1960)	2 (1964)	2300 (1963)
Turkey	259	75 (1960)	45 (1963)	21 (1960)	9 (1964)	7600 (1963)
Some developed countries						
Japan	684	27 (1964)	439 (1964)	97 (1960)	91 (1964)	920 (1963)
United States	3166	7 (1964)	314 (1963)	98 (1960)	354 (1964)	690 (1963)

a/ See Appendix 1-2 for sources of data. Dates in parenthesis indicate reference period for each country.

b/ Korea, Philippines, Thailand, Turkey or any of these with available data.

c/ Excluding Indonesia.

* Not available for years between 1960 and 1964.

TAICHUNG: THE SETTING FOR THE STUDY

Taichung, the island's third largest city, has shared in Taiwan's social and economic development.[19] Since it is an important administrative, educational, and market center, there is every reason to expect that the forces of modernization sweeping Taiwan would be even stronger in this city. As an illustration of this, the educational attainment of women of childbearing years is significantly higher for Taichung than for Taiwan as a whole (see data top of page 22). There is no reason not to expect that Taichung would be above the average in terms of almost any other indicator of modernization.

Taichung's couples of childbearing age are the population of immediate concern for our study. The extent to which the forces of modernization have affected them is reflected in such characteristics as family structure, literacy, and consumption patterns. A description of

[19] Many of the statistical measures used for Taiwan are not available for a city, but where comparable data are available Taichung is significantly above the average for the country.

	% distribution of women 15-49 years old in 1965	
	Taiwan	*Taichung*
Less than primary school graduation	45	31
Primary school graduation	42	47
Junior high school	8	12
Senior high school graduation or more	5	10
Total	100%	100%

how this population is distributed on a variety of such measures will indicate the background of Taichung's young adults, while introducing the categories which will be used in later analyses.

RURAL BACKGROUND

Like most Asian cities, Taichung has a significant number of farmers within its administrative boundaries.[20] Most of those couples not presently on farms have a rural background; either the husband or the wife or both have lived on a farm at some time. Only 16 per cent of the couples have a purely urban personal history. A background of peasant life is very recent for most of the city's population:

Rural background	*% distribution*
Farmer now	18
Not farmer now	82
Both husband & wife have farm background	38
Either husband or wife has farm background	28
Neither husband nor wife has farm background	16
Total	100%

[20] Taichung covers a large geographic area. In some suburban areas a large part of the population lives on farms. However, farmers are found in almost every part of the city except the central business district. Even the majority of the farmers who live in outlying areas are closely linked to the markets and other urban facilities in the central areas by frequent bus service and by the bicycles that most farm households have.

FAMILY STRUCTURE

Whether the Chinese historically have actually lived in the large extended families idealized by their literature and folklore, or whether this was an ideal not often realized, is a matter of considerable controversy.[21] It is likely that not many married couples could live in the complex multiunit families prescribed by tradition, because high mortality often meant that the relatives required for the extended unit simply were not available. Secondly, poorer families probably did not have the means to maintain the larger familial unit in one household.

In 1962 about one-quarter of the Taichung couples were living in an extended familial household—that is, in a common household with either the parents of the couple or with other married couples of the same generation.[22] As prescribed by tradition, the parents were almost always the husband's, and the same-generation relatives were usually the married brothers of the husband or, less often, his married cousin. Another substantial minority of couples—21 per cent—had lived in an extended familial arrangement for some time after marriage, but were living in a nuclear family unit when interviewed. The nuclear unit is the common Western type of family: a husband and wife, their unmarried children, and possibly other unmarried persons, usually relatives. About half of the couples had always lived in such a nuclear unit since their marriage. The distribution in 1962 of young married couples looked like this with respect to family structure:

Family type	*% distribution*
Living in extended unit	27
Living in nuclear unit	73
Once lived in extended unit after marriage	21
Always nuclear	52
Total	100%

[21] See especially Olga Lang, *Chinese Family and Society*, New Haven: Yale University Press, 1950; Marion Levy, *The Family Revolution in Modern China*, Cambridge, Mass.: Harvard University Press, 1949.

[22] Much of this discussion of family type is based on unpublished analyses by Solomon Chu, done as part of his graduate work at the University of Michigan.

About half the couples, then, had lived under the immediate influence of the traditional extended family during some part of their married life. This figure underestimates the influence that the extended family environment must have had. A large proportion of those living only in nuclear units after marriage had had some experience of the extended family as children. Further, many of those who had lived only in nuclear units had no real choice, because neither parents nor married brothers were alive and available in Taiwan in the period after their marriage. This is particularly true of the husbands who had migrated from the Mainland after the war. In the case of 12 per cent of the couples, both husband and wife were from the Mainland. For another 12 per cent of the couples, one spouse, usually the husband, was a Mainlander.

That some experience in an extended family is common after marriage when possible is indicated by the fact that 88 per cent of the Taiwanese couples had lived in an extended unit at some time after marriage, if either the husband's parents were alive and in Taiwan or if he had married brothers in Taiwan. The almost universal pattern was to begin married life in the extended family if possible, and to break off into a separate nuclear unit only later. Once the break was made, there was very seldom a return to the larger unit. The real tie to the extended unit was through the husband's parents. If the husband's parents were in Taichung, the couple was very likely to live with them. Joint families involving several married brothers were common only if the parents were also in the household or had once been there.

EMPLOYMENT STATUS OF THE HUSBAND

In Taiwan, as in other developing societies, kinship ties and influence permeate all other institutions. Nepotism is common and expected. Therefore, our classification of the husband's employment status takes this into account in an attempt to distinguish more and less modern labor-force participation (see data at top of page 25).

The most traditional status in this scale is that of farmer, since the farms are almost invariably family enterprises, and farmers consistently took a more traditional position on almost every attitude and behavior measured in our study. At the opposite extreme, having the most modern status, are the small group of professionals (6 per cent), whose advanced education and ties to larger impersonal associa-

Husband's employment status	*% distribution*
Farmer	18
Other traditional employment	26
Employed by non-relatives	50
Professional	6
Total	100%

tions were consistent with their advanced position on most of the attitudes and behavior considered. It is the remaining majority of husbands whose positions appear to be improperly represented for our purpose by the Western occupational classifications. We have defined as in "other traditional employment" those husbands who worked for their relatives or who were self-employed, usually in small family enterprises (excluding the self-employed professionals). Those who were employed by non-relatives are regarded as being in the impersonal work situation typical of the modern economy. On this basis, then, about half of the husbands are in the two groups regarded as more traditional, and about half in the two groups that are more modern.

A more conventional occupational classification, which we will also use occasionally, yields the following distributions:[23]

Farmers	21
Non-farm manual workers	40
Proprietors of small businesses	12
White-collar workers	26

The category "white-collar workers" is relatively large for Taichung, since this city is a provincial administrative center and also contains some large educational institutions.

The distributions on family structure and on employment status indicate that while a substantial number of the husbands live and work in the newer, Western style, there is still a considerable involvement in extended family relationships. The attitudes expressed by wives about a number of traditional familial values are also indicative of such involvement:

[23] In this classification based on data from the Household Survey the number of farmers is somewhat greater than in the employment status classification, based on the pre-program Intensive Survey. The latter is believed to be more accurate, because it was possible to ask more questions and the work of the interviewers could be supervised more closely.

% distributions of answers:

Questions	*Definitely yes*	*Probably yes*	*Uncertain*	*Probably no*	*Definitely no*	*Total*
Do they want to live with their children in their old age?	64	13	16	4	3	100%
Do they expect that their children will support them if they don't live together in their old age?	58	11	20	7	4	100%
Would they like their married sons to live together in a joint family?	41	17	23	9	10	100%

	Very important	*Important*	*Uncertain*	*Not important*	
How important it is for their family to have a male heir?	67%	25%	2%	6%	100%

INCOME

A classification of the families by household income is carried along in our analysis. We do not regard it as a very useful indicator of modernization, partly because our confidence in its accuracy is not great, but mainly because household income is not as well correlated as some other indicators with modern types of behavior.[24] This fact is in accord with the logic of the situation. Income differences have existed for centuries, and high incomes can be used to support traditional values as well as modern ones. How money is spent seems to be more important for modernization than how much money the household has.

[24] Income is difficult to measure accurately in a developing society, because there is a considerable amount of income in kind and because there are extensive and varied patterns of income-pooling among relatives. Further, we were unable to probe in the detail required to maximize the accuracy of income reporting. This would have involved questions for each member of the household about each possible source of income in cash or in kind. Income is not as well correlated as education is with the ownership of modern objects. It is not as well correlated as the ownership of modern objects with economic innovation or modern economic attitudes.

Household income per month 1962, in New Taiwan Dollars	*% distribution of Couples who reported income*	*All couples*
Less than 1,000	25	23
1,000–1,499	30	29
1,500–1,999	17	15
2,000–2,499	12	11
2,500 or more	16	14
Not determined	—	8
Total	100%	100%

OWNERSHIP OF MODERN CONSUMER OBJECTS

A more useful economic modernization measure was derived from a count of the number of small modern consumer durable objects owned in the respondent's household. Each couple was asked whether they had the following objects. The numbers in parentheses indicate the proportion that owned each:

- Bicycle (89%)
- Radio (55%)
- Radio with record player (18%)
- Electric fan (57%)
- Sewing machine (68%)
- Electric iron (57%)
- Clock or watch (88%)
- Electric rice cooker (16%)
- Motorcycle (5%)

Ownership of these objects is regarded as a significant indicator of modernization. They are involved in the transition to a larger market economy. Their possession shows a willingness to adopt new methods; the desire to own them draws people into the modern economy in a variety of ways; and the demand for them leads to the creation of modern business enterprises. It is significant that the number of these objects owned is much more closely related to the educational level of the couple than to their household income. Adjustment to allow for the effect of income diminishes the relation between education and ownership of these objects much less than adjustment for education diminishes the relation between income and ownership. Our confidence in the utility of an inventory of these items as an accurate indicator of modernity is enhanced by a separate study of husbands from this same sample,[25] which shows that the number of objects owned is associated, independent of income, with a variety of behaviors that can be regarded as modern in the economic area:

1. Innovation in business and work.
2. The belief that "what you do" is important in addition to "who you know."
3. Saving more out of current income and saving in modern investment media.
4. Increased income during the three years following the pre-survey.

We will use the following distribution of ownership of the objects as one index of consumption-modernization:

No. of modern objects owned	*% distribution*
0	2
1	6
2	6
3	16
4	16
5	16
6	22
7 or more	16
Total	100%

EDUCATION AND LITERACY

Education is widely regarded as an important force for modernization.[26] Educational attainment, especially for women, has been found to be related to lower fertility and to the use of birth control in a variety of settings. The educational distribution of the husbands and wives in our sample is as indicated in the table at top of page 29. The husbands are more highly educated than the wives, so we use different cutting points in the classifications. While the Taichung couples are relatively well educated for members of a developing so-

[25] For an extensive analysis of the economic and social correlates of the ownership of these objects, see D. Freedman, *The Role of Modern Consumption Durables in a Developing Economy*, Ph.D. Dissertation in Economics, University of Michigan, 1967.

[26] For example, see C. A. Anderson and M. J. Bowman, eds., *Education and Economic Development*, Chicago: University of Chicago Press, 1965.

Husband's education	*% distribution*
Less than primary school graduate	19
Primary school graduate	41
Junior high (some schooling beyond primary school but not a senior high graduate)	13
Senior high graduate	15
Some college	12
Total	100%

Wife's education	*% distribution*
None	31
Primary school, not graduate	12
Primary school graduate	35
Junior high (some schooling beyond primary school but not a senior high graduate)	13
Senior high graduate or higher	9
Total	100%

ciety, it is clear that a substantial minority, especially among the women, have little education, and the high school graduate is in an elite group.

One important functional aspect of education is the ability and motivation it gives for contact with the outside world by reading. In Taiwan, where there is a considerable circulation of newspapers, this should be reflected in the frequency of reading newspapers:

	% distribution of:	
Frequency of reading newspapers	*husbands*	*wives*
Can't read	13	42
Can read but never does	10	14
Reads		
less than once a week	18	14
more than once a week	10	11
almost every day	49	19
Total	100%	100%

About three-quarters of the husbands and a little less than half of the wives read a newspaper sometimes. About two-thirds of the husbands and about one-third of the wives read the paper often enough (more than once a week) to be considered regular members of the newspaper audience.

MODERNIZATION INDICES

With the exception of income, all the social characteristics we have discussed in this section will be treated as rough measures of the participation of Taichung's couples in the modern sector of their society —that is, of their modernization. Broadly speaking, we define modernization as a shift from dependence on relatively self-contained local institutions to interdependence in larger social, economic, and political units. Such a shift implies a change in the division of labor from one in which the kinship unit is necessarily central, to that of a larger social system in which such local units as family and village give up many functions to larger, specialized units not based on kinship ties.

We consider each of the social classifications as providing some indication of the participation of the individual in larger, more modern systems of interchange. For example, education and literacy are relevant because they link the individual to the ideas and institutions of a larger modern society. If the individual is, or believes that he is, part of a larger non-familial system, he begins to find rewards in activities and relationships to which children are irrelevant. Obviously literacy will facilitate the dissemination of information about the ideas and means of family limitation, but education plays a more basic role through its general relation to modernization.

The type of family in which the individual lives and the employment status of the husband are pertinent, because they help to indicate whether traditional family ties may limit participation in new impersonal institutions. The inventory of modern objects has been discussed as an indicator of involvement in the modern economy. The rural background of the couple is pertinent, too, because the more recent the migration to the city, the greater the probability that the couple's experience has been limited by the traditional and local world of the village and the farm.

Apart from their obvious conceptual significance, we can give the specific modernization measures some further empirical validation by showing that they are associated very strongly with a measure of traditional attitudes toward family life (Table I-3). Those who are modern by any of the indices used also have more modern attitudes on such matters as whether they expect to live with or depend on their children in their old age. Those who hold traditional attitudes about such general familial values may also be expected to be more traditional in the areas of family limitation and family size.

Table I-3. Attitudes of Wives Toward Traditional Family Values, by Indicators of Modernization for Couples in Taichung Intensive Pre-Survey, 1962

	Attitude toward traditional family values[a]			Total	
Measures of modernization	Very traditional	Moderately traditional	Less traditional	Percentage	Number of couples
Wife's education					
None	82	17	1	100	767
Primary school, not grad.	81	18	1	100	303
Primary school grad.	67	28	5	100	842
Junior high school[b]	31	46	23	100	320
Senior high school grad. or higher	13	57	30	100	211
Husband's education					
Less than primary school grad.	84	16	*	100	450
Primary school grad.	78	20	2	100	1002
Junior high school	63	30	7	100	324
Senior high school grad.	40	45	15	100	375
Some college	21	51	28	100	292
Farm background					
Farmer now	92	8	--	100	448
Not farmer now					
Both husband and wife have farm background	67	25	8	100	919
Either husband or wife has farm background	55	36	9	100	677
Neither has farm background	43	44	13	100	399
Family type					
Living in extended unit	70	24	6	100	1263
Living in nuclear unit					
Once in extended unit	67	24	9	100	658
Always nuclear	47	42	11	100	522
Husband's employment status					
Farmer	92	8	--	100	448
Other traditional employment	66	28	6	100	641
Employed by non-relative[c]	58	33	9	100	1199
Professional	26	47	27	100	155

Table I-3 (continued).

Measures of modernization	Attitude toward traditional family values[a] Very traditional	Moderately traditional	Less traditional	Total Percent-age	Number of couples
Household income in New Taiwan Dollars					
Less than 1,000	77	21	2	100	559
1000-1499	67	28	5	100	698
1500-1999	61	28	11	100	367
2000-2499	45	41	14	100	258
2500 or more	47	36	17	100	332
Not determined	78	20	2	100	229
Number of modern objects owned					
0 or 1	86	14	*	100	191
2 or 3	78	20	2	100	572
4	75	22	2	100	375
5	65	28	7	100	380
6	55	35	10	100	537
7 or more	35	43	22	100	388
All wives	64	28	8	100	2443

a/ This classification of attitudes toward traditional family values is based on their responses to the following two questions, which could be answered "definitely yes," "probably yes," "uncertain," "probably no," or "definitely no":

(a) Do they want to live with their children in their old age?
(b) Do they expect that their children will support them if they don't live together in their old age?

They were classified as "most traditional" if their responses to both of these questions were either "definitely yes" or "probably yes," and "less traditional" if both of their responses were either "definitely no" or "probably no," or "uncertain" or a combination of them. All other combinations of responses were grouped as representing a "moderately traditional" attitude.

b/ In this and subsequent tables, "Junior high school" includes all those who had education beyond primary school but were not graduates of a senior high school.

c/ Exclusive of professionals.

* Less than 1 per cent.

The several indicators of modernization are related in the following chapters first to fertility and to the practice of birth control before the Taichung program began. It is not surprising that we find that the couples in the more modern sector of the population are more likely to use birth control and to have lower fertility than the average. This is consistent with the experience in the West, although we can document this more completely for Taichung than for any Western city at a similar stage of development. The more surprising finding is that once the program began, these indicators of modernization no longer served to distinguish those who accepted family planning in the program. This fact is of very great importance, because the mass of the population of the developing countries is in the less modern categories. If it were necessary to wait for this group to acquire more modern characteristics, the adoption of family planning on a mass scale would be long delayed. That is why we are especially concerned to compare how modern traits affect the adoption of family planning when organized help is not available and their effect under the influence of an intensive program.

PART 2. FERTILITY AND BIRTH CONTROL BEFORE THE ORGANIZED PROGRAM

II. The Number of Children Wanted and the Number Born: Ideal and Reality

HOW MANY CHILDREN ARE WANTED: THE IDEAL

Most Taichung wives wanted only a moderate number of children in 1962, even before the organized family planning program began.[1] Relatively few wanted a large number of children or believed that family growth is determined solely by fate or divine powers. The unlimited number of children (and especially of sons) called for by fabled Chinese tradition are not in practical evidence now in Taichung, and perhaps they never were. However, many women are having more than the moderate number they say they want. Probably this is partly a result of falling death rates, which keep many more children alive than was the case in the last generation; it is also partly a result of the lack of effective means[2] to limit families to the desired size.

[1] As Appendix I-3 explains in detail, the Intensive Survey covering a probability sample of all the couples in Taichung was conducted both just before and just after the year-long experiment in Taichung. The materials in Chapters II through V refer to the situation as it existed before the first Intensive Survey, in which 2,713 couples were interviewed. However, in most cases we have used the data only for those 2,443 couples who were interviewed both before and after the survey. As Appendix I-3 indicates, this does not bias the results. In some of the materials that follow we refer to birth control practice before the first interview, but we consider those sterilized up to the second interview for technical reasons that will be clear later. Whether sterilization at first or second interview is used makes no real substantive difference in the results.

For most questions the "not ascertained" category is very small. Therefore, N.A. is not shown as a separate category in most tables, although such cases are included in the total row or column where possible. Only in those few instances where N.A. responses are numerous or intrinsically significant are they shown separately.

We have not distinguished between Mainlanders and native Taiwanese in any of the analyses presented in this book, in spite of the fact that there are significant differences in the characteristics of these peoples. The overall patterns described in this book do not differ much for the sample as a whole as compared with Taiwanese only, since the proportion of Mainlanders is relatively small. For a brief discussion of some of the differences in background, see Appendix II-1.

[2] Theoretically, the technical means are available in drugstores and from doctors in Taiwan, but for many this is not really effective availability, which requires that couples who want to limit family size must know what to do and where to get supplies and service. Most importantly, if they are to be led to act in a new way not specifically sanctioned by tradition, they must feel that this action is sufficiently safe and respectable.

About two-thirds of the wives want three or four children (Table II-1). A small group—perhaps part of the wave of the future—want

Table II-1. Number of Children Ever Born, Alive and Wanted, by All Wives and by Wives 30-34 and 35-39 Years Old: Percentage Distributions and Mean Values

	Wives 20-39			Wives 30-34			Wives 35-39		
	Number of children			Number of children			Number of children		
Number of children	ever born	alive	wanted[a]	ever born	alive	wanted	ever born	alive	wanted
0	6	6	0	2	2	0	3	3	0
1	12	14	1	4	4	1	4	5	1
2	15	17	7	6	9	7	6	5	7
3	17	19	28	15	20	23	9	13	18
4	17	18	38	26	27	38	12	19	41
5 or more	33	26	26	47	38	31	66	55	33
Total per cent	100	100	100	100	100	100	100	100	100
Number	2443	2443	2443	684	684	684	589	589	589
Mean value	3.6	3.3	3.9	4.5	4.1	4.1	5.5	4.8	4.3

[a] 75 responses of "Up to God," "Up to Fate," etc. were included here with "5 or more," 15 cases not responding were assigned values of four. These 90 cases are not included in the computation of mean number of children wanted.

only two. Less than two is outside the pale; no woman said that she wanted no children, and less than 1 per cent chose one. On the other hand, only one woman in four said that she wanted more than four children or that such matters were out of her hands. Even among those choosing more than four children, most wanted five, and only 2 per cent chose seven or more.

It is significant that only 3 per cent could not give a specific numerical answer, saying that such matters were up to God, fate, or chance.[3] This is far fewer than might have been expected on the basis of the advice of some experts (both Chinese and Western), who insisted when these studies were begun that Chinese women either had strong preferences for high fertility or were fatalistic about it, and that they would therefore consider a question about the number of children wanted ridiculous. Some critics said that the many women

[3] A number of initial responses of this kind were replaced by a specific number when the interviewer used a probe like this: "Many people feel as you do, but still they have an idea of what they want fate (God, chance) to bring. How about in your case?"

who already had large families would be unwilling to express a preference for fewer children than they had, because according to folklore this would mean that they wished their last children dead. This turned out to be a myth. While those with the larger families did express a preference for a larger number of children than the average, there was no general reluctance to report wanting smaller numbers than were alive. For example, among the wives in the sample who were 35-39 years old, 38 per cent reported that they would prefer fewer children than they had alive already.[4]

Some critics of surveys like ours contend that the answers the women give may be only polite words to please the interviewer rather than a statement of real convictions. Undoubtedly it is true that some answers were influenced by politeness and by perceptions of what was expected by the well-regarded young women conducting the interviews. But at the very least this means that most respondents are aware of a "small family value"; and this awareness is in itself a social fact that can have some influence on behavior. We shall see that those who express such small or moderate family values appear to be validating them not only by the consistency of other attitudes expressed, but by action as well. It is true that many couples do not act in a rational way to achieve what they say they want, and that the action may come late or be ineffective. Even in the rationalistic West, wishes and actions frequently do not match. An even larger discrepancy between the wish and the act should not be surprising in a population where only recently has low mortality made it unnecessary to bear a large number of children to have a moderate number survive.

The preference for a moderate number of children was expressed by the wives in response to a variety of probing questions about how many children they would want or consider ideal for themselves, how many were ideal for Taiwanese generally, and how many their husbands would consider ideal for the family (Table II-2). As usually happens in such interviews, the questions about the ideal for others (for Taiwanese generally) elicited an even stronger consensus, in this case on three or four children, than the questions about the ideal for

[4] Of course, the respondent was not asked directly: "Would you prefer fewer children than you have?" or "Are some of your children unwanted?" The classification we are using was derived by comparing responses to separate sets of questions about the number of children alive and the number wife (or husband) wanted if they could start married life over again.

Table II-2. Values About Family Size: Number of Children Wife Wants, Number She Considers Ideal for Self, Number She Considers Ideal for Taiwanese in General, and Number of Children Husband Considers Ideal: Percentage Distributions

Number of children	Number of children wife: wants for self	considers ideal for for self	considers ideal for Taiwanese in general	Number of children husband considers ideal
0 or 1	*	*	*	*
2	8	7	3	7
3	29	30	25	28
4	38	41	51	42
5	15	14	14	13
6	5	4	4	5
7	2	1	1	1
Up to God, fate, chance	3	3	2	4
Total per cent	100	100	100	100
Number[a/]	2697	2693	2623	2310
Mean value[b/]	3.9	3.8	3.9	3.8

[a/] These are the number of wives, among the total sample of 2713 interviewed in the first survey, who gave determinate responses to the pertinent questions.

[b/] Computed only for cases giving a specific numerical answer.

* Less than 1 per cent.

the respondent's own family. The more general question may represent the prevailing social value more accurately, because what the woman wants for her own family is affected also by its particular situation and history. The wife's report about her husband's values often may be a projection of her own values. An earlier pilot study in Taichung, however, obtained similar results for husband and wife when each was interviewed separately.[5] No matter which of the four value measures are considered, slightly less than four is the average number of children desired or seen as ideal. The range around this number varies with the measure used, but the distributions are generally similar.

[5] See R. Freedman, J. Y. Peng, J. Y. Takeshita, and T. H. Sun, "Fertility Trends in Taiwan: Tradition and Change," *Population-Studies*, 16, No. 3, March 1963, 219-36.

Number of Children Wanted vs. Number Born

Although they prefer to have only a moderate number of children, many of the Taichung couples have a larger number than they want. In the whole sample of wives (including the young and the recently married), 18 per cent wanted fewer children than they already had alive. The proportion wanting fewer than they already had increases substantially with the age of the wife, with the number of years married, and especially with the number of children already born (Table II-3). The critical point in dissatisfaction with family growth

Table II-3. Comparison of Number of Children Alive and Wanted by Wife, by Age of Wife, by Duration of Marriage, and by Number of Children Already Born: Percentage Distributions

Demographic characteristics	Wife has alive: fewer children than she wants	just the number wanted	more children than she wants	Wife says this is "up to God, fate, chance" or doesn't answer	Total: Percentage	Number of wives
Age of wife						
20-24	88	8	*	4	100	427
25-29	66	22	7	5	100	743
30-34	33	38	26	3	100	684
35-39	24	34	38	4	100	589
Duration of marriage						
0-4 years	92	4	*	4	100	610
5-9 years	61	29	6	4	100	648
10-14 years	28	39	30	3	100	642
15 or more years	20	36	40	4	100	543
Number of live births						
0	96	0	0	4	100	134
1	97	1	0	2	100	301
2	86	10	0	4	100	379
3	59	34	2	5	100	408
4	34	52	11	3	100	414
5 or more	13	34	49	4	100	807
All wives	51	27	18	4	100	2443

* Less than 1 per cent.

is when the couples have four living children. The proportion of these who would prefer fewer children jumps sharply after four are alive. About half of those with large families (five or more children) prefer fewer, and a very large majority would prefer no more than they have. Further, there is little evidence that the women of the older generation or those with very large families are especially traditional

No. of children alive	*% who would prefer less*[6]	*% who want no more*
2	0	10
3	2	36
4	11	63
5 or more	49	83

in expressing the view that the number of children wanted is out of their hands. In no demographic category considered did more than 5 per cent express the conviction that such matters were in the hands of God, fate, or chance.

Chinese tradition, like that of most preindustrial societies, has placed a high value on sons. Over and over again in the Taichung study we found that the desire for a son, and preferably for two, was important not only in values stated but in the action taken to limit family size, both before and during the official program.

After the wife indicated how many children she preferred, she was asked how many of these should be sons and how many daughters. There is a strong preference for sons, although by no means to the exclusion of daughters. Perhaps the attitudes can best be summarized as: "We want both sons and daughters, but it is better to have more sons than daughters, and it is essential to have at least one son and preferably two." About half preferred more sons than daughters, about half wanted equal numbers, but very few chose more daughters than sons (Table II-4). No one wanted to be without a son, and only 1 or 2 per cent did not want a daughter (Table II-5). However, while less than 10 per cent were willing to settle for one son, more than 40 per cent thought one daughter was enough. At the other extreme, while about one in four wanted three or more sons, only about 5 per cent wanted that many daughters.

While having one or two sons is clearly considered essential, very few considered an unlimited number of sons ideal, just as very few considered an unlimited number of children ideal. In their situation of demographic pressure, even the weight of Chinese tradition was insufficient to prevent our respondents from saying that they had more sons than was ideal or than were wanted. It seems hardly plausible that this was only a polite response, since it is very much affected by

[6] We exclude from the base here (and under "% who want no more") approximately 4 per cent who said that these matters were up to God, fate, or chance.

Table II-4. Comparison of Number of Sons and Daughters Wife Wants, Husband Wants, and Number Wife Considers Ideal for Taiwanese in General: Percentage Distributions

Comparison of number of sons and daughters preferred	Number of children and sons: wife wants	husband wants	wife considers ideal for Taiwanese in general
Prefers equal number of sons and daughters	42	43	54
Prefers more sons than daughters	50	49	46
Prefers more daughters than sons	8	8	*
Total per cent	100	100	100
Number[a]	2214	1858	2288

[a] These are the wives, among the total sample of 2443 interviewed in both the first and the second survey, who gave determinate responses to the pertinent questions.

* Less than 1 per cent.

Table II-5. Number of Sons and Daughters Wanted by Wives and Husbands: Percentage Distributions

	Number of sons:		Number of daughters:	
	wife wants	husband wants	wife wants	husband wants
Number of sons or daughters				
0	0	0	1	2
1	8	7	43	41
2	66	65	50	50
3	22	24	5	5
4 or more	3	3	0	1
Up to God, Fate, Chance	1	1	1	1
Total per cent	100	100	100	100
Number of couples[a]	2564	2155	2563	2152
Mean number wanted[b]	2.2	2.2	1.6	1.6

[a] These are the wives, among the total sample of 2713, who answered the pertinent questions. The excluded cases are those who had no sex-preference or who were unable to give an answer (especially when the wife was asked to respond for her husband).

[b] Computed only for cases giving a specific numerical answer.

their demographic situation and also later influenced response to the program.

When we compared the number of sons alive and the number considered ideal, no one without a son and only 11 per cent of those with only one son thought that this was ideal. However, the proportions of those who thought the number of sons they had alive was either ideal or already greater than the ideal rose rapidly with the number of living sons as follows:

No. of living sons	*% who felt that ideal is no greater than this*	*ideal is less than this*
2	77	2
3	94	39
4	95	73

Whether more children were actually wanted at the time of the interview (regardless of what might be ideal) depended very much not only on the number of children alive but also on how many of these were sons. It is particularly striking that among those with three or four children, the proportion of those who wanted no more children rises rapidly with the number of sons. The total number of children makes a difference, too. Few couples with no sons will stop before four children; but about 25 per cent of those with four children wanted no more, even if they had no sons (see data on page 45).

This evidence that Taiwanese couples wanted fewer children and fewer sons than they were having was one of the facts that led the Taiwan Health Department to carry forward the Taichung City family planning experiment on a much larger scale than had been planned originally and later to expand it to the whole island. These action efforts have since been validated by the special interest in family limitation of those with large numbers of children and sons.

HOW MANY CHILDREN ARE BORN: THE REALITY

Taichung wives, like those of Taiwan generally, bear more children than the wives in such Western countries as the United States. However, the Taichung fertility is not exceptionally high for a developing country. Taichung's gross reproduction rate in 1962 (2.3) and that of

Number of Children Wanted vs. Number Born

No. of living children and sons	*% who want no more children*
None	0
One child	
No son	0
One son	1
Two children	
No son	2
One son	15
Two sons	7
Three children	
No son	2
One son	25
Two or more sons	56
Four children	
No son	24
One son	51
Two or more sons	83
Five or more children	91

Taiwan (2.5) were both higher than the rates of most developed countries, but they were already on the low side for developing countries—among the lower 15 or 20 per cent of the countries covered in a comprehensive United Nations inventory (Table II-6). Taiwanese fertility even in 1962 was certainly far below estimates of the physiological maximum. Such high fertility groups as the inhabitants of the Cocos Islands or the American Hutterites have had total fertility rates 66 to 83 per cent higher than that of Taichung for 1962. Even before the recent fertility declines in Taichung, its fertility never reached the high levels reported for some populations.

During the years immediately preceding the new family planning program, fertility had already begun to decline substantially both in Taichung and in Taiwan as a whole. In the period between 1959 and 1962 alone, the crude birth rate fell by 12 per cent and the general fertility rate by 9 per cent in Taichung and at a somewhat lesser rate in the rest of Taiwan. The decline in fertility among married women was almost entirely a result of rapidly falling birth rates among

Table II-6. Comparison of Gross Reproduction Rates in Taichung and Taiwan for 1962 with Frequency Distributions of Such Rates for the World, and for the Less Developed and More Developed Regions, About 1960[a]

Gross reproduction rates	Percentage distributions of gross reproduction rates for countries with data available about 1960			
	The world	More developed areas	Less developed areas	
Under 1.0	0.8	2.8	0.0	
1.0-1.2	11.5	37.3	1.1	
1.3-1.5	10.6	31.4	2.3	
1.6-1.9	8.2	20.0	3.4	
2.0-2.3	5.7	2.8	6.9	Taichung-2.3 (1962)[b]
2.4-2.6	9.8	0.0	13.8	Taiwan-2.5 (1962)[b]
2.7-2.9	19.8	0.0	27.7	
3.0-3.2	15.6	0.0	21.8	
3.3-3.5	16.4	5.7	20.7	
3.6 and over	1.6	0.0	2.3	
Total per cent	100.0	100.0	100.0	
Number	122	35	87	

[a] Data from Table 1.3 of Population Bulletin of the United Nations, No. 7, 1963. New York: United Nations, 1965.

[b] Taichung and Taiwan fit into the distributions at the indicated places. The few countries listed as "developed" and with gross reproduction rates of 3.0 or more are not truly developed places in any accepted definition of that concept; they are small less developed countries classified as "developed," because they are part of larger regions so classified on arbitrary geographical grounds.

women over 30, with the rate of decline especially high for the older women (Table II-7). While the pattern in the rest of Taiwan was similar, the Taichung decline from 1959 to 1962 was much more precipitous, ranging from 24 to 68 per cent in the successive age groups over 30.

This pattern of birth rate declines—the fact that the decline occurs first among older rather than younger women—surprises many who expect that the younger women will be more innovative and will lead the way. It is, however, the pattern to be expected if, in a period of rapid social and mortality change, many women want a moderate number of children, have them alive by age 30 due to lower mortality, and only then begin to try to do something about family limitation under the joint pressures of more children surviving and higher aspirations for them. There is earlier evidence of such a pattern at the be-

Table II-7. Percentage Changes in Various Fertility Measures Between 1959 and 1962 for Taichung and Taiwan

Rates	Percentage change: 1959-1962			
	Taichung		Taiwan	
	All women	Married women	All women	Married women
Age-specific fertility rate				
15-19	-14	+ 4	- 2	+ 1
20-24	+13	+16	+ 3	+ 5
25-29	+ 9	+ 9	+ 1	+ 2
30-34	-22	-24	-13	-13
35-39	-46	-46	-23	-24
40-44	-49	-50	-30	-24
45-49	-68	-68	-34	-36
Total fertility rate	-13	- 7	- 9	- 5
General fertility rate	- 9	-11	- 5	- 7
Crude birth rate	-12		- 9	

ginning of the modern fertility decline in a number of Western countries.

The younger Taichung (or Taiwan) women generally have considerably lower fertility rates than are found in many other developing high-fertility societies (Table II-8). This results from a much higher age-at-marriage in this Chinese society than in most other high-fertility countries; fewer of the younger women are married and at risk of having children (Table II-9). However, when only married women are considered, Taichung's birth rates at these younger ages are very high indeed (Table II-10), and there is no question about the fecundability of the Taichung women (Table II-11). But by age 30, when almost all women are married, both Taichung and Taiwan in 1962 had significantly lower fertility rates than most of the other developing societies. This results, as we shall see later, from action to limit family size after the number of children wanted are born. The decline in fertility that had occurred already before the new family planning program was not a result of a change in the age-at-marriage. The higher age-at-marriage in Taiwan as compared with India, for example, is not a new phenomenon. The birth rate decline resulted

Table II-8. Age-Specific Fertility Rates, Total Fertility, and Crude Birth Rates for Taichung, for Taiwan, and for Selected Other Populations

Rates	Taichung 1962	Taiwan 1962	Mexico[a] 1960	India[a] 1958-59	Upper[a] Volta 1960-61	Cocos[b] Islands 1942	American[c] Hutterites 1946-50	United[b] States 1960	Hong[e] Kong 1965	Japan[d] 1960
Age-specific fertility rates										
15-19	42	45	105	145	169	130	12	88	45	4
20-24	248	255	299	263	308	378	231	257	237	107
25-29	326	337	314	244	265	442	383	198	276	181
30-34	194	235	271	188	220	294	391	113	180	80
35-39	97	145	200	128	154	280	345	56	107	24
40-44	46	65	74	50	84	216	208	15	31	5
45-49	7	10	21	20	21	24	42	1	2	*
Total fertility rates	4799	5460	6421	5192	6105	8820	8060	3644	4390	2007
Crude birth rate	34	37	46	39	49	58	46	24	27	17

[a] Data from Population Bulletin of the United Nations, No. 7, New York: United Nations, 1965.

[b] Data from T.E. Smith, "The Cocos-Keeling Islands: A Demographic Laboratory," Population Studies, Vol. XIV, No. 2, 1960, pp. 94-130.

[c] Data from J.W. Eaton and A.J. Mayer, Man's Capacity to Reproduce, the Demography of a Unique Population, Glencoe: Free Press, 1954.

[d] Data from Standardized Vital Rates for All Japan 1920-1960, Institute of Population Problems (Tokyo) Research Series, No. 155, August 1, 1963, Table 2.

[e] Data from a special field study of birth records by Hong Kong Family Planning Association and University of Michigan Population Studies Center.

Table II-9. Proportion of Women Currently Married, by Age, for Taichung, for Taiwan, and Selected Other Countries

Age of wife	Taichung 1962	Taiwan 1962	Pakistan[a] 1961	U.A.R.[a] (Egypt) 1960	Singapore[a] 1959	United[a] States 1960	Hong[b] Kong 1961	Japan[c] 1961
15-19	9	12	73	32	20	15	6	1
20-24	55	60	92	73	66	67	51	31
25-29	86	89	94	89	89	83	83	76
30-34	92	92	92	90	92	86	91	86
35-39	91	90	87	89	88	85	90	86
40-44	87	86	77	80	80	83	84	82
45-49	82	81	70	76	69	80	76	77

[a] Data from Population Bulletin of the United Nations, No. 7 (with special reference to conditions and trends of fertility in the world), New York: United Nations, 1965.

[b] Data from K.M.A. Barnett, The Census and You, Hong Kong: Government Printer, 1961.

[c] Data from 1964 White Paper on Welfare, Ministry of Health and Welfare, Tokyo, 1965.

mainly from family limitation in the ages over 30, when almost all women are married in Taiwan as in other developing societies.

Although fertility has been falling in Taichung and is lower than in most other developing societies, it is still high enough to produce many large families, more children than are wanted for many families, and many more children per family than are born in the United

Table II-10. Age-Specific Fertility Rates for Currently Married Women, for Taichung, for Taiwan, and Selected Other Countries

Age of wife	Taichung 1962	Taiwan 1962	Singapore[a] 1957	Albania[a] 1955	United States 1962	American[b] Hutterites 1946-50	Hong[c] Kong 1965	Japan[d] 1960
15-19	456	375	395	277	476	92	(705)	322
20-24	452	424	459	369	335	336	464	342
25-29	372	380	400	382	214	498	331	237
30-34	210	256	316	318	120	443	197	93
35-39	107	161	221	277	58	370	119	28
40-44	53	76	101	146	16	215	37	6
45-49	9	12	17	92	0	43	3	*

[a] Data from United Nations, Population Bulletin No. 7.

[b] Data from J.W. Eaton and A.J. Mayer, Man's Capacity to Reproduce, Glencoe: Free Press, 1954.

[c] Data from a special field study by Hong Kong Family Planning Association and University of Michigan Population Studies Center. The data for age group 15-19 are in parentheses because they may be in error. They appear to be unreasonably high. The error is probably in the estimate of number of married women, not in the number of births.

[d] Data from 1964 White Paper on Welfare, Ministry of Health and Welfare, Tokyo, 1965, p. 8.

* Less than 1 per cent.

Table II-11. Comparison of Number of Children Ever Born to Taichung and U.S. Wives,[a] 30-34 and 35-39 Years Old: Percentage Distributions and Means

Number of children ever born	Wives 30-34		Wives 35-39	
	Taichung 1962	U.S.A. 1960	Taichung 1962	U.S.A. 1960
0	2	10	3	10
1	4	14	4	14
2	6	28	6	27
3	15	23	9	22
4	26	13	13	13
5 or more	46	12	66	14
Total per cent	100	100	100	100
Mean value	4.5	2.7	5.5	2.7

[a] For wives married only once, currently living with husband. Data from 1960 U.S. Census.

States. Both fecundity and the desire to have at least some children must be high, as indicated by the fact that only 2 or 3 per cent of the women over 30 are childless and only 4 per cent have an only child (Table II-1). By age 35-39, 66 per cent have had five or more live births and 55 per cent five or more living children, although only 33 per cent say that they want that many. The mean number of children alive per couple is about 10 per cent above the number wanted for women 35-39, and the discrepancy is almost certain to increase before childbearing ends. Childbearing has certainly not ended for these older women, since 13 per cent were pregnant at the time they were interviewed.

Survival rates[7] have increased greatly in Taiwan, so that most children born now survive to be adults. Of course, the older women had many of their first children when death rates were much higher. Still, in the case of women 35-39, 88 per cent of all the children they ever bore were still alive. This compares, for example, with 76 per cent in a high mortality situation such as that in a 1952 study of Mysore, India.[8] If the Taiwanese survival rate in 1962 had been that low, then the mean number of children alive for women 35-39 would have been lower than the number they wanted and the interest in family limitation might therefore have been less.

Fertility is still much higher in Taichung (or Taiwan) than in a Western country like the United States. The United States is chosen for comparison not only because data are easily available, but also because its fertility is much above the average for industrialized countries. This permits us to say that the differences are minimized. The contrasts could be much greater if we used countries like Great Britain or France or Hungary as the basis for comparison.

Taichung wives in their thirites had borne more than twice as many children as wives of the same age in the United States (Table II-11). By age 35-39 the proportion of those who had borne five or more children was 66 in Taichung and 14 in the United States. At the other extreme, 73 per cent of the American women but only 22 per cent of the women in Taichung had fewer than four children.

A much higher proportion of the Taichung than of American women of each age group was pregnant at the time of the survey (Table II-12). This means that the differences in fertility should grow larger by the end of the childbearing period. We can compare the timing of family growth for the two societies by contrasting the cumulative number of children ever born at successive periods after marriage for cohorts of women married approximately the same length of time (Table II-13). One year after marriage the American women had more children than the Chinese (presumably because of the higher rate of premarital pregnancy in the United States). But by the end

[7] Shown here by the ratio between the number of children currently alive and the number ever born.

[8] Computed from data in United Nations, *The Mysore Population Study*, New York: United Nations Population Studies, No. 34, ST/SOA/ Series A/34, 1961.

Table II-12. Proportion Currently Pregnant at Interview by Age of Wife: Taichung, 1962 and U.S. White Population, 1955

Age of wife	Per cent currently pregnant: Taichung 1962	Per cent currently pregnant: U.S.A.[a] 1955	Per cent by which Taichung proportion pregnant exceeds that for U.S.A.
20-24	28	20	40
25-29	26	14	86
30-34	13	7	86
35-39	6	3	100
All ages	18	10	80

[a]Unpublished data from 1955 Growth of American Families study.

Table II-13. Number of Children Ever Born per 1000 Women Currently Married: Taichung, 1962 and United States White Women,[a] Married 10-14 and 15-19 Years in 1959

Duration of marriage	Women married 10-14 years			Women married 15-19 years		
	Taichung	U.S.A.	Ratio: Taichung/ U.S.A.	Taichung	U.S.A.	Ratio: Taichung/ U.S.A.
1 year	300	323	93	210	242	87
2 years	830	654	127	720	529	136
3 years	1220	940	130	1060	771	137
4 years	1660	1208	137	1450	999	145
5 years	2040	1455	140	1780	1216	146
6 years	2430	--		2160	--	
7 years	2830	1871	151	2540	1606	158
8 years	3190	--		2920	--	
9 years	3530	--		3270	--	
10 years	3820	2328	164	3580	2023	177
11 years				3920	--	
12 years				4200	--	
13 years				4470	--	
14 years				4740	--	
15 years				4970	2454	203

[a]Data for U.S. refer to White Women married once and husband present. U.S. Bureau of the Census, Current Population Reports, Series P-20, No. 108, "Marriage, Fertility, and Childspacing."

--Data not available.

of the second year of marriage, the Taiwanese women had borne 27 to 36 per cent more children than the Americans. The differential widens steadily from this time onward, reaching more than 50 per cent after seven years of marriage, 77 per cent after ten years, and more than 100 per cent after fifteen years.

Taichung and Taiwan have not had exceptionally high fertility levels as compared with other developing societies. However, the fertility rates are still substantially higher than those of more developed Western societies such as the United States. If Taiwan's modernization was to bring its fertility levels within the range of recent Western experiences, considerable change was still necessary in 1962. The fertility declines which took place before the establishment of the organized program were only a beginning.

III. Family Limitation Before the Program: Reconciling the Ideal and the Actual

AN INITIAL OVERVIEW

A LARGE minority of Taichung couples—36 per cent—had done something on their own[1] to limit family size by 1962, before the organized family planning program began. This may seem to be merely the most obvious, rational course of action for these couples, so many of whom said they wanted a moderate number of children, and especially for the large number who already had all the children they wanted. However, in this area of behavior, as in many others, what is logical, rational, and consistent may not be what is true.

Many surveys in other developing countries[2] have also found that couples want only a moderate number of children and that many have more than the number they want, but in many of these countries there is little evidence as yet of very much practice of family planning, either before or after an organized family planning program is instituted.[3] Taiwan happens to be one of the places where inconsistency between what is desired and the reality has been associated by many with action to reconcile the two. Of course, even in Taichung or Taiwan in 1962, family planning was not universally or very effectively used, but the practice was sufficient to have produced the fertility decline already underway at that time.

Alternative patterns of family planning involving different major

[1] There had been a small experimental program to bring traditional methods of contraception to Taiwan women before the 1963 Taichung experiment. This "Pre-Pregnancy Health Program" was an important, if small-scale, beginning which helped to train workers, but it reached relatively small numbers and very few in Taichung itself. For a description of this program see J. Y. Takeshita, J. Y. Peng, and P.K.C. Liu, "A Study of the Effectiveness of the Prepregnancy Health Program in Taiwan," *Eugenics Quarterly*, 11, No. 4, December 1964, 222-33.

[2] For a review of such studies see B. Berelson, "KAP Studies on Fertility" in Berelson et al., *Family Planning and Population Programs*, Chap. 51, and also the review by Parker Mauldin in *Studies in Family Planning*, No. 7, June 1965.

[3] For a critique of the use of attitude studies without behavioral validation, see P. Hauser, "Family Planning and Population Programs," *Demography*, 4, No. 1, July 1967, 397-416.

methods and different timing sequences were sufficiently complex even by 1962 to make an initial summary view of the major facts useful before a more detailed discussion:

1. A significant minority of couples used contraception, abortion, and sterilization in various combinations.
2. The proportion using one or more of these methods increased with successive stages of family growth. The relatively late stage at which family planning was used by most of the couples who took it up is consistent with the fact that fertility had declined only in the older age groups.
3. The practice of family limitation was still rather ineffective if the criterion is attaining the desired family size. This is indicated by the following facts:
   a. Many couples had more children than they wanted.
   b. Many couples who said that they wanted no more children were doing nothing about it.
   c. Most of those who used family limitation began rather late, usually only after all of the children they wanted were alive, and often only when they had more than were wanted.
   d. Many couples who did something about family limitation had experimented with several radically different methods.
   e. A significant minority of couples used induced abortion for family limitation, although a very large majority regarded abortion as undesirable.
4. The differences in fertility between Taichung and a country like the United States are matched by differences in contraceptive practice: far fewer Taichung than American couples used family planning at any stage of family growth, and those who did use it in Taichung began much later in married life.
5. Despite all these limitations, the practice of family limitation was sufficiently effective to increase substantially for those using it the interval between successive pregnancies and the period without any pregnancies at all. There is also some evidence that younger women were beginning to use contraception earlier.
6. Those more modern and higher status couples who have relatively low fertility were also those who had used family limitation the earliest and to the greatest extent. (This issue is the subject of Chapters IV and V.)

HOW MANY COUPLES PRACTICED EACH MAJOR TYPE OF FAMILY LIMITATION?

Thirty-six per cent of all the couples had already practiced one or more of the major methods of birth control:

	% who had ever practiced:
contraception[4]	28
abortion	12
sterilization	9
any of these	36

Contraception was used more than any other method: three out of four couples who had done anything to limit family growth chose this means. About one-third of the women who had ever used any of the three major methods used more than one, perhaps an indication of experimentation to find a satisfactory method. In particular, few women relied on abortion alone. Eighty-eight per cent of the women who had ever had an abortion had also used contraception and/or sterilization. Among those ever using contraception or sterilization, a substantial but much smaller proportion, about 40 per cent, had used one of the other major types.

Most (80 per cent) of the women who had ever had an abortion had also used contraception, and among these, two-thirds used contraception either just before or just after the pregnancy terminated by an abortion.[5] Some women had an abortion when contraception failed. About an equal number took up contraception only after an unwanted pregnancy was terminated by abortion. These various facts about abortion appear to validate the meaningfulness of the responses to one of our questions; these responses indicated that abortion was

[4] The term "contraception" refers to any method used to avoid conception, including mechanical and chemical methods, periodic or prolonged abstinence, and coitus interruptus. It does not include induced abortion, which is a method of birth control (not conception control). Sterilization (either wife or husband or both) can be considered to be a permanent method of contraception. However, because it is radically different from other methods, we will usually treat it separately. The term "birth control" is used to refer to any of these major methods. "Family planning" and "family limitation" are used interchangeably to refer to fertility control in general, when methods are not being distinguished.

[5] "Just before" and "just after" refer to use at any time in the specific pregnancy intervals immediately preceding or immediately following an induced abortion.

considered very undesirable,[6] that better methods should be used, but also that sometimes abortion is necessary. While abortion is illegal in Taiwan, the law is not enforced very often, and many well-established doctors are known to perform such operations.

The proportion of women ever having an abortion (12 per cent) is much greater than the proportion of pregnancies terminated by abortion, since most women have several pregnancies but either have no abortion or only one.

WHEN WAS FAMILY LIMITATION BEGUN AND WHAT PART OF FAMILY LIFE DID IT AFFECT?

At a very liberal estimate, contraception and sterilization protected the Taichung couples from additional pregnancies during only about 20 per cent of that period of their married life in which they were subject to the risk of conception.[7] Two-thirds of this coverage was by contraception and one-third by sterilization. The total period covered varies from about 9 to 22 per cent, depending on how long the couple had been married. Even if we consider only those who had ever used either contraception or sterilization, about 40 per cent of the period at risk was covered. (See Table III-1.) One reason for the fact that a relatively small part of the risk period was covered is that most couples married for less than ten years had never done anything to limit family growth, and even among couples married for more than ten years the proportion of those who had done something was only slightly more than half.

Another reason is that even those who use family limitation methods begin quite late in married life (Table III-2). The proportion of couples ever using contraception was much smaller in Taichung than in the United States, but the differences are even greater in the early

[6] Seventy-seven per cent of all respondents indicated that they disapproved of abortion and 50 per cent that they disapproved strongly.

[7] The period at risk was defined as the total number of months since the wife's first marriage, excluding: (a) periods when the husband was away for three months or more, (b) periods between marriages, and (c) the months of pregnancy. The months of contraceptive protection are defined as including *all* months in any interpregnancy period (or during the open pregnancy interval) during which contraceptives were used at any time, excluding those months taken out of the risk base as above. Since contraceptive practice was intermittent in many cases, this is a liberal estimate of protection.

Table III-1. Proportion of Net Months of Exposure Covered by Sterilization or Contraception, by Duration of Marriage for All Wives and for Wives Who Have Ever Used Contraception and/or Sterilization Prior to First Interview

	Proportion of net months of exposure covered by:					
	Sterilization		Contraception		Sterilization and/or contraception	
Duration of marriage	All couples	Couples sterilized only	All couples	Couples ever using contraception only	All couples	Couples ever using contraception and/or sterilization
0-4 years	*	22	9	57	9	54
5-9 years	2	43	12	42	14	43
10-14 years	5	38	16	41	22	44
15 years or more	8	40	12	36	21	41
Total	6	39	13	40	19	43

* Less than 1 per cent.

Table III-2. Proportion of Couples Who Ever Used Contraception or Who Were Sterilized at Time of Interview, Taichung (1962) and U.S.A. (1955)[a/]

Characteristics of couples	Proportion who ever used contraception		Proportion sterilized by time of interview	
	Taichung	U.S.A.	Taichung	U.S.A.
Duration of marriage				
0-4 years	12	65	1	1
5-9 years	26	75	5	7
10-14 years	38	73	14	13
15 years or more	35	65	20	24
Parity at interview				
0	4	42	4	8
1	11	71	1	5
2	22	77	2	8
3	33	81	8	12
4	40	73	11	15
5	31	67	21	16
6 or more	33	56	14	16
All couples	28	70	9	9

[a/] For Taichung wives 20-39 and U.S. wives 18-39. Unless otherwise indicated, all data on family limitation practices in the United States in this chapter are from R. Freedman, P.K. Whelpton, and A.A. Campbell, Family Planning, Sterility, and Population Growth, New York: McGraw Hill, 1959.

stages of married life, when few Taichung couples but most Americans had begun to do something. For example, among those who had only one child, 11 per cent of the women of Taichung and 71 per cent of the Americans reported use of contraception. While the proportion of Taichung women who ever used contraception rises with the duration of marriage, or parity, it never reaches the U.S. levels, although the differences are narrowed in these later stages of married life. At comparable later stages of married life, the ratio by which the American use exceeds that in Taichung is still about two to one.

Sterilization is about equally common in Taichung and in the United States. However, again the American couples had much higher rates in the early years of married life. The proportion sterilized is similar only after five children have been born.

While we have no data for the United States on abortion, it is clear that this method was used in Taiwan only under considerable demographic pressure, in the later stages of married life. The proportion of pregnancies aborted intentionally rises from less than 1 per cent among first pregnancies to more than 17 per cent for pregnancies of the sixth order or higher.

The Taichung couples generally used family limitation to end childbearing rather than to space their births (Table III-3). About two-

Table III-3. Proportion of Wives Ever Using Various Methods of Family Limitation Who Began in the Open Interval, the Last Preceding Interval, or Earlier

	Percentage of all users who began in				
				Total	
Type of method used	the open birth interval	last completed birth interval	earlier birth intervals	Percent-age	Number
Contraception	61	22	17	100	(684)
Abortion	69	20	11	100	(299)
Sterilization	100	0	0	100	(220)
Any method	65	20	15	100	(882)

thirds of those using any one of the three major methods had begun only since the last birth, in what we call the "open birth interval." Another 20 per cent had begun only in the last completed birth interval. It is likely that most of these were couples who had intended to make that interval an open one, but the interval was closed by an "accidental" unwanted pregnancy. The figure of 15 per cent for those who had begun family limitation in a completed birth interval earlier than the last matches rather closely the percentage of Taiwanese women who have reported in other surveys that they were accepting help from a family planning program in order to space their children.

The proportion of those who used family limitation depended on whether the couples wanted no more children, whether they had all the children they wanted or more (Table III-4). Given the preceding

Table III-4. Proportion of Couples Who Have Ever Used Various Types of Family Limitation by Comparison of Number of Children Alive and Wanted, by Number of Living Children and Sons, for Wives 20-29 and 30-39 Years Old

Characteristics of couples	Wives 20-29 years old: Percentage who have ever used: any method	contra-ception	abor-tion	steril-ization	Number of couples	Wives 30-39 years old: Percentage who have ever used: any method	contra-ception	abor-tion	steril-ization	Number of couples
Comparison of number of children alive and wanted by wife										
Wants 2 more	8	7	2	1	494	21	11	6	12	103
Wants 1 more	25	21	7	2	374	33	26	9	8	266
Has wanted number	49	38	16	10	200	56	44	23	16	464
Has more than wants	44	33	17	13	52	63	45	24	18	400
Wanted number unknown, "up to God," "up to fate," etc.	6	4	2	0	50	23	18	3	7	40
Number of living children and sons										
None	7	6	0	2	108	6	3	0	6	35
One child										
No son	3	3	0	0	118	39	28	0	11	36
One son	13	12	1	1	150	23	23	0	0	26
Two children										
No son	10	8	3	0	79	18	12	0	6	17
One or two sons	22	20	5	1	249	49	44	21	7	71
Three or four children										
No son	23	19	5	2	43	21	18	7	0	28
One son	25	22	8	1	100	42	34	15	9	117
Two or more sons	40	30	11	9	255	60	46	23	18	364
Five or more children	37	25	17	10	68	51	36	20	16	579
All women	22	18	6	3	1170	49	37	18	14	1273

evidence about the late start in the use of family planning and the large proportion never starting, it is not surprising that only among those older women who had all or more than the children they wanted had a majority done something about keeping reality from getting too far out of line with their ideals. Even so, one-third of the older women (and more than half of the younger women) who had more children than they wanted had still done nothing about family limitation. Even among the older women, more than half of those who had never done anything about family limitation already had all children they wanted or more (Table III-5).

Table III-5. Proportion of Couples Who Want Fewer, More, or Same Number of Children as Are Alive, by Types of Family Limitation Ever Used, for Couples with Wife 30-39 Years Old

	Wife wants				Total	
Types of family limitation ever used	more children	the number of children she has	fewer children than she has	Number wanted unknown, "up to God, fate," etc.	Percentage	Number of couples
Never used anything	40	32	23	5	100	643
Used some type of family planning	18	41	40	1	100	625
Sterilized only	20	37	41	2	100	109
Sterilized after using abortion or contraception	16	47	36	1	100	75
Used contraception only	21	38	39	2	100	263
Used abortion only	21	32	47	0	100	19
Used contraception and abortion	11	47	41	1	100	159
All couples	30	36	31	3	100	1268

Family limitation, then, was used by only a minority, was begun late, and was often used ineffectively. That is why the Taichung fertility levels were still as high as they were in 1962. But even at this time, fertility levels were lower than in most developing societies and were falling. In the next chapter, we shall see that the practice of family limitation had brought fertility to levels much lower than average in the case of those more modern groups that used it most. We can also show that, on the average, those using any of the methods effectively lengthened the intervals between pregnancies and births, and especially that they were successful in lengthening the open pregnancy or open birth intervals, that is, the period since the last pregnancy or birth.

First of all, the interval between pregnancies was much longer for users of contraception or of any of the other methods after first use than before (Table III-6). The large differences remain even when we remove the first pregnancy interval (which is shorter, because, unlike the other intervals, it does not start out with a period of amenorrhea). The differences are considerably diminished if we eliminate also the open pregnancy interval, since that is very long. But that period is long precisely because of the use of family limitation, and so its elimination would probably give us too conservative a picture. It probably is more reasonable to compare instead the average length of pregnancy intervals after the first pregnancy but before the use of family limitation is begun, with the average length of pregnancy intervals after family limitation is begun. On this basis, the average

Table III-6. Average Length in Months of Pregnancy Intervals Before, After, or During Use of Various Family Limitation Methods for Wives Using Various Methods, Ages 30-39, by Pregnancy Order at the Time of Survey

	Present pregnancy order						
Use of family limitation	1	2	3	4	5	6+	Total
For users of contraception only							
Before using contraception	*	*	14	15	16	13	14
After using contraception	*	39	44	38	31	19	26
Before using contraception (excluding first interval)	c/	*	19	18	18	15	16
After using contraception (excluding open interval)	*	*	25	29	24	16	19
For users of any limitation methods[a]							
Before starting to use anything	*	35	14	14	16	14	14
After starting use of any method	*	41	48	44	34	21	28
Before starting to use anything (excluding first interval)	c/	*	18	17	18	15	16
After starting use of any method (excluding open interval)	*	*	25	29	24	15	18
Mean length of pregnancy intervals[b] during which contraception was							
Used	*	44	49	42	32	21	28
Not used	*	26	15	15	16	14	14
Wives never using any family limitation method	55	37	30	21	19	16	20
All wives	54	38	28	22	20	16	19

a/ Includes contraception, sterilization, and abortion.

b/ Excluding the open interval for sterilized cases.

c/ No cases in this category.

* Less than 20 pregnancy intervals.

pregnancy intervals are about one year (about 75 per cent) longer after the first practice of family limitation than before, whether we consider all of the women or only those of similar pregnancy orders at the time of interview.

The comparisons considered so far have referred to all intervals after first use of some type of birth control, regardless of whether contraception was actually used in every interval following its first use. We wanted to see what the total effect is if we compare by gravidity the intervals in which contraception was used or not used (in this case excluding the open interval for sterilized cases):

Number of pregnancies by time of interview	*Mean length of the pregnancy interval in months for:*		
	Women never using any method	*Women ever using contraception*	
		Intervals in which not used	*Intervals in which used*
2	37	26	44
3	30	15	49
4	21	15	42
5	19	16	32
6	16	14	21
Total	20	14	28

Clearly, the intervals during which contraception was used are much longer than those during which it was not. Those who later became users initially had much shorter intervals than those who remained non-users, so the longer intervals during periods of use are probably produced despite high fecundability. We can speculate that those using contraception may have been motivated to begin by the quick succession of their pregnancies.

The average length of pregnancy intervals tends to decrease somewhat as the pregnancy order attained increases, because a large number of pregnancies is possible only if the intervals between them are relatively short. However, all the comparisons we have made are valid not only on the average but also for those couples who had reached each particular pregnancy order at the time of the interview. The ratio of interval length as between periods of use and non-use ranges between two to one and three to one throughout.

About two-thirds of those using contraception and, of course, everyone sterilized began these practices after the last pregnancy, in the open interval. Therefore, the facts about its length are particularly important (Table III-7). The open pregnancy interval is much longer for those using contraception or sterilized at any time in that interval, than for those using nothing since the last pregnancy.

For fertility comparisons the open birth interval is more important than the open pregnancy interval, since fetal deaths, whether by induced abortion or otherwise, may have a significant effect on the interruption of late childbearing. P. S. Mohapatra has made a thorough

Table III-7. Average Length in Months of Open Pregnancy Interval for Those Sterilized and for Those Using and Not Using Contraception in the Open Pregnancy Interval, by Number of Completed Pregnancies

Present pregnancy order	Not using contra-ception	Using contra-ception	Ster-ilized	Using either contra-ception or ster-ilized	All couples
0	76	*	*	*	77
1	23	*	*	*	25
2	17	30	*	31	20
3	21	48	*	51	29
4	19	37	62	44	36
5	21	31	49	37	29
6 or more	16	25	47	33	16
Total	22	31	52	38	28

* Less than 20 pregnancy intervals.

analysis of the open birth interval and its correlates.[8] If any birth control method was used during the open birth interval, the interval was substantially longer than when nothing had been used:

Parity at interview	*Mean length of open interval in months*		
	Use of birth control methods in open interval		
	Used none	*Used some*	*Total*
2–4	42	62	53
5–6	26	50	38
7 or more	17	36	24
Total	30	53	41

It may seem an obvious and fatuous exercise to demonstrate that using birth control methods lengthens the period without a pregnancy. But this is only obvious after the fact, since with the less effective methods often used and the intermittent character of much contraceptive practice, the impact could be quite trivial.

Abortions are not likely to lengthen average pregnancy intervals,

[8] P. S. Mohapatra, *The Effect of Age at Marriage and Birth Control Practices on Fertility Differentials in Taiwan*, Ph.D. Dissertation in Sociology, University of Michigan, 1966 (published in microfilm form).

unless they are performed under unsafe conditions that decrease fecundability by the damage done. Instead, it is likely that abortions shorten interpregnancy intervals, since they do not involve a period of amenorrhea. A. K. Jain[9] has demonstrated that for the Taichung couples interpregnancy intervals were significantly shorter if the preceding pregnancy was terminated by an induced abortion than if it ended in a live birth, so any untoward effects of abortions under Taichung conditions must be less on the average than the compensating factors. However, it is still possible that birth intervals are lengthened by abortions which prevent pregnancies from coming to term as a live birth. The average difference in the open birth interval was considerably greater than the difference in the open pregnancy interval, indicating that induced abortions did lengthen birth intervals.

We cannot use simply the average number of pregnancies or births of those using and not using birth control methods to demonstrate the effects of the limitation actions. The fact is that at any given age those who used birth control methods had more, rather than less, than the average number. This is because it is precisely high fertility that motivates the use of family limitation in a place like Taiwan. Those who use contraception, abortion, or sterilization do so after having had a rather quick succession of pregnancies and births. Therefore, the argument must be that without the use of family limitation procedures fertility would have been even higher. The evidence for this has just been seen. Pregnancy and birth intervals—and especially the crucial open intervals—were lengthened by birth control.

DEMOGRAPHIC CORRELATES OF FAMILY LIMITATION

Use of family limitation methods increased with both the number of living children and the number of sons (Table III-4). With minor exceptions, the proportion using family limitation in general or any of the three major methods increased with the number of sons, among those having any specific number of living children. For example, among those with two living children the proportion using some method was more than twice as great for those with sons than for those without. For those with three or four children, the proportion

[9] "Fecundity Components in Taiwan: Application of a Stochastic Model of Human Reproduction," Ph.D. Dissertation in Sociology, University of Michigan, 1968 (published in microfilm form).

of users rose rather steeply with the number of sons. This is an important consistency validation of the general attitudes about sons examined earlier.

By now it should not be necessary to say much in detail about the fact that the proportions of those using contraception, abortion, or sterilization rose with such other family life-cycle measures as wife's age, duration of marriage, number of children ever born, or number of pregnancies for either younger or older women (Tables III-8 and III-9). That abortions were more a crisis action than any of the other

Table III-8. Proportion of Couples Who Have Ever Used Various Types of Family Limitation, by Duration of Marriage, Number of Pregnancies, and Number of Live Births: All Wives

	Percentage who have ever used:				
Characteristics of couples	any method	contra-ception	abor-tion	steril-ization	Number of couples
Duration of marriage					
0-4 years	13	12	2	1	610
5-9 years	32	26	8	5	648
10-14 years	50	38	20	14	642
15 years or more	52	35	20	20	543
Number of pregnancies					
0	6	3	0	3	68
1	8	7	0	1	237
2	19	18	1	2	328
3	30	25	3	6	360
4	38	29	9	9	378
5	49	34	15	15	379
6 or more	54	39	29	16	693
Number of live births					
0	8	4	0	4	138
1	11	11	1	1	297
2	26	22	7	2	380
3	40	33	12	8	408
4	49	40	20	11	415
5	49	31	18	21	358
6 or more	47	33	17	14	447
All couples	36	28	12	10	2443

major methods is indicated by the fact that abortions were much rarer in the early stages of married life and that they were used much more often by couples who also used other methods sooner or later. Relative to the other methods there was a much sharper jump in practice of abortion after ten years of marriage, after four or five pregnancies, or after three births. The proportion of those using abortion increased much more regularly with the number of pregnancies than with the number of births, since the abortions prevented higher order pregnancies from becoming higher order births. This is only somewhat less true for contraception, since contraception failures for

Table III-9. Proportion of Couples Who Have Ever Used Various Types of Family Limitation by Duration of Marriage, Number of Pregnancies, and Number of Live Births, for Wives 20-29 and 30-39 Years Old

	Wives 20-29 years old					Wives 30-39 years old				
	Percentage who have ever used:					Percentage who have ever used:				
Characteristics of couples	any method	contra- ception	abor- tion	steril- ization	Number of couples	any method	contra- ception	abor- tion	steril- ization	Number of couples
Duration of marriage										
0-4 years	13	11	2	1	582	29	29	4	0	28
5-9 years	29	24	8	23	487	42	35	11	7	161
10-14 years	46	26	13	15	100	52	40	21	14	542
15 years or more	*	*	*	*	1	52	35	19	20	542
Number of pregnancies										
0	9	4	0	4	46	0	0	0	0	22
1	4	4	0	0	199	26	21	0	5	38
2	16	15	1	1	271	35	30	0	5	57
3	18	19	3	3	252	50	41	3	13	108
4	29	23	8	4	213	50	36	10	15	165
5	41	29	13	11	122	52	37	16	17	257
6 or more	51	37	34	10	67	54	39	28	17	626
Number of live births										
0	8	6	0	2	104	9	0	0	9	34
1	7	7	1	0	249	33	29	0	4	48
2	22	19	5	1	306	43	35	16	8	74
3	26	21	7	4	250	62	51	20	16	158
4	34	32	12	7	161	56	45	24	13	254
5	40	27	13	13	77	51	32	15	23	281
6 or more	26	4	9	13	23	48	34	18	14	424
All couples	22	18	6	3	1170	50	37	18	15	1273

* Base less than 20 cases.

higher order pregnancy intervals were often followed by an induced abortion.

Young women with only a few pregnancies or births were much less likely than older women with similar histories to begin any method of family limitation, but the differences were less in the case of those with more years of married life or more pregnancies (Table III-9). Apparently, older women who marry late or who for other reasons have had only a few births or pregnancies are much readier to use family limitation methods than younger women at the same stage of family growth.

These cross-sectional comparisons may be misleading, because, for example, the older women with few births are the select small group who did not go on to have larger families, although at risk for many years. More generally, when we compare older and younger women of the same parity at the time of interview, the older women will have taken much longer to arrive at the same family-building stage. Presumably this results at least partly from the use of contraception over a longer period of time.

What we really want to know is whether the older women or the younger ones were more likely to have used family limitation when they were at similar family-building stages. For example, among women who have all had two or more pregnancies, what proportion began contraception before the first pregnancy or the second, and how do older and younger women compare? (Table III-10). On this basis

Table III-10. Proportion of Women Ever Having a Given Number of Pregnancies or More Who Started Using Contraception, Abortion, Sterilization, or Any of the Three Methods for the First Time Before That Pregnancy,[a] by Age of Wife

Number of pregnancies preceding first use of each type of method	Contraception			Abortion			Sterilization			Any method		
	Age of wife			Age of wife			Age of wife			Age of wife		
	20-29	30-39	20-39	20-29	30-39	20-39	20-29	30-39	20-39	20-29	30-39	20-39
0	1	1	1	0	0	0	*	*	*	1	1	1
1	4	2	3	*	*	*	*	*	*	4	2	3
2	6	4	5	1	*	*	*	*	*	6	4	5
3	7	7	7	2	1	2	1	1	1	9	8	8
4	10	8	8	6	4	4	2	2	2	14	10	11
5	12	10	10	10	6	6	8	5	6	19	14	15
6 or more	12	26	24	20	22	21	12	18	17	23	38	37

[a] For example, among women 20-29 who had 2 or more pregnancies 4 per cent began first use of contraception after one but before two pregnancies.

* Less than 1 per cent.

the results are rather different from the cross-sectional view. Younger women were more likely than the older to have used a method of family planning before any given pregnancy up to the sixth. Further, for any one of the three major types of limitation, the proportion of all younger women beginning use before any particular pregnancy order was usually greater and never less than that of the older women. The situation is reversed only when we consider those with six or more pregnancies and ask how many began before the sixth, presumably because young women can only have that large a number of pregnancies if they begin family limitation late or never. We interpret the table as a whole as indicating that the younger women are beginning to use contraception in larger numbers at earlier stages of family growth. This probably means that more of them will eventually take up family planning.

IV. Modernization, Fertility, and the Timing of Childbearing

THE PROBLEM AND THE DATA

BIRTH rates were only moderately high in Taichung by 1962, because of the relatively low fertility of the more modern couples. In this chapter we describe the differences between major social strata in the total number of children born and how these differences develop over the family life-cycle. We shall see in the next chapter that the more modern couples have lower fertility because more of them use family planning and use it at earlier stages of married life than is common in the more traditional sectors of the population.

The differences between social strata in fertility are large and important. Much of the information about these differences presented here is unique for a developing country with respect to the social classifications used, the combinations of fertility measures available, or both. To analyze the relative influence of each social variable and to link the net influence of these variables with the various fertility measures is beyond the scope of this book.[1] Since our primary purpose is to give the background for the Taichung family planning experiment, we have limited ourselves to a more elementary but essential task: that of discussing the distinctive family growth patterns for important social classifications, without trying to determine which of the interdependent social variables are primary and which are secondary.

Fortunately, the major fertility patterns are so consistent for a variety of social or modernization criteria that we can usually generalize from different sets of data without repetitious discussions of each. To be sure, there are significant differences in specific details, and we try to provide enough statistical evidence to permit independent examination of any facts of special interest to the reader.

The data on fertility are presented only for the women over 30 years of age. Up to 1962, significant fertility differentials appear mainly during these later childbearing years, when family planning measures

[1] T. H. Sun carried out such a multivariate analysis of the factors affecting fertility in Taichung in his "Socio-Structural Analysis of Fertility Differentials in Taiwan," Ph.D. Dissertation in Sociology, University of Michigan, 1968.

were used most often. Further, since our sample includes only currently married women, it does not represent at the younger ages the single women who will marry later. By age 30, however, almost all the women who will ever marry have done so. While the data do not cover those over 30 whose marriages are currently broken, this is not a very large group in Taiwan.

The data are presented separately for women 30-34 and 35-39, because fertility of these two age groups differs significantly and because in the 35-39 group we can study women who have almost completed childbearing. Most of our discussions, therefore, will be based on the results for the women 35-39, although the comparable data for the women 30-34 are presented too. The relationships are generally similar in pattern, if not in size, for the two age groups.

DIFFERENTIALS IN CHILDREN EVER BORN

The couples who are most modern by any of our criteria had the smallest number of children by the time the wife was in her thirties (Tables IV-1 to IV-8). The closer to the modern end of any scale, the

Table IV-1. Mean Number of Live Births, Living Children, Children Wanted by Wife, and Survival Ratios, by Wife's Education, for Wives 30-34 and 35-39 Years Old

Wife's education	Average number of: live births	living children	children wife wants	Survival ratio	Number of wives
			Wives 35-39 years old		
None	5.8	5.0	4.5	86	224
Primary school, not grad.	5.2	4.7	4.2	90	40
Primary school grad.	5.4	4.8	4.3	89	180
Junior high school	4.6	4.1	3.7	89	75
Senior high school grad. or higher	3.6	3.4	3.4	94	70
All wives	5.2	4.6	4.2	88	589
Correlation ratio	0.32	0.26	0.30		
			Wives 30-34 years old		
None	4.9	4.3	4.5	88	206
Primary school, not grad.	4.8	4.3	4.4	90	52
Primary school grad.	4.3	4.0	4.0	93	262
Junior high school	3.9	3.7	3.6	95	101
Senior high school grad. or higher	3.3	3.1	3.3	93	63
All wives	4.4	4.0	4.1	91	684
Correlation ratio	0.28	0.23	0.34		

Table IV-2. Mean Number of Live Births, Living Children, Children Wanted by Wife, and Survival Ratios, by Husband's Education, for Wives 30-34 and 35-39 Years Old

	Average number of:				
Husband's education	live births	living children	children wife wants	Survival ratio	Number of couples
		Wives 35-39 years old			
Less than primary school grad.	5.8	4.8	4.5	83	127
Primary school grad.	5.6	5.0	4.5	89	216
Junior high school	5.4	4.8	4.1	89	79
Senior high school grad.	4.8	4.4	3.8	92	67
Some college	3.7	3.4	3.4	92	100
All couples	5.2	4.6	4.2	88	589
Correlation ratio	0.34	0.29	0.34		
		Wives 30-34 years old			
Less than primary school grad.	4.6	4.1	4.3	89	104
Primary school grad.	4.7	4.3	4.3	91	299
Junior high school	4.5	4.3	4.1	96	93
Senior high school grad.	3.7	3.4	3.7	92	106
Some college	3.3	3.2	3.2	97	82
All couples	4.4	4.0	4.1	91	684
Correlation ratio	0.31	0.27	0.34		

fewer the children. For example, by the time the wife was 35-39 the difference in number of children ever born was considerable for the extreme categories in each classification:

Categories compared for wives 35-39 years old with:	*Difference in average no. of births*	*Percentage by which the least modern exceeds the most modern in average no. of live births*
Least and most educated wives	2.2	61
Least and most educated husbands	2.1	57
Farmers and always urban couples	1.4	28
Husband's job: farmers & professionals	2.3	58
Lowest and highest household income	0.0	0
Fewest and most modern objects	1.6	33
Extended families and those always nuclear	1.8	32

Table IV-3. Mean Number of Live Births, Living Children, Children Wanted by Wife, and Survival Ratios, by Couple's Farm Background, for Wives 30-34 and 35-39 Years Old

Couple's farm background	Average number of: live births	living children	children wife wants	Survival ratio	Number of couples
			Wives 35-39 years old		
Farmer now	6.3	5.5	4.9	87	100
Not farmer now					
Both husband and wife have farm background	5.1	4.5	4.1	88	245
Either husband or wife has farm background	4.8	4.3	3.9	90	146
Neither has farm background	4.9	4.4	4.0	90	98
All couples	5.2	4.6	4.2	88	589
Correlation ratio	0.23	0.21	0.26		
			Wives 30-34 years old		
Farmer now	5.1	4.5	4.5	88	119
Not farmer now					
Both husband and wife have farm background	4.4	4.0	4.0	91	266
Either husband or wife has farm background	4.0	3.7	3.9	92	182
Neither has farm background	4.0	3.8	3.9	95	117
All couples	4.4	4.0	4.1	91	684
Correlation ratio	0.23	0.18	0.18		

These sizable differences are likely to increase by the end of the childbearing period, because the proportion currently pregnant was generally higher for the less modern couples (Tables IV-9 to IV-14). As we shall see, the more modern couples were using birth control most extensively and successfully in the later years of married life and this probably will further increase the differentials by the time childbearing ends.

Income does not differentiate high- and low-fertility couples in the same way as other measures used. This further strengthens the argument made earlier, on other grounds, that income is not a very good measure of modernity. We shall carry along some tabulations relating to income, however, because it is so widely used as a measure of social and economic position.

The less modern couples not only had higher average fertility; they were also much more likely to have large numbers of children. This fact is clear if we consider the distributions of couples by the specific

Table IV-4. Mean Number of Live Births, Living Children, Children Wanted by Wife, and Survival Ratios, by Husband's Employment Status, for Wives 30-34 and 35-39 Years Old

Husband's employment status	Average number of: live births	living children	children wife wants	Survival ratio	Number of couples
			Wives 35-39 years old		
Farmer	6.3	5.4	4.9	86	100
Other traditional employment	5.7	5.1	4.5	89	159
Employed by non-relative	4.8	4.2	3.9	88	278
Professional	4.0	3.7	3.4	92	52
All couples	5.2	4.6	4.2	88	589
Correlation ratio	0.30	0.29	0.34		
			Wives 30-34 years old		
Farmer	5.1	4.5	4.5	88	119
Other traditional employment	4.4	4.2	4.2	95	172
Employed by non-relative	4.2	3.8	3.9	90	348
Professional	3.0	3.0	3.4	100	45
All couples	4.4	4.0	4.1	91	684
Correlation ratio	0.28	0.24	0.24		

Table IV-5. Mean Number of Live Births, Living Children, Children Wanted by Wife, and Survival Ratios, by Household Income, for Wives 30-34 and 35-39 Years Old

Household income in New Taiwan dollars	Average number of: live births	living children	children wife wants	Survival ratio	Number of couples
			Wives 35-39 years old		
Less than 1000	5.5	4.6	4.3	84	111
1000-1499	5.1	4.5	4.1	88	177
1500-1999	5.0	4.4	4.0	88	102
2000-2499	5.0	4.7	4.3	94	61
2500 or more	5.5	5.0	4.1	91	94
Not determined	5.3	4.7	4.5	89	44
All couples	5.2	4.6	4.2	88	589
Correlation ratio	0.10	0.10	0.11		
			Wives 30-34 years old		
Less than 1000	4.8	4.2	4.3	88	148
1000-1499	4.3	3.9	4.0	91	208
1500-1999	4.1	3.7	3.8	90	99
2000-2499	4.0	3.7	3.9	92	73
2500 or more	4.1	3.9	4.0	95	93
Not determined	4.8	4.5	4.4	94	63
All couples	4.4	4.0	4.1	91	684
Correlation ratio	0.18	0.15	0.17		

Table IV-6. Mean Number of Live Births, Living Children, Children Wanted by Wife, and Survival Ratios, by Number of Modern Objects Owned, for Wives 30-34 and 35-39 Years Old

Number of modern objects owned	Average number of: live births	living children	children wife wants	Survival ratio	Number of couples
		Wives 35-39 years old			
0 or 1	6.4	5.2	4.8	81	42
2 or 3	5.7	4.8	4.4	84	154
4	5.5	5.0	4.3	91	80
5	4.7	4.2	4.1	89	93
6	4.7	4.4	3.9	94	130
7 or more	4.8	4.3	3.9	90	90
All couples	5.2	4.6	4.2	88	589
Correlation ratio	0.24	0.17	0.21		
		Wives 30-34 years old			
0 or 1	5.0	4.3	4.3	86	75
2 or 3	4.6	4.1	4.2	89	152
4	4.7	4.3	4.4	91	86
5	4.4	4.1	4.1	93	90
6	4.3	4.0	4.1	93	148
7 or more	3.5	3.4	3.5	97	133
All couples	4.4	4.0	4.1	91	684
Correlation ratio	0.27	0.19	0.27		

Table IV-7. Mean Number of Live Births, Living Children, Children Wanted by Wife, and Survival Ratios, by Family Type, for Wives 30-34 and 35-39 Years Old

Family type	Average number of: live births	living children	children wife wants	Survival ratio	Number of couples
		Wives 35-39 years old			
Living in extended unit	5.6	4.9	4.3	88	288
Living in nuclear unit					
Once in extended unit	5.6	5.0	4.3	89	181
Always nuclear	3.7	3.3	3.6	89	120
All couples	5.2	4.6	4.2	88	589
Correlation ratio	0.35	0.34	0.22		
		Wives 30-34 years old			
Living in extended unit	4.5	4.1	4.1	91	346
Living in nuclear unit					
Once in extended unit	4.5	4.1	4.2	91	212
Always nuclear	3.6	3.5	3.7	97	126
All couples	4.4	4.0	4.1	91	684
Correlation ratio	0.20	0.16	0.16		

Table IV-8. Percentage Distributions of Number of Live Births, Number of Children Wife Wants, by Wife's Education, for Wives 35-39 Years Old

Wife's education	Number of children or births: Less than 2	2	3 or 4	5	6 or more	Total: Percentage	Number
	Percentage distribution by live births						
None	5	4	10	21	60	100	224
Primary school, not grad.	10	5	15	22	48	100	40
Primary school grad.	8	4	19	21	48	100	180
Junior high school	3	11	34	23	29	100	75
Senior high school grad. or higher	8	10	56	17	9	100	70
All wives	6	6	22	21	45	100	589
	Percentage distribution by living children						
None	8	4	24	22	42	100	224
Primary school, not grad.	10	5	22	28	35	100	40
Primary school grad.	8	4	28	25	35	100	180
Junior high school	10	7	39	23	21	100	75
Senior high school grad. or higher	8	10	64	12	6	100	70
All wives	8	5	32	22	33	100	589
	Percentage distribution by children wife wants						
None	1	4	51	23	21	100	224
Primary school, not grad.	2	10	53	20	15	100	40
Primary school grad.	0	5	60	21	14	100	180
Junior high school	0	12	75	9	4	100	75
Senior high school grad. or higher	4	16	71	6	3	100	70
All wives	1	7	60	18	14	100	589

numbers of children (Table IV-8) rather than only by the average number of children. For example, among wives 35-39 years old, 60 per cent of those with no education had already borne six or more children, as compared with 9 per cent of those who were high school graduates. Since not many wives wanted to have fewer than two children, it is not surprising that the proportion having that few does not vary with educational level. While not many women wanted to have only two children, there were enough for significant differences to be evident between the two most educated groups of women and the others in this respect (about 10 per cent of the better educated and about 5 per cent of the less educated had borne just two children). What really distinguishes the better-educated women is that so many of them had just three or four children. The proportion having this

Table IV-9. Age at Marriage, Open Birth Interval, Fecundability, and Current Pregnancy, by Wife's Education, for Wives 30-34 and 35-39 Years Old

Wife's education	Mean age at marriage (in years)	Fecundability rate per 1000 women[a]	Mean open birth interval: in months	Mean open birth interval: as percentage of mean number of months married	Percentage pregnant at first interview	Number of couples
			Wives 35-39 years old			
None	19.0	94	48	23	9	224
Primary school, not grad.	20.2	90	44	23	0	60
Primary school grad.	19.5	109	64	31	5	180
Junior high school	20.1	129	70	36	5	75
Senior high school grad. or higher	21.4	153	86	47	1	70
All wives	19.7	108	60	29	6	589
Correlation ratio	0.25		0.26		0.12	
			Wives 30-34 years old			
None	19.5	130	25	17	23	206
Primary school, not grad.	19.2	215	28	19	15	52
Primary school grad.	20.1	152	39	28	10	262
Junior high school	20.6	203	42	31	4	101
Senior high school grad. or higher	21.3	141	47	38	8	63
All wives	20.0		35	25	13	684
Correlation ratio	0.20		0.23		0.20	

[a] Fecundability refers to the monthly probability of conceiving in the absence of contraception during the period at risk; is computed for wives pregnant at least once and not premaritally pregnant, and is based on the duration between marriage and the beginning of first pregnancy. For simplicity, average fecundability of a group of women, which is the unweighted mean of individual fecundabilities, is expressed in terms of 1000 women.

moderate number increases from 10 per cent among the least educated to more than 50 per cent for the best-educated women. There are similar differentials for the other modernization criteria.[2] Many more of the professionals than of the farmers had fewer than three children (21 per cent and 2 per cent). The major differences are that 42 per cent of the professionals had three or four children, as compared with only 12 per cent of the farmers; and only 37 per cent of the professionals had five or more children, as compared with 86 per cent of

[2] Unpublished tables show similar results for husband's employment status and family type.

Table IV-10. Age at Marriage, Open Birth Interval, Fecundability, and Current Pregnancy, by Husband's Education, for Wives 30-34 and 35-39 Years Old

Husband's education	Mean age at marriage (in years)	Fecundability rate per 1000 women	Mean open birth interval: in months	Mean open birth interval: as percentage of mean number of months married	Percentage pregnant at first interview	Number of couples
			Wives 35-39 years old			
Less than primary school grad.	19.3	95	47	22	12	127
Primary school grad.	19.2	96	55	26	5	216
Junior high school	19.5	132	64	31	3	79
Senior high school grad. or higher	20.0	127	70	35	3	67
Some college	21.1	120	77	42	4	100
All couples	19.7	108	60	29	6	589
Correlation ratio	0.23		0.21		0.14	
			Wives 30-34 years old			
Less than primary school grad.	19.8	153	22	16	17	104
Primary school grad.	19.6	147	32	22	17	299
Junior high school	20.1	152	33	24	7	93
Senior high school grad. or higher	20.8	152	45	34	9	106
Some college	20.7	208	52	40	9	82
All couples	20.0	155	35	25	13	684
Correlation ratio	0.17		0.27		0.13	

the farmers. The pattern, then, is that irrespective of their characteristics, almost all the couples had some children, and generally they had at least three or four. What differentiates the more modern couples is that they do not go on to have five or six or more, as the more traditional couples do.

THE TIMING OF CHILDBEARING

The more modern couples had fewer children mainly because they ended childbearing earlier in married life. They were not less fecundable[3] than the more traditional couples; they did not have fewer children in the first five to ten years of marriage; the average interval between their births was not longer. The decisive difference was

[3] See footnote *a*, Table IV-9 for definition.

Table IV-11. Age at Marriage, Open Birth Interval, Fecundability, and Current Pregnancy, by Couple's Farm Background, for Wives 30-34 and 35-39 Years Old

Couple's farm background	Mean age at marriage (in years)	Fecundability rate per 1000 women	Mean open birth interval: in months	Mean open birth interval: as percentage of mean number of months married	Percentage pregnant at first interview	Number of couples
			Wives 35-39 years old			
Farmer now	19.3	94	35	17	8	100
Not farmer now						
Both husband and wife have farm background	19.6	103	66	33	6	245
Either husband or wife has farm background	19.8	95	66	33	7	146
Neither has farm background	20.0	117	60	30	1	98
All couples	19.7	108	60	29	6	589
Correlation ratio	0.07		0.22		0.10	
			Wives 30-34 years old			
Farmer now	19.6	143	21	15	17	119
Not farmer now						
Both husband and wife have farm background	19.7	149	36	25	12	266
Either husband or wife has farm background	20.4	164	37	27	13	182
Neither has farm background	20.6	162	43	31	12	117
All couples	20.0	155	35	25	13	684
Correlation ratio	0.13		0.20		0.05	

that the interval since the last birth—the open birth interval—was longer for the more modern couples.

Since fecundability was generally above average for the more modern couples, it is not likely that their lower fertility was due to sterility or to fecundity impairments (Tables IV-9 to IV-15). The operational measure used is such that the higher fecundability of the more modern couples means that, on the average, they became pregnant more quickly after they were married. It is possible that the lower fecundability measures for the more traditional couples could result from their greater failure to report early pregnancies or births, par-

Table IV-12. Age at Marriage, Open Birth Interval, Fecundability, and Current Pregnancy, by Husband's Employment Status, for Wives 30-34 and 35-39 Years Old

Husband's employment status	Mean age at marriage (in years)	Fecundability rate per 1000 women	Mean open birth interval: in months	Mean open birth interval: as percentage of mean number of months married	Percentage pregnant at first interview	Number of couples
			Wives 35-39 years old			
Farmer	19.3	92	36	17	8	100
Other traditional employment	19.2	105	62	29	6	159
Employed by non-relative	19.8	114	64	32	5	278
Professional	21.1	110	80	43	4	52
All couples	19.7	108	60	29	6	589
Correlation ratio	0.18		0.23		0.05	
			Wives 30-34 years old			
Farmer	19.6	144	21	15	17	119
Other traditional employment	19.9	154	36	26	14	172
Employed by non-relative	19.9	129	38	27	11	348
Professional	22.2	208	42	38	20	45
All couples	20.0	155	35	25	13	684
Correlation ratio	0.21		0.19		0.08	

Table IV-13. Age at Marriage, Open Birth Interval, Fecundability, and Current Pregnancy, by Household Income, for Wives 30-34 and 35-39 Years Old

Household income in New Taiwan Dollars	Mean age at marriage (in years)	Fecundability rate per 1000 women	Mean open birth interval: in months	Mean open birth interval: as percentage of mean number of months married	Percentage pregnant at first interview	Number of couples
			Wives 35-39 years old			
Less than 1000	19.5	86	42	20	9	111
1000-1499	19.7	98	60	30	5	177
1500-1999	19.8	114	62	31	2	102
2000-2499	20.3	142	66	34	5	61
2500 or more	19.1	124	73	35	5	94
Not determined	19.7	95	61	30	9	44
All couples	19.7	108	60	29	6	589
Correlation ratio	0.10		0.19		0.10	
			Wives 30-34 years old			
Less than 1000	19.8	146	23	16	20	148
1000-1499	19.8	134	35	24	15	208
1500-1999	20.2	192	43	31	4	99
2000-2499	20.4	143	44	32	10	73
2500 or more	20.3	159	44	32	11	93
Not determined	20.2	160	28	19	11	63
All couples	20.0	155	35	25	13	684
Correlation ratio	0.09		0.24		0.14	

ticularly those that produced no surviving child.[4] But if this were true, then the fertility differences between the modern and traditional couples would be even greater than those we report.

How childbearing proceeds over the family life-cycle is evident in the birth rates for successive periods after marriage (Table IV-16). During the first five years or so of marriage, there are no significant consistent differences between social strata. During the next five years differences begin to appear, particularly in lower rates, for the most advanced or modern categories. Then, after ten years of marriage, very large differences appear, with fairly large, monotonic decreases in fertility as we proceed to the more modern categories of our classifications. We illustrate with the following comparisons of the extreme categories for three variables[5] for women 30-39:

Categories compared for wives 30-39 years old:	*% by which fertility rate for the least modern exceeds the fertility rate for the most modern in the following periods of married life: (Number of years after marriage):*		
	0-4	*5-9*	*10 or more*
Least and most educated wives	(–5%) *	41%	172%
Farmers and professionals	(–1%) *	40%	125%
Extended families and those always nuclear families	12%	38%	55%

* Less modern group has lower fertility

It is useful also to consider fertility rates for periods of married life counted backwards from the present to the time of the marriage rather

[4] See Appendix IV-1.

[5] For these tabulations and several others we have selected three social variables: wife's education, husband's employment status, and family structure. Wife's education is the most consistently useful measure in our wide range of work with the Taiwan data, so we will restrict some of the later tabulations to that variable alone. Husband's employment status differentiates the couples quite well on many fertility

Table IV-14. Age at Marriage, Open Birth Interval, Fecundability, and Current Pregnancy, by Number of Modern Objects Owned, for Wives 30-34 and 35-39 Years Old

Number of objects owned	Mean age at marriage (in years)	Fecundability rate per 1000 women	Mean open birth interval in months	Mean open birth interval as percentage of mean number of months married	Percentage pregnant at first interview	Number of couples
			Wives 35-39 years old			
0 or 1	19.6	95	25	12	12	42
2 or 3	19.1	84	48	23	6	154
4	20.2	100	48	25	9	80
5	20.1	99	72	36	4	93
6	19.9	112	69	34	4	130
7 or more	19.5	149	81	40	3	90
All couples	19.7	108	60	29	6	589
Correlation ratio	0.14		0.31		0.11	
			Wives 30-34 years old			
0 or 1	19.3	139	23	15	20	75
2 or 3	19.8		27	19	19	152
4	19.7	160	30	21	21	86
5	20.1	141	33	23	10	90
6	20.0	178	42	29	6	148
7 or more	20.9	157	48	37	8	133
All couples	20.0	155	35	25	13	684
Correlation ratio	0.17		0.26		0.18	

than the reverse (Table IV-17). This may be the view of the couples themselves, standing in the present. They may be most influenced in decisions about family planning by their recent fertility, since this is what makes them aware of a continuing risk of pregnancy and child-bearing. There are fertility differences very much larger in the three years or so immediately preceding the survey. In the categories of wife's education and husband's employment status, fertility rates are

---

variables and gives a measure of important differences in the economic sphere. The family structure variable is included both because presumably it represents a principle important in Chinese traditional thinking about family life and because it is the subject of much speculation but little data in discussions of developing societies.

Table IV-15. Age at Marriage, Open Birth Interval, Fecundability, and Current Pregnancy, by Family Type, for Wives 30-34 and 35-39 Years Old

Family type	Mean age at marriage (in years)	Fecundability rate per 1000 women	Mean open birth interval: in months	Mean open birth interval: as percentage of mean number of months married	Percentage pregnant at first interview	Number of couples
			Wives 35-39 years old			
Living in extended unit	19.2	112	56	27	6	288
Living in nuclear unit						
Once in extended unit	19.1	116	54	26	6	181
Always nuclear	20.7	88	78	42	6	120
All couples	19.7	108	60	29	6	589
Correlation ratio	0.19		0.18		0.01	
			Wives 30-34 years old			
Living in extended unit	19.9	148	32	22	12	346
Living in nuclear unit						
Once in extended unit	19.8	146	37	25	14	212
Always nuclear	20.8	202	40	31	17	126
All couples	20.0	155	35	25	13	684
Correlation ratio	0.13		0.08		0.06	

three to five times higher for the least modern than for the most modern classes. The differences in the category based on wife's education, for example, are quite large for the most recent five years of marriage and still sizable for the five years before that. Going back ten to fourteen years, the differences are much smaller and only the most educated women have distinctively low fertility that far back. For periods more than fifteen years ago, the fertility rates are actually higher for the better educated than for the less educated. Differentials similar in pattern but varying in size are also found, using this same view from present back into past, for categories based on husband's employment status or the family structure.

The family structure differentials are especially interesting. Those who had always lived in nuclear units had lower fertility than the other

Table IV-16. Duration-Specific Birth Rates for Wives 30-39 Years Old, by Selected Social Characteristics

Social characteristics	Fertility rates per annum per 1000 woman-years, by number of years since marriage[a]		
	0-4 years	5-9 years	10-14 years
Wife's education			
None	368	380	332
Primary school, not grad.	395	383	312
Primary school grad.	394	359	274
Junior high school	426	323	205
Senior high school grad. or higher	386	269	122
Husband's employment status			
Farmer	394	415	373
Other traditional employment	385	385	282
Employed by non-relative	391	325	254
Professional	380	297	166
Family type			
Living in extended unit	396	374	299
Living in nuclear unit			
Once in extended unit	397	373	287
Always nuclear	355	271	190
Use of family limitation			
Sterilized by 2nd interview	428	386	227
Used contraception and/or abortion by 1st interview	418	266	281
Never used birth control	340	321	277
All wives (30-39 years old)	389	355	277

[a] Rates for each period computed only for women married throughout that period.

couples—by a very wide margin for whatever period we consider, and whether we measure the time periods backwards from the present or forward from the time of marriage. As compared with those always living in nuclear families, fertility was not much higher even late in married life for those who lived in a nuclear unit when interviewed but who began married life in an extended family.[6] The couples who moved from extended to nuclear units did have significantly lower

[6] Unpublished work by Solomon Chu demonstrates that those families which are now nuclear but were once extended almost invariably began married life living in the extended unit (usually in a stem family or a stem-joint family) involving the husband's parents. Very rarely did extended family experience begin after marriage or involve a move back into the extended unit after an initial period of living alone. Unfortunately, we cannot date the various stages except with reference to the time of marriage and the time of the survey.

Table IV-17. Specific Birth Rates for Periods of Time Counted Backwards from Time of First Interview for Women 30-39 Years Old, Married at Least 10 Years, by Selected Social Characteristics

Social characteristics	Duration-specific birth rates for indicated periods of months preceding first interview[a]							
	0-11	12-23	24-35	36-47	48-59	60-119	120-179	180 or more
Wife's education								
None	248	268	296	316	351	375	382	340
Primary school, not grad.	207	256	268	305	280	376	380	371
Primary school grad.	170	183	252	255	287	354	397	375
Junior high school	105	98	168	182	189	327	410	446
Senior high school grad. or higher	88	49	69	157	137	245	355	441
Husband's employment status								
Farmer	301	296	342	357	408	405	416	358
Other traditional employment	187	163	262	269	316	351	406	359
Employed by non-relative	155	194	212	234	240	337	367	381
Professional	74	59	88	176	118	282	390	395
Family type								
Living in extended unit	222	214	259	279	312	358	419	384
Living in nuclear unit								
Once in extended unit	169	209	249	256	310	369	390	386
Always nuclear	107	117	174	219	153	293	292	287
Use of family limitation								
Sterilized by 2nd interview	104	93	124	212	197	353	459	397
Used contraception and/or abortion by 1st interview	100	186	257	252	303	363	421	433
Never used birth control	285	243	273	289	299	337	332	320
All wives (30-39 years old)	184	196	241	262	283	350	388	371

[a] The rates in each period are calculated only for those women married throughout that period. For example, the first period is for the 11.9 months immediately preceding the first interview, the second is for the 12.0 to 23.9 months period before the first interview, etc.

fertility than those remaining in extended families, but this is a recent difference and it disappears after five years in the view backwards in time. Those couples who eventually broke away from the extended family initially were no different from those who did not make the break. It is only after ten years or so of married life that their fertility rates appear lower than those of couples in the extended families, but even then they do not have the much lower fertility rate of those always in a nuclear family setting.

Another view of the family-building process comes from a consideration of the cumulative number of children that have been born after various periods of marriage (Table IV-18). In this view, for the three categories of modernization characteristics considered, cumulative fertility differentials begin to appear after eight to ten years of marriage. These differentials are much larger and more systematic fifteen years or so after marriage.

Table IV-18. Cumulative Birth Rates (per Woman) by Periods After First Marriage, by Selected Social Characteristics for Women 30-39 Years Old

	Cumulative rates per woman						Number of women					
	Number of complete years after first marriage[a]											
Social characteristics	2	6	8	10	13	15	2	6	8	10	13	15
Wife's education												
None	0.7	2.2	3.0	3.7	4.7	5.2	431	429	424	404	344	274
Primary school, not grad.	0.8	2.4	3.1	3.9	4.8	5.2	92	88	86	83	68	53
Primary school grad.	0.8	2.3	3.1	3.7	4.5	5.0	444	433	422	399	315	226
Junior high school	0.9	2.5	3.2	3.7	4.4	4.7	175	172	164	151	119	92
Senior high school grad. or higher	0.8	2.3	2.9	3.2	3.6	3.8	133	126	118	109	94	63
Husband's employment status												
Farmer	0.7	2.4	3.2	4.0	5.1	5.7	220	218	214	199	168	124
Other traditional employment	0.8	2.3	3.1	3.8	4.6	5.1	330	325	316	304	251	198
Employed by non-relative	0.8	2.3	3.0	3.5	4.3	4.7	630	617	601	569	462	343
Professional	0.7	2.3	2.9	3.3	3.9	4.3	95	88	83	74	59	43
Family type												
Living in extended unit	0.8	2.4	3.1	3.8	4.7	5.3	636	623	613	574	470	356
Living in nuclear unit												
Once in extended unit	0.8	2.4	3.1	3.8	4.6	5.1	394	389	377	363	302	237
Always nuclear	0.8	2.1	2.7	3.1	3.6	3.8	245	236	224	209	168	121
Use of family limitation												
Sterilized by 2nd interview	0.8	2.6	3.4	4.0	4.8	5.1	204	202	201	196	174	144
Used contraception and/or abortion by 1st interview	0.8	2.5	3.2	3.9	4.7	5.2	475	466	455	429	346	244
Never used birth control	0.7	2.1	2.8	3.4	4.2	4.7	596	580	558	521	420	320
All wives (30-39 years old)	0.8	2.3	3.1	3.7	4.5	5.0	1275	1248	1214	1146	940	708

[a] Rates computed in each period only for women married throughout the period. For example, the first period covers the first two years of marriage, that is the first 1.99 years.

It is consistent with these differentials over time that the less and more modern couples should differ with respect to the average time since their last birth but not with respect to the average interval between births. The proportions of the more modern classes who tried to space their children were apparently too small to affect the average interval between births. However, the proportions of these classes trying to stop further family growth were large enough and sufficiently correlated with the social characteristics to make for differences of 100 per cent or more in the length of the open interval. The long open interval for the more modern couples is consistent, of course, with the low fertility rates during the last few years before the interview. Since the wives with the most education married later than others, the differentials are even more pronounced when the open interval is expressed as a proportion of the total months married (Tables IV-9 to IV-15).

The very last closed interval is somewhat longer for the more modern couples, when we compare couples who had had a similar number of births as of the interview. This is consistent with the fact that these couples were also more likely than others to begin the use of family planning in that last interval. We believe that for many of these couples the intent was probably to end childbearing rather than to lengthen the time between the last two children, but an interval that was meant to be open was closed by an unplanned pregnancy.

These conclusions about the relation of birth intervals and the open interval to modernization are taken from an extensive analysis by Mohapatra.[7] The following data for wives 30-39 with at least two live births are illustrative:

Wife's education	*Average birth interval in months*	*Interval since last birth in months*
None	28.7	31.0
Primary, not graduate	27.5	35.6
Primary, graduate	26.7	40.8
Jr. high	27.2	52.8
Sr. high graduate or higher	27.1	66.4
Husband's employment status		
Farmer	26.9	27.7
Other traditional employment	26.8	41.8
Employed by non-relatives	28.1	45.0
Professional	26.6	55.3

Differences in age at marriage can account for some of the fertility differentials (Tables IV-9 to IV-15). The age at marriage was moderately higher for the more modern couples, especially if education or family structure or husband's employment status is the classifying

[7] Mohapatra, *op.cit.* These data are for all birth intervals except the open interval. Mohapatra demonstrates similar results when particular birth intervals (e.g., that between second and third birth) are considered.

principle. We illustrate below by comparing, again, extreme categories of the variables:

Categories compared for wives 35-39 years old:	*Differences in months for extreme groups in:* average age at marriage	*the open birth interval*
Least- and most-educated wives	20	38
Least- and most-educated husbands	21	30
Farmers and always urban couples	8	25
Husband's job: farmers & professionals	21	44
Fewest and most modern objects	4	33
Extended families and those always nuclear	18	22

The differences in the length of the open interval are much larger than those in the age at marriage. However, the months in the early years of marriage when fecundability is high are more important for fertility than those later in the marriage. Mohapatra, in his detailed analysis of the role of marriage age and open birth interval, comes to the conclusion that both have an effect on the fertility differentials, but that the open interval is more important even for those characteristics related most closely to age at marriage.

We have already seen that for similar durations of marriage the fertility rates of the more modern were considerably lower late in marriage. This reduction of the later fertility rates has a considerably greater effect on fertility than the later age at marriage. For example, ten to fourteen years after marriage the best-educated women had fertility rates so much lower than the least-educated women as to make a difference of 1,050 births per thousand over this five-year period. Those women with the least education married on the average two years earlier than the best educated. If they had postponed their marriages by two years and then borne babies at the rate found for their first five years of marriage, they would have had 780 fewer births, a reduction significantly smaller than the number of births averted by the longer open interval of the best educated, the effects of which were still not all recorded at the time of the interview.

We have no reason to believe that the differences in age at marriage in relation to modernization have been changing very much in recent years. In any case, they do not account for any substantial part of the fertility decline in either Taichung or Taiwan in recent years.[8]

COMPARISON OF THE NUMBER OF CHILDREN BORN AND WANTED

The more and less modern couples differed more in the number of children ever born than in the number alive (compare the averages in Tables IV-1 to IV-7). The less modern couples bore more children, but fewer of them survived. The families with larger numbers of children are probably less able to give them adequate care, since they are poorer and know less about modern health practices. Another possibility is that the experience of higher child mortality may encourage higher fertility in order to insure the survival of a desired minimum number.

The difference between the more and less modern couples is even less in terms of the number of children wanted than it is for the numbers alive or ever born:

	Differences in the average number of:		
Categories compared for couples with wives 35-39 years old:	*children ever born*	*children alive*	*children wife wants*
Least- and most-educated wives	2.2	1.6	1.1
Least- and most-educated husbands	2.1	1.4	1.1
Farmers and always urban couples	1.4	1.1	0.9
Husband's work: farmers & professionals	2.3	1.7	1.5
Lowest and highest household income	0.0	–0.4	0.2
Fewest and most modern objects	1.4	0.9	0.7
Extended families and those always nuclear	1.0	1.6	0.7

So the less and more modern couples differ least in the number of children wanted and most in the number ever born. The fact that the less modern say that they want more children than others is sometimes said to be a rationalization for the larger number they have alive.

[8] See R. Freedman and J. Muller, "The Continuing Fertility Decline in Taiwan: 1965," *Population Index*, 33, No. 1, January-March 1967, 3-16.

This explanation is not very plausible, because when couples with the same number of births are considered, the number who want more children is greater for the less educated.

The averages may be less meaningful than the distributions of specific numbers of children born, alive, and wanted. This is illustrated for the categories based on wife's education in Table IV-8. For example, of the wives with no education, only 20 per cent wanted six or more children but more than 60 per cent had borne that many already. Among the high school graduates, only 3 per cent wanted and 9 per cent had borne six or more children. The number of women who wanted fewer than two children was very small. The number wanting just two children increased with education, perhaps a sign of what the future will bring when many more will be better educated. At least 50 per cent of every educational group, however, wanted three or four children, and this proportion rose to over 70 per cent among the better-educated wives.

Every class of couples, including the more modern, had been unsuccessful, on the average, in limiting births to the number wanted. By the time the wife was between 35 and 39, the average number of children ever born exceeded the number wanted in thirty of thirty-two categories considered (Tables IV-1 to IV-7). The number of children alive also exceeded the number wanted in thirty of thirty-two categories. The only exceptions are the couples who always lived in nuclear families and those with the best-educated wives. It is likely that the discrepancy between the number alive and number wanted will increase by the end of the childbearing period.

These comparisons do not specify the size of the rather large minority of couples in all social strata who already had more than the number of children they wanted (Table IV-19). This proportion varies from 20 to 46 per cent among the various groups considered. In view of the fact that many of the couples who said they had just the wanted number were either using no birth control or using ineffective methods, it is likely that many of those giving this satisfied response will be among the dissatisfied, with "too many" children, before the wife passes through the menopause.

The more modern couples were not much more successful than others in having just the number of children they wanted, because although they had substantially fewer children, they also wanted fewer, and those they had were more likely to survive. For example,

Table IV-19. Percentage Distributions, Comparison of Number of Children Alive and Wanted, by Wife's Education, Husband's Employment Status, Family Type, and Number of Modern Objects Owned, for Wives 35-39 Years Old.

Characteristics of couples	Comparison of number of children alive and wanted: number of children alive is: fewer than wife wants	the number wife wants	more than wife wants	up to God, Fate, etc.	Total: Percentage	Total: Number
Wife's education						
None	21	39	34	6	100	224
Primary school, not grad.	30	23	45	2	100	40
Primary school grad.	24	28	46	2	100	180
Junior high school	27	30	40	3	100	75
Senior high school grad. or higher	26	48	23	3	100	70
Husband's employment status						
Farmer	19	33	42	6	100	100
Other traditional employment	21	32	42	5	100	159
Employed by non-relative	26	37	34	3	100	278
Professional	31	29	38	2	100	52
Family type						
Living in extended unit	18	35	43	4	100	288
Living in nuclear unit						
Once in extended unit	44	32	20	4	100	181
Always nuclear	20	36	41	3	100	120
Number of modern objects owned						
0 or 1	17	52	29	2	100	42
2 or 3	23	31	39	7	100	154
4	23	31	41	5	100	80
5	29	37	30	4	100	93
6	20	38	41	1	100	130
7 or more	30	28	40	2	100	90
All couples	24	34	38	4	100	589

the better-educated women were much more likely than others to say that they wanted no more children when they still had only a few (Table IV-20). Twenty-seven per cent of the best-educated wives with only two births wanted no more children, as compared with 4 per cent of the least-educated wives. The differences between the educational classes narrow with the number of children already born, but there is always a significant rise in the proportion who want no more children as education increases. Obviously, many of the better-educated women wanted to limit childbearing to a level that is low as judged either by Chinese tradition or by the standards of the less educated.[9]

[9] Unpublished tables show similar result for employment status and family type.

Table IV-20. Proportion of Wives Who Want No More Children[a] by Wife's Education, by Number of Live Births

Wife's education	Number of live births: 0 or 1	2	3	4	5	6 or more	All wives	Number of wives
Primary school, not grad.	0	4	28	50	74	85	44	1070
Primary school grad.	0	8	33	60	76	92	45	842
Junior high school	3	14	48	83	88	97	52	320
Senior high school grad. or higher	0	27	55	94	85	*	47	211
All wives	**	10	36	62	77	88	46	
Number of wives	435	379	408	414	358	449		2443

[a] Includes wives who said they wanted fewer children than they had alive. Wives who said "up to God," "fate", or "Chance" or gave no answer are counted as wanting more children in this tabulation.

* Base less than 20 cases.

**Less than 1 per cent.

V. Modernization and Birth Control Before the Organized Program

Even before the organized program, a large proportion of the more modern couples had used some form of birth control. The traditional couples were much less likely to begin on their own initiative in this pre-program period, even if they had all the children they wanted or more (Tables V-1 to V-3). For example, among those having just the number of children wanted at the time of the survey, 83 per cent of the most educated and 36 per cent of the least educated had used some form of birth control. Among those who had more children than they wanted, virtually all (97 per cent) of the best educated had done something, as compared with 40 per cent of the least educated.

Table V-1. Proportion Who Ever Used Any Form of Birth Control (Contraception, Induced Abortion, or Sterilization), by Comparison of Children Alive and Wanted, by Three Social Characteristics

	Comparison of number of children alive and wanted: number of children alive is:					
Social characteristics	fewer than wife wants	the number wife wants	more than wife wants	up to God, Fate, etc.[a/]	All couples	Number of couples
Wife's education						
Primary school, not grad.	10	36	40	7	22	1070
Primary school grad.	19	58	64	*	38	842
Junior high school	30	77	84	*	56	320
Senior high school grad. or higher	56	83	97	*	72	211
Family type						
Living in extended unit	14	46	57	12	31	1263
Living in nuclear unit						
Once in extended unit	21	55	61	10	40	658
Always nuclear	29	71	72	*	45	522
Husband's employment status						
Farmer	6	33	34	8	17	448
Other traditional employment	16	49	58	16	34	641
Employed by non-relative	23	60	69	14	41	1199
Professional	47	79	84	*	63	155
All couples	19	54	60	13	36	
Number of couples	1237	664	452	90		2443

[a/] Includes indeterminate cases.

* Base less than 20 cases.

Table V-2. Proportion Who Ever Used Contraception, by Comparison of Children Alive and Wanted, by Three Social Characteristics

Social characteristics	Comparison of number of children alive and wanted: number of children alive is: fewer than wife wants	the number wife wants	more than wife wants	up to God, Fate, etc.[a/]	All couples	Number of couples
Wife's education						
Primary school, not grad.	5	25	25	3	14	1070
Primary school grad.	15	46	47	*	29	842
Junior high school	26	66	60	*	46	320
Senior high school grad. or higher	55	74	88	*	66	211
Family type						
Living in extended unit	11	39	42	9	24	1263
Living in nuclear unit						
Once in extended unit	17	37	47	5	29	658
Always nuclear	24	59	45	*	36	522
Husband's employment status						
Farmer	2	23	25	4	11	448
Other traditional employment	11	37	42	8	25	641
Employed by non-relative	19	48	47	14	32	1199
Professional	46	70	77	*	59	155
All couples	16	42	44	10	28	
Number of couples	1237	664	452	90		2443

[a/] Includes indeterminate cases.

* Base less than 20 cases.

We have already seen that the better-educated couples wanted fewer children and that among those with any specific number of children, more of the better-educated wives were willing to say that they wanted no more. Now we see that those who were better educated were also much readier than others to try to realize their desires by taking action to prevent further births. The use of some form of birth control before the program began increases substantially with the degree of modernization, by any of the criteria used (Tables V-4 to V-5).

The relationship between preventive action and modernization is much stronger for the use of contraception than for abortion or sterilization. Contraception is probably the most flexible and rational response to the problem of how to limit family size. Abortion is action taken only after a conception, to remove a pregnancy that wasn't wanted in the first place. Given the circumstances surrounding the procuring of an abortion in Taiwan, this is understandably not the

Table V-3. Proportion Sterilized or Using Contraception at First Interview, by Comparison of Children Alive and Wanted, by Three Social Characteristics

	Comparison of number of children alive and wanted: number of children alive is:					
Social characteristics	fewer than wife wants	the number wife wants	more than wife wants	up to God, Fate, etc.[a/]	All couples	Number of couples
Wife's education						
Primary school, not grad.	6	30	28	6	16	1070
Primary school grad.	12	51	54	*	30	842
Junior high school	18	68	69	*	44	320
Senior high school grad. or higher	33	76	85	*	55	211
Family type						
Living in extended unit	9	39	45	5	34	1263
Living in nuclear unit						
Once in extended unit	14	48	48	10	32	658
Always nuclear	17	61	65	*	34	522
Husband's employment status						
Farmer	3	31	28	0	14	448
Other traditional employment	9	42	46	12	26	641
Employed by non-relative	15	51	55	11	32	1199
Professional	28	72	74	*	49	155
All couples	12	46	49	8	28	
Number of couples	1237	664	452	90		2443

[a/] Includes indeterminate cases.

* Base less than 20 cases.

method of choice. Sterilization tends to be reserved for those financially better off, because of its cost, and it is almost always an irreversible step. Furthermore, sterilization tended to be used only rather late in family growth. The facts are that contraception was the primary method of birth control in Taichung and that its use was strongly related to levels of education and modernization existing before the organized program began.

Apparently, among the elite minority of the most modern couples a significant number had begun to use contraception as a method for spacing births. Among those who still wanted more children, half of the best-educated wives had already used contraception (Table V-2). This proportion was substantially less for each progressively lower level of education, declining to 5 per cent among the least-educated group.

Table V-4. Proportion of Couples Who Have Ever Used Any or Specific Methods of Birth Control, by Selected Measures of Modernization, for Wives 20-39 Years Old

Measures of modernization	Percentage who have ever used: contra-ception	abor-tion	steril-ization	any of three	Number of couples
Wife's education					
None	11	7	5	19	767
Primary school, not grad.	19	9	12	30	303
Primary school grad.	29	13	9	38	842
Junior high school	46	20	13	57	320
Senior high school grad. or higher	66	22	12	72	211
Correlation ratio	0.36	0.15	0.09	0.34	
Husband's employment status					
Farmer	11	5	5	17	448
Other traditional employment	25	12	10	34	641
Employed by non-relative	32	14	10	41	1199
Professional	59	21	8	63	155
Correlation ratio	0.24	0.12	0.06	0.23	
Family type					
Living in extended unit	24	10	8	31	1263
Living in nuclear unit					
Once in extended unit	29	14	11	40	658
Always nuclear	36	16	10	45	522
Correlation ratio	0.10	0.08	0.06	0.12	
Husband's education					
Less than primary school grad.	11	6	5	18	450
Primary school grad.	19	9	8	27	1002
Junior high school	38	18	11	51	324
Senior high school grad.	40	17	12	49	375
Some college	58	21	12	64	292
Correlation ratio	0.34	0.16	0.09	0.33	

If abortion and sterilization are added to contraception as methods of birth control, among those who wanted more children the proportion that ever practiced any methods of birth control varies from 10 per cent among the least educated to 56 per cent among the best educated (Table V-1). Among those who by their own definition already had too many children, less than half of the least educated had made any attempt to do anything about it; virtually all of the best educated had done something.

Failure to continue birth control practices after beginning use, even when no more children are wanted, is one of the persistent problems

Table V-4 (continued).

Measures of modernization	Percentage who have ever used contra-ception	abor-tion	steril-ization	any of three	Number of couples
Farm background					
Farmer now	12	5	5	18	448
Not farmer now					
Both husband and wife have farm background	29	13	10	38	919
Either husband or wife has farm background	31	13	9	38	677
Neither has farm background	38	17	12	48	399
Correlation ratio	0.18	0.11	0.07	0.20	
Household income in New Taiwan dollars					
Less than 1000	17	6	5	23	559
1000-1499	24	12	8	31	698
1500-1999	35	17	13	46	367
2000-2499	41	15	13	50	258
2500 or more	44	18	11	53	332
Not determined	17	9	9	25	229
Correlation ratio	0.23	0.13	0.10	0.24	
Number of modern objects owned					
0 or 1	12	5	3	17	191
2 or 3	16	7	5	22	572
4	18	8	8	26	375
5	28	13	9	36	380
6	36	16	11	46	537
7 or more	52	22	16	63	388
Correlation ratio	0.30	0.17	0.14	0.32	
All couples	28	12	9	36	2443

of family planning programs in developing countries—especially among the lower-status, more traditional couples. Therefore, the proportion ever using contraception may be less significant than the proportion of those currently protected, either permanently by sterilization or temporarily by contraception (Table V-3).

The proportion of all couples thus currently protected varies from 16 per cent among the least educated to 55 per cent among the best educated. This difference depended very much on the number of children alive and wanted. Very few women of any educational class wanted fewer than two children. However, even among those with fewer than two births, 20 per cent of the best-educated women were currently protected, as compared with 2 to 4 per cent of the less-educated women (Table V-6). This still means that the overwhelming ma-

Table V-5. Proportion of Couples Who Have Ever Used Any or Specific Methods of Birth Control by Measures of Modernization, for Wives 20-29 and 30-39 Years Old

Measures of modernization	Wives 30-39: Percentage who have ever used: contra-ception	abor-tion	steril-ization	any of three	Number of couples	Wives 20-29: Percentage who have ever used: contra-ception	abor-tion	steril-ization	any of three	Number of couples
Wife's education										
None	16	9	9	26	430	6	5	1	9	337
Primary school, not grad.	32	20	23	48	92	14	4	6	22	211
Primary school grad.	39	20	15	52	442	19	5	3	22	400
Junior high school	60	29	20	76	176	30	9	4	33	144
Senior high school grad. or higher	75	29	15	81	133	51	9	5	55	78
Correlation ratio	0.10	0.20	0.13	0.40		0.30	0.07	0.10	0.28	
Husband's employment status										
Farmer	18	9	8	27	219	5	2	3	9	229
Other traditional employment	31	18	15	45	331	18	5	4	22	310
Employed by non-relative	42	20	16	55	626	21	7	3	25	573
Professional	69	28	12	75	97	41	9	2	43	58
Correlation ratio	0.26	0.13	0.09	0.26		0.21	0.10	0.03	0.19	
Family type										
Living in extended unit	33	15	12	44	634	14	4	3	18	629
Living in nuclear unit										
Once in extended unit	37	20	17	53	393	17	5	3	20	265
Always nuclear	46	23	16	58	246	26	10	5	33	276
Correlation ratio	0.10	0.08	0.06	0.12		0.13	0.10	0.06	0.15	
Husband's education										
Less than primary school	16	10	7	25	231	5	3	3	10	219
Primary school grad.	26	14	14	38	515	11	3	2	14	487
Junior high school	45	24	17	63	172	30	12	5	37	152
Senior high school grad.	58	27	20	74	173	25	8	5	30	202
Some college	68	29	17	77	182	41	9	3	43	110
Correlation ratio	0.38	0.18	0.11	0.38		0.29	0.15	0.08	0.28	
Farm background										
Farmer now	19	9	8	27	219	5	1	3	8	229
Not farmer now										
Both husband and wife have farm background	37	20	16	51	511	19	5	2	22	408
Either husband or wife has farm background	43	19	14	53	328	20	7	4	24	349
Neither has farm background	47	24	19	62	215	27	9	4	33	184
Correlation ratio	0.19	0.12	0.09	0.21		0.18	0.11	0.12	0.18	
Household income in New Taiwan dollars										
Less than 1000	22	9	8	31	259	12	4	3	17	300
1000-1499	32	18	13	43	385	14	5	2	17	313
1500-1999	44	23	21	61	201	24	10	4	28	166
2000-2499	54	23	20	69	134	27	6	4	31	124
2500 or more	55	25	14	66	187	30	10	6	37	145
Not determined	26	18	16	40	107	10	1	2	12	122
Correlation ratio	0.25	0.14	0.12	0.28		0.19	0.12	0.07	0.19	

jority of even the best-educated women did nothing to limit births if they had had fewer than two. The proportion of the best-educated women beginning that early—20 per cent—is much smaller than the corresponding figure for a Western country such as the United States,

Table V-5 (continued).

Measures of modernization	Wives 30-39: Percentage who have ever used: contra-ception	abor-tion	steril-ization	any of three	Number of couples	Wives 20-29: Percentage who have ever used: contra-ception	abor-tion	steril-ization	any of three	Number of couples
Number of modern objects owned										
0 or 1	16	6	3	21	117	5	3	3	9	74
2 or 3	21	10	7	28	306	9	4	4	15	266
4	25	13	16	40	166	12	4	1	15	209
5	38	20	17	52	183	18	7	3	21	197
6	51	25	19	66	278	21	5	3	25	259
7 or more	61	30	22	77	223	40	12	7	44	165
Correlation ratio	0.33	0.22	0.19	0.40		0.27	0.12	0.11	0.24	
All couples	37	18	14	49	1273	18	6	3	22	1170

Table V-6. Proportion Sterilized or Using Contraception at First Interview, by Number of Live Births, by Three Social Characteristics

Social characteristics	Number of live births: 0 or 1	2	3	4	5	6 or more	All couples	Number of couples
Wife's education								
Primary school, not grad.	2	6	16	20	24	25	16	1070
Primary school grad.	4	13	27	40	51	48	30	842
Junior high school	3	29	49	63	62	70	44	320
Senior high school grad. or higher	20	48	65	88	75	*	55	211
Family type								
Living in extended unit	5	11	21	33	34	35	34	1263
Living in nuclear unit								
Once in extended unit	2	12	34	35	48	41	32	658
Always nuclear	8	29	42	61	55	33	32	522
Husband's employment status								
Farmer	3	0	9	15	22	26	14	448
Other traditional employment	2	8	21	35	44	36	25	641
Employed by non-relative	5	22	38	47	45	43	32	1199
Professional	14	50	58	71	*	*	49	155
All couples	5	16	30	39	42	37	28	
Number of couples	435	379	408	414	358	449		2443

* Base less than 20 cases.

but even action by one in five at such an early stage may be a significant sign of what the future will bring.

Educational level made a very great difference also in the proportion currently protected after only two, three, or four births—small to moderate numbers of children, even by Western standards. The gradient in terms of wife's education was very steep. The ratio between the best-educated and least-educated wives in the proportions currently protected was:

10 to 1 for those with fewer than two live births
8 to 1 for those with two live births
4 to 1 for those with three or four live births
3 to 1 for those with five or more live births

More than three-quarters of the women with least education (about 40 per cent of all the women) were not currently protected even when they had five or more children. The proportions protected among the poorly educated did increase with the number of live births, but a large majority was currently doing nothing about stopping family growth regardless of the number of previous births.

Presumably this was not because the poorly educated wanted unlimited numbers of children, since the proportion of those currently protected was less than one in three, even among those who had all the children wanted or more. The proportion currently protected increased considerably with education among those who have all children wanted or more. Nevertheless, there were still substantial numbers of even the better-educated women not protected at that stage. Twenty per cent of the women who were senior high school graduates and about 35 per cent of those who were primary school graduates (but not senior high graduates) were not currently protected at this late stage of family growth (Table V-3).

The dimensions of the discrepancy between the numbers of children wanted and the numbers already born can be illustrated with reference to relatively large families, defined for this purpose as those with five or more live births. For women over 30 years of age, the number wanting five or more children and the number who had already borne five or more varied with education as follows:

Education of wife	*% who wanted 5 or more children*	*% who had borne 5 or more children*	*Excess: the percentage by which the proportion with 5 or more born exceeds the proportion wanting 5 or more*
Primary, not graduate	44	68	24
Primary, graduate	34	57	23
Jr. high	12	40	28
Sr. high graduate, or higher	8	22	14

The proportion of those who wanted five or more children and the proportion that had borne five or more both decline sharply with education. The result is that the discrepancy between what was wanted and the number borne did not vary much with education. The more educated were much more successful in limiting their births to fewer than five, but since many more of them wanted fewer than five children, the dicrepancy is not much affected by education except for the group with the most education.

The association of education and birth control practice depends not only on the number of children already born, but also on whether some of those children were sons (Table V-9). A very large proportion of the better-educated couples had begun birth control even before they had three children, if at least one of those children was a son. Among the poorly educated, having a son made relatively little difference in relation to contraceptive practice until they had three or four children.

Table V-7. Proportion Who Ever Used Any Form of Birth Control (Contraception, Induced Abortion, or Sterilization), by Number of Live Births, by Three Social Characteristics

	Number of live births							
Social characteristics	0 or 1	2	3	4	5	6 or more	All couples	Number of couples
Wife's education								
Primary school, not grad.	2	9	22	28	31	33	22	1070
Primary school grad.	5	21	37	51	56	59	38	842
Junior high school	10	43	62	76	72	85	56	320
Senior high school grad. or higher	48	70	73	94	90	*	72	211
Family type								
Living in extended unit	8	17	30	42	40	45	31	1263
Living in nuclear unit								
Once in extended unit	6	19	42	44	54	51	40	658
Always nuclear	14	45	51	72	64	43	45	522
Husband's employment status								
Farmer	6	2	11	21	25	29	17	448
Other traditional employment	4	16	29	46	50	46	34	641
Employed by non-relative	9	32	47	56	53	56	41	1199
Professional	33	64	77	79	*	*	63	155
All couples	10	25	39	49	49	47	36	
Number of couples	435	379	408	414	358	449		2443

* Base less than 20 cases.

Table V-8. Proportion Who Ever Used Contraception, by Number of Live Births, by Three Social Characteristics

Social characteristics	Number of live births: 0 or 1	2	3	4	5	6 or more	All couples	Number of couples
Wife's education								
Primary school, not grad.	1	5	14	21	16	21	14	1070
Primary school grad.	4	18	31	42	40	42	29	842
Junior high school	10	39	55	65	48	62	46	320
Senior high school grad. or higher	48	68	69	82	70	*	66	211
Family type								
Living in extended unit	7	16	25	35	27	32	24	1263
Living in nuclear unit								
Once in extended unit	5	15	32	34	39	36	29	658
Always nuclear	14	38	47	62	34	20	36	522
Husband's employment status								
Farmer	3	0	5	15	22	18	11	448
Other traditional employment	4	13	22	36	29	35	25	641
Employed by non-relative	8	28	40	49	34	37	32	1199
Professional	33	64	74	64	*	*	59	155
All couples	9	22	32	40	32	33	28	
Number of couples	435	379	408	414	58	449		2443

* Base less than 20 cases.

Table V-9. Proportion Ever Using Any Form of Birth Control, by Wife's Education, by Number of Living Children and Sons

Wife's education	0-2 children: No sons	0-2 children: Sons	3 or 4 children: No sons	3 or 4 children: Sons	5 or more children	Total
None	4	5	8	23	26	17
Primary school, not grad.	4	14	10	32	40	25
Primary school grad.	5	16	25	43	55	34
Junior high school	13	30	29	65	73	48
Senior high school grad. or higher	38	63	67	78	73	66
All wives	9	20	22	42	44	32

(Number of living children and sons)

We have illustrated the relationships between birth control and modernization mainly by discussing the data for education, but similar relationships exist with both employment status and family type (Tables V-1 to V-8). The more modern the employment relationship or family type, the more likely it was that a birth control method had been used, that it was being used currently, that it was used while more children were still wanted, and that it was used with fewer children already born. For these criteria, too, while it is true that the more modern the category the more advanced the fertility behavior, even the most modern categories had a significant number of couples unprotected currently, even when all the children wanted or more than this number were alive.

The relative influence of the demographic modernization variables on birth control practice in this pre-program period depended on the type of method used. For example, K. Srikantan[1] estimates on the basis of a multivariate analysis that the proportion of total variance in birth control practice explained by the demographic and social characteristics of the individual couples is as follows for different methods:

	Proportion of the total variance explained by all individual characteristics of the couples which can be attributed to:	
Type of birth control ever used	*demo-graphic variables*	*social or modernization variables, after controlling for demographic variables*
Contraception	37%	63%
Abortion	57%	43%
Sterilization	71%	29%
Any method	51%	49%

Thus, the relative influence of demographic and modernization variables is about equal if all methods are considered, but the modernization variables are much more important than the demographic methods for contraception, the most rational method; about equally important as the demographic variables for abortion; and much less important than the demographic variables for sterilization. Since abortion and contraception often preceded sterilization, and since steriliza-

[1] In his *Effects of Neighborhood and Individual Factors on Family Planning in Taichung,* Ph.D. Dissertation in Sociology, University of Michigan, 1967 (published in microfilm form). The "demographic variables" used in this multivariate analysis include numbers of living children and sons, comparison of numbers of children alive and wanted, the duration of marriage, and wife's age. The social variables used include: wife's education, number of modern objects, couples' rural background, husband's occupation, and family structure. While based on the same set of data, the classifications used by Srikantan differ in detail from those used here.

tion was used relatively late, as a final method of family limitation, it is not strange that it should be more closely related than the others to demographic variables. Sterilization tended to be used when other methods had failed and when the pressure of demographic events motivated a more drastic solution.

The use of abortion, like that of other methods, increased with the educational level of the wives, regardless of whether the desired family size had been attained (Table V-10). However, only a few couples at

Table V-10. Proportion Who Ever Had Induced Abortion, by Wife's Education, by Comparison of Children Alive and Wanted

	Comparison of children alive and wanted					
Wife's education	Fewer than wife wants	The number wife wants	More than wife wants	Up to God, Fate, etc.[a]	All couples	Number of couples
Primary school, not grad.	3	13	14	3	8	1070
Primary school grad.	4	21	26	*	13	842
Junior high school	7	36	28	*	20	320
Senior high school grad. or higher	9	35	38	*	22	211
All couples	4	21	23	2	12	
Number of couples	1237	664	452	90		2433

[a] Includes indeterminate cases.

* Base less than 20 cases.

any educational level had ever used abortion if they still had fewer children than they wanted. At every educational level the proportion reporting at least one abortion was very much higher for those who had all the children they wanted or more. Abortion was obviously used to limit the number of children, not to space them.

MODERNIZATION AND THE TIMING OF BIRTHS

The more educated the wives, the earlier in married life they begin to use family limitation, if they begin at all. This is illustrated below for women 30-39 years old with at least two live births.[2] There is quite a steep gradient, but note that even the best-educated women began only after three births, on the average.

For those who had done something to limit family growth, education was also important in determining whether the action was begun

[2] These data and those below on the interval in which birth control was begun are from the analysis by P. S. Mohapatra, *op.cit.*

Education of wife	*Mean no. of live births before first use of birth control*
Primary, not graduate	5.3
Primary, graduate	4.6
Jr. high	3.8
Sr. high graduate, or higher	2.9

only in the current open interval, in the last completed birth interval, or earlier than that:

	For women with at least two live births, the % who first practiced birth control in:			
Education of wife	*the open interval*	*the last closed birth interval*	*earlier intervals*	*Total*
Primary, not graduate	77	16	7	100
Primary, graduate	69	17	14	100
Jr. high	59	21	20	100
Sr. high graduate, or higher	48	22	30	100

A majority of all those practicing birth control began only in the open interval. A large majority in all educational groups began no earlier than the last closed birth interval, and we have suggested earlier that most of these had probably intended that interval to be an open one. The steep gradient of the relationship with education in the percentages of those who began in a still earlier birth interval is undoubtedly related to the greater efforts made to space births in the higher educational strata. These figures may give a rather exaggerated picture of the situation, since they refer only to those who actually did do something about limiting the number of births. The following data indicate what percentage of all wives (30-39 years old with at least two live births) had practiced birth control for the first time in the indicated intervals:

Education of wife	*% who first practiced birth control in:* the open birth interval	the last closed birth interval	earlier intervals	*% who had not begun*
Primary, not graduate	22	4	2	72
Primary, graduate	37	9	17	47
Jr. high	45	15	16	24
Sr. high graduate, or higher	39	17	25	19

A final indication of the earlier use of contraception by the better educated is the fact that among those ever having had any specific number of pregnancies, the percentage of those who began contraception before that pregnancy increased sharply with education (Table V-11).

Table V-11. Proportion of Women Ever Having a Given Number of Pregnancies or More Who Started Using Contraception, Abortion, Sterilization or Any of the Three Methods for the First Time Before That Pregnancy[a/] by Wife's Education

Number of pregnancies preceding first use of each type of method	Contraception — Wife's education[b/] A	B	C	D	All	Abortion — Wife's education A	B	C	D	All	Sterilization — Wife's education A	B	C	D	All	Any method — Wife's education A	B	C	D	All
0	0	0	3	10	1	0	0	0	0	0	*	0	0	0	*	*	0	2	10	1
1	0	2	5	13	3	*	*	*	*	*	0	*	0	0	*	*	3	5	13	3
2	2	4	9	16	5	0	*	2	2	*	*	*	*	0	*	2	4	10	18	5
3	3	6	14	19	7	*	1	3	7	2	1	1	1	2	1	4	7	15	20	8
4	4	9	14	16	8	2	4	7	10	4	1	2	2	8	2	6	13	16	21	11
5	4	14	16	10	10	3	7	11	11	6	4	5	11	6	6	9	17	25	13	15
6 or more	17	30	30	31	24	13	25	31	33	21	12	19	24	21	17	28	43	46	33	37

a/ For example, among women who are primary graduates, and had 2 or more pregnancies, 4 percent began first use of contraception after 1 but before 2 pregnancies.

b/ Education categories are as follows:

A - less than primary school graduate
B - primary school graduate
C - junior high school
D - senior high school

* Less than 1 per cent.

SUMMARY

The birth control practices of the more modern couples were consistent with their lower fertility. More of them practiced contraception or other forms of birth control. They began earlier than other couples. Many of them were currently protected by sterilization or contraception, and this undoubtedly explains their longer open birth intervals. They had successfully avoided additional births for relatively longer periods of time.

The more modern couples were beginning contraception earlier than the less modern for at least three reasons: (1) they wanted fewer children; (2) they were more likely to use birth control if they had all the children wanted; and (3) a significant minority of them began birth control even before they had all the children wanted.

Nevertheless, the more modern couples were not much more successful than the less modern in having just the number of children wanted, as we have seen in the preceding chapter. The most important reason for this is that the more modern couples set much more difficult goals for themselves: they wanted relatively few children. Apart from this, however, the fact was that many couples—even the most modern—were using methods that were not very effective, using them late, and using them sporadically. While it is true that the more modern couples did begin birth control much earlier than others, many of them still began only *after* they had the number of children they wanted.

Both demographic and modernization variables were associated with birth control practice. Modernization made the most difference at early demographic stages. Under greater demographic pressure, modernization made less difference. Modernization was most strongly correlated to use of contraception and least correlated to sterilization. Despite these differences, it is clear that at all demographic stages, and for any method of birth control, modernization was associated with action to limit family growth before help was available from the program.

PART 3. THE PROGRAM: AN EXPERIMENT TO INCREASE THE PRACTICE OF FAMILY PLANNING

VI. The Taichung Experiment: Design and Major Results

THE EXPERIMENT: QUESTIONS TO BE ANSWERED

THE Taichung family planning program was a unique, large-scale experimental effort to make family planning available quickly to the whole population of an Asian city and to observe the effects systematically.[1] It may be one of the largest social science studies as yet conducted under some approximation to experimental conditions. It was unique among studies of fertility and family planning in its combination of a number of characteristics: a program to bring family planning to a large, concentrated population rather than to small urban areas or small village populations; systematic observation of the experiment and its effects using social science methods; a design which would allow the testing of some basic ideas about family planning programs; an emphasis on bringing family planning to those who wanted to limit family size rather than on attempting to change ideas about the number of children desired; concentration of a large effort in a rather short period of time and in one place in order to build up multiple, reinforcing stimuli.

Other large-scale family planning programs have also had some of these features, but have unfortunately made little provisions for systematically studying their own progress in such a way as to guide either their own development or new programs elsewhere. Furthermore, the Taichung experiment, because of its early starting date, has a fairly long time reference, an advantage that is still lacking for some of the cities and countries with more recent intensive programs.

The principal objectives of the Taichung study were to answer the following major questions:

1. *To what extent can the practice of family planning be increased by a massive information and service campaign of short duration?* For this general purpose the whole of Taichung can be considered as a single case to be compared with the other cities of Taiwan

[1] For earlier preliminary reports on the experiment, see B. Berelson and R. Freedman, "A Study in Fertility Control," *Scientific American*, 210, No. 5, May 1964, 3-11; and R. Freedman and J. Y. Takeshita, "Studies on Fertility and Family Limitation in Taiwan," *Eugenics Quarterly*, 12, No. 4, December 1965, 233-50.

and with Taiwan as a whole, where intensive programs began a year or more later. When the program was begun in Taichung there were no examples anywhere in the world of a large population in which a program organized for this purpose had changed substantially the proportion practicing family limitation. Whether it is possible to produce such a change in a relatively short time was the single most important question to be answered by the study.

2. *Is it necessary to approach both husbands and wives in an educational program, or is it enough to approach the wife alone?* It is widely believed that in the poor, high-fertility populations husbands are dominant and make the important family decisions, so that no program will succeed which does not involve communication with them. Most programs have concentrated on reaching wives, and their failure to attain very significant results has often been attributed to the hostility or indifference of the husbands. This view, while plausible, has rarely been tested. Since reaching husbands as well as wives is often difficult and expensive, it is important to know whether this additional effort is necessary and worthwhile.

3. *Can family planning ideas be spread cheaply and simply by written communication, through the mails?* Most family planning programs involve expensive person-to-person contacts by fieldworkers. The potential benefits of influencing couples by a mail campaign are great. Even if results per person reached are much less than in the intensive person-to-person approach, the total results could be substantially greater. Given a fixed budget, it is possible that the increase in the number of people reached might outweigh the decrease in the proportion influenced to accept. This approach requires at least minimal levels of literacy in the neighborhood units, so that the written message may be communicated by others to the person to whom it is addressed if necessary.

4. *Can direct communication to systematically spaced subgroups of a population indirectly affect a much larger population by diffusion from the initial foci of direct contact?* How much "circulation" effect can be expected in a program of this kind? To what extent can one depend on the population itself to spread the de-

sired innovation, and how large an initial effort is needed to prime this process? To communicate directly with each couple of childbearing years is prohibitively expensive in terms of both money and personnel, so it is important to know whether word-of-mouth communication will spread the necessary information and move the couples to meet their own needs. Word-of-mouth diffusion was probably mainly responsible for spreading ideas about family planning in the West and in Japan, over a rather long period of time and without any organized program for this purpose. Can this natural network of informal communication be used to bring about a much faster diffusion of information, if it is connected to intensive, planned, focal centers of direct communication and influence?

5. *Does a new method of contraception, the intrauterine contraceptive device (IUD), have distinctive advantages in terms of acceptance and diffusion?* The use of this new type of contraceptive by significant numbers of women was just beginning at the outset of the Taichung study. It had what appeared to be rather obvious advantages, but it was necessary to test empirically whether it would be uniquely acceptable, whether this innovation would diffuse rapidly, and whether some potential disadvantages would create special problems.

6. *If there is a significant adoption of family planning, will it accelerate the decline of fertility already begun in Taichung and Taiwan?* Family planning programs may be fully justified apart from their effects on the birth rate. In the poorly developed countries the rapid decline of child mortality means that tens of millions of couples have more children than they want or can care for given the rising standards of family welfare and education to which many of them aspire. Helping these families to meet their own problems is in itself a legitimate humane concern—particularly for those who have unwittingly precipitated the problem by helping to reduce child mortality. Family planning that improves family living standards may make a substantial direct contribution to social and economic development by improving both the morale of the parents and the contribution which each child can make to its society as a result of better education and other advantages. In addition, there is an increasing interest in many de-

veloping countries in limiting population growth as an aid to development programs. From this point of view, how many people are helped to solve a personal problem by adoption of family planning is less important than how much effect the family limitation program has on the birth rate.

The present chapter gives some answers to these six questions. The Taichung study, however, has a rich body of data on other important questions as well, and these will be treated in succeeding chapters. To place the present chapter in context, these questions are listed briefly here:

7. *Which demographic and social characteristics of the couples are most important in determining whether they accept family planning in an organized program?*
8. *What are the characteristics of the large proportion of the couples who express an intention to accept family planning but fail to do so?*
9. *Was the recent fertility of those accepting family planning high enough so that their use of effective contraception could have produced a distinctively large reduction in birth rates?*
10. *Which characteristics of the couples are related to persistence in effective use of family planning once it is adopted?*
11. *How did the discussion and perception of what others were doing about family planning affect information and acceptance?*

Taiwan in general (and Taichung in particular) seemed to be an appropriate place to study these major questions. As we saw in Chapter I, Taiwan has had for some time the low mortality and significant progress in social and economic development which are probably facilitating, if not necessary, conditions for fertility decline. In fact, the fertility decline was already underway.

On the basis of the pre-program survey, Taichung's young married couples appeared to be ready for a successful family planning program. They wanted a moderate number of children, but were having more than they wanted. An overwhelming majority approved of family planning and a significant minority were attempting to use it, but they were not well informed and their practice was too late and too ineffective to achieve their own stated goals.

The Taichung Experiment

THE DESIGN OF THE EXPERIMENT

Since the pre-program survey had indicated so clearly that a large part of the population wanted help in family limitation, the Taiwan Provincial Health Department organized an experimental program for this purpose. The essential design of that program involved four "treatments," involving anywhere from much to little effort, which were directed to the approximately 36,000 married couples in Taichung with wives 20-39 years old. These treatments were allocated by *lin,* a neighborhood unit containing an average of about 20 households which usually include about 12 married women aged 20-39. (Taichung is divided into about 2,400 such neighborhood units.) These four treatments were:

1. Everything—husband and wife (Ehw) : In these lins all of the stimuli of the program were combined: personal visits to both husbands and wives by trained health workers,[2] to provide information and to support motivation; mailings of information to newlyweds and to those couples with at least two living children; and meetings in the neighborhoods[3] that mixed entertainment and information about family planning, using slides, film strips, flip-charts, etc.
2. Everything—wife only (Ew) : This involved all the major stimuli except the personal visit to the husband.
3. Mailings (M) : No personal visits (unless requested)[4] or meetings in the neighborhood; instead, a series of mailings of letters and pamphlets to newlyweds and to those couples with at least two living children provided general information on methods, rationale,

[2] Eighteen fieldworkers were responsible for the home visits. They ranged in age from 21 to 45; most of them were in their late twenties and about two-thirds of them were married. Nearly all had senior high school education and/or previous nursing or midwifery experience. Nine had worked in the health stations as PPH workers prior to the experiment. In addition to these fieldworkers, there were nine supervisors who were regular employees of the Provincial Maternal and Child Health Institute. Apart from supervising the fieldworkers, they were responsible for keeping records, carrying out home visits requested by mail, and holding the various meetings. They ranged in age from 22 to 43; about a third of them were married and nearly all had had nurses' training in senior high school or junior colleges.

[3] The meetings were scheduled to be held in the Everything lins before the fieldworkers started their home visits. However, as noted later in this report, not all of the originally scheduled meetings were held, thus inadvertently introducing an additional experimental variation into the design of the study.

[4] Less than 2 per cent of those receiving letters actually requested a home visit.

location of clinics, etc., and included a postal device for requesting more information or a personal visit from a fieldworker.

4. Nothing (N) : No effort was made to reach the couples directly; there were posters in the area, since these were distributed throughout the city, and some meetings were held at the *li* level (a larger neighborhood unit of about 350 households), cutting across treatment boundaries.

In addition to assignment to one of these four treatments, each lin was also located in one of three "density" sectors. These sectors differed, so far as possible, only in the proportion of lins getting the more intensive Everything treatments, which included the personal home visit. For this purpose, the city was divided into three pie-shaped sectors, roughly equal initially in terms of fertility, rural-urban distribution, occupational composition, and educational level. Within each of the three sectors all the lins were distributed randomly among the four treatments in the proportions indicated in Table VI-1. In

Table VI-1. Distribution of Taichung Lins, by Treatment, by Density Sector in the Family Planning Program

Treatment	Density sector I Heavy	II Medium	III Light	Total
	Numerical distribution			
Everything: husband and wife (Ehw)	232	122	73	427
Everything: wife only (Ew)	232	122	73	427
Mail (M)	232	244	292	768
Nothing (N)	232	243	292	767
Total	928	731	730	2389
	Percentage distribution			
Everything: husband and wife (Ehw)	25	17	10	18
Everything: wife only (Ew)	25	17	10	18
Mail (M)	25	33	40	32
Nothing (N)	25	33	40	32
Total	100	100	100	100

Sector I the largest proportion (50 per cent) and in Sector III the smallest proportion (20 per cent) of the lins were assigned to the

Everything treatments. These sectors will be referred to as the "Heavy," "Medium," and "Light" sectors, indicating the intensity of effort involved (see Figure 1).

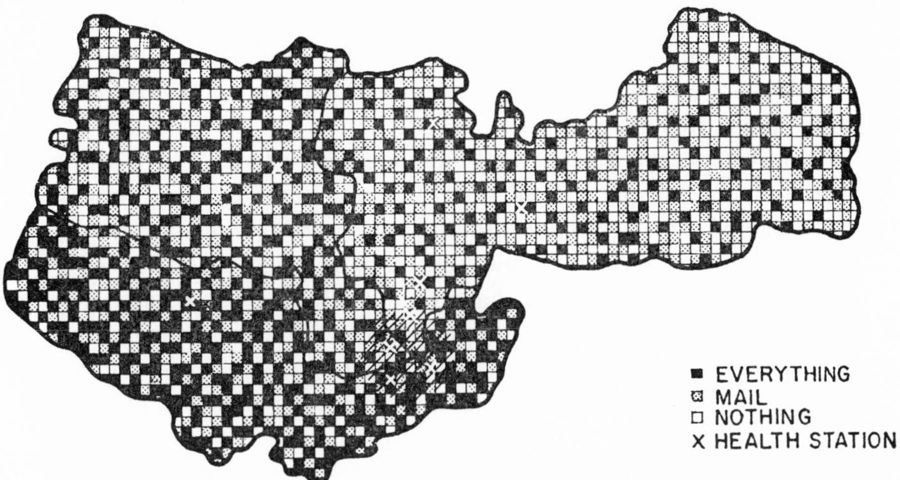

Figure 1. A Schematic Map of the Experimental Design

All the couples in the lins of a particular treatment type supposedly got the same set of prescribed stimuli, (or, in the Light sector, no stimuli), regardless of the density sector in which they were located. Only the percentage of the surrounding lins getting other treatments differed. For example, those in the Nothing lins in the Heavy sector had an environment in which many of the neighboring lins were receiving the intensive treatment; Nothing lins in the Light sector had an environment in which relatively few of the surrounding lins were getting the intensive treatment.

In addition to the specific treatments, there were some city-wide mass media messages, limited, however, to a very small number by a local policy decision. In view of the literacy of the population and the excellent mass media available, major supporting use of such media would probably have increased the success of the program considerably. Fifty thousand copies of a set of sixteen posters were placed in prominent locations throughout the city. They presented the idea of family planning in simple, attractive form with an invitation to come to the nearest health station for further information.[5] (See Figure 2 for an example of these posters.) There were also some meetings with community leaders and with occupational groups such as the farmers' association and the pedicab drivers' association.

As some indication of the overall scope of the program, nearly twelve thousand first home visits and some five hundred neighborhood meetings were held. Follow-up visits of various kinds probably ran to more than twenty thousand.

Family planning services and supplies were offered at ten clinics located in various parts of the city. Information, services, and supplies were offered with respect to the diaphragm, jelly, foam tablets, condom, withdrawal, rhythm, oral pills, and the new IUD. No effort was made to set up a design that would rigidly test the attractiveness of different methods, but the interest in the IUD was so great, as we shall presently see, that its attraction for this population can hardly be doubted.[6] It should be added that except for the oral pills and the IUD, which were available only at the clinics, the other methods were available on request from the fieldworkers at the time of the home visit or group meeting. With a few exceptions for indigent cases, there was a nominal charge for any contraceptive devices or chemicals that were accepted.[7]

The timing of the experimental program in Taichung may be divided into three major phases:

1. The intensive experimental program, running from February to October 1963, involved the large-scale effort just described. The first effects of this intensive effort were observed through March 31, 1964. Between October 1963 and March 31, 1964, there was no additional informational or educational effort made. However, the clinic services of the program were available throughout this period and in the succeeding periods as well.

[5] However, many of the posters were torn down, quickly covered over by others, or otherwise had a short life. Very few respondents mentioned the posters in the post-program survey at the end of 1963.

[6] The intrauterine type of contraceptive is not new to Taiwan. The Ota ring has been widely known and used there for some time. The type of IUD introduced in this program is the Lippes loop. (The Margulies spiral and the silkworm gut were inserted for a few women at the start of the program.)

[7] A charge of 75 cents (U.S.) was made for an IUD insertion and for a month's supply of oral pills. The charges for other methods were nominal and generally below the market price.

祖母說：「看！我的兒子和媳婦只有三
個子女，他們多麼健康幸福！」
請向附近的衛生所詢問

Figure 2. A poster used in the program. The caption reads, "A wise grandmother says: 'Look! My son and his wife have only three children. How healthy and happy they are!' If you have any questions, go to the nearest health station."

2. An "extension" program (April 1 to December 31, 1964) involved a very limited number of home visits and group meetings, mostly in the neighborhoods where these were not scheduled during the

intensive experimental period.[8] In addition to the clinic services started during the experiment, some private obstetricians and gynecologists were brought into service during this period as part of the expanded, island-wide IUD program.[9]

3. A second-round effort, beginning in March 1965, involved a new attempt to stimulate acceptances by providing IUD services without cost to the acceptors. We have detailed observations on this "free-insertion" period through July 31, 1965,[10] and a summary set of acceptance figures through April of 1966. The input of personnel and resources in this third period was much smaller than that of the initial, intensive effort of the experimental period but larger than that of the diffuse effort of the "extension" period.[11] Acceptances have continued to come in during the period since April 1966, but they are not part of the present analysis.

THE RESULTS OF THE EXPERIMENT: A SUMMARY OVERVIEW

A cumulative total of 3,362 women accepted[12] family planning services in the program by August 1963, when most of the intensive edu-

[8] The home visits and group meetings have since April 1, 1964 been conducted by the regular family planning workers. Known locally as the Prepregnancy Health (PPH) Workers, they are assigned to the city's nine health stations, one per station. These workers were originally recruited and trained as fieldworkers before the Taichung experiment, as part of an island-wide family planning program which involved only traditional methods. During the Taichung experiment they formed the nucleus of a team of fieldworkers which numbered twenty-seven in all (including nine supervisors). For an evaluation of the PPH work before the Taichung experiment and before the introduction of the IUD, see J. Y. Takeshita, J. Y. Peng, and P.K.C. Liu, "A Study of the Effectiveness of the Prepregnancy Health Program in Taiwan," *Eugenics Quarterly*, 11, No. 4, December 1964, 222-33.

[9] For an early description of the island-wide IUD program, see L. P. Chow, "A Programme to Control Fertility in Taiwan: Setting, Accomplishment and Evaluation," *Population Studies*, 19, No. 2, November 1965, 155-66. Chapter XIII summarizes the more recent experience of the general Taiwan program.

[10] Although the free insertion period actually started in March 1965 and the "extension" period lasted until then, for convenience of tabulation we present our data as if the change had occurred as of January 1, 1965. We happened to receive the data from the field at the end of 1964 and again at the end of July 1965, and we processed them for analysis as they were received.

[11] Not only the regular family planning (PPH) workers but also the nursing staffs of the City Health Department and of the nine health stations, as well as the city's private midwives were authorized during the free period to distribute coupons which exempted the recipients of paying the 75 cents (U.S.) ordinarily charged for an IUD insertion.

[12] An acceptance is defined as being fitted with an IUD or receiving supplies and/or instructions for other methods, presumably with intent to use them.

cational effort was completed in Taichung. Of these, 2,838 acceptors were from the city itself and 524 from elsewhere.[13] By March 1964, the cumulative acceptances reached 5,453. With the resumption of some educational effort after April 1, 1964, new acceptances continued so that by the end of December 1964 the cumulative total reached 8,715. Finally, as the second-round effort in the form of a free offer of the IUD was started in early 1965, the acceptances soared and by July 1965 reached a cumulative total of 10,776, with 7,522 from the city and 3,254 from outside. An additional 3,345 IUD insertions were made between August 1965 and April 1966.[14] By April 1966 there was a grand total of 14,121 acceptances. The cumulative figures for the several significant dates are summarized below:

	Cumulative number of acceptors		
Period	*City*	*Outside*	*Total*
Feb. 1963 – Aug. 1963	2,838	524	3,362
– Mar. 1964	4,026	1,427	5,453
– Dec. 1964	5,559	2,616	8,175
– July 1965	7,522	3,254	10,776
– Apr. 1966	10,069	4,052	14,121

Of the 7,522 acceptors from the city as of July 1965, 7,110 were in the 20-39 age group, representing about 20 per cent of all the married women of these ages in the city. Not all of the women in the base group were equally eligible for the program, of course. For example, those couples in which either the husband or the wife had been sterilized would certainly be ineligible. We might further exclude as ineligible those currently using contraception who did not become acceptors. Together the two groups might be defined as those already protected against unwanted family growth. When the sterilized (approximately 9 per cent) and satisfied contraceptors (approximately 20 per cent) are successively removed from the base, the acceptance rates come to 21 per cent and 27 per cent, respectively. In short, by

[13] Most of the acceptors from outside the city came from Taichung Hsien, the administrative unit surrounding the city, and the next two adjacent hsiens. For example, of all the acceptors from outside as of October 15, 1963, 65 per cent came from Taichung Hsien, 25 per cent from the next two adjacent hsiens, and the remaining 10 per cent from more distant places all over the island.

[14] Approximately 7 per cent of the IUDs inserted in this latest period were Ota rings, which have been added to the program since November 1965 because of their popularity in Taiwan.

July 1965 approximately one out of every four women not already protected against unwanted family growth had taken advantage of the services extended by the program. The proportion of the "eligible" women accepting rises, of course, with the further narrowing of the criterion of eligibility. If we additionally exclude as ineligible women who wanted more children at the beginning of the program, the acceptance rates rises to 31 per cent.[15]

The acceptance rates for Taichung based on the three criteria of eligibility just considered increase systematically as follows:

	Acceptance rate
All wives 20-39	20%
Non-sterilized wives 20-39	21%
Non-sterilized wives 20-39 not using satisfactory contraception already	27%
Non-sterilized wives 20-39 not using satisfactory contraception and not wanting any more children at the beginning of program	31%

Eligibility can be defined in various ways, but the important point is that an acceptance rate using *all* married women of a given age range as the base underestimates the impact of a program vis-à-vis its objectives. A range of alternate acceptance rates calculated on such bases as we have suggested is more realistic and sensitive in measuring the impact of the program than rates based on all married women regardless of their eligibility.

THE PREDOMINANT ROLE OF THE *IUD*

The experiment in Taichung serves as a bench mark for family planning programs in several ways, but especially because it introduced

[15] The number of Taichung wives in the 20-39 age group eligible by the different criteria was estimated from the results of the intensive sample surveys made just before and after the experiment. If we exclude the sterilized, 91 per cent were eligible. Excluding, additionally, those already using contraception who did not switch to the IUD, 71 per cent were eligible. Excluding in addition to this those who wanted more children leaves 63 per cent eligible. The incidence of sterilization and the use of satisfactory contraception was based on the report at the second survey. The proportion of those wanting more children was based on the report at the first interview.

the new IUD to the population of a developing country on a large scale for the first time. What is more, it served to demonstrate the importance of the type of method offered to the success of a program. In spite of the fact that a variety of methods were offered during most of the program, the great majority (86 per cent) of all acceptances by July 1965 were for the IUD.

The proportion of IUD acceptances was high in every period and in every area, except in the Everything lins during the early, intensive phase of the program (February through August 1963), when the first-round home visits were made. During this early home visit phase in the Everything lins, nearly half of the acceptances were for traditional methods, but even there the IUD was chosen by most people once the home visits were completed. The great majority of the acceptances in the Mail and Nothing lins and nearly all of the acceptances from outside Taichung were for the IUD from the very start, as the following data indicate:

Proportion of all acceptances that were IUD, by period and treatment:

Period	All places	Taichung City: Total	Taichung City: Everything lins	Taichung City: Mail & Nothing lins	Outside Taichung
Feb.-Aug. 1963	71	67	52	88	97
Sept. 1963-Mar. 1964	93	88	86	90	99
Apr.-Dec. 1964	92	88	86	88	98
Jan.-July 1965	92	90	88	91	95
Entire period	86	80	69	90	97

In the course of the home visit in the Everything lins, each woman was asked whether she intended to come to the clinic for family planning service, and if so whether she intended to ask for the IUD or for other methods. While large numbers of women who expressed an intention to act did not do so, those choosing the IUD were more likely than others actually to come to the clinic. The proportion of those expressing positive intentions and acting on them by July 1965 was 39 per cent for those choosing the IUD and 26 per cent for those initially choosing other methods. Further, changes at the clinic from the method initially elected were in the direction of more changes to the IUD. While 21 per cent of those initially intending to get an IUD switched to other methods at the clinic, 56 per cent of those originally expressing a preference for the other methods switched to the IUD.

In the intensive survey a subsample representing all women throughout the city was interviewed both before and after the experiment about their awareness of various methods of contraception. As Table VI-2 indicates, before the experiment very few women had heard about the new IUD; several of the traditional methods were known to about 25 to 50 per cent of the women, but very large pro-

Table VI-2. Proportion of Married Women 20-39 in Taichung Who Became Aware of Different Methods of Contraception Before and During the Experimental Program in 1963[a]

Contraceptive method	Percentage who became aware of method: Before the experiment	Percentage who became aware of method: During the experiment
Ligation	96	4
Ota ring	84	4
Foam tablet	53	16
Condom	50	15
Vasectomy	50	4
Rhythm[b]	41	9
Jelly	29	12
Diaphragm	26	9
Pill	19	21
Coitus interruptus	13	1
IUD	2	47
Number of cases interviewed before and after experiment	1227	1227

[a] Data based on subsample of 1227 cases who were interviewed originally in October-December 1962 and reinterviewed a year later after the experiment.

[b] Includes basal temperature method.

portions had heard about the Ota ring and about ligation. The high level of previous awareness about the Ota ring probably facilitated the diffusion of information about the IUD and its adoption.

In the experimental period of about a year, almost half the women had become aware of the IUD, 20 per cent said they had learned of the pill, and lesser proportions ranging from 1 to 16 per cent had learned of other, older methods.

While the study seems to demonstrate the overwhelming appeal of the IUD in Taichung, it might be argued that its popularity resulted from more emphasis on this method by the fieldworkers. This seems very unlikely on several grounds. In the first place, IUD acceptance rates were lowest in the Everything lins where the workers had the closest and most direct interaction with the women. During the intensive home visit phase of the program (February through August 1963) 48 per cent of the acceptors in these lins chose methods other than the IUD, as compared with 12 per cent in the lins where home visits were not made. Furthermore, in our informal observation of the workers in action it was not so much that they chose to emphasize the IUD, but rather that the prospective cases urged them to get on with the details of the newest methods available rather than to talk about the older methods "we already know about."

The appeal of the new IUD apparently lies in its simplicity and general effectiveness, as well as in the fact that it requires no continuing supply and that it has no immediate connection with the sexual act.[16] In these respects it probably appears to most of the population studied as superior to the traditional methods available to them.

Oral pills were available as part of the program, with few takers, but these results should not be interpreted as indicating a preference for the IUD as against the pills. The program was not designed to make such a test. There were not adequate supplies of the pills to meet a mass demand if it had developed, and the program's educational information stressed the IUD and the traditional methods rather than the pill. It is quite possible that a similar mass campaign based on the pills might have equal or greater success in such a

[16] There is now considerable literature on the IUD. For example, see the proceedings of the 1962 and 1964 conferences on the IUD, sponsored by the Population Council: C. Tietze and S. Lewit, eds., *Intra-Uterine Contraceptive Devices*, Amsterdam: Excerpta Medica International Congress Series No. 54, 1962, and S. J. Segal, A. L. Southam, and K. D. Shafer, eds., *Intra-Uterine Contraception*, Amsterdam: Excerpta Medica International Congress Series No. 86, 1965.

population. Since even the relatively high acceptance rates attained still leave a substantial part of the eligible women unprotected and since a substantial minority removed the IUD after a time for various reasons, it would be very improper to conclude from the Taichung experiment that the IUD answers all questions about the most suitable methods in such a population. However, the IUD was much more attractive than the other methods available, and knowledge and use of it diffused quite rapidly. While we do not have experimental evidence on this point, it seems quite unlikely that the success of the program would have been nearly as great if only the traditional methods had been available. When this experiment was completed there were no examples of acceptance rates this high for any other method in a large, high-fertility population. However, since 1966 the official family planning program in Singapore has achieved high acceptance rates with a program that is based mainly on the oral contraceptives, although other methods are also offered.[17]

RESULTS OF THE EXPERIMENT: VARIATION BY TREATMENT AND DENSITY

The cumulative acceptance rates in Taichung for married women 20-39, by treatment and by density sector, provide the test of the effects of the major experimental variables. In Table VI-3 these rates are shown for all methods to the end of the experimental period (March 1964) and to the last date of observation (July 1965).[18] Four conclusions stand out:

1. *Contacting both the husband and the wife in the home visit (Ehw) had no discernibly greater effect than contacting just the the wife (Ew).* The fact that the principal method involved was the IUD, a female method, may have had something to do with this result. It may also be that there was already such a considerable consensus between the spouses about the need for family

[17] For a description of the Singapore program and results to date see K. Kanagaratnam, "Singapore: The National Family Planning Program," *Studies in Family Planning*, No. 28, April 1968, 1-15. Although Singapore has some unusual advantages in its compact population and its concentration of obstetrical services under the aegis of one hospital, the acceptance rate achieved in 1966-67 is exceptionally high and uniquely associated with the contraceptive pill.

[18] The four major conclusions based on data for these two periods are also applicable in the case of unpublished data for other, intermediate time periods and for rates calculated separately for IUD and other methods.

planning that it made the additional contacts with the husbands redundant.[19] In any case, it is clear that the additional effort to reach the husbands did not increase acceptance rates. Since it is usually much more difficult to contact husbands than wives, the saving in program cost is considerable if home visits can be restricted to wives.

2. *The direct personal contacts in the Everything lins definitely produced more acceptances, although the advantage was not increased by visiting both husband and wife.* The higher acceptance rate in the Everything neighborhoods, however, is perhaps less remarkable than the substantial, if lower, acceptance rate in the neighborhoods in which the influence was almost entirely by diffusion.

3. *The use of letters did not prove effective in Taichung.* The acceptance rate in the Mail lins was no higher than that in the Nothing lins. The letters did not include any statement about the new IUD; they mentioned only that family planning services could be obtained from a fieldworker upon request or by going to the nearest health station. It may be that the letters would have been more effective had they been keyed specifically to the IUD, which turned out to be almost the only attraction for the cases that did not receive home visits. In Seoul, Korea, however, mailings specifically keyed to the IUD were used in a similar experiment but also failed to produce any significant effect.[20] On the other hand, Palmore has reported that letters were very effective in an experiment in the United States.[21] Certainly the mass use of letters did not pay dividends in the early Taichung and Seoul trials. This is not to say that a more selective use of this medium would not work if directed, say, to the highly literate or to those with a recent birth. However, whether in a mass program in a developing country the

[19] According to the sample survey before the program, 63 per cent of the wives had discussed birth control with their husbands at least occasionally.

[20] See E. Hyock Kwon et al., *Seoul National University Sungdong Gu Action-Research Project on Family Planning: A Progress Report (For Period July 1964-December 1965)*, The School of Public Health, Seoul National University, Seoul, Korea, April 1966.

[21] J. Palmore, "The Chicago Snowball: A Study of the Flow and Diffusion of Family Planning Information," pp. 272-363 in D. Bogue, ed., *Sociological Contributions to Family Planning Research*, Chicago: University of Chicago Community and Family Study Center, 1967.

additional cost is justified in terms of the probable overall effect on acceptances is still a moot point.[22]

4. *The heavy density of effort yielded acceptance rates that are distinctively higher than the lighter densities of effort.* However, contrary to expectation, the Medium and the Light sectors did not differ in any consistent, meaningful way.

Table VI-3. Cumulative Acceptance Rates[a/] for All Methods Among Married Women 20-39 in Taichung, from February 1963 through March 1964, and February 1963 through July 1965, by Treatment and by Density Sector

Treatment	Density sector			
	Heavy	Medium	Light	All sectors
	February 1963 - March 1964			
Everything: husband and wife (Ehw)	20	12	14	17
Everything: wife only (Ew)	18	14	14	17
Mail (M)	8	7	8	8
Nothing (N)	9	7	7	8
Total	14	9	8	11
	February 1963 - July 1965			
Everything: husband and wife (Ehw)	29	18	21	25
Everything: wife only (Ew)	28	21	24	26
Mail (M)	18	13	16	16
Nothing (N)	23	13	17	18
Total	24	16	18	20

[a/] In this and subsequent tables acceptance rates are given per 100 married women 20-39.

These observations lead us to the conclusion that for most purposes we can collapse our twelvefold experimental design into a four-

[22] Our sample survey taken immediately following the experiment shows that as many as 40 per cent of the couples to whom letters were sent during the program did not even remember receiving them. Recently, the Taiwan island-wide program has had an extensive mailing campaign directed mainly to women who have recently had babies. This does produce acceptances at a small cost per acceptance, although only a very small number of those receiving the mail respond. Mailings to women in the postpartum period definitely appear to be worthwhile.

fold one by: (a) reducing the four treatments to a dichotomy: Everything and Nothing, the latter including the original Mail and Nothing treatments, and (b) reducing the three density sectors into another dichotomy: Heavy and Light, the latter including the original Medium and Light sectors.

Before doing this, however, we want to examine how the effects of the experimental variables may be altered by successively removing from consideration groups of couples that are probably ineligible for acceptance in the sense that the program cannot or does not aim to reach them at a particular stage. For this purpose, five different eligibility definitions were used. Eligibility definition 1 simply includes all the couples in which the wife is 20-39. The other definitions successively remove from consideration couples with certain characteristics,[23] as follows:

Eligibility definition 2: excludes couples who have had a sterilizing operation or believed themselves to be sterile. (That such couples are ineligible is obvious.)

Eligibility definition 3: excludes additionally those cases where the husband and/or the wife said that they wanted more children. (The program aimed at helping those who wanted no more children, rather than at trying to change this attitude. Acceptance rates were very much higher in the short run for those who didn't want more children than for those who did, although the latter group had rising acceptance rates as time went on.)

Eligibility definition 4: excludes additionally those who were pregnant at the time of the first home visit. (Such couples, while highly motivated for later acceptance, had low acceptance rates in the short period to April 1, 1964.)

Eligibility definition 5: excludes additionally couples who were using contraception at the time of the first home visit. (While some of these couples became acceptors in the course of searching for a better method, the acceptance rate was persistently low for such couples, suggesting that they already had a satisfactory solution. Acceptance rates were much higher among couples who had once used contraception but were not currently doing so—an indication of motivation with no satisfactory solution yet found.)

23 The number of couples in each category is estimated from the information obtained during home visits to those living in the Everything lins.

Tables VI-4 and VI-5 show how the relationship between treatment or density and acceptance rates varied with the five eligibility criteria. The variations are also shown in the bottom panels of the tables, in the form of indices with the average rate for each ineligibility definition as 100.

Table VI-4. Acceptance Rate to April 1, 1964, Among Married Women 20-39 in Taichung, by Type of Method Accepted, by Density Sector, by Five Eligibility Definitions

Eligibility definition[a]	Density sector			All sectors
	Heavy	Medium	Light	
	Acceptance rate: all methods			
1	14	9	9	11
2	16	10	10	13
3	22	14	14	17
4	26	17	17	20
5	35	24	25	29
	Acceptance rate: IUD			
1	9	7	7	8
2	10	8	9	9
3	14	11	12	13
4	16	14	15	15
5	24	20	22	22
	Index: all methods			
1	129	82	82	100
2	129	82	83	100
3	129	82	81	100
4	127	83	84	100
5	122	84	89	100
	Index: IUD			
1	112	90	96	100
2	111	90	96	100
3	112	90	96	100
4	108	91	98	100
5	106	91	101	100

[a] Eligibility definitions are as follows:

1. All couples with wife 20-39.
2. Excludes couples who were sterilized or believed themselves to be sterile.
3. Excludes additionally those cases where husband and/or wife wanted more children.
4. Excludes additionally those who were pregnant at the time of the first home visit.
5. Excludes additionally those who were using contraception at the time of the first home visit.

Table VI-5. Acceptance Rate to April 1, 1964, Among Married Women 20-39 in Taichung, by Type of Method Accepted, by Treatment, by Five Eligibility Definitions

Eligibility definition[a]	Treatment				All treatments
	Ehw	Ew	M	N	
	Acceptance rate: all methods				
1	16	16	8	7	11
2	19	19	9	9	13
3	27	26	12	12	17
4	31	29	15	15	20
5	40	37	23	23	29
	Acceptance rate: IUD				
1	10	10	7	7	8
2	12	12	8	8	9
3	16	16	11	11	13
4	18	18	13	14	15
5	26	24	20	21	22
	Index: all methods				
1	156	153	72	69	100
2	154	152	71	69	100
3	155	149	71	71	100
4	151	144	74	75	100
5	141	129	80	81	100
	Index: IUD				
1	127	126	87	86	100
2	125	125	86	85	100
3	128	125	85	87	100
4	121	117	88	91	100
5	116	109	92	95	100

[a] Eligibility definitions are as follows:

1. All couples with wife 20-39.
2. Excludes couples who were sterilized or believed themselves to be sterile.
3. Excludes additionally those cases where husband and/or wife wanted more children.
4. Excludes additionally those who were pregnant at the time of the first home visit.
5. Excludes additionally those who were using contraception at the time of the first home visit.

Of course, acceptance rates rise steadily as we narrow the population considered to the more eligible couples. This is true in each density sector and each treatment whether for all methods or for the IUD only. By April 1, 1964, the most eligible group (eligibility definition 5) had a total acceptance rate in the heaviest density sector of

35 per cent as compared to 14 per cent for all couples. For the IUD alone the rise is from 9 per cent to 24 per cent. Similarly, for the Everything lins the acceptance rates rise from 16 to 40 per cent for all methods and from 10 to 25 per cent for the IUD, when we move from the first to the fifth eligibility definition.

Collapsing the twelvefold experimental design to a fourfold one appears to be justified even after taking eligibility into account. Regardless of the eligibility base or method, Ehw and Ew rates are not significantly different from each other, although there is a slight advantage for Ehw as compared with Ew as the eligibility base is narrowed. Similarly, the rates for the Mail and Nothing treatments do not differ significantly. Furthermore, the rates are significantly higher for the Heavy sectors than for the Medium and Light for every eligibility and method comparison, but there is no consistent distinction between the Medium and Light sectors.

The advantage of the Everything and the Heavy density lins is much greater for all methods than for the IUD alone. (This is clear from a comparison of the relative indices in the bottom panels of Tables VI-4 and VI-5.) We interpret this to mean that the IUD diffused much more easily than the traditional methods across treatment and density boundaries.

The effects of treatment and density sector are significantly less as the definition of eligibility is narrowed. (Compare, again, the indices in the bottom panels of Tables VI-4 and VI-5.) Apparently the experimental variables make less difference when we have a population group that is ready in the sense that its members want no more children, are not currently pregnant, and do not already have an effective means to limit family growth in sterilization or current contraceptive practice. The most consistent narrowing of the treatment or density variations comes in the shift from the fourth to the fifth eligibility criterion—that is, when we add to other criteria of readiness the condition that the couples are not currently using contraception. This is particularly true for the IUD. This probably means that the IUD diffuses most readily across treatment and density boundaries to those who are both ready in terms of family size goals and without a satisfactory solution to attain those goals. (In Chapter VII we show that acceptances are especially high among couples who had once used contraception but had given it up—that is, among motivated but unsatisfied couples—but below average among those currently using contraception.) Table VI-6 summarizes the results, after

Table VI-6. Acceptance Rate to April 1, 1964, Among All Married Women 20-39 and Among the Non-sterile, Non-pregnant Wives 20-39 Who Did Not Want Any More Children but Were Not Using Any Contraception, by Type of Method Accepted, by Treatment and Density Sector in Taichung

Eligibility definition[a]	Everything lins		Nothing lins		All lins
	Heavy	Light	Heavy	Light	
	Acceptance rate: all methods				
1	19	14	8	7	11
5	44	33	26	22	29
	Acceptance rate: IUD				
1	10	10	8	6	8
5	24	26	23	20	22
	Index: all methods				
1	178	127	80	66	100
5	153	114	91	76	100
	Index: IUD				
1	125	127	97	80	100
5	110	116	103	89	100

[a] Eligibility definitions are as follows:

1. All couples with wife 20-39.
5. Non-sterile, non-pregnant wives 20-39 who did not want any more children but were not using any contraception.

collapsing the twelvefold design to a fourfold one, for the two extreme eligibility bases, definitions 1 and 5.

We are now prepared to present the findings in terms of the fourfold experimental design for the three different periods of observation for the different contraceptive methods. Table VI-7 contains the cumulative acceptance rates to the end of each period and Table VI-8 the acceptance rates within each period.[24]

The Everything treatment, which included the home visit, was especially effective in gaining acceptances for more traditional methods, compared to the other treatments. In fact, a large part of the difference in overall acceptance rates for various treatments is accounted for by the traditional methods.

During the intensive initial program period, the Everything treatment resulted in substantially higher acceptance rates than the other

[24] In Table VI-8 we excluded from the base in each period after the first those who had accepted in a previous period.

Table VI-7. Cumulative Acceptance Rates,[a/] Among Married Women 20-39 in Taichung, from February 1963, to March 31, 1964, December 31, 1964, and July 31, 1965, by Type of Method Accepted, by Treatment and Density Sector

	Feb. 63 - Mar. 64			Feb. 63 - Dec. 64			Feb. 63 - July 65		
Treatment	Heavy	Light	Total	Heavy	Light	Total	Heavy	Light	Total
					All methods				
Everything	19	14	16	23	18	20	28	21	25
Nothing	8	7	7	13	11	11	21	15	17
Total	14	9	11	18	12	15	24	16	20
					IUD				
Everything	10	10	10	13	13	13	18	16	17
Nothing	8	6	7	12	10	10	19	13	15
Total	9	7	8	12	10	11	18	14	16
					Other methods				
Everything	9	4	7	10	4	7	11	4	8
Nothing	1	1	1	2	1	1	2	2	2
Total	5	2	3	6	2	3	6	2	4

[a/] The sum of IUD and other acceptance rates does not always add up to the total acceptance rate due to rounding.

treatments. However, the advantage was much greater for traditional methods than for the IUD, and it disappeared completely once the intensive program support ended. Since the direct stimuli were used mainly in the Everything lins, this must mean that the IUD diffused so well into the Nothing lins from the Everything lins as to minimize the treatment differences.

The easy availability of the traditional methods from the home visitor no doubt contributed to the greater acceptance of these methods in the Everything lins. The supplies and instructions for traditional methods could be obtained directly from the fieldworkers during the home visits or at the time of the group meetings. The IUD, on the other hand, had to be inserted at the clinics. While many women were prepared to take the trouble to go to the clinics for an IUD insertion, few came for traditional methods. That the IUD acceptors came to the clinics nearly as often from the Nothing as from the Everything lins is a striking testimony, in terms of diffusion, to the special appeal this new method must have had.

The Heavy density sector yielded higher acceptance rates than the Light density sector, but the proportional difference is much

Table VI-8. Acceptance Rates,[a] Among Married Women 20-39 in Taichung, for Each of the Three Periods of Observation, by Type of Method Accepted, by Treatment and Density Sector[b]

	Feb. 63 - Mar. 64			Apr. 64 - Dec. 64			Jan. 65 - July 65		
Treatment	Heavy	Light	Total	Heavy	Light	Total	Heavy	Light	Total
					All methods				
Everything	19	14	16	5	4	4	7	4	6
Nothing	8	7	7	5	4	4	9	5	6
Total	14	9	11	5	4	4	8	5	6
					IUD				
Everything	10	10	10	4	4	4	6	4	5
Nothing	8	6	7	4	4	4	8	4	5
Total	9	7	8	4	4	4	7	4	5
					Other methods				
Everything	9	4	7	1	*	1	1	*	1
Nothing	1	1	1	1	*	*	1	*	*
Total	5	2	3	1	*	*	1	*	*

[a] The sum of IUD and other acceptance rates does not always add up to the total acceptance rate due to rounding.

[b] In each period after the first we excluded from the base those who had accepted in a previous period.

* Less than 1 per cent.

greater for the traditional methods than for the IUD. For the period of the experiment, for example, the acceptance rate in the Light sector was lower than that in the Heavy sector by as much as 70 per cent for the traditional methods but by only 16 per cent for the IUD. A similar pattern persists into the later periods of observation (see Table VI-7).

In the Heavy sector there is relatively little difference between the Everything and Nothing lins regarding the volume of IUD acceptances. The small advantage held by the Everything lins in the first period had disappeared by the second period and was reversed by the third. Diffusion must have been extremely effective with this heavier concentration of effort. During the free insertion period, the rate of IUD acceptance was actually slightly higher in the Nothing than in the Everything lins for the Heavy sector, and by then these High density Nothing lins also had a higher IUD acceptance rate than the Nothing lins in the Light sector (see Table VI-8).

Our conclusion is that the intensive treatment made a significant difference initially, but as time went on the IUD diffused so widely throughout the city as to minimize the initial treatment differences. That there should have been some substantial difference initially is not surprising. After all, there must be some focal centers from which the diffusion occurs. We were surprised, however, that diffusion was so powerful and operated so quickly, virtually obliterating the initial differences.

DIFFUSION OF THE *IUD*

The fact that diffusion played a key role in the success of the Taichung program is extremely important, since it indicates that it is unnecessary to approach each couple by means of expensive individual contacts. Systematically spaced efforts have considerable effect on parts of the population not approached directly.

We have just seen that the IUD acceptance rates varied little between treatments and between density sectors, indicating that the IUD diffused throughout the city, cutting across boundaries between areas of intensive and little effort. In fact, diffusion did not stop at the borders of the city. As much as 26 per cent of all the acceptances in the experimental period came from outside Taichung, where no formal effort was made to recruit them. By July 1965, 30 per cent of all the acceptances were from outside. From the very start nearly all (97 per cent) of the acceptors from outside Taichung came for the IUD.

Other striking evidence of diffusion is the fact that 16 per cent of those who accepted up to April 1, 1964, though coming from the Everything lins in the city, accepted even before the home visitors could get to them. Most of them (87 per cent) were attracted by the IUD.

Diffusion is also evident when we compare the acceptance rate in a lin with the average for the lins that are immediately adjacent. Diffusion into a neighborhood ought to be greater if the nearby neighborhoods have high acceptance rates. Conversely, the neighborhoods which have high acceptance rates ought to produce higher rates in the areas around them. By computing for each lin the average acceptance rate in the immediately adjacent lins, we were able to get some measure of the probable supporting force of relevant behavior in the immediate environment. The crude measure we use is based only on immediately adjacent neighborhoods. Therefore, it is probably most relevant for the neighborhoods in the Light density sector. In the Heavy sector, even if the immediately adjacent neighborhoods do not have high rates, it is likely that there are such high rate neighborhoods in the very next row of lins. In retrospect, it also seems plausible that in the case of the Everything lins influence should move outward to the Nothing lins; while for the Nothing lins influence should move mainly in from the adjacent lins. Data to test these ideas are shown in Tables VI-9 and VI-10.

Table VI-9. Percentage Distribution of Lins According to Average Level of Acceptance of All Methods to April 1, 1964, in the Adjacent Lins, for Married Women 20-39 in Taichung, by Level of Acceptance, by Treatment and Sector

Level of acceptance in the lin	Number of lins	Average level of acceptance in adjacent lins: Under 5%	5-14%	15% or more	Total
Heavy sector	937	4	61	35	100%
Everything lins	465	3	64	33	100%
Under 5%	43	0	53	47	100%
5-19%	229	4	67	29	100%
20% or more	193	3	63	34	100%
Nothing lins	472	4	57	39	100%
Under 5%	190	6	59	35	100%
5-19%	229	2	57	41	100%
20% or more	53	8	49	43	100%
Light sector	1479	21	67	12	100%
Everything lins	396	22	68	10	100%
Under 5%	83	26	71	2	100%
5-19%	194	24	68	8	100%
20% or more	119	16	66	18	100%
Nothing lins	1083	20	68	12	100%
Under 5%	519	20	69	11	100%
5-19%	467	20	68	12	100%
20% or more	97	16	65	19	100%
All sectors	2416	14	65	21	100%

In the Light density sector the acceptance rates in the adjacent lins do increase with higher rates in the Everything lins (Table VI-9); and acceptance rates in the Nothing lins rise with higher acceptance rates in the adjacent lins (Table VI-10). In the Heavy density sector there is no such consistent pattern, perhaps because there the close spacing of the Everything lins with their more intense treatments makes distance less relevant and our adjacent-lin concept less ap-

Table VI-10. Percentage Distribution of Lins According to Their Levels of Acceptance of All Methods to April 1, 1964, for Married Women 20-39 in Taichung, by Average Level of Acceptance in the Adjacent Lins, by Treatment and Sector

Average level of acceptance in the adjacent lins	Number of lins	Level of acceptance in the lin: Under 5%	5-19%	20% or more	Total
Heavy sector	937	25	49	26	100%
Everything lins	465	9	49	42	100%
Under 5%	14	*	*	*	*
5-14%	298	8	51	41	100%
15% or more	153	13	44	43	100%
Nothing lins	472	40	49	11	100%
Under 5%	20	60	20	20	100%
5-14%	268	41	49	10	100%
15% or more	184	36	52	12	100%
Light sector	1479	41	44	15	100%
Everything lins	396	21	49	30	100%
Under 5%	88	25	53	22	100%
5-14%	268	22	49	29	100%
15% or more	40	5	40	55	100%
Nothing lins	1083	48	43	9	100%
Under 5%	216	49	44	7	100%
5-14%	735	48	43	9	100%
15% or more	132	43	43	14	100%
All sectors	2416	35	46	19	100%

* Base is less than 20.

propriate. Nevertheless, even in the Heavy density sector the increase in acceptance rates in adjacent lins was associated with a systematic shift from very low to moderately high acceptance rates for the Nothing lins (Table VI-10).

Word-of-mouth communication by neighbors, friends, and relatives played an important role in the diffusion of the IUD. (See Table VI-11.) About half of those from the city who accepted up to the end of the extension period, without the benefit of home visits, mentioned that they heard about the program from such informal primary group sources. The acceptors served as informal information sources for others. Over 60 per cent of the women in the intensive survey who had accepted an IUD by the second survey said that they had recommended it to at least one other person, and 20 per cent to two or more.

The informal communication channels played an even more dominant role in the diffusion of the IUD beyond the borders of the city. From 65 to 67 per cent of the acceptors from outside the city gave

Table VI-11. Sources of Information About the Program Reported by Acceptors Who Did Not Have a Home Visit Before Accepting, by Place of Residence

	Taichung City			Outside Taichung		
Sources of information	Feb. 63- Mar. 64	Apr.- Dec. 64	Jan.- July 65	Feb. 63- Mar. 64	Apr.- Dec. 64	Jan.- July 65
Primary relations	49.3	51.5	22.4	65.0	64.8	66.8
Neighbors	22.1	20.4	6.4	19.4	18.9	19.3
Friends	17.9	22.9	12.1	25.2	28.6	31.0
Relatives	9.3	8.2	3.9	20.4	17.3	16.5
Program treatment	39.7	33.5	53.9	6.1	4.1	18.9
Home visitor	19.3	28.5	52.7	3.8	3.8	18.9
Meeting	8.0	1.1	0.3	2.0	0.1	--
Letters	11.3	3.5	0.8	0.1	0.2	--
Posters	1.1	0.4	0.1	0.2	--	--
Mass media	3.0	4.4	1.5	1.8	2.6	2.1
Newspaper	2.1	3.8	1.3	1.4	2.3	1.9
Radio	0.5	0.4	0.1	0.3	--	0.2
Movie spots	0.4	0.2	0.1	0.1	0.3	--
Health agency	26.1	14.4	27.5	29.9	27.9	13.0
Health station	24.4	13.8	27.2	29.3	27.8	12.8
MCH Institute	1.7	0.6	0.3	0.6	0.1	0.2
Medical personnel	0.8	0.4	1.6	0.5	0.5	0.9
Private doctor	0.2	0.2	0.4	0.1	0.2	0.4
Private midwife	0.6	0.2	1.2	0.4	0.3	0.5
Others	3.3	1.1	0.6	1.2	1.3	1.1
Total per cent[a/]	122.2	105.3	107.5	104.4	101.1	102.8
Number of cases	2272	1246	1645	1427	1189	638

[a/] Total percentages exceed 100% because some cases gave more than one source.

their neighbors, friends, and relatives as their source of knowledge about the program.

Other important information sources were the regular health station personnel, who presumably had good relations with the public in their routine health service activities. We are referring here to regular workers not involved in the special program of home visits for family planning. Some of the health station nurses in outlying areas brought in groups of women for IUD insertion.

Finally, the home visitors of the program, who apparently talked to people outside of the Everything lins on their rounds in addition to making their scheduled home visits, helped to circulate the message. Their influence increased after the experimental period, as they began to make home visits in areas where such visits were not originally scheduled. In the last period they were cited more often, even among the cases coming from outside Taichung. Apparently the home visits made under the national program in the outlying areas led some women to seek an IUD insertion in Taichung. Sources other than the primary relations, regular health station personnel, and home visitors were mentioned infrequently. The small number citing the mass media is not surprising, since there was little notice of the program in these media.

Multiple sources of influence were mentioned more often during the experimental period than later and more often among city acceptors than among those from outside.[25] Presumably, the high acceptance rate in the city during the experiment was brought about by the mutually reinforcing influences of the various stimuli, both formal and informal, which were set in motion by the intensive effort of the program.

Both the IUD and the oral pill diffused more through primary relations than through any other means. This is indicated in the following data regarding methods learned by at least 10 per cent of the population between the two surveys:

Proportion of All Married Women 20-39 in Taichung Who Learned About a Method From Primary Contacts and From Direct Program Sources During the Experiment in 1963. (Data based on 1,227 cases who were interviewed originally in October-December 1962 and reinterviewed a year later, after the experiment):

	Percentage of all women who learned about the method first from		*Ratio of primary relations to direct program sources*
Method learned	*primary contacts: friends, neighbors, relatives, or husband*	*direct program sources: home visitors and group meetings*	
IUD	16	24	.67
Oral pill	8	8	.98
Condom	4	9	.42
Foam tablet	3	11	.25
Jelly	2	9	.19

[25] Indicated by the extent by which the total percentage figures at the bottom of Table VI-11 exceed 100.

For every three women who learned about the IUD from a direct program source, two more reported hearing about it through informal contacts—from friends, neighbors, relatives, or husbands. This ratio of diffusion was much lower for the three traditional methods. The ratio was even higher for the other new attractive method, the oral pill. But the proportion of those who had heard about the oral pill at all was smaller, so the total impact and diffusion were less.

Many more women remembered learning about the IUD from either the major formal or informal sources than was the case for any other method. However, the relative advantage of the IUD was greater in terms of informal than formal program sources. The IUD was better known initially from direct program sources, and it therefore had at that point a considerable additional advantage in diffusion.

PERCEPTION OF SOCIAL SUPPORT AND ACCEPTANCE

One of the consequences of the circulation effect of a program, we believe, is the increased perception of support from others—such as relatives, friends, neighbors—whose opinions count and facilitate readiness to accept what the program has to offer.

The wives interviewed before and after the intensive program were asked whether some or many of their relatives, friends, and neighbors were using family limitation methods. We can therefore compare the "before" and "after" responses on these questions to determine whether there were changes in the direction of perceiving more or fewer users among these important primary group members. We can also determine whether the number answering "don't know" to these questions decreased as a result of the program, which presumably made family limitation more salient.

As Table VI-12 indicates, there were definite shifts toward perceiving more use of contraception among relatives, friends, and neighbors. Also, the proportion of those answering "don't know" to questions about use of contraception in these groups decreased during the program period. The Everything treatment was definitely associated with a greater rise in the proportion perceiving an increase in the use of family limitation than were the Nothing and Mail treatments. The Everything treatment also produced a greater change from "don't know" to a definite perception of some kind. Significant increases in perception of use were not confined to the Everything treatment. Even in the Mail and Nothing treatments there were significant changes, indicating the pervasiveness of the circulation effect.

The increase in the perception that significant "others" were practicing contraception was related positively to acceptance in the program. Table VI-13 summarizes this relationship for "eligible" women (those not using contraception at the first survey or sterilized by the

Table VI-12: Changes Between the First and Second Survey in the Perceptions of Contraceptive Practice of Relatives, Friends, and Neighbors by Married Women 20-39 Years Old in Taichung, by Treatment in the Experiment

Change in perception about use of contraception between first and second survey (beginning and end of experiment)	Relatives			Friends			Neighbors		
	Everything	Nothing	Total	Everything	Nothing	Total	Everything	Nothing	Total
For those giving definite answers:									
Percent seeing an increase	45	35	40	32	27	30	47	39	42
Percent seeing no change	36	44	40	44	46	45	32	37	34
Percent seeing a decrease	19	22	20	23	26	25	21	25	23
Net percent changing upward	26	13	19	9	1	5	25	14	19
Net percent changing from "don't know" to definite answer	14	6	10	18	10	14	15	9	12

Table VI-13. Cumulative Acceptance Rates, by Changes in Perception of the Number of Friends, Relatives, and Neighbors Practicing Contraception (for Women Not Using Contraception by First Interview and Not Sterile by Second Interview)[a]

Changes in perception of contraceptive use among three groups: friends, relatives, and neighbors	Number in base group	Acceptance rate by date			
		Second survey	April 1, 1964	December 31, 1964	July 31, 1965
At second interview, woman gave an answer of a higher number practicing contraception for two or three of the three groups than she gave at the first interview	241	15	19	23	29
At second interview, woman gave an answer of a higher number practicing contraception for one of the three groups than she gave at first interview	352	13	17	18	22
At both interviews, woman answered that "some" or "many" of at least one of the three groups was practicing contraception	114	10	13	18	22
All other women, including those for whom we had insufficient information to categorize their change in perception of numbers of others practicing contraception	854	5	7	9	12
Total, all categories	1561	9	12	14	17

[a] In this tabulation, prepared by Dr. James Palmore, couples who had used contraception by the first interview or with either husband or wife sterilized by the second interview were considered "ineligible."

second survey).[26] The greater the perception of change and the larger the number of groups (relatives, friends, or neighbors) that were perceived to have changed, the greater the likelihood of acceptance. The change in perception during the experiment influenced acceptances not only during that period but also in the subsequent periods.

Acceptance rates were related less to increased discussion about family limitation than to increased perception of use by others. Apparently, whether more discussion takes place is less important than whether people believe that more of their primary contacts are actually adopting family limitation.[27]

GROUP MEETINGS AND THEIR EFFECTS: AN INADVERTENT EXPERIMENT

Group meetings were originally scheduled in all the Everything lins. The shortage of personnel and the unexpected difficulty of getting a group together in some areas, however, resulted in only about 500 of the 854 scheduled meetings actually being held.[28] This situation provided us with an unforeseen opportunity to test the influence of group meetings apart from the effect of the other stimuli that went into the program.

The meetings were rated as "effective," "somewhat effective," and "ineffective" by the fieldworkers who conducted them. These ratings were given immediately after the meetings were held and hence before the workers could know what the response in acceptances would be.[29] Whether a meeting was effective depended very much on the density of the treatment. (See Table VI-14.) Apparently, people living in the Heavy density sector must have been drawn to attend meetings by the activities in nearby neighborhoods. It is also likely that under these circumstances people from one neighborhood attended meetings in one of the several nearby neighborhoods where

[26] In this case the tabulation excludes couples who had used contraception before the first interview or those in which either husband or wife had been sterilized by the time of the second interview.

[27] See Chapter IX.

[28] Meetings were to be held in the Everything lins before the fieldworkers began their home visits, but when the scheduling got behind these were cancelled in order to avoid delaying the home visits.

[29] See Appendix I-3 for the specific procedure used in making this classification. The number of Everything lins add up to 860 rather than 854 in Tables VI-14 and VI-16. This is because the city readjusted some of the lin boundaries after our initial allocation of treatments.

Table VI-14. Percentage Distribution of the Everything Lins by Group Meeting Effectiveness[a] by Treatment by Sector in Taichung

Treatment	Number of lins	Percentage distribution by group meeting effectiveness: Total	Effective	Somewhat effective	Ineffective	No meeting
			Heavy sector			
Ehw	230	100	26	25	7	42
Ew	233	100	25	21	8	46
Total	463	100	26	23	8	43
			Medium sector			
Ehw	124	100	4	25	10	61
Ew	126	100	9	18	16	57
Total	250	100	6	21	13	60
			Light sector			
Ehw	72	100	1	51	18	30
Ew	75	100	5	42	20	33
Total	147	100	3	46	19	32

[a] A group meeting was coded as "effective" if the field worker in her evaluation checked all of the following "1"; "somewhat effective" if a combination of "1" and "2" or all "2"; and "ineffective" if she checked any of them either "3", "4", "5", or "N.A.":

Number of questions raised:

1 many 2 some 3 a few 4 none

Discussion among participants:

1 much 2 some 3 little 4 none

Overall interest generated among participants:

1 very much 2 much 3 neither much nor little

4 little 5 very little

such gatherings might be held. In any case, the proportion of meetings that were effective was much greater in the high density lins than elsewhere. Despite the fact that a somewhat larger proportion of the low density lins had meetings, the proportion of effective meetings was eight times as large in the Heavy density sector as in the other two.

The acceptance rates up to April 1, 1964 were influenced by a group meeting only if it was effective or somewhat effective. (See Table VI-15.) If the meetings were ineffective, the lins did no better than if meetings were not held at all. Effective meetings yielded higher acceptance rates for both the IUD and the traditional methods, but somewhat effective meetings influenced only the acceptances of the IUD. The higher acceptance rates for the IUD in the Everything lins were

Table VI-15. Acceptance Rate to April 1, 1964, Among Married Women 20-39 in Taichung, by Type of Method Accepted, by Treatment and Group Meeting Effectiveness[a]

Treatment and group meeting effectiveness	All methods	IUD	Others
Everything with:			
Effective meeting	21	13	8
Somewhat effective meeting	17	11	6
Ineffective meeting	14	7	7
No meeting	14	8	6
Mail	8	7	1
Nothing	7	7	1
All treatments	11	8	3

[a] See footnote under Table VI-14 for definition of effectiveness.

due almost entirely to the lins with either an effective or a somewhat effective meeting, while the high acceptance rates for the traditional methods in the Everything lins were due to the home visits. The IUD acceptance rates are significantly higher in the lins where effective or somewhat effective meetings were held than in any of the other types of lins. The acceptance rates for traditional methods, on the other hand, are uniformly high in the lins receiving home visits, with only the effective meeting lins doing somewhat better.

Despite the relatively high acceptance rates in the Everything lins taken as a whole, almost one-third of the Everything neighborhoods had had no acceptances by the end of the first period. (See Table VI-16.) But this phenomenon was much less common in the neighborhoods with effective or somewhat effective meetings. Conversely, the more effective the group meetings in the area, the more likely it was that the acceptance rate was exceptionally high.

THE EFFECT OF THE PROGRAM ON CONTRACEPTION AND FERTILITY

The success of the program in Taichung is indicated in part by the increase in the proportion of active users of contraception. According to the surveys taken just before and immediately after the experimental phase of the program (at the end of 1962 and the end of 1963, respectively), the proportion reporting current use of contraception increased from 19 per cent to 26 per cent. By mid-1965 an estimated 33 per cent were active users, if we count all the cases that

Table VI-16. Percentage Distribution of the Everything Lins by Level of Acceptance of All Methods[a/] to April 1, 1964 by Group Meeting Effectiveness

Group meeting effectiveness	Number of lins	Level of acceptance to April 1, 1964						
		None	Very low	Low	Medium	High	Very high	Total
Effective meeting	140	21	6	9	32	19	13	100
Somewhat effective meeting	226	26	6	10	30	17	11	100
Ineffective meeting	96	40	6	10	28	12	4	100
No meeting	398	33	4	13	32	12	6	100
All everything lins	860	30	5	12	31	14	8	100

a/ The levels of acceptance were categorized on the basis of the distributions of the acceptance rates of the non-zero lins using cut-off points at approximately the first decile, the first quartile, the third quartile, and the 90th percentile as follows:

None	0.0
Very low	1.0 - 5.4
Low	5.5 - 7.1
Medium	7.2 - 19.9
High	20.0 - 30.9
Very high	31.0 -100.0

accepted within the program by July 31, 1965 and those who reported current use of contraception in the second survey but did not become acceptors in the program (presumably because they were satisfied with whatever methods they were using).[30] Not all the acceptors in the program remained active users up to July 31, 1965, of course; but then, not all active users are included in this estimate, since we do not know how many started use of contraception on their own outside the program after the second survey was completed in the last months of 1963. In any case, the evidence on acceptance points to a substantial increase in the number of active users of contraception as a result of the program, and the majority of these active users were protected by the IUD, a much more effective method than those previously used by many.

One immediate consequence of the increase in the number of active users of contraception and of those using a more effective method was a decline in the proportion of women reporting a current preg-

[30] These data relate to the couples in the pre-program survey, a probability sample of married couples with wife 20-39, as of just before the program began in the fall of 1962. By July 1965 these wives were approximately 23-42 years old. These estimates relate to this initial panel, which therefore does not include acceptors who were migrants into the city during this period, nor does it adjust for those leaving.

nancy between the two surveys: from 17 per cent just before the program to 12 per cent immediately after, one year later.

The whole question of the program's effect on the use of birth control and then on the fertility of both the acceptors and the general population of Taichung is so important and complicated that we will postpone its further treatment until Chapter XII.

SUMMARY

We can now summarize our findings with respect to the questions raised at the outset as well as several additional major findings that have emerged:

1. *A large information and service campaign of a short duration can increase the practice of family planning in a large population of a developing country.* An intensive campaign in Taichung of only nine months' duration in 1963 was accompanied by a rise in the proportion of married women 20-39 who were using contraception from 19 per cent before the campaign to 26 per cent at the end of nine months and to at least 33 per cent within two and a half years. Actual acceptances in the program itself amounted to 20 per cent of Taichung's married couples with wife 20-39 years old as of two and a half years after the start of the program.

2. *It may not be necessary to approach both husbands and wives in a family planning program.* At least, the additional effort of approaching the husband did not prove worthwhile in Taichung. The acceptance rate in the neighborhoods where both the husband and wife were visited was no higher than that in the neighborhoods where only the wife was visited. This may be due to the fact that the principal method accepted was the IUD, a female method, and that there was already considerable consensus between the spouses about family planning.

3. *Letters were not effective in increasing the acceptance rate, although the population is fairly literate.* The letters were not keyed specifically to the IUD, and this may account for their lack of influence. But in an experiment in Seoul, Korea, where letters specifically referred to the IUD, the results were no better than in Taichung. More recent efforts directed to new mothers are giving more promising results.

4. *Diffusion played a major part in circulating the message and effect far beyond the couples directly influenced by the program.* The influence was mediated largely by the word-of-mouth communications of friends, neighbors, and relatives. The regular personnel of the health stations, those not assigned specifically to family planning work, were also important.

   Apparently, one important way in which diffusion operated was by increasing the perception that other, significant people—friends, neighbors, and relatives—were practicing contraception. This provided social support that facilitated acceptance. In any case, acceptances were highest where such perceptions increased. Such increased perceptions of contraceptive practice were more important than whether discussion about family planning increased.

   There is evidence of the power of diffusion not only in these data on increased perceptions, but also in the large number of acceptances by those from outside the city, in the relatively high acceptance rate in city areas without direct program influences, in the rather large number of acceptors who came to the clinics before the program workers reached them, and in reports of sources of information other than the direct program influences—especially for the IUD.

   While the acceptance rate was higher in the sector with the heaviest density of direct program effort than in the other two sectors, the most important finding is probably that the differences in the acceptance rates in relation to either treatment or density sector are relatively small. Together with the direct evidence on diffusion, we take this to indicate the power of diffusion, especially with a new method like the IUD, in cases where the total effort provides enough mutually reinforcing foci from which the message can be spread.

5. *Effective small group meetings had an important role in increasing the acceptance of the IUD.* Further, it is important that the fieldworkers were able to judge the effectiveness of the meetings at the time these occurred, as indicated by the later high acceptance rate in neighborhoods with such meetings.

6. *The new intrauterine device was chosen by a large majority of the acceptors.* In particular, acceptance by diffusion depended almost

entirely on the IUD, with primary contacts playing an especially important role in the diffusion of this innovation.

7. *Taichung's fertility decline was accelerated in the year following the experiment, and for 1963-64 exceeded that of the other cities or of the province by a considerable margin. By 1965, however, Taichung's advantage was minimized, presumably because of the rapid expansion of the family planning program in other parts of the island and the continuous adoption of family planning methods outside of the program.* While there are problems with respect to the long-term retention rate of the IUD and the proper evaluation of the precise effect of a family planning program on the birth rate in a dynamic situation, the initial effect of the large-scale adoption of the IUD in Taichung in 1963 apparently was to speed up the decline in fertility that was already under way there before the program began. Chapter XII presents the evidence on this issue.

8. *An important result of the program was that many families strongly interested in family planning were helped to adopt more satisfactory and effective methods.* Since many of these families were already limiting family size by such methods as abortion, the effect on the birth rate was less than might have been anticipated. For the 40 per cent of acceptors who had previously been using unsatisfactory methods there may have been some further reduction in fertility, but the major gain may have been in terms of the health and greater security of such families.

9. *One of the most important findings of the study was that such a large-scale effort could be carried out according to plan, with measured results, without political repercussions, and in such a way as to provide a secure basis for the much larger island-wide effort that immediately followed it.* There is some reason to believe that this is one of several efforts in various places that have encouraged workers in this field to begin their programs on the larger scale and with the intensity of effort which we believe to be necessary if a program is to set in motion the kind of diffusion that occurred in Taichung.

These are only the high points of the experiment. In succeeding chapters we shall deal in more detail with such important questions as how the characteristics of the people affected the acceptance rate and the persistence of use, how the informal communication process facilitated the diffusion that occurred, to what degree the acceptors were a selected high-fertility group, to what extent birth control and fertility were affected by the program, and what happened when the program was extended to the whole island.

VII. Who Accepts Family Planning Services: Demographic and Social Characteristics of the Acceptors

INTRODUCTION: AN OVERVIEW

WHO were the acceptors in the Taichung family planning program? Which demographic and social characteristics were associated with high acceptance rates? Which was more important: the pressures of growing family size, or education and other signs of modernization? How did the characteristics of the acceptors in the program compare with those of couples who had adopted family limitation before the program began, and did such previous practice lead to participation in the program? Were the younger women readier than others to adopt family planning?

Answers to these questions come from analysis of extensive sets of data and must take into account several important conditioning variables, especially whether the couples were ineligible for the program because they were already protected.

It may be useful, first, to have a broad summary of results as a framework for the detailed analysis which follows:

1. *Demographic variables are much more important than social and economic variables in determining who becomes an acceptor.* The demographic variables are those which indicate in various ways the stages of the family life-cycle and their relation to the desired number of children and the sexes wanted. Included among the demographic variables is the fact of prior use of birth control, which indicates demonstrated motivation to limit family growth. Acceptance rates increased markedly:

a. with increasing numbers of children, especially after an essential few.
b. with increasing numbers of sons.
c. among couples who had alive all the children they wanted or more: the more children that were still wanted, the lower the acceptance rate.
d. among couples who had already tried to limit family size but had given up the effort.

e. with increasing age or years of marriage, once eligibility is taken into account; but age and marriage duration are mainly significant in reflecting increasing numbers of children and prior use of birth control.

2. *The correlation between acceptance and social status or modernization is relatively weak, where it exists at all.* In the earlier preprogram period of individual action, the use of some method of family limitation was associated with measures both of modernization and of demographic status. The demographic variables were strongly associated with family limitation practice both before and during the period of the organized program. A plausible interpretation of these findings is that demographic pressures provide the constant incentive for family limitation both with and without the existence of an organized program. The more modern couples were better able to deal with these pressures without an organized program. The organized program provides the less advanced strata with resources and support they apparently require to meet similar needs.

3. *That acceptance rates are not high for the more modern couples is partly a reflection of the fact that more of them were already using more or less effective family limitation methods.* Therefore, many of them were ineligible for the program. If we consider only those couples not already practicing family limitation satisfactorily, a somewhat more positive correlation between acceptance and modernization appears in the program effort, too.

4. *However, this result cannot explain away the greater effect of demographic than social variables.* Even for couples fully eligible for the program, the modernization variables have lower correlations with acceptance in the program than with prior use of family limitation, and the association with acceptance is much greater for the demographic than for the modernization variables. In addition, since the groups under demographic pressure are much larger than the advanced, modern categories, the higher acceptance rates based on demographic criteria have a much greater impact on total acceptance rates.

5. *The relation of acceptance rates to demographic and social characteristics is substantially different for the younger (20-29) and*

the older (30-39) wives. In part, this simply reflects differences in eligibility. Younger wives are less likely to have been subject as yet to the demographic pressures which had already led many older women to some type of limitation effort. But even when eligibility is taken into account, substantial differences remain:

a. Younger wives are more likely than the older wives to be acceptors at an earlier demographic stage. They are readier to adopt family planning even with very few children and before they have the wanted number.
b. There is a stronger association between demographic variables and acceptance rates for the older couples than for the younger ones.
c. The modernization variables have a much more positive relation to acceptances for the younger couples than for the older ones. This may reflect the fact that the much greater demographic pressures faced by the greater majority of older couples transcend the influence of modernization.

6. *The contribution that any demographic or social stratum makes to the total number of acceptances depends on three component variables for each stratum:* (a) *the proportion of couples who are eligible;* (b) *the proportion of eligible couples who are acceptors; and* (c) *the proportion of all couples in the stratum.* The first two components determine the total acceptance rate for the stratum, but the contribution which the stratum makes to the total number of acceptances in the population often depends more on the number of couples in the stratum than on the acceptance rates. The advanced demographic categories have both high acceptance rates and a large representation in the population. Even if advanced social strata have high acceptance rates, they can not contribute very much to the total volume of acceptances, because they have small populations.

7. *The demographic and social characteristics of the acceptors differ by the type of treatment.* The intensive Everything treatment brought into the program more couples who were under less demographic pressure and who might not have accepted without strong program support, such as those with few children and sons and no previous birth control experience. Those accepting from the Nothing lins and from outside the city, on the other hand, were se-

lected to a greater extent from among the demographically advanced and highly motivated. They were younger and had been married for shorter periods, but had more children and sons and already had experience with birth control.

8. *The effective group meetings were successful in bringing into the program the lower status, less modernized couples who were demographically advanced but not yet protected against further growth of their families.* The effective meetings helped to bring in more IUD acceptances regardless of background, but they were especially successful with the still-unprotected lower status couples under strong demographic pressure.

9. *The program was successful in reaching younger women with fewer children and sons as time went on.* Although the more demographically advanced and the more highly motivated accepted in relatively larger numbers throughout the period of observation, the program reached progressively larger numbers of those at earlier stages of family life as time passed. There was no such constant trend toward greater success with lower status groups. Instead, the evidence indicates that the acceptance rate is highest for lower status groups during periods of more intensive program support.

THE DATA

The generalizations about the characteristics of the acceptors are drawn from three different sets of data:

1. The Intensive Survey data for the 2,443 women interviewed just before and just after the program—a probability, cross-section sample of all the wives of childbearing years in the city.
2. The Household Survey interview of the more than 11,000 women in the Everything lins. Since the Everything lins were chosen in such a way as to represent the whole city, characteristics obtained through this survey, such as education and prior fertility, can be taken as representative of the population as a whole. However, since the acceptance rates were higher in the Everything lins, the rates based on the Household Survey characteristics cannot be generalized in this way.
3. The clinic records of all the women who were acceptors, regardless of where they came from. These records include answers to the

household interview questions, even if the women did not come from the Everything lins.

The clinic records were linked to the interview records for those acceptors who fell into either the Household Survey sample or the Intensive Survey sample. Therefore, it is possible to relate the characteristics of the respondent as recorded by a survey to whether she later became an acceptor.

The details about data collection are set forth in Appendix 1-3. In addition, some problems in using these data are discussed in an unpublished technical memorandum available on request from the University of Michigan Population Studies Center. However, for the general reader a few special problems must be mentioned here to help in understanding what follows:

1. Both the Intensive Survey and the Household Survey somewhat underestimate the level of acceptance in the population, because the system for linking survey and clinic records did not permit us to follow respondents who moved from one lin to another. Also, acceptors among couples who moved into the city after the surveys could not be linked directly to survey cases, of course. But these problems arising from migration probably had only a small effect on acceptance rates or on their patterns of relationship with other variables.
2. However, the rates for the city as a whole (as in Tables VII-1 and VII-2) are generally not affected by the migration problem, because we do have in the clinic records all of the acceptors and their characteristics as obtained by the Household Survey items, even if we do not know their migration status. Generally, we were able to construct denominators for city-wide rates based on these clinic records by using either the Intensive Survey or the Household Survey to estimate the distribution of relevant characteristics for the population of the whole city. In this way we could relate the number of acceptors having specific characteristics to an estimate of the total number of wives with these characteristics. The data in Table VII-1 were put together on this basis. Such rates, based on relating different groups, differ in their construction from those based completely on the surveys. In the latter the characteristics of each individual acceptor and non-acceptor are known, so that

Table VII-1. Acceptance Rates of All Methods and IUD to July 31, 1965, by Demographic and Social Characteristics[a/] (Household Survey)

Characteristics	Acceptance rate to July 31, 1965 — All methods	IUD
All wives	20	16
Age of wife		
20-24	22	19
25-29	22	19
30-34	20	16
35-39	13	9
Duration of marriage		
Under 5 years	21	18
5-9 years	23	19
10-14 years	19	15
15 years or more	14	10
Number of living children		
0	3	1
1	7	5
2	16	13
3	25	20
4	24	20
5 or more	23	18
Number of living sons		
0	7	5
1	17	14
2 or more	24	20

Characteristics	Acceptance rate to July 31, 1965 — All methods	IUD
Number of living children and sons		
No children	3	1
One child		
No son	5	4
One son	9	6
Two children		
No son	10	8
One or two sons	18	14
Three or four children		
No son	16	12
One son	20	16
Two or more sons	27	22
Five or more children	23	18
Number of additional children and sons wife wanted		
No more	26	21
One more of any sex	13	11
One more son	13	11
Two or more of any sex	10	7
Two or more with at least one son	6	4

[a/] The 36,417 married women 20-39 years of age estimated to be living in Taichung at the start of the experiment were distributed in the various demographic and social strata according to the distributions found in the household survey of the Everything lins, which by the way the treatment allocation was made constituted a random sample of all the lins and married women 20-39 in the city.

the numerator and denominator for the rates are derived from a single sample and body of data.

3. The characteristics of the couples are almost always taken as of the time of the survey, just before the program began in the case of the Intensive Survey and during the first half of the program period for the Household Survey. Such characteristics as education or farm background are not likely to change during the period of observation, but there is a problem regarding such changing characteristics as number of living children, use of contraception, or de-

Table VII-1 (continued).

Characteristics	Acceptance rate to July 31, 1965	
	All methods	IUD
Birth control experience		
Sterilized	--	--
Currently using contraception, no abortion	12	7
Currently using contraception, had abortion	19	13
Past use of contraception, no abortion	53	42
Past use of contraception, had abortion	83	64
Abortion only	58	49
Never used anything	18	15
Wife's education		
Less than primary school graduate	18	15
Primary school graduate	19	15
Junior high school	24	18
Senior high school grad.	23	16

sire for more children. In the absence of a continuous flow of observations, it seemed best to fix all characteristics as of the outset of the program. This means, for example, that a woman who said in the survey that she wanted another child may have had that child before accepting family planning in the program a year later. We will refer at several points to possible effects of this limitation of the data.

4. Data from two different surveys are used. The Intensive Survey data are more detailed, of higher quality, and represent the whole city, but the small size of this sample limits cross-tabulations and increases sampling fluctuations. We therefore draw also on the Household Survey, which has a much larger sample; but since this survey represents only the women in the Everything lins, some of the tables refer only to these areas. By and large, patterns of relationship for the city as a whole are not much different from those for the Everything lins, but acceptance rates are significantly higher in the Everything areas.

In the present analysis, we deal with cumulative acceptances up to July 31, 1965. In unpublished tabulations for various earlier dates of reference the levels of acceptance differ, but the basic patterns of relationship are similar. The cumulative acceptances over several years

Table VII-2. Acceptance Rates of All Methods and IUD to July 31, 1965, by Demographic and Social Characteristics (Intensive Survey)

Characteristics	Acceptance rate to July 31, 1965: All methods	Acceptance rate to July 31, 1965: IUD
All wives	17	13
Number of living children and number wanted		
Wanted at least 2 more	10	8
Wanted 1 more	20	16
Had number wanted	16	12
Had more than wanted	25	20
N.A., up to God, etc.	11	10
Family limitation practice and open birth interval		
Used contraception or abortion		
0-8 months	44	30
9-11 months	29	17
12-23 months	26	17
24-59 months	21	15
60 months or more	12	7
Never used anything		
0-8 months	21	18
9-11 months	18	16
12-23 months	20	17
24-59 months	12	10
60 months or more	1	1
Family type		
Living in extended unit	18	14
Living in nuclear unit		
Once in extended unit	17	14
Always nuclear	16	11
Husband's employment status		
Farmer	20	18
Other traditional employment	15	11
Employed by non-relative	17	13
Professional	16	12

represent the results after the initial program effect had had some chance to diffuse and develop.

DIFFERENTIALS ON A CITY-WIDE BASIS FOR ALL COUPLES

We consider first how the acceptance rates vary for the demographic and social strata of the whole city. This initial view of total rates provides the gross differences between major strata, before we explain or qualify by taking into account the ages of the women and their eligibility.

Acceptance rates vary markedly from one demographic category to another or among categories based on prior use of family limitation methods, but there is little difference between modernization categories. These summary statements are based on data from the Household Survey found in Table VII-1 and from the Intensive Survey data in Table VII-2.[1] Let us now consider the specific evidence on which these generalizations are based.

Number of living children and sons: Acceptance rates increased markedly with number of living children and sons at the outset of the program (Table VII-1). Acceptance rates are highest among those who initially had three or more children; after three children, the specific number is not important. Also, the largest difference in acceptance rates is between those who initially had no son and those who had one. Having at least a second son is associated with an additional but lesser increase in acceptance rates.

Obviously, there will be interdependence between these two variables, since the probability of having at least one son increases with the number of children. When considered simultaneously, the number of children and the number of sons have independent effects, within limits. Acceptances increased with number of children both for those who did and those who did not have sons. Conversely, among those with any specific number of children, acceptances were higher for those with at least one son than for those without a son. The highest acceptance rates were recorded among those with at least three or four children and at least two sons.

These results validate the significance of the values expressed by the respondents in the survey carried out before the program. They indicated then that three or four children and one or two sons was the family composition they preferred for themselves and considered ideal for Taiwanese generally.

Comparison of number of children alive and number wanted: In a population much more interested in limiting the number of children than in spacing them, a crucial question is how many couples already have all the children they want or more. In the Intensive Survey it was possible to compare the number of children alive with the

[1] The acceptance rates by the characteristics available from the Household Survey (and the clinic records) were computed for the city as a whole on a base population estimated according to the distribution of the cases in the Everything lins by these characteristics. The Intensive Survey, of course, was a random sample representative of the city as a whole. Whenever measures of the variables are available from both sources, those from the Household Survey are used because of the larger sample size (and hence the smaller sampling errors involved).

number the wife said she would want, if "she could start over and have just the number wanted by the time she was 45."

Acceptance rates varied substantially according to this comparison of number of children alive and number wanted, reaching a maximum of 25 per cent among those who already had more children than they wanted (Table VII-2). That acceptance rates were higher for those who wanted one more child than for those with just the number wanted results from the fact that a large proportion of those having just the number wanted were already sterilized or using contraception and therefore were not really eligible for the program. Once this is taken into account (Table VII-4, Panel A), the rates increase as expected. While the discrepancy between actual and desired family size is important, the interest in birth control cut across all the categories. Even among those wives who initially declared that the number of children born is up to God, fate, etc., 11 per cent had become acceptors by July 1965.

The Household Survey data do not indicate whether wives wanted fewer children than they already had. However, the number of additional children and sons they wanted is known (Table VII-1). Acceptance rates were much higher for those who wanted no more children than for those who wanted more. If they wanted only one more child, acceptance rates did not depend on whether a son was preferred. But if two or more children were wanted, acceptance rates were significantly lower among couples who wanted at least one more son, presumably because more than half of them had no sons. The large majority of the other couples already had at least one son and many had more, as we can see from the data presented on page 159.

The acceptance rate among those who did not want any more children is much higher when eligibility is taken into account, as we shall presently see.

It is important that the proportion of couples who already had the wanted number of children or more at the start of the program was so large (46 per cent) and that the acceptance rate among them was high. This means that if these couples are reached by the program, there will be a large contribution to the total volume of acceptors from couples whose values about family size need not be changed by any effort of the program.

Prior practice of family limitation: Whether the couples had already begun to practice some form of family limitation before the

No. of additional children and sons wife wanted	*Percentage distribution, by no. of living sons at first home visit*							
	None	*One*	*Two*	*Three*	*Four*	*Five or more*	*N.A.*	*Total*
No more	3	18	41	24	10	4	*	100%
One more of any sex	2	22	49	19	6	2	–	100%
One more son	23	68	8	1	*	–	*	100%
At least two more of any sex	15	21	40	17	4	2	1	100%
At least two more, with at least one a son	57	37	6	*	*	*	*	100%

* Less than 1 per cent.

program began had a powerful effect on whether they would become acceptors, especially if we take into account the method used and whether its practice was current. Obviously, the sterilized could not become acceptors. Those already sterilized aside, couples were classified in the Household Survey by whether contraception and induced abortion had ever been used (Table VII-1).

Couples currently practicing contraception with no history of induced abortion had the lowest acceptance rates. Since at least 50 per cent of all induced abortions followed unsuccessful use of contraception, it is plausible to consider the current contraceptors with no abortion history as a relatively successful group least in need of the program effort. It may also be, however, that some of these couples had not resorted to abortion because their motivation was weaker.

Couples not currently using contraception as of just before the program began had high acceptance rates if they had previously used either contraception or abortion or both. Acceptance was especially likely among those who had tried both contraception and abortion. Presumably these are highly motivated couples, since they had demonstrated their interest in birth control in two different ways but were not currently protected. Acceptance rates were lower, but still notably higher than the average, for the couples who had once used either abortion or contraception but not both. We demonstrate later that the couples who had once tried contraception but had then given it up had much higher fertility than the other couples during the years immediately preceding the program. They probably had the strong motivation that comes from continuing high fertility, which their attempts at birth control had failed to limit.

The acceptance rate of 18 per cent for those who had never previously used anything is low as compared to the rates for some of the categories of former users, but it is not negligible. It is especially important that this group has a reasonably high rate, because it includes a large proportion of the population. The proportion of all acceptances coming from this group should be, and was, quite high, as we shall presently see.

The open birth interval and prior birth control: How recently a couple has had a child is an important determinant of interest in family limitation, since it is the most recent reminder to the couples of the continuing risk of additional family growth. It is also important to know whether the couple has used birth control, since such practice may produce a long open interval, making the couple less interested in the program. Couples with long open birth intervals and no prior birth control practice are likely to have low fecundability. It was possible to use both open interval and prior family limitation action to classify the cases in the Intensive Survey sample[2] (Table VII-2).

There is a powerful inverse association between the length of the open interval and the acceptance rate among those who have previously used some form of family limitation, presumably because the longer open interval among such couples indicates either greater success in family planning or lower fecundability or both. The proportion of current contraceptors was significantly smaller among those with short rather than long open intervals. Among those who have never used family limitation, there is little difference in acceptance rates between those with more births within the preceding two-year period and those with fewer. However, the acceptance rate drops sharply if there has been no birth for two years or more. Such a long period without a birth probably indicates very low fecundability and little recent demographic pressure.

In any specific open interval category, acceptance rates are much

[2] In this classification, couples sterilized by the time of the second interview are excluded entirely from consideration.

higher for those who have used family limitation previously than for those who haven't, presumably because the former group is more strongly motivated and has not been able to postpone recent births any more successfully than those who were using nothing.

Age and duration of marriage: Neither age nor duration of marriage has a consistent relation to acceptance for all couples, although the oldest wives (35-39) and those married for the longest periods (more than ten years) have significantly lower acceptance rates than the younger women and those married for shorter periods (Table VII-1). We shall see later that when eligibility is taken into account, acceptance rates do increase monotonically with increasing age or marriage duration.

Measures of modernization: A wide variety of social status and modernization variables were considered in relation to acceptance rates in tabulations not presented here. Data are presented for only three measures used in earlier analyses of birth control practice before the program began, because none of the modernization variables had a very large correlation to acceptance rates. The education measure we used can alone account for most of the acceptance variance explained by a group of nine social and modernization variables. The three characteristics to be considered are wife's education (from the Household Survey), family type, and employment status (from the Intensive Survey).

These three measures of modernization, as well as others, were previously found to be correlated positively to prior use of family limitation and negatively to fertility before the program. However, there is very little relationship between modernization and the acceptance rates in the program for the city as a whole (Tables VII-1 and VII-2). We shall see later that there are somewhat more significant relationships when eligibility and age are taken into account. Even then, however, the association is far less than is the case with demographic measures.

ELIGIBILITY AND ACCEPTANCE RATES

Some couples are temporarily or permanently ineligible for family limitation assistance. If the husband or the wife has been sterilized, the couple is permanently ineligible. Couples who are currently using a family limitation method adopted outside the program which satisfies them are much less likely to become acceptors than others, although some may choose to change to a method or source of supply associated with the program. Various criteria of eligibility may be used, and we have illustrated in Chapter VI that acceptance rates vary with the criterion.

In the present analysis, the definition of eligibility will be based on two criteria. For the Intensive Survey, we exclude as ineligible the couples who either (a) had been sterilized by the time of the second interview (October-December 1963) or (b) were currently using contraception adopted outside the program at the time of second interview and did not become acceptors by July 31, 1965. The basis for excluding the first group is obvious. The second group is excluded on the assumption that those current users of contraception who did not become acceptors by July 31, 1965 were probably satisfied with their current practice. Unfortunately, we have no data for periods beyond the second interview to validate this inference. The definition of eligibility for the Household Survey could be only roughly comparable. It excludes as ineligible not only (a) those who were sterilized, but also (b) those who believed themselves sterile at the time of the household interview (February-October 1963)[3] and (c) current users of contraception at the time of the household interview who did not become acceptors in the program by July 31, 1965. This additional exclusion from the eligible group of those who believed themselves sterile permits a more plausible interpretation of some of the findings.

With any definition of eligibility, it is possible to decompose the acceptance rates into two useful components:

$$\frac{A}{N} = \frac{E}{N} \times \frac{A}{E}$$

where: N = total number of wives 20-39
A = total number of acceptors among N
E = number of wives among N who are eligible.

The total acceptance rate (A/N) is a function of:

[3] About 10 per cent of the couples in the Household Survey reported that they were sterilized because of an operation. Those who only reported that they "believed" themselves to be sterile were much older and had fewer children than the other couples on the average, so their self-classification has some factual basis. They were also treated as ineligible in the Household Survey analysis.

1. the proportion of wives in the total population who are eligible (E/N), and
2. the rate of acceptance among those who are eligible (A/E).

The same function can be applied in each subgroup with the corresponding lower-case letters, as follows:

$$\frac{a_i}{n_i} = \frac{e_i}{n_i} \times \frac{a_i}{e_i}$$

where: n_i = total number of wives 20-39 in a given subgroup i
a_i = total number of acceptors among n_i
e_i = number of wives among n_i who are eligible.

The acceptance rate in a given subgroup (a_i/n_i) is a function of:

1. the proportion of wives in the subgroup who are eligible (e_i/n_i), and
2. the rate of acceptance among those eligible in the subgroup (a_i/e_i).

In other words, the acceptance rate in a subgroup is affected not only by the acceptance rate among the eligible wives, but also by the proportion of all the wives in the subgroup who are eligible.

When the acceptance rates are broken down into these component parts, the source and dynamics of observed differences in the overall rates are clarified. More specifically, removing the eligibility component sharpens further the important association that was noted between demographic variables and acceptance rates. It also reveals a modest positive association between modernization and acceptance rates. The strata under demographic pressure and the more modern strata have low proportions of eligible couples because many in these categories are already sterilized or using satisfactory contraception. This obscures or minimizes differences between categories. If only eligible couples are considered, the basic demographic differences increase and some social differences emerge that were not apparent initially. Table VII-3 summarizes pertinent selected data from the Household Survey, and Table VII-4 from the Intensive Survey. Since the data from the Household Survey are restricted to the Everything

Table VII-3. Acceptance Rates of All Methods to July 31, 1965, in the Everything Lins, for All Wives and Eligible Wives Only, Percentage of Wives Eligible, and Distribution of All Wives and Acceptors, by Demographic and Social Characteristics (Household Survey)

Characteristics	Acceptance rate among: All wives (1)	Acceptance rate among: Eligible wives (2)	Percentage eligible (3)	Percentage distribution[a] All wives (4)	Percentage distribution[a] Acceptors (5)
All wives	23	33	70	100	100
Panel A					
Age of wife					
20-24	20	21	94	19	16
25-29	26	31	83	30	33
30-34	26	41	62	28	31
35-30	21	48	44	23	20
Panel B					
Duration of marriage					
Under 5 years	19	20	94	24	20
5-9 years	27	33	81	28	31
10-14 years	26	44	60	26	29
15 years or more	21	48	44	22	20
Panel C					
Number of living children					
0	3	4	74	4	1
1	11	12	89	13	6
2	19	24	81	18	14
3	28	39	72	19	22
4	27	45	61	19	22
5 or more	30	50	59	27	35

[a] N.A.'s are distributed proportionately in the various categories.

lins, we shall be concerned mainly with the patterns rather than with the specific levels of the values.[4]

Moving now from the city-wide differentials to more refined analyses such as that of data concerning eligible couples or specific age groups, we present only a selected few among the tabulations available, fewer than those presented in Tables VII-1 and VII-2 for the city as a whole. Our purpose is to spare the general reader unneces-

[4] We have already noted that the acceptance rates are higher in these Everything lins; the Household Survey rates are therefore higher than those from the Intensive Survey, which covers the whole city. The eligibility rates also differ somewhat for these two sources of data, because in the Everything areas current users were more likely to become acceptors, and therefore to be eligible by our definitions.

Table VII-3 (continued).

Characteristics	Acceptance rate among: All wives (1)	Eligible wives (2)	Percentage eligible (3)	Percentage distribution[a] All wives (4)	Acceptors (5)
			Panel D		
Number of living children and sons					
No children	3	3	74	4	1
One child					
No son	8	9	90	6	2
One son	14	16	88	7	4
Two children					
No son	13	15	89	4	2
One or two sons	21	26	79	14	12
Three or four children					
No son	23	26	90	3	3
One son	25	32	76	10	11
Two or more sons	30	50	60	25	31
Five children or more	30	50	59	27	34
			Panel E		
Wife's education					
Less than primary school grad.	23	30	76	41	40
Primary school grad.	23	33	69	41	40
Junior high school	26	42	63	10	11
Senior high school grad.	26	48	54	8	9

sary detail and repetition.[5] We have selected variables which illustrate general conclusions or which produce different results.

The proportion of those who are ineligible varies with social and demographic characteristics in much the same way as the proportion ever using birth control did in Chapters III and V.[6] The proportion ineligible thus increases rather sharply with either increasing demographic pressure or modernization (see column 3 in Tables VII-3 and VII-4).

Number of living children and sons (Table VII-3, Panels C and D): The proportion eligible decreases consistently with increasing number of living children. It drops from 89 per cent for those with one child to 59 per cent for those with five or more. The proportion eligible among those without any living children is relatively low (74

[5] More detailed tabulations are available for the interested specialist on request.

[6] The proportion of those who had ever used birth control and the proportion ineligible are not identical, because: (a) couples who used only abortion were not defined as ineligible, and (b) couples who were not currently using contraception by the second interview were not defined as ineligible, irrespective of prior practice.

Table VII-4. Acceptance Rates of All Methods to July 31, 1965, for All Wives and Eligible Wives Only, Percentage of Wives Eligible, and Distributions of All Wives and Acceptors, by Demographic and Social Characteristics (Intensive Survey)

Characteristics	Acceptance rate among: All wives (1)	Acceptance rate among: Eligible wives (2)	Percentage eligible (3)	Percentage distribution[a/] All wives (4)	Percentage distribution[a/] Acceptors (5)
All wives	17	23	73	100	100
			Panel A		
Number of living children and number wanted					
Wanted at least 2 more	10	11	93	24	14
Wanted 1 more	20	24	83	26	31
Had number wanted	16	28	58	28	26
Had more than wanted	25	45	54	18	27
N.A., up to God, etc.	11	12	91	4	2
			Panel B		
Family limitation practice and open birth interval					
Sterilized	--	--	--	9	--
Used contraception or abortion					
0-8 months	44	65	66	3	7
9-11 months	29	42	69	1	2
12-23 months	26	51	51	6	10
24-59 months	21	46	45	10	13
60 months or more	12	37	34	6	4
Never used anything					
0-8 months	21	23	94	22	27
9-11 months	18	20	91	7	8
12-23 months	20	21	96	18	21
24-59 months	12	12	94	11	8
60 months or more	1	1	99	7	*

[a/] N.A.'s are distributed proportionately in the various categories.

* Less than 1 per cent.

per cent), because the women who believed themselves to be sterile, many of them childless, are classified as ineligible in the Household Survey.[7] The acceptance rates among eligible couples increase with increasing numbers of living children from 4 to 50 per cent as compared with a range of 3 to 30 per cent among all couples. The sharper

[7] By age 30-34, less than 3 per cent of all the women in the intensive sample had never had a live birth. This must be rather close to the minimum sterile group. Almost all childlessness in Taiwan is involuntary.

Table VII-4 (continued).

Characteristics	Acceptance rate among: All wives (1)	Eligible wives (2)	Percentage eligible (3)	Percentage distribution[a/] All wives (4)	Acceptors (5)
			Panel C		
Family type					
Living in extended unit	18	24	76	52	54
Living in nuclear unit					
Once in extended unit	17	23	71	27	26
Always nuclear	16	23	70	21	20
			Panel D		
Husband's employment status					
Farmer	20	23	88	18	22
Other traditional employment	15	20	73	26	23
Employed by non-relative	17	24	71	50	49
Professional	16	27	57	6	6

gradient among the eligible results from the large increase in acceptance rates among those with more children when we set aside the ineligible couples. For those who had fewer than three children the two sets of acceptance rates differ little, because a large proportion of the couples are eligible. But in the case of those who already had at least three children the rates for the eligible couples are much higher, since so many of these couples with larger families are ineligible. To illustrate for the extreme categories:

	Total acceptance rate	=	*Acceptance rate among eligible*	×	*Proportion of all couples eligible*
Had one child	11		12		.89
Had five or more children	30		50		.59

Similarly, by the time couples have two or more sons, 40 per cent are already satisfactorily protected. Therefore, the acceptance rate increases more sharply in relation to the number of sons when the ineligible are set aside.

When the number of children and the number of sons are considered jointly, the rates for eligible couples show still larger differences, because both the number of children and the number of sons affect the proportion eligible. At one extreme, among couples with three or four children and at least two sons, only 60 per cent were eligible, but 50 per cent of these couples became acceptors. At the other extreme, 90 per cent of the couples with one daughter and no sons were eligible, but only 9 per cent of these eligibles were acceptors. The decomposition of the total acceptance rates for these two rather extreme categories looks like this:

No. of living: *children*	*sons*	*Total acceptance rate*	=	*Acceptance rate among the eligible*	×	*Proportion of all couples eligible*
1	0	8		9		.90
3 or more	2 or more	30		50		.60

Comparison of number of children alive and number wanted (Table VII-4, Panel A): Nearly half of those who had just the number of children they wanted or more were ineligible, and acceptance rates for the eligible among them are therefore much higher than for all couples. The great majority of those who wanted more children were still eligible, so that the two types of rates differ only slightly for them.

The comparison of number of children alive and number wanted was made before the program began, and it is possible that a woman who wanted more children might have had one or more of them and then become an acceptor. By that time, she may have had all the children she wanted. Such changes would not appear in the data shown in Table VII-4, and their omission minimizes the relationship found. We do have data obtained by the Intensive Survey on whether an additional child was born between the pre-program and post-program interviews (that is, between the end of 1962 and the end of 1963, approximately). We can take this additional data into account and relate the revised classification to acceptance rates at a point shortly afterward (March 31, 1964). The results are as follows:

Comparison of no. of living children and no. wanted and whether had a live birth during the first year of the program	*% accepted by March 31, 1964*
Wanted at least 2 more	
had none	5
had one	6
Wanted 1 more	
had none	12
had one	22
Had no. wanted	23
Had more than wanted	30
N.A., up to God, etc.	12

Among those who initially wanted one more child, those who had this child accepted at a rate much higher than those who didn't. Presumably, those having the additional child then had the number wanted. It is striking that their acceptance rate was almost identical with that of couples who had just the number wanted before the program began. The acceptance rate for those who initially wanted two or more additional children did not become very much higher when they had just one of the several additional children they wanted. The substantial relationship between the acceptance rates and whether more children were wanted is minimized in most of our tables, because we cannot take into account for later periods the additional births which gave many couples all the children they wanted.

Among eligible couples, those not already protected against further births, the acceptance rate rises sharply in relation to increasing felt demographic pressure, defined by the wife's own perception that she has all the children she wants or more.

Family limitation practice and open birth interval (Table VII-4, Panel B): Couples currently using contraception at the time of the second interview were ineligible.[8] Therefore, among those practicing birth control before the program, acceptance rates were substantially

[8] However, if they subsequently became acceptors, they were defined as eligible on the grounds that their acceptance indicates dissatisfaction with prior practice—that is, they were not satisfactorily protected. Admittedly, this operational definition introduces some circularity.

higher for the eligible than for all couples for every open interval category. The proportion ineligible is highest (66 per cent) among those without a birth for five years or more, presumably because these are couples who have used an effective method to avoid births for a long time.[9]

Nevertheless, there are a considerable number of couples who are eligible even though they had once used contraception or abortion. These were couples who had previously used only abortion, those who had given up their former contraceptive practice by the second Intensive Survey interview, or those who had switched from another contraceptive method to one in the program after the second interview. The proportion of such eligible couples increases as the length of time since the last birth grows shorter. This is to be expected, because most of those with recent birth had presumably not practiced birth control very successfully. It is significant, therefore, that the shorter the open birth interval, the higher the acceptance rate. For the shortest interval the rate was very high: 65 per cent. Those who have tried birth control previously and have nevertheless had a recent birth must be very highly motivated to accept what a family planning program has to offer.

Among those who had not previously used birth control by the time of the first interview the proportion eligible is uniformly high,[10] of course, so the acceptance rates differ little between all couples and the eligible couples. The acceptance rates decline very rapidly to close to zero among the couples without a birth for five years. This simply means that couples who can go for long periods of time without a birth even though they don't practice birth control do not have a family planning problem. Low fecundity takes care of the situation for them. Those who had not practiced birth control but had a relatively recent birth did have a problem, and the more recent the birth, the higher their acceptance rates. However, at equivalent open intervals their rates are always lower than those of persons previously trying something else. Again, it is the combination of recent demon-

[9] Mohapatra, *op.cit.*, has shown that most of the couples who ever used contraception had used it in the open interval, and that the open interval is much longer for such couples.

[10] These couples who had used no birth control method before the first interview could only be classified as ineligible if they adopted contraception outside of the program or were sterilized between the first and second Intensive Survey interviews.

stration of fertility and motivation proven by previous birth control efforts which produces the higher receptivity to the program.

Age and duration of marriage (Table VII-3, Panels A and B): Progressively fewer women remain unprotected or fecund with advance in age or length of marriage. While 94 per cent are eligible in the 20-24 age group or among those married for less than five years, only 44 per cent are eligible in the 35-39 range or among those married at least fifteen years or longer. Among the eligible couples, the acceptance rates rise consistently with age and duration of marriage. Demographic pressure, unless already checked, increases with additional exposure to the risk of fertility, and acceptance rates in the program rose accordingly.

Measures of modernization (Table VII-3, Panel E and Table VII-4, Panels C and D): No significant correlations were observed between modernization measures and acceptance rates when all women were considered. With eligibility taken into account, there is a significant and consistent correlation between the wife's education and acceptance rates, previously obscured, because eligibility decreases as education increases. Acceptance is still not correlated with family type, although eligibility is higher among the more modern family types. As to husband's employment status, among those in non-farm occupations the rates for the eligible couples do increase consistently with modernization.

The position of the farmer is distinctive and important. Initially, farmers have a higher acceptance rate than any other employment status category. This is partly due to their high eligibility rate, since very few farm families were already protected. However, even among the eligible couples, the farmer's acceptance rate is close to the average for the whole population. The farmers responded to the program as well as any other urban group, with the exception of the professionals, even after allowing for eligibility differences.

A MULTIVARIATE ANALYSIS OF FACTORS AFFECTING ACCEPTANCE RATES AMONG ELIGIBLE COUPLES

That acceptance rates depend much more on demographic than on social or modernization variables can be demonstrated more precisely in a multivariate analysis of eligible couples, which also specifies the difference in patterns followed by older and younger women. The interval since the last birth, when considered jointly with prior family limitation practice, is found to be the best basis for predicting acceptance. This and other demographic factors are related to acceptance much more strongly for the older women than for the younger. Apparently the younger women may accept in the absence of strong demographic pressure, while the older women are more likely to respond only under such demographic pressure.

Table VII-5 shows how much of the variance in acceptance rates is explained by each of three demographic and nine social variables.[11]

Table VII-5. Proportion of Variance in Total and IUD Acceptance Rates to July 1965 "Explained" (Eta Squared)[a/] by Various Demographic and Social Characteristics for "Eligible"[b/] Couples, by Age of Wife

	Total acceptances			IUD acceptances		
	Age of wife			Age of wife		
Characteristics	20-39	20-29	30-39	20-39	20-29	20-39
Demographic characteristics						
Open birth interval and whether ever used family limitation before	10	5	19	6	2	12
Number of living children and sons	7	6	7	5	5	5
Comparison of number of children alive and wanted	7	5	9	5	4	7
Other social characteristics						
Wife's education	2	3	2	*	1	*
Husband's education	1	3	*	*	1	1
Wife's newspaper reading	1	2	*	*	1	*
Husband's newspaper reading	*	1	*	*	*	*
Number of modern objects owned	2	3	1	*	2	*
Husband's employment status	*	*	*	*	*	*
Household income	*	1	*	*	1	2
Family type	*	*	*	*	*	*
Ethnic background	*	*	*	*	*	*
Joint effect of all 3 demographic variables[c/]	15	9	22	10	5	14
Joint effect of all 9 social variables[c/]	3	5	2	2	3	3

[a/] Eta is a measure of correlation requiring no assumptions about linearity or ordering of variables.

[b/] Unless otherwise indicated the data in all succeeding tables also refer to eligible women and to acceptances to July 1, 1965.

[c/] The measure used here is the square of the multiple correlation from the multiple classification program, adjusted for the degrees of freedom.

* Less than 1 per cent.

11 The technique of multivariate analysis used here is "multiple classification" analysis, which is described in detail in F. Andrews, J. Morgan, and J. Sonquist,

No adjustment has been made in this first table for the overlapping influence of the other variables.

It is immediately obvious that the demographic variables are much more important than the social ones. Any one of the three demographic measures accounts for more of the variance than any one of the social variables, usually by a very wide margin.[12] In fact, each of the demographic variables explain as much as or more than all nine of the social variables considered jointly either for all women (20-39) or for each of the two broad age groups (20-29 and 30-39). The joint explanatory power of the three demographic variables greatly exceeds that of the nine social variables.

Dealing with eligible couples should maximize the possible influence of the social variables.[13] If we had not excluded the in-

---

Multiple Classification Analysis, Institute for Social Research, The University of Michigan, May 1967. Essentially, this is a regression procedure in which each category of each independent variable is a predictor (having the value zero or one). It is unnecessary to consider the categories as having any order by rank, and there are no assumptions about the scaling or linearity of the variables. We have also analyzed total and IUD acceptances up to the end of the action program (late 1963), and to April and December of 1964, as well as to July 31, 1965, using the same social and demographic variables in the multivariate analysis discussed here. Since there is little difference between patterns for the three time periods, the latest date is used in order to take the maximum number of cases under consideration. This multivariate analysis includes a few variables not previously used in this chapter. Since they did not seem to add to the understanding of the problem, they are not discussed separately.

[12] The measure used is the square of eta, derived as a by-product of the multiple classification computer program described in the source cited in the preceding footnote. We cite eta-squared rather than eta in these tables, because we are interested in discussing the amount of variance explained. Eta requires no assumptions about ordering of categories or linearity.

[13] The eta values for the social variables are almost always higher for the eligible couples than for the total sample, e.g.:

	Eta values for correlation of acceptance rates to July 1965	
	All couples	*Eligible couples*
Wife's education	.06	.14
Number of modern objects owned	.09	.14
Household income	.03	.08
Husband's employment status	.04	.04

eligible couples it might have been argued, for example, that the better educated have lower acceptance rates because they are more likely to be protected against unwanted family growth already by sterilization or effective contraception.

In confining ourselves to eligible couples it was our intention to eliminate as a factor in the situation the varying proportions eligible in different social and demographic strata. It could be argued that in the high status groups the definition leaves as eligible only those women less motivated to accept. This seems unlikely, but if it is true, then this is a fact with which family planning programs must deal. Whether or not eligibility is taken into account, it remains true that acceptances in the program as it was conducted were not strongly associated with social characteristics. In any case, the same argument could be made in the case of the demographic variables, because the large numbers of couples who are ineligible in the advanced demographic strata must include many of the highly motivated couples also.

The relative power of various combinations of demographic and social variables to explain the variance of the rates is shown in Tables VII-6 and VII-7. In Table VII-6 the main multivariate analysis is based on the three demographic variables used in Table VII-5 and on four selected social variables. The maximum percentage of the variance explained by all seven variables combined is 16 per cent for all ages, 11 per cent for the younger women, and 22 per cent for the

Table VII-6. Proportion of Variance in Total Acceptance Rates "Explained" by Various Combinations of Demographic and Social Variables

Characteristics	Age of wife 20-39	20-29	30-39
Three demographic variables	15	9	22
Three demographic variables and wife's education	16	11	22
Three demographic variables and wife's education and three other social variables[b]	16	11	22
Three demographic variables plus wife's education and number of modern objects	16	11	22

[a]/Number of living children and sons, comparison of number of children alive and wanted, open interval-family limitation.

[b]/Husband's employment status, ethnic background, and family type.

Table VII-7. Proportion of Variance in Total Acceptance Rates "Explained" by Various Combinations of Basic Demographic Variables

Demographic variables	Age of wife		
	20-39	20-29	30-39
A: Open interval family limitation	10	5	19
B: Comparison of number of children alive and wanted	7	5	9
C: Number of living children and sons	7	6	7
A and B	14	7	21
A and C	14	8	20
B and C	8	6	11
A and B and C	15	9	22
A and B and C and four social variables[a]	16	11	22

[a] Wife's education, husband's employment status, ethnic background, and family type.

older women. While these are quite respectable values for a social investigation, they indicate that even a set of crucial demographic and social variables leaves most of the variance unexplained. We suspect that the addition of other available variables would add little statistically, because it appears that the program has an appeal for all kinds of people and that the final decision to accept rests on idiosyncratic factors in the lives of the individuals and in the operation of the program.

Adding other social variables to the four considered in Table VII-6 could contribute very little, since nine social variables (including the four in Table VII-6), collectively explain only 3 per cent of the variance in acceptances. The crucial social variable in Table VII-6—wife's education—accounts for about two-thirds of the amount of the variance explained by all nine social variables.[14]

Of the total amount of variance explained by the three demographic and four social variables considered in Table VII-6, the three demographic variables alone can account for 94 per cent for all ages, 82 per cent for the younger women, and 100 per cent for the older

[14] We did try adding number of modern objects owned to the four social variables used in Table VII-6, since it has been useful in other analyses, but nothing further was gained in amount of explained variance.

women. Adding the social variable of wife's education to the three demographic variables leaves the three other social variables with no explanatory power.

In short, once we have taken the three demographic variables into account, the social variables add nothing for the older women, and the relatively small increment in the case of the younger women is completely accounted for by either wife's education or number of modern objects owned. The social variables predict very little about acceptances among eligible women that cannot be attributed to demographic variables.

Since the demographic variables are clearly the most important, we have shown in Table VII-7 the amount of variance explained by various combinations of them. How recently a woman has borne a child, when considered together with whether she has ever used family limitation, is the best single basis for predicting acceptance rates. For more convenient reference we call this open interval-family limitation. This variable alone accounts for 62 per cent of the variance explained by all seven variables for women of all ages, 45 per cent for the younger women, and 86 per cent for the older.

It is not surprising that the open interval-family limitation variable, as well as the other demographic variables, should be more relevant at the older ages than at the younger. At any interval after a previous birth, the older woman is more likely to be interested in preventing further births. If she has recently had a birth she will be especially responsive, because she has demonstrated to herself her risk of childbearing at a time when the probability is high that she already has as many children as she wants or more. The older women are less likely to have had a recent birth, but if they have had one they are likely to be highly motivated to accept family limitation.[15]

Of secondary importance are the two other demographic variables considered: (1) the number of children and sons alive at the initial interview, and (2) the comparison of the number of children wanted and the number alive at that time. There is a great deal of overlap between these two variables, so that their joint effect is only a little more than the separate effects of either considered alone (see Table

[15] Several other demographic variables were considered in relation to acceptance, but were not carried into the multivariate analysis because they did not have a very strong association with acceptance rates. These included the duration of marriage and the length of interpregnancy intervals before first use of contraception.

VII-7). Also, adding either one of these variables to open interval-family limitation yields about the same total explanatory power. Since the children-sons variable is more objective and more generally available, it should be more useful. Omitting either one of these two variables makes relatively little difference. However, the open interval-family limitation variable is indispensable; it adds a substantial increment to the joint influence of the other two variables.[16]

Since nine social variables considered together accounted for only about 3 per cent of the variance in acceptance, any extended discussion of the individual social variables is unjustified. However, we can say briefly that the wife's education and the number of modern objects owned can account together for all of the variance explained by the nine social variables. This is indicated by the following:

	% of variance explained		
		wife's age	
	Total	*20-29*	*30-39*
(a) wife's education	2	3	2
(b) *a* plus husband's education	2	3	2
(c) *b* plus newspaper reading by husband and wife	2	4	2
(d) *c* plus number of modern objects owned	3	5	2
(e) *d* plus family type, ethnic classification, household income, and husband's employment status	3	5	2

Once we have taken into account the education-literacy variables and number of modern objects owned, nothing is gained by adding four other pertinent variables. Furthermore, among the education-

[16] The multivariate analysis was also tried with the open interval and prior use of contraception treated as separate variables. Since each of these variables could be divided into more classes when treated separately, they explained more of the variance than the single interaction variable we have used, but the net gain was too small to compensate for the conceptual loss in separating the two variables.

literacy variables, wife's education alone is adequate to account for most of the effect. The most important conclusion is that none of the social variables, considered alone or in combination, have much explanatory power in this analysis.

The social variables do explain more of the variance for younger women (5 per cent) than for older women (2 per cent). This may be a small indication that modernization variables such as education of women are becoming more relevant in the younger generation to decisions about spacing and timing of births as well as to limiting them.

The most important conclusions arrived at from the preceding analyses are that the appeal of the program is determined more by the demographic than by the social characteristics of respondents, and that demographic factors are more important at older ages than at younger. We interpret this to mean that the program's appeals penetrate to all social strata, including the traditional and disadvantaged. The common conditions determining acceptance are related to the demographic situation of the couple, which is most likely to involve frustrating pressures on family resources (social, economic, psychological) when the woman is past 30. The fact that at younger ages acceptance is much less conditioned by demographic factors leads us to infer that the program has enabled some young women who anticipate this frustration to take effective action to prevent it. The fact that the small social influences are most important at these younger ages suggests that acceptance is facilitated by such modern characteristics as higher education, which is more prevalent among women under 30.

Many of the same social factors which have so slight a relationship to acceptance among eligible couples in the program have a very considerable relationship with whether birth control was adopted prior to the program in the "natural" demographic process of change already underway in Taiwan. This is important, because it indicates that while modernization and higher social status may have been preconditions for individual acceptances previously, where a program exists such characteristics are less important. The pre-program phase in Taiwan was presumably similar to the early stages of the fertility decline in Japan and the Western countries. Those in the advanced sectors of the population felt a need for family limitation and found ways to meet this need, even if available solutions were sometimes unsatisfactory. The less modern and disadvantaged parts of the population also felt demographic pressures during this period, but they needed social support and encouragement to define their problem, to become receptive to information about suitable solutions, and to be motivated to use them.

We have analyzed the relationship of demographic and social factors to pre-program use of family limitation in earlier chapters. Now we want to document the fact that the social factors just found to have relatively little association with program acceptances have a much greater relation to the pre-program use of contraception.

In Table VII-8 we compare the associations of selected social and demographic variables with use of contraception prior to the program and with acceptances in the program.[17]

Table VII-8. Proportion of Variance Explained (Eta Squared) by Selected Social and Demographic Variables for Use of Contraception Prior to Program and for Acceptances in Program

	Use of contraception for wife:					
	20-39		20-29		30-39	
Demographic and social variables	Before program	Acceptance in program	Before program	Acceptance in program	Before program	Acceptance in program
Wife's education	13	*	9	2	16	1
Number of modern objects	9	1	7	2	11	1
Husband's employment status	6	*	4	*	7	1
Household income	5	*	4	1	6	*
Four social variables[a/]	15	1	11	3	18	1
Nine social variables[b/]	17	1	14	4	18	1
Number of living children -- sons	7	2	6	3	4	3
Open interval	9	3	6	1	6	7
Comparison of children alive and wanted	11	2	10	2	6	3
All three demographic variables	17	6	14	3	13	8
All twelve social and demographic variables	29	7	26	7	27	8

[a/] Four listed above.

[b/] Nine listed in Table VII-5.

* Less than 1 per cent.

Clearly, the social variables are much more important in relation to prior use of contraception than for acceptances in the program. Either the individual social variables or groups of them have much greater associations with prior use of contraception than with acceptances in the program.

[17] In this analysis all the data are necessarily for the total sample rather than being restricted to eligible couples, since we would otherwise be eliminating many prior users of contraception. Also, we use the open interval without simultaneous classification by prior use of family limitation, since prior use of contraception is one of our dependent variables.

In relation to prior use of contraception, the social variables are important independent of the demographic variables. The nine social variables collectively have about the same relation as the three demographic variables to the prior use of contraception in the total sample, and a much larger relation in the older ages. Moreover, the associations with the social variables are largely independent of the demographic variables, since the proportion of variance explained is increased substantially when we add the effect of the social variables to that of the demographic variables. This is not true for the acceptance rates, mainly because the social variables add nothing to the amount of explained variance in acceptance rates for the older women, precisely the group where the social variables have the greatest associations with prior contraception.

When we deal with the total sample, as in Table VII-8, the amount of variance in acceptances explained by individual variables or by groups of variables is less than when we were concerned with the eligible couples only. This follows from the fact that in the latter case we had eliminated a group of couples who could add nothing to the relationship.

Our final conclusion based on the multivariate analysis is that neither the demographic nor the social variables predict individual acceptances in the program very well, certainly not as well as they predict use of contraception prior to the program. Adoption of family limitation in a program is less restricted by demographic and social characteristics of the couples than is the "natural" process of acceptance prior to the development of a program. However, it is true that of the variables considered, those most accurate in predicting acceptances among couples eligible for the program are demographic and not social.

JOINT EFFECTS OF NUMBER OF CHILDREN AND OTHER VARIABLES ON ACCEPTANCE RATES

It is useful to examine how several of the variables considered together affect acceptance rates. For this purpose, we have taken the number of children alive as a primary demographic variable known to have a major effect on acceptance rates. We will then consider successively how the association of some other variables with acceptances depends on the number of children. Conversely, we want to know whether the relationship between number of children and acceptances differs depending on the category of the other variables considered. For example, does the association between number of children and acceptances differ according to the educational level? Conversely, does the relationship of education and acceptances differ for those with small and large numbers of children? This problem of interaction is not necessarily handled by the kind of multivariate analysis just considered.

Wife's education and number of living children (Table VII-9): Since both education and number of living children affect eligibility very much, these data are examined for only the eligible women. An age control is introduced, since the association of acceptance rates with education, and to a lesser extent with number of living children, differs somewhat for the younger and the older women.

For both age groups, the acceptance rates generally rise consistently within each educational level with number of living children (Table

Table VII-9. Acceptance Rates of All Methods to July 31, 1965, in the Everything Lins, for Eligible Wives, by Wife's Education, by Number of Living Children, by Wife's Age Group (Household Survey)

	Number of living children						
Wife's education	None	One	Two	Three	Four	Five or more	Total
				All ages			
Less than primary school grad.	2	7	17	32	39	47	30
Primary school grad.	4	14	21	38	46	51	33
Junior high school	4	17	36	58	62	62	42
Senior high school grad.	8	24	52	66	68	68	48
Total	4	12	24	39	45	50	33
				Ages 20-29			
Less than primary school grad.	2	7	17	35	37	45	23
Primary school grad.	4	15	21	40	44	49	27
Junior high school	5	19	36	56	58	*	35
Senior high school grad.	10	29	49	66	*	--	43
Total	4	13	23	40	42	48	27
				Ages 30-39			
Less than primary school grad.	*	0	14	24	41	48	40
Primary school grad.	*	6	23	30	48	52	43
Junior high school	*	*	36	61	65	62	54
Senior high school grad.	*	0	58	67	67	60	55
Total	0	3	27	37	47	50	44

* Base is less than 20.

VII-9). The gradients, however, are considerably steeper for the lower education categories than for the higher, especially for the first three children. In the case of those with more than a primary school education, the acceptance rates vary within a narrow range at a very high level (58 to 68 per cent) if the couples already have at least three children. While the number of living children is generally more important than education, higher education has the effect of narrowing the range of variation by bringing more women with few children into the program.

Acceptance rates rise with education within each parity, whatever the age of the woman. However, the rise is much greater for the parities under three, and especially for the younger women with only one child or none. Better education has the effect, especially, of bringing the younger women into the program at an extremely early stage of the family life-cycle. Most of the older women, of course, could not accept at that early demographic stage, long since past for them.

Joint effect of number of children and marriage duration (Table VII-10): How many children a woman had was much more important for acceptance rates than how long she had been married. For any given duration of marriage there is a very marked increase in acceptance rates with the number of children. Within parity groups there

Table VII-10. Acceptance Rates of All Methods to July 31, 1965, in the Everything Lins, for All Wives and Eligible Wives Only, by Wife's Length of Marriage, by Number of Living Children (Household Survey)

Years since wife's first marriage	Number of living children: None	One	Two	Three	Four	Five or more	Total
				All wives			
Under 5	4	14	23	41	45	*	19
5-9	0	4	16	32	33	34	27
10-14	0	1	17	19	27	32	26
15 or more	0	1	7	12	18	27	21
Total	3	11	19	28	27	30	23
				Eligible wives only			
Under 5	4	14	25	45	*	*	20
5-9	0	5	19	39	42	43	33
10-14	0	2	28	35	47	50	44
15 or more	0	4	26	43	49	52	48
Total	4	12	24	39	45	50	33

* Base is less than 20.

is no systematic variation of acceptance rates with marriage duration for eligible couples. The results are essentially similar if age rather than duration of marriage is considered jointly with the number of children.

Birth control experience and number of living children (Table VII-11): For the couples who had never used any form of family

Table VII-11. Acceptance Rates of All Methods to July 31, 1965, in the Everything Lins, by Birth Control Experience Before the Program, by Number of Living Children (Household Survey)

	Number of living children						
Birth control experience	None	One	Two	Three	Four	Five or more	Total
Sterilized	*	0	0	0	0	0	0
Currently using contraception, no abortion	*	20	25	30	24	24	25
Currently using contraception, had abortion	-	*	32	31	31	25	29
Past use of contraception, no abortion	*	23	34	35	50	52	42
Past use of contraception, had abortion	*	*	33	62	50	47	46
Abortion only	*	*	15	42	38	49	39
Never used anything	3	10	17	26	30	35	22
Total	3	11	19	28	27	30	23

* Base is less than 20.

limitation before, the chances of accepting in the program rise consistently and sharply as the number of living children increases. If, on the other hand, they had already tried something in the past, their chances of accepting are much higher regardless of the number of children they have. Acceptances are especially high, after the third or fourth parity, for those who had tried either contraception or induced abortion in the past but were not currently protected. These results suggest that the greatest impetus to acceptance for the Taichung couples was the combination of a growing family size and past effort to control it, especially if that effort was made with unsatisfactory methods. That it is not the size of the family alone that moves couples to acceptance is indicated by the fact that the level of acceptance for those who had five or more children and had never used any form of family limitation is nearly matched by that of past users of contraception with only two children and exceeded by that of couples who had three children and were past users of either contraception or induced abortion. The demonstration of concern by previous trials of birth control is as important for acceptance in the program as the fact of family growth itself.

CONTRIBUTION TO TOTAL ACCEPTANCE FROM THE DIFFERENT STRATA

A high acceptance rate in a given category may have relatively little impact on the future course of fertility in the population if that category includes relatively few couples. On the other hand, a moderate or even low acceptance rate may have a large impact simply because it applies to many couples. The functional relationship between these component parts of the total acceptance rate can be summarized as follows:

$$\frac{a_i}{N} = \frac{a_i}{n_i} \times \frac{n_i}{N}$$

where: a_i = total number of acceptors in a given subgroup i

N = total number of wives 20-39 in the population

n_i = total number of wives 20-39 in the given subgroup i

$$\frac{a_i}{n_i} = \frac{e_i}{n_i} \times \frac{a_i}{e_i}$$, as previously defined.

The expression tells us that the proportion of the total number of married women 20-39 who are acceptors from any particular subgroup (a_i/N) is a function of:

1. the acceptance rate in the subgroup (a_i/n_i), which in turn is a function of:
   a. the proportion of wives in the subgroup who are eligible (e_i/n_i), and
   b. the rate of acceptance among those eligible in the subgroup (a_i/e_i).
2. the proportion of all the wives who are members of this subgroup (n_i/N).

The sum of these rates (a_i/N) from all the subgroups equals the total acceptance rate in the population (A/N). In the present analysis, we shall use the function (a_i/A) to show the contribution from each subgroup instead of a_i/N, because it is more easily compared with the function (n_i/N), which shows the distribution of all the wives in the population. This is justified by the following:

$$\frac{a_i}{N} = \frac{A}{N} \times \frac{a_i}{A}$$

Because the total acceptance rate (A/N) is constant over all subgroups, a_i/N is completely determined by a_i/A. In short, we can compare the relative contributions from the subgroups by evaluating a_i/A as well as by evaluating a_i/N. In Tables VII-3 and VII-4, we have in column 5 the percentage distributions of all acceptors in these subgroups (a_i/A). These columns are examined in relation to the others which, as we saw, give the total acceptance rates in the subgroups (column 1: a_i/n_i), the acceptance rates in the subgroups who are eligible (column 2: a_i/e_i), and the proportions eligible in the subgroups (column 3: e_i/n_i).

In summary, then, the contribution that any demographic or social stratum makes to the total number of acceptances in the program depends on three component variables for each stratum: (1) the proportion of couples who are eligible, (2) the proportion of eligible couples who are acceptors, and (3) the proportion of all couples in the stratum. The first two of the three components determine the total acceptance rate for the stratum, but the contribution which the stratum makes to the total number of acceptances in the population may—and often does—depend more on the number of couples in the stratum than on the acceptance rate.

The greatest contributions to the total number of acceptances come from those strata which are apparently under strong demographic pressure. From the Household Survey (Table VII-3), we see that the largest proportions of acceptors come from among those who already have at least three children and two sons (Panels C and D). Large contributions come from these demographic strata in spite of the fact that many of the couples were already ineligible. This happens in part because of the high acceptance rate among those who were still eligible, but the fact that many of the wives visited (52 per cent) were in these strata to begin with was also very important. From the Intensive Survey (Table VII-4, Panel A), we see that the contribution from those who already had the wanted number of children or more is also very substantial (43 per cent), for similar reasons. In spite of the low rates of eligibility in these categories, the acceptance rates were high among the eligible (28 and 45 per cent) and many of the women in Taichung were in these categories to start with (45 per cent).

The contribution from those couples who had never used any form of family limitation before the program is unusually high (62 per cent), in spite of the low acceptance rate (1 to 23 per cent) among them (Table VII-4, Panel B). This results from the fact that as many as 65 per cent of the couples visited were in this category and more than 95 per cent were still eligible. By contrast, the contributions from those who had used either contraception or abortion, but only in the past, are insignificant in spite of the high acceptance rates among them. Too small a proportion of the couples visited were in these categories to have much impact on total acceptances.

One category that contributed rather little to total acceptances in spite of a high acceptance rate is the group of past users of family limitation who had had a live birth recently (Table VII-4, Panel B). The relatively small numbers in this category and the relatively low eligibility rates contribute to this result. By contrast, the contribution is rather large (55 per cent of all acceptances) from those couples who had not used any family limitation before and had had a live birth within the past two years. Nearly half (47 per cent) of the couples in Taichung were in this category and only a few of them were satisfactorily protected already, so that their contribution to total acceptances is considerable even if the acceptance rate was only moderately high.

The contributions from the more modern social strata have been small as compared with those from the strata under demographic pressure. The less modern social strata have contributed considerably more than the more modern strata, in spite of their generally lower acceptance rates. This happens because there were considerably more couples in the less modern strata and many of them were still eligible for the program. For example, consider wife's education (Table VII-3, Panel E). The acceptance rate is 30 per cent for the least-educated eligible wives and 48 per cent for the best-educated. But the contribution to total acceptances from the least educated is 40 per cent and that from the best educated only 9 per cent. The moderate level of acceptance among the least educated is compensated for by the large proportion of wives in this category (41 per cent) and their high eligibility rate (76 per cent). By contrast, the high acceptance rate among the best educated is less significant because there were only a few women in this category (8 per cent) and a large proportion of them (46 per cent) were ineligible.

We can demonstrate the much greater importance of demographic as compared with social and modernization variables by taking a rather extreme example. About one-third of all acceptances in the Everything lins came from women with five or more living children, although only 59 per cent of such couples were eligible (Table VII-3, Panel C). This happened partly because the eligible high-parity women had a high acceptance rate (50 per cent), but also because 27 per cent of the women visited were in this high-parity group. On the other hand, the best-educated women made a much smaller contribution to total acceptances (9 per cent), although the rate of acceptance among the eligible (48 per cent) and the proportion eligible (54 per cent) did not differ much from those among women with five or more children (Table VII-3, Panel E). The difference is that only 8 per cent of all women were in the best-educated stratum, while 27 per cent had five or more living children. So the rather similar eligibility and acceptance rate components are multiplied by a factor of three to one for the women with many children as compared to those with the best education.

These examples illustrate the fact that a high acceptance rate in any particular stratum will not have a significant effect on total acceptance rates unless it occurs in a population category that is large or that contains a high proportion of eligible couples. It may be efficient for a program to concentrate on categories in which acceptance rates are moderate or even low, if they have large numbers eligible for acceptance.

OVERALL TREATMENT EFFECTS ON CHARACTERISTICS OF ACCEPTORS

The characteristics of the acceptors differed by the type of treatment. Those who accepted from the Everything areas, which received the most intensive treatment, were likely to have characteristics indicating less demographic pressure, and hence less motivation than those from other areas. Conversely, those who accepted from areas of little or no program effort, such as the Nothing lins or areas outside Taichung, were selected to a greater extent from among the more highly motivated, as suggested by their presence in more advanced demographic strata. Intensive program support apparently helped the less highly motivated.

EVERYTHING LINS VS. NOTHING LINS IN THE CITY

In either the Heavy or Light sectors, the Everything lins, as compared with the Nothing lins, had more acceptors (Table VII-12):[18]

Table VII-12. Demographic and Social Characteristics of All Acceptors to July 31, 1965, by Sector and Treatment in Taichung (Percentage Distribution)

	Heavy sector			Light sector			All sectors		
Characteristics[a]	Everything lins	Nothing lins	All lins	Everything lins	Nothing lins	All lins	Everything lins	Nothing lins	All lins
All acceptors									
Number	2002	1546	3548	1314	2607	3921	3316	4153	7469
Percentage	100	100	100	100	100	100	100	100	100
Age of wife									
Under 20	1	4	3	3	3	3	2	4	3
20-24	19	22	20	19	22	21	19	22	21
25-29	31	33	32	33	34	33	32	33	32
30-34	28	26	27	28	27	28	28	27	27
35-39	19	13	16	15	12	13	17	12	15
40 and over	2	2	2	2	2	2	2	2	2
Years since wife's first marriage									
Under 5	25	31	28	25	28	27	25	29	28
5-9	28	31	29	32	32	33	30	32	31
10-14	28	22	25	23	24	23	26	23	24
15 or more	19	16	18	20	16	17	19	16	17
Number of living children									
0	1	*	1	1	*	1	1	*	1
1	7	4	6	7	4	5	7	4	5
2	16	16	16	15	15	15	16	15	15
3	22	23	23	24	23	23	23	23	23
4	21	24	22	22	24	23	21	24	23
5 or more	33	33	32	31	34	33	32	34	33

[a] N.A.'s are distributed proportionately in the various categories.

* Less than 1 per cent.

[18] In this and subsequent tables of this chapter, wherevei percentage distributions by characteristics are shown, the few cases whose characteristics could not be ascertained (N.A.s) were distributed proportionately in the various categories. For no characteristic did the N.A.s exceed 2 per cent of the total.

Table VII-12 (continued).

Characteristics	Heavy sector Everything lins	Heavy sector Nothing lins	Heavy sector All lins	Light sector Everything lins	Light sector Nothing lins	Light sector All lins	All sectors Everything lins	All sectors Nothing lins	All sectors All lins
Number of living sons									
None	8	7	7	8	6	6	8	6	7
One	30	25	28	26	25	26	28	25	27
Two or more	62	68	65	66	69	68	64	69	66
Number of additional children and sons wife wants									
No more	71	83	77	72	84	81	72	84	78
One more, any sex	6	4	5	7	4	5	6	4	5
One more son	13	8	11	11	7	8	12	7	10
Two or more, any sex	1	*	*	1	*	*	1	*	*
Two or more, at least one a son	9	5	7	9	5	6.	9	5	7
Birth control experience									
Using contraception currently	19	10	15	19	10	13	20	10	14
Used contraception in the past	11	19	14	10	18	15	11	19	14
Used abortion only	7	12	9	6	15	12	7	14	11
Never used anything	63	59	62	65	57	60	62	57	61
Wife's education									
Less than primary school grad.	37	37	37	40	38	38	39	37	38
Primary school grad.	43	41	42	37	41	40	40	41	41
Junior high school	11	14	12	12	12	12	11	13	12
Senior high school grad. or higher	9	8	9	11	9	10	10	9	9

1. with fewer than three children or two sons.
2. who still wanted more children, and especially who still wanted sons.
3. who had never tried any form of birth control before, or who were currently using contraception.
4. among somewhat older wives married for somewhat longer time periods.

Conversely, the Nothing lins had more acceptors:

1. with more than three children or two sons.
2. who did not want any more children.
3. who had previously tried either contraception or induced abortion but were not protected currently.
4. among somewhat younger wives married for somewhat shorter time periods.

Taken together, all of these characteristics indicate that the acceptors from the Nothing lins were more motivated to accept without program support. Although they were somewhat younger and had been married for shorter periods of time, they had more children and more sons than the Everything area acceptors.[19] They wanted fewer additional children and sons. More of those from the Nothing lins had already used birth control, but so many had given up the methods used or had used abortion only that fewer were currently using contraception. The total picture of the acceptors from the Nothing area is one of a group that was under demographic pressure at younger ages both because they had more children and because they had been unsuccessful with previous birth control practice. Conversely, then, it would appear that the Everything treatment helped to bring into the program at earlier life-cycle stages couples who might otherwise not have accepted.

There were no significant differences in the social characteristics of acceptors in terms of treatment and density sectors. The generally similar pattern for wife's education shown in Table VII-12 is repeated for husband's education and occupation in unpublished tabulations.

CITY VS. OUTSIDE

A notable feature of the Taichung experiments is the large number of acceptors that came from outside the city, although there was no organized effort to recruit them.[20] While most of the outside acceptances came from counties relatively close to Taichung, some acceptors traveled a considerable distance. We might expect acceptors from outside the city who traveled a substantial distance to accept an innovation[21] about which they had heard only indirectly to be a highly motivated group, as compared with either the acceptors in Taichung or the non-acceptors at their places of origin. Table VII-13 provides some basis for comparing the acceptors from outside Taichung both with all married women and with the Taichung acceptors.

19 Unpublished data reveals that more of the acceptors from the Nothing lins had three or more children while still under 25 years of age or married less than five years. We also examined the educational composition of the acceptors to see whether more of the better educated were in the youngest ages for those coming from the Nothing lins, but this was not the case.

20 An island-wide program of family planning was started in early 1964, but no attempt has been made to send outside cases to the clinics in Taichung.

21 Ninety-seven per cent of the acceptors from outside accepted the IUD, which was introduced in Taiwan on a mass basis through the Taichung experiment.

The data for all married women outside Taichung are estimates based on a 1965 sample survey covering the entire island.[22]

Table VII-13. Demographic and Social Characteristics of All Acceptors to July 31, 1965, Among Wives 20-39, for Taichung and Outside Taichung, Compared with Characteristics of All Wives 20-39 (Percentage Distribution)

	Taichung		Outside Taichung	
Characteristics[a]	All wives 20-39[b]	All acceptors 20-39	All wives 20-39[c]	All acceptors 20-39
All wives				
Number	11,393	7,097	3,184	3,105
Percentage	100	100	100	100
Age of wife				
20-24	19	22	16	17
25-29	30	34	30	36
30-34	28	29	28	32
35-39	23	15	26	15
Years since wife's first marriage				
Under 5	24	26	21	19
5-9	28	32	29	34
10-14	26	26	25	29
15 or more	22	16	25	18
Number of living children				
0	4	*	5	*
1	13	4	11	2
2	18	15	17	9
3	19	24	19	22
4	19	24	20	26
5 or more	27	33	28	41
Number of living sons				
0	17	7	19	3
1	29	26	27	18
2 or more	54	67	54	79

[a] N.A.'s are distributed proportionately in the various categories.

[b] These are women who were home-visited in the Everything lins, which comprised a random sample of all the lins in Taichung.

[c] These are women who comprised a probability sample of all married women 20-39 in Taiwan from an island-wide survey in 1965.

* Less than 1 per cent.

22 The island-wide survey by the Taiwan Population Studies Center covered all married women 20-44 years of age. Special tabulations were made for those aged 20-39 for comparability with the data from the present study.

Table VII-13 (continued).

Characteristics	Taichung: All wives 20-39	Taichung: All acceptors 20-39	Outside Taichung: All wives 20-39	Outside Taichung: All acceptors 20-39
Number of additional children and sons wife wants				
No more	58	79	56	91
One more, any sex	7	5	6	2
One more son	14	10	12	4
Two or more, any sex	1	*	3	*
Two or more, at least one a son	20	6	23	3
Birth control experience				
Sterilized	9	---	5	--
Using contraception currently	18	15	19	10
Used contraception in the past	5	14	2	19
Used abortion only	3	11	2	14
Never used anything	65	60	72	57
Wife's education				
Less than primary school grad.	40	38	58	52
Primary school grad.	42	41	33	33
Junior high school	10	12	6	9
Senior high school grad. or higher	8	9	3	6
Husband's education				
Less than primary school grad.	16	13	26	22
Primary school grad.	48	44	51	47
Junior high school	12	13	10	10
Senior high school grad. or higher	24	30	13	21
Husband's occupation				
Farmer	21	18	33	41
Nonfarm manual worker	41	40	42	27
Proprietor	12	11	8	8
White collar worker	26	31	17	24

Clearly, the acceptors from outside Taichung were in even more advanced demographic stages than the acceptors within the city. Although younger and married for less time than Taiwan women in general, the acceptors from outside already had more children and sons than average, and considerably more of them did not want any more children. They were even more strongly selected than the Taichung acceptors from among those who had used some form of birth control in the past but were not protected at the time of their acceptance. Finally, relative to the general population from which they were drawn, they were more highly educated and more often from among both white-collar and farm workers. The unusually high representation of the farmers presumably reflects the important influence of demographic pressure on acceptance for these couples. On the whole, it was the demographically advanced and the more modernized couples who accepted in disproportionate numbers from outside the city, suggesting their selectivity with respect to both strong motivation and greater awareness.

SPECIAL EFFECTS OF GROUP MEETINGS ON CHARACTERISTICS OF ACCEPTORS

In the Everything lins, as part of the treatment, meetings were scheduled to be held before the start of home visits. As indicated earlier, only about half of the scheduled meetings could be held, permitting a test of the influence of group meetings apart from the other stimuli of the program. Meetings were classified by their effectiveness as perceived at the time they were held.

The success of a meeting was probably influenced both by the quality of the fieldworkers and by the characteristics of the people in attendance. While some fieldworkers were less able than others, there were other factors making for poor response in some of the lins. There was considerable variation, among the districts of the city, in the ease with which a group of women could be called together for a meeting. It was difficult to hold meetings in the three congested and busy districts that comprise the central core of the city (Central, West, and North), and it was especially difficult to hold effective meetings in the Central District (the business center of the city). (See page 194, top.)

Whether a meeting was held and whether it was effective did not depend at all on such characteristics of the lin inhabitants as age, number of living children or sons, or how many additional children were wanted. The higher the number of couples who had never used birth control, the greater the probability that a meeting would be held and that it would be effective. The lins with meetings and with effective meetings also tended to be those in which the couples were less modern or less urban, as indicated by education or occupation.

Presumably the more modern, urbanized couples were less interested in coming to a group meeting, partly because they were already prac-

District	*Percentage of Everything lins without a meeting*	*Percentage of meetings that were ineffective*
Central	62	55
West	68	18
North	77	34
East	37	14
South	32	4
North Rural	24	30
West Rural	30	30
South Rural	50	36
All Districts	50	21

	Percentage of couples who:		
Everythings lins with:	*had never used birth control*	*had wives with more than primary education*	*had husbands who were proprietors or white-collar workers*
effective meetings	68	13	31
ineffective meetings	65	15	33
no meetings	59	23	46

ticing contraception or had alternate sources of information and entertainment.

We saw in Chapter VI that the influence of the group meetings on eventual acceptance in the program was confined almost exclusively to the acceptance of the IUD and that lins with ineffective meetings showed little advantage over lins with no meetings at all. This selective influence of effective meetings is evident throughout with but a few exceptions, even when demographic and social characteristics of the couples are controlled. Table VII-14 shows that with only a few exceptions, the IUD acceptance rates are highest in the lins with effective meetings in the various demographic and social strata for which data are shown illustratively. There is no such consistent pattern for the traditional methods.

The one important exception is that there is no systematic difference in IUD acceptance rates according to group meeting effective-

Table VII-14. Acceptance Rates of IUD and Other Methods to July 31, 1965, by Group Meeting Effectiveness in the Everything Lins, by Selected Demographic and Social Characteristics (Household Survey)

Characteristics	IUD			Other methods		
	Effective meeting	Ineffective meeting	No meeting	Effective meeting	Ineffective meeting	No meeting
All wives	18	13	13	8	8	8
Number of living children and sons						
No children	1	2	1	1	—	3
One child						
No son	5	7	6	2	4	2
One son	9	6	9	6	3	5
Two children						
No son	12	6	6	4	4	6
One or two sons	17	9	13	6	6	7
Three or four children						
No son	18	10	12	9	—	9
One son	19	17	14	6	7	10
Two or more sons	24	16	17	10	13	8
Five or more children	22	15	16	12	9	9
Number of additional children and sons wife wants						
No more	22	16	16	11	11	9
One more, any sex	20	13	13	5	5	5
One more son	18	9	13	7	6	6
Two or more, any sex	13	—	8	10	8	8
Two or more, at least one a son	7	6	6	3	3	4
Birth control experience						
Using contraception currently	17	13	11	13	12	14
Used contraception in the past	29	26	24	20	21	14
Used abortion only	29	28	19	13	17	14
Never used anything	18	11	14	7	7	6
Wife's education						
Less than primary school grad.	19	11	14	7	8	5
Primary school grad.	17	13	13	8	8	7
Junior high school	21	16	13	11	6	10
Senior high school grad. or higher	14	15	2	12	15	13

ness either in the lowest parities or among those wanting several more children including a son. Otherwise, the IUD acceptance rates are generally highest in the effective meeting lins and the acceptance rates for the traditional methods were generally at a similar level for all types of lins. Lins with ineffective meetings generally did no better than lins with no meetings, whatever the methods involved. In short, if the couples were beyond the earliest stages of family building, the probability of accepting the IUD was increased by an effective meeting.

The effective meetings were especially successful in bringing into the program more couples who had never used birth control before, and among such couples their success was especially great with the less modern. Table VII-15 indicates that for those not using contracep-

Table VII-15. Rate of Acceptance of All Methods to July 31, 1965, for Wives Not Sterilized or Not Currently Using Contraception at the Time of First Survey, by Selected Demographic and Social Characteristics, by Treatment and Group Meeting Effectiveness (Intensive Survey)

	Everything lins			
Characteristics	Effective meeting	Ineffective or no meeting	Other lins	Total
All wives	26	19	15	18
Number of living children and sons				
No children	--	5	8	6
One child				
No son	7	4	9	7
One son	25	17	12	16
Two children				
No son	4	--	4	3
One or two sons	27	15	17	19
Three or four children				
No son	*	*	6	10
One son	19	26	21	22
Two or more sons	33	30	20	26
Five or more children	38	25	17	25
Number of living children and number wanted				
Want at least 2 more	13	10	10	10
Want 1 more	33	19	18	21
Have number wanted	21	29	16	20
Have more than wanted	44	34	24	32
N.A., up to God, etc.	21	*	10	12
Wife's education				
Less than primary school grad.	21	19	13	16
Primary school grad.	34	18	17	21
Junior high school	28	15	20	20
Senior high school grad. or higher	17	35	18	24

* Base is less than 20.

tion and not sterilized at the first survey of the Intensive Sample, for almost every demographic and social characteristics considered the couples in the effective meeting lins had higher acceptance rates than those either in other Everything lins or in the Nothing lins. In general, the influence of the effective meetings in this group not protected before was greatest among couples who had many children or sons and among those in the less modern strata. So it would appear that the support of the effective group meeting brought in the lower status couples whose demographic problem was most acute.

Table VII-15 (continued).

Characteristics	Everything lins: Effective meeting	Everything lins: Ineffective or no meeting	Other lins	Total
Family type				
Living in extended unit	27	20	15	19
Living in nuclear unit				
Once in extended unit	27	20	13	18
Always nuclear	20	13	17	17
Husband's employment status				
Farmer	27	22	14	20
Other traditional employment	28	14	13	16
Employed by non-relative and professional	24	21	17	19

THE CHANGING CHARACTERISTICS OF ACCEPTORS OVER TIME

We have found that acceptors in the program tended to be older, married for longer periods of time, with more than average numbers of children and sons, and with some previous birth control experience. It is logical that such couples, being under the most demographic pressure, have a rather high probability of becoming acceptors, and this can be the basis for a significant initial decline in fertility for a population. However, for a continuing or accelerating fertility decline a family planning program will aim to reach couples at earlier stages of family life—younger, married for shorter lengths of time, with fewer children and sons, and with less previous birth control experience.

Therefore, it is significant that as time went on the acceptors in the Taichung program were younger, married for shorter periods, more likely to have fewer than three children or two sons, less likely to have ever used contraception or to be using it currently (Table VII-16). These trends are more pronounced for the people inside the city than for those from outside.[23] This is plausible, since the program

[23] The data for the Nothing lins and for outside the city are based on the characteristics of the acceptors at the time of acceptance, and are therefore valid indicators of trends. The characteristics of the acceptors in the Everything lins are as of the initial interview date, and therefore the trends are exaggerated somewhat, since by the time of acceptance the acceptors were older, married longer, and might have more children. However, the similarity of the basic trends for the Nothing and Everything lins is reassuring.

Table VII-16. Demographic and Social Characteristics of All Acceptors in Taichung, by Time of Acceptance, by Treatment Area

Characteristics[a] and area	Experimental period	Extension period	Free insertion period
Percentage under 25 years of age			
City			
Everything lins	15	31	32
Nothing lins	19	29	33
Outside city	15	20	23
Percentage under 30 years of age			
City			
Everything lins	45	64	68
Nothing lins	51	64	66
Outside city	49	54	59
Percentage married less than 5 years			
City			
Everything lins	18	37	40
Nothing lins	20	34	39
Outside city	16	22	27
Percentage married less than 10 years			
City			
Everything lins	47	67	71
Nothing lins	52	67	69
Outside city	48	55	59
Percentage with less than 3 children			
City			
Everything lins	19	31	31
Nothing lins	17	23	21
Outside city	12	12	14
Percentage with less than 2 sons			
City			
Everything lins	31	46	46
Nothing lins	29	34	34
Outside city	20	23	24

[a] For the Everything lins only, the characteristics are either as of October 1, 1962, or as of the home visit during the experimental period; otherwise, they are as of the time of acceptance.

was within the city and the cumulation of acceptances and program influence there presumably was sufficient to provide social support for acceptances among those with less demographic pressure to motivate them. On the outside of the city there was much less support of this kind, so the importance of high motivation and demographic pressure remained more constant.

There is no consistent time trend in the proportion wanting additional children. The acceptors were presumably selected in all periods

Table VII-16 (continued).

Characteristics and area	Experimental period	Extension period	Free insertion period
Percentage wanting more children			
City			
Everything lins	23	37	40
Nothing lins	15	20	17
Outside city	9	10	8
Percentage currently using contraception			
City			
Everything lins	23	15	10
Nothing lins	14	10	5
Outside city	12	11	5
Percentage never used any form of birth control			
City			
Everything lins	60	65	71
Nothing lins	55	57	63
Outside city	58	58	60
Percentage wife with primary education or less			
City			
Everything lins	80	73	80
Nothing lins	80	75	80
Outside city	86	84	83
Percentage husband with primary education or less			
City			
Everything lins	60	54	62
Nothing lins	56	51	54
Outside city	68	67	67
Percentage husband in farming			
City			
Everything lins	21	15	17
Nothing lins	20	16	14
Outside city	39	44	40

from among the couples who did not want any more children, but as the program advanced they came increasingly from among those who were satisfied with fewer children and sons. Unfortunately, we cannot tell whether this represented a change in goals for these couples.

In the city both the experimental and the free insertion periods attracted more of the poorly educated than did the interim extension period. The more intensive program support of the first and third periods apparently helped a larger number of the poorly educated to accept within the program. With only diffuse program effort in the second period, the acceptors during that period were selected to a somewhat greater extent from among the better educated. Time made little difference for the outside cases. They were selected from among the better educated from the start and throughout the program, just as they were selected from among the more demographically advanced and the more highly motivated. The proportion of farmers attracted to the program from outside also differed little over time. On the whole, even where there was systematic variation over time it was substantially less for the social than for the demographic characteristics.

VERY EARLY ACCEPTANCE: BEFORE OR DURING THE HOME VISIT

About 2 per cent of those who were visited at home in the Everything lins during the experimental period had already accepted before the home visit, and another 3 per cent accepted at the time of the home visit. Though few in number, they constitute an especially interesting group for analysis; presumably they were a highly motivated group. Those who came to the clinics to accept before the home visit were led to action by the diffusion of information very quickly—even before the fieldworker could get to them during the first five months of the program, when substantially all home visits were completed. Those accepting at the time of home visit took traditional contraceptives, but they were not postponing this action, as some others did. In this analysis, we consider the early acceptors first as a proportion of all couples (Table VII-17). Then we consider them as a proportion of those not already using satisfactory contraception, since those types of couples who were likely to accept at these two early points included many who had already worked out their own family planning solution. Presumably, the same factors in their situations which had earlier led some of these couples to adopt contraception on their own might lead others in the same situation to accept very quickly when the program made the opportunity available.

Acceptance before or at the time of the home visit is especially high for those couples who were under demographic pressure, as indicated by the number of children and sons, by the fact that no more children are wanted, and by previous action to limit family size. While the proportion that were early acceptors is modest, it increases considerably for the groups under the most demographic pressure, especially if we set aside those who have already solved their problem by adopt-

Table VII-17. Percentage of Wives Who Accepted At or Before the First Home Visit, by Demographic and Social Characteristics, for All Wives[a] and for Wives Not Already Using Satisfactory Contraception (Household Survey)

Characteristics	Percentage of all wives who accepted[a]			Percentage of all wives not already using satisfactory contraception who accepted[b]		
	Before visit	At visit	Before or at visit	Before visit	At visit	Before or at visit
All wives	2	4	6	2	5	7
Number of living children and sons						
No children	0	0	0	0	0	0
One child						
No son	*	2	2	*	2	2
One son	1	4	5	1	4	5
Two children						
No son	1	3	4	1	3	4
One or two sons	2	3	5	2	3	5
Three or four children						
No son	1	3	4	1	3	4
One son	3	4	7	4	5	9
Two or more sons	4	5	9	6	7	13
Five or more children	3	5	8	4	7	11
Number of additional children and sons wife wants						
No more	4	6	10	6	9	15
One more, any sex	1	1	2	1	1	2
One more son	1	2	3	1	2	3
Two or more, any sex	1	3	4	1	3	4
Two or more, at least one son	*	2	2	*	2	2
Prior birth control experience						
Contraception						
Now using, no abortion	2	3	5	22	33	55
Now using, had abortion	2	4	6	14	29	43
Past use, no abortion	7	8	15	7	8	15
Past use, had abortion	11	10	21	11	10	21
Abortion only	5	8	13	5	8	13
Never used anything	2	4	6	2	4	6
Wife's education						
Less than primary school grad.	2	3	5	2	3	5
Primary school grad.	2	4	6	3	5	8
Junior high school	4	5	9	6	7	13
Senior high school grad.	2	5	7	4	9	13

[a] Excludes sterile and those with indeterminate characteristics.

[b] Excludes additionally those who said they did not intend to accept, because already using satisfactory contraception.

* Less than 1 per cent.

ing contraception satisfactory to them. (See right-hand column of Table VII-17). For example, among those wanting no more children, 10 per cent were early acceptors in the total sample and 15 per cent among those not already using satisfactory contraception: twice as many early acceptors as was the average for all categories.

Those who have previously used contraception or have had an abortion are also likely to be early acceptors. Our interpretation is that these are people who have demonstrated that they are aware of the existence of a problem which a solution previously tried did not solve. Those who had indicated the seriousness of their concern about family growth by previous use of both abortion and contraception had the highest of all early acceptance rates.

Those who were currently using contraception have a very low early acceptance rate, since more than 80 per cent of them said that their current practice made it unnecessary for them to participate in the program. However, there was also a minority of 20 per cent who either accepted a program method at the very early stages we are considering or said that they would do so sooner or later. Among this minority of the current users, more than one-third accepted at or before the first home visit. Current users of contraception outside of the program were very likely to accept very early or not at all.

Better-educated wives had somewhat higher than average early acceptance rates, especially if we exclude those already using satisfactory contraception. However, the differences associated with wife's education (or any other social characteristics) were, again, much less than those for the demographic characteristics.

VIII. Intentions to Accept Family Planning: Correlates and Consequences

DEFINITIONS AND DISTRIBUTIONS

THE MORE than 11,000 women in the Everything lins who were visited in their homes were asked at that time whether they intended to accept family planning within the program. Their intentions can be compared with their behavior over several years to see whether such intentions predict behavior. We can determine whether the reasons given to explain intentions help to discriminate between acceptors and non-acceptors. We can also see how the demographic and social characteristics of the couples affect both what they intend to do and whether their intentions are followed by appropriate action.

In the initial home visits, the great majority of the women said that they intended to accept contraception from the program[1] sooner or later,[2] if they were not protected already by sterilization or the use of a satisfactory method of contraception. Sixteen per cent of all the women were uninterested because they said they were sterilized or believed themselves to be sterile[3] (Table VIII-1, Sample A). Another 16 per cent said that they would not accept because they were already using a satisfactory method of contraception. An additional 5 per cent either had already accepted at the clinics before the first home visit or accepted a traditional method at that visit.[4] This leaves 63 per cent of the initial panel presumably eligible to become acceptors in the program. Among these, 15 per cent said they expected to accept "soon," and 38 per cent said they would accept later. This means that about 86 per cent of those not already protected by sterilization or contraception intended to accept soon or later. Of those not already protected, 24 per cent said that they would accept "soon" and 62 per cent said "later" (Table VIII-1, Sample C).

[1] We use the terms "acceptor" or "acceptance" to refer to an acceptor of, or acceptance of, contraception from the organized program.

[2] See Appendix VIII-1.

[3] Ten per cent of the women reported that they or their husbands had had a sterilizing operation. An additional 6 per cent believed that they were sterile, although they did not report such an operation.

[4] "Acceptance at the home visit" means that supplies for a traditional method were accepted.

Table VIII-1. Percentage Distributions of Wives 20-39 Who Were Home Visited in the Everything Lins of Taichung, by Acceptance Intention in the Program (Using Three Different Bases)[a/]

Intention status	Percentage distribution using as base: Sample A	Sample B	Sample C
All wives			
Number	11,393	8,810	7,031
Percentage	100	100	100
Sterilized or believes self sterile	16	--	--
Accepted before home visit	2	--	--
Accepted on home visit	3	--	--
Stated intention to accept:			
soon	15	20	24
eventually	38	49	62
Total intending to accept	53	69	86
Stated intention never to accept because:			
already using contraception	16	20	--
ambivalent or undecided	5	6	8
opposed to general idea and others	4	5	6
Total intending never to accept	25	31	14
Indeterminate[b/]	1	--	--

[a/] The three different bases used are:

Sample A: all home-visited cases
Sample B: excludes the sterilized or sterile, those accepting before or on home visit, and the indeterminate cases
Sample C: further excludes those not intending to accept because already using contraception.

All of the data in this chapter refer to the home-visited wives 20-39 years old in the Everything lins. Therefore, this fact will not be repeated in the titles of succeeding tables in this chapter.

[b/] These are acceptors whose records could not be matched with the home visit interviews.

Apart from those already protected, only 9 per cent of the initial panel (about 14 per cent of those not already protected) did not intend to accept at all. This small group of uninterested couples was divided about evenly between those who gave ambivalent or undecided responses on the one hand, and those who were opposed to the idea or gave other reasons for not accepting, on the other.

In Table VIII-1 the percentage distributions of the home-visited cases[5] into these major categories are shown on three different bases.

[5] Unless otherwise indicated, all data and statements in this chapter refer to the 11,393 home-visited cases in the Everything lins.

Sample A provides the distribution of the total initial sample. For more meaningful comparisons over time, Sample B excludes from the total initial sample the following categories: (1) the sterilized or those believing themselves sterile (only 2 per cent of this group eventually accepted), (2) those who accepted at the very outset of the program (at or before the home visit), and (3) those few whose status could not be determined for lack of relevant information. Finally, a third distribution, Sample C, eliminates additionally those couples who said they were not accepting because they were already protected by contraception.

ACCEPTANCE RATES BY INITIAL INTENTIONS

If the intentions are taken at face value, the acceptance rates should have been much higher than they proved to be. The total cumulative acceptance rate was 19 per cent for all the home-visited cases by July 31, 1965, thirty months after the program began. This is considerably less than the expected result if action had been taken by the 15 per cent of the total sample who said that they would act "soon" and also by a sizable minority of the 38 per cent who said they would accept "later." The fact is that after two years a majority even of those who said they intended to accept soon had not done so. On the other hand, a significant minority of those who had said that they did *not* intend to accept had done so.

Obviously, there is a considerable discrepancy between verbal intentions presented to a friendly interviewer and actual behavior. This is not too surprising in a situation where a new form of behavior and new standards and values are at issue and where the passage of time may change the circumstances to which the attitudes refer. Yet, as we shall see, statements of intention were much better predictors of behavior than the social or demographic characteristics of the couples alone. Our problem is to see how intentions and behavior correspond for different kinds of couples after different periods of time. It seems worthwhile first to see how acceptance rates varied over time in relation to stated intentions and then to see how the results are affected by the reasons for the intentions.

The variations in acceptance rates over time are considered for four periods of time:

1. the first thirty days after the home visit.
2. the intensive experimental phase of the program (February 1963 through March 1964), but at least thirty days after the home visit.
3. the extension period (April through December 1964).
4. the free insertion period (January through July 1965).

Table VIII-2 shows the acceptance rates for each of these periods (excluding from the base in each period those who accepted in an earlier period), and Table VIII-3 shows the cumulative rates to the end of each successive period.

Table VIII-2. Acceptance Rates for Four Time Periods, by Initial Acceptance Intention[a/]

Intention status	Number in base group	Acceptance rate in: Experimental period: Within 30 days of home visit	Feb. 1963–Mar. 1964	Extension period: Apr. 1964 Dec. 1964	Free insertion period: Jan. 1965–July 1965
Sterilized or believes self sterile	1,839	*	1	*	*
Accepted before home visit	226	100	-	-	-
Accepted on home visit	374	100	-	-	-
Stated intention to accept:					
soon	1,703	13	28	6	6
eventually	4,307	1	7	4	4
Total intending to accept	6,010	4	12	4	5
Stated intention never to accept because:					
already using contraception	1,779	2	12	2	3
ambivalent or undecided	573	3	15	3	4
opposed to general idea and others	448	1	5	4	2
Total intending never to accept	2,800	2	12	3	3
Total intending never to accept excluding those already using	1,021	2	11	4	3
Indeterminate	144	-	100	-	-
Total (Sample A)[b/]	11,393	6	13	3	3
Total (Sample B)[b/]	8,810	4	12	3	3
Total (Sample C)[b/]	7,031	4	12	3	4

[a/] In each period those accepting previously are excluded from the base.

[b/] Sample A includes all home-visited cases; Sample B excludes the sterilized or sterile, those accepting before or on home visit, and the indeterminate cases; Sample C further excludes those not intending to accept because already using contraception.

For those intending to accept soon, acceptance rates were especially high during the first thirty days and during the rest of the intensive experimental phase of the program. By the end of this phase, 38 per cent of this group had accepted. During the two following periods

Table VIII-3. Cumulative Acceptance Rates to End of Each of Four Time Periods, by Initial Acceptance Intention

Intention status	Number in base group	Cumulative acceptance rate to end of: Experimental period: Within 30 days of home visit	Experimental period: Feb. 1963–Mar. 1964	Extension period: Apr. 1964–Dec. 1964	Free insertion period: Jan. 1965–July 1965
Sterilized or believes self sterile	1,839	*	1	2	2
Accepted before home visit	226	100	100	100	100
Accepted on home visit	374	100	100	100	100
Stated intention to accept:					
soon	1,703	13	38	41	44
eventually	4,307	1	8	11	15
Total intending to accept	6,010	4	16	19	23
Stated intention never to accept because:					
already using contraception	1,779	2	14	16	19
ambivalent or undecided	573	3	18	21	24
opposed to general idea and others	448	1	6	10	12
Total intending never to accept	2,800	2	14	16	19
Total intending never to accept excluding those already using	1,021	2	13	16	19
Indeterminate	144	-	100	100	100
Total (Sample A)[a]	11,393	6	18	21	24
Total (Sample B)[a]	8,810	4	15	18	22
Total (Sample C)[a]	7,031	4	16	19	23

[a] Sample A includes all home-visited cases; Sample B excludes the sterilized or believes self sterile, those accepting before or on home visit, and the indeterminate cases; Sample C further excludes those not intending to accept because already using contraception.

* Less than 1 per cent.

they continued to have the highest acceptance rates, but the margin of difference was much smaller. By the last date of observation, 44 per cent were acceptors, a much higher rate than that for any other group. Still, this means that a large proportion of even those intending to act soon[6] had not done so as of more than two years after the program began.[7] Some of these couples may have taken action outside of the program.

Over 4,000 couples, 38 per cent of the total sample, indicated that they would accept "eventually" but gave various reasons for not do-

[6] The reader should bear in mind that we are using such phrases as "intending to act soon" as abbreviations for "statement to interviewer of an intention to act soon." We do not know if these were "real" or "true" intentions, even at the time of interview.

[7] As we have already indicated, those who moved out of the lin where they were living initially could not be matched up if they accepted after moving, so that these rates understate by an estimated 15 per cent the actual acceptance rates. However, there is no reason to believe that this source of error was correlated with the intention categories.

ing so "soon." This is the largest single group, constituting almost two-thirds of the eligible couples of Sample C. Very few of these couples (only 1 per cent) accepted during the first thirty days. A larger proportion accepted during the experimental phase of the program, but even in this period their acceptance rate was below the average for the whole sample. In the last two periods, however, the rates for this group had risen to just about average; and cumulatively, 15 per cent had accepted by 1965.[8] This is only about one-third the rate of those intending to accept soon, so the initial difference in intention makes a real difference in acceptance over a period of two or more years. As we shall see, many of these women had very good reasons for postponing acceptance, so the rise in acceptance rates over time is plausible. Over the whole period of observation there is some convergence between the rates for the two groups who intended to accept (soon or later). At the end of the first thirty days the ratio of their acceptance rates was thirteen to one; by 1965 it was three to one. Despite this convergence, it makes a substantial difference to the very end of the observation period whether the respondent initially said "soon" or "later."

Almost 20 per cent of those who initially said that they did not expect to accept had done so by 1965. In part, this is simply due to changes to contraceptive practice in the program by those who initially said that they were already using contraception. In this group of former contraceptors almost half of the acceptances were of traditional methods and may reflect only a shift in the source of supply. But even excluding acceptances by these former contraceptors, the final cumulative acceptance rate for those initially not intending to accept at all was 19 per cent.

An especially interesting subgroup consists of the more than 500 wives who refused to make a commitment because they had doubts, were undecided, wanted to talk it over with their husbands, or expressed ambivalence in other ways. Very few in this group were acceptors during the first thirty days. However, in the remaining months of the intensive campaign period their acceptance rate (15 per cent) was higher than average, and it remained at about the average level from that time on. Presumably, it took a month or so for these women to gain the assurance they needed from other acceptors and from the increasing amount of supporting information about the program. By

[8] We shall use "1965" in this chapter to refer to the final reference date, July 31, 1965.

1965 almost a fourth of these ambivalent women had accepted. This is the second highest final cumulative rate (Table VIII-3).

The residual group of women who expressed opposition to the idea of family planning or gave various other reasons for not accepting[9] did have a relatively low final acceptance rate: 12 per cent. However, the time trend indicates that they were being won over gradually. Their rate was one-sixth of the average during the first thirty days, one-third during the rest of the experimental period, and about at the average for the two final periods. Their cumulative rate at the end of the observation period was just half of the average for the total panel.

The general picture that emerges is that intentions did make a difference, especially in the very early phases of the program. There is, however, a marked convergence of the cumulative rates over a two-year period. Relative variability in the first thirty days (range: 1 to 13 per cent) was much greater than in the final period (range: 12 to 44 per cent).

This cumulative convergence results from the continuing reduction in the range of the rates during successive periods:

Period	*Range* (*ratio of maximum to minimum rates*)[10]
First 30 days	13 to 1
Rest of experimental period	28 to 5
Extension period	6 to 2
Free insertion period	6 to 2

[9] In the residual group of 448 women classified as "opposed to general idea" and "others" in Tables VIII-1 to VIII-3, only 68 women, or approximately 15 per cent, actually flatly stated opposition to the general idea of contraception. The other subcategories shown in detail in Table VIII-4 produce the following percentage distribution for the category "never accept-opposed to general idea" and "other":

	%
Wants more children	18
Pregnant	13
Lactating or menstrual irregularity	24
Disapproves of idea	15
Miscellaneous or unspecified	30
Total	100

[10] Excludes the small groups with zero rates, the sterilized, and those accepting at or before the first home visit.

Tables VIII-4 and VIII-5 present more details on acceptances in terms of the major reasons given to explain the stated intentions. Table VIII-4 shows cumulative rates by initial reasons, by the method of contraception chosen in advance, and by the method actually selected, up to the end of the experimental and the free insertion periods. Table VIII-5 shows the rates for all methods combined in each of the four periods, excluding from the base in each period those who accepted earlier.

Table VIII-4. Cumulative Acceptance Rates by Method, Preferred and Actually Selected, to End of Experimental and "Free Insertion" Periods, by Initial Acceptance Intention and Reason or Circumstance for Intention

		Cumulative acceptance rate by end of:					
		Experimental period			Free insertion period		
			Actually chose:			Actually chose:	
Intention status	Number in base group	All methods	IUD	Others	All methods	IUD	Others
All wives[a]	8,810	15	10	5	22	16	6
Stated intention to accept soon, and preferring:							
IUD	1,481	39	31	8	46	37	9
others	222	26	15	11	34	22	12
All methods	1,703	38	29	9	45	35	10
Stated intention to accept eventually but not soon because:							
lactating or menstruating irregularly	360	25	17	8	34	25	9
pregnant	1,059	12	10	2	23	20	3
wanted more children	2,888	4	3	1	10	8	2
Total intending to accept eventually	4,307	7	5	2	15	12	3
Stated intention never to accept because:							
already using contraception	1,779	14	6	8	19	10	9
ambivalent or undecided	573	18	13	5	24	19	5
lactating or menstruating irregularly	109	10	6	4	21	16	5
pregnant	57	4	2	2	16	12	4
wanted more children	79	0	0	0	2	2	0
opposed to general idea	68	6	3	3	9	6	3
other reasons	135	7	5	2	10	7	3
Total intending never to accept	2,800	14	7	7	19	11	8

[a] Excludes those sterilized or sterile, those that accepted before or on home visit, and the indeterminate cases.

Table VIII-5. Acceptance Rates for All Methods for Each of Four Time Periods[a] by Initial Acceptance Intention, by Reason or Circumstance for Intention

		Acceptance rate in:			
		Experimental period		Extension period	Free insertion period
Intention status	Number in base group	Within 30 days of home visit	Feb. 1963-Mar. 1964	Apr. 1964-Dec. 1964	Jan. 1965-July 1965
All wives[b]	8,810	4	12	3	3
Stated intention to accept soon	1,703	13	28	6	6
Stated intention to accept eventually but not soon because:					
lactating or menstruating irregularly	360	2	23	8	5
pregnant	1,059	*	11	7	7
wanted more children	2,888	1	3	2	4
Total intending eventual acceptance	4,307	1	7	4	5
Stated intention never to accept because:					
already using contraception	1,779	2	12	2	3
ambivalent or undecided	573	3	15	3	4
lactating or menstruating irregularly	109	2	8	8	4
pregnant	57	0	4	11	2
wanted more children	79	0	0	0	3
opposed to general idea	68	1	4	3	0
other reasons	135	1	7	2	1
Total intending never to accept	2,800	2	12	3	3

[a] In each period those accepting previously are excluded from the base.

[b] Excludes those sterilized or sterile, those that accepted before or on home visit, and the indeterminate cases.

* Less than 1 per cent.

Selection of the new IUD rather than of a traditional method was related both to whether intention was followed by action and to the method actually adopted. Those intending to accept soon were asked which method they preferred. Acceptance rates were much higher among those intending to use the IUD than among those initially preferring traditional methods. Of course, those interested in the traditional methods might have obtained supplies from non-program sources, but those interested in the IUD could also have obtained one outside the official program by getting an Ota ring, an older type of IUD long known in Taiwan and available from many doctors in Taichung.

Among those initially expressing interest in the IUD, only a small proportion (about 20 per cent) switched to other methods when they came to the clinics. On the other hand, a majority (about 65 per cent) of those acceptors who initially intended to use the traditional methods took the IUD when they came to the clinics. We cannot rule out, of course, the possibility that sometimes the clinic staff influenced clients to choose the IUD.

After the initial period the choice was almost exclusively for the IUD, regardless of initial method preference or intention. The choice of the traditional methods was confined mainly to the intensive experimental period. The reader should also bear in mind that the proportion choosing the traditional methods even in the first period is much higher in the present analysis than was true for Taichung as a whole, because we are considering in this chapter only the Everything lins, where these methods had their major appeal.

REASONS FOR POSTPONEMENT AND ACCEPTANCE

Among those intending to accept later rather than soon, the reasons given[11] for the postponement made a substantial difference in acceptance rates. Women who had borne a child recently and who were lactating or menstruating irregularly had a very low acceptance rate in the first thirty days even if they had indicated that they intended to accept eventually, presumably because they believed that they were unlikely to conceive at this time. But during the rest of the experimental period they had an above average acceptance rate of 23 per cent, and after that their acceptance rate continued to be substantially above average. It is to this postpartum group that some new family planning programs are devoting considerable attention in Taiwan and elsewhere; this is additional evidence that women with a recent birth have a high acceptance potential after a short postpartum delay. The cumulative acceptance rate for this group as a whole was 34 per cent by 1965. Among all the women classified as lactating or menstruating irregularly, 77 per cent intended to accept. Even among the 23 per cent of those in this category who said that they would not accept, about one in five were actually acceptors by the end of the observation period—a proportion higher than the average for the whole panel.

Women pregnant at the time of the home visit had also demonstrated their fecundity recently, but they were not in a position to become acceptors as early as the postpartum cases. They had lower than average acceptance rates until the very last period, when their

[11] See Appendix VIII-1 for a further explanation of the "reasons" categories.

rate was above the average for that period. Of those pregnant at the home visit, 95 per cent said they would accept eventually. Perhaps the reason this figure was so much higher than the one for the post-partum group was that the required action was more remote for the pregnant wives, who could more lightly give what they thought was the expected response.

Women who were postponing their acceptance because they wanted more children had very low acceptance rates in the first three periods, presumably because they did not yet have the wanted number of children. By the last period the rates for this group were somewhat above the average, but their final cumulative rate was still very low; it had reached 10 per cent as compared with 22 per cent for the total panel.

Among those who initially said that they would never accept, the rates varied considerably with the explanation given. By 1965, 19 per cent of all those who first said "never" had accepted, despite their initial negative statement. However, the final cumulative acceptance rates varied from 2 to 24 per cent according to the reason given. The high rate after an initial delay by the ambivalent-undecided group has been mentioned already. We have referred also to the significant number of acceptances by those who initially said that they were already using a satisfactory method of contraception.

The lowest acceptance rate was for the small number of women who said that they wanted more children and intended never to use contraception. Their very low cumulative acceptance rate of 2 per cent, however, applies to a very small group, less than 1 per cent of the total sample. More than 97 per cent of *all* home-visited cases who said that they wanted more children also said that they intended to accept later, so wanting more children was not linked to a repudiation of family planning.

The few women who either simply indicated opposition to contraception or did not specify reasons for not accepting also had relatively low rates. These were very small groups: together they amounted to less than 2 per cent of the total sample. Even these extreme negative groups had acceptance rates of about 10 per cent by 1965.

The contribution of any subgroup to the total number of acceptances depends, of course, not only on its specific rate of acceptance but also on its proportionate size in the total sample. After the initial, intensive phase of the program, there was a great increase in the proportion of acceptances coming from groups other than the "accept soon" group (Table VIII-6). Only 28 per cent of all acceptances in

Table VIII-6. Percentage Distributions of All Wives and of All Acceptors in Each of Four Time Periods[a/] by Initial Acceptance Intentions (Using Three Different Bases)[b/]

Intention status	Percentage distribution of all cases in sample: A	B	C	Percentage distribution of acceptors in sample: Sample A, period: 1	2	3	4	Sample B, period: 1	2	3	4	Sample C, period: 1	2	3	4
All wives															
Number	11,393	8,810	7,031	695	1,416	285	313	319	1,028	279	304	275	816	241	261
Percentage	100	100	100	100	100	100	100	100	100	100	100	100	100	100	100
Sterilized or believes to be sterile	16	--	--	*	1	2	3	--	--	--	--	--	--	--	--
Accepted before or after home visit	5	--	--	54	16	0	0	--	--	--	--	--	--	--	--
Stated intention to accept:															
soon	15	20	24	33	29	21	19	72	40	21	20	83	50	25	23
eventually	38	49	62	3	21	52	56	7	29	53	57	8	37	61	66
Total intending to accept sometime	53	69	86	36	50	73	75	79	69	74	77	91	87	86	89
Stated intention not to accept because:															
already using contraception	16	20	--	6	15	13	14	14	21	14	14	--	--	--	--
ambivalent or undecided	5	6	8	3	6	5	6	6	8	5	6	7	10	6	8
opposed to general idea and others	4	5	6	1	2	7	3	1	2	7	3	2	3	8	3
Total intending never to accept	25	31	--	10	23	25	23	21	31	26	23	--	--	--	--
Total excluding those already using	9	11	14	4	8	12	9	7	10	12	9	9	13	14	11
Indeterminate	1	--	--	--	10	--	--	--	--	--	--	--	--	--	--

[a/] The four time periods are: (1) within 30 days of home visit; (2) experimental period, excludes acceptors in period 1; (3) extension period; (4) free insertion period.

[b/] Cf. Table VIII-1 for definition of samples.

* Less than 1 per cent.

the first thirty days came from those planning not to accept or to accept only later, but this percentage increased to 60 per cent in the intensive period and to 80 per cent in the last two periods.[12] This shift was in part a result of changes in the acceptance rates, but also it reflects the large proportion of the base population (about 80 per cent) in these two categories.

The acceptance rates for the "accept soon" group were substantially above those for the rest of the sample in every period. However, the increase in rates for the rest of the sample over time was great enough

[12] These rates are for Sample B (Table VIII-6), which excludes the sterile and those accepting at or before the first home visit.

to shift most acceptances in the population to these other groups, because their numbers were large enough to make up for their lower acceptance rates.

Clearly, intentions to accept or not to accept are far from infallible predictors, even when we take into account the reasons put forward originally by the respondent as an explanation for her attitude. Although rates are much higher for those intending to accept soon, a serious question can be raised as to whether these initial subjective responses can tell the analyst more than he would know from the objective demographic and social classification of the couples. We will return to this question after we have prepared the way by considering how the demographic and social characteristics of the couples affected their statements of intentions and whether action corresponded to intention.

HOW THE DEMOGRAPHIC AND SOCIAL CHARACTERISTICS AFFECT THE INTENTION TO ACCEPT

Stated intentions regarding acceptance are rather strongly related to the demographic characteristics of the couples but much less so to their social characteristics. This corresponds to our findings in Chapter VII about the factors affecting actual acceptance. As evidence for these broad generalizations we illustratively present data in Table VIII-7 for three demographic characteristics (number of living children and sons, whether more children are wanted, and prior family limitation experience) and for wife's education—the social characteristic generally found most useful in our analyses.[13]

It is necessary to consider not only all the couples stating their intentions concerning future action, but also, separately, the group not already using satisfactory methods of contraception.

Since most couples in most categories said that they intended to accept family planning soon or later, this total statistic does not produce very interesting or significant differentials. However, some more specific measures are highly differentiating.

The couples already characterized as under demographic pressure—those with more children and sons, those who want no more children,

[13] We have also examined in unpublished tables the following demographic characteristics: number of living children, number of living sons, wife's age, and duration of marriage; and the following social characteristics: husband's education, occupational classification. These data are not presented, because the results differ little from those shown.

and those who have unsuccessfully tried family limitation—are all distinguished by three facts:

1. The proportion intending to accept soon was much higher than average.
2. Among those intending to accept either soon or later, a much higher than average proportion said "soon." This is important, because the actual subsequent acceptance rate is much higher for those saying "soon" than for those who answered "later." For at least a significant minority of those saying "later," this was probably a convenient way for the respondent to say what she thought the interviewer wanted to hear with little risk or commitment.
3. Among those intending to accept soon, a much higher than average proportion said they would accept the IUD rather than other traditional methods. This is also important because preference for the IUD was more often validated by an actual acceptance. Further, the action required to get an IUD involved traveling to a clinic and submitting to a minor medical procedure. To reverse this action requires still another specific action. The intention to adopt a traditional contraceptive, even if followed by an actual acceptance, may not provide any contraceptive protection, since there is no certainty that the traditional contraceptive will be used even if a supply is taken.

So in the situations of demographic pressure, those not already protected by satisfactory contraception were much more likely than other couples both to make a positive statement that they would take action soon and to plan to use the contraceptive which commits them to a more difficult and serious action, one which is likely to have a contraceptive effect. For example, among all women not already using satisfactory contraception (see Table VIII-7):

1. 55 per cent of those who wanted no more children intended to act soon (as compared with 3 to 9 per cent of those who want more children).
2. 43 per cent of those with three or four children and two or more sons intended to accept soon (as compared with 9 per cent of those with three or four children and no sons, or 14 per cent of those with two children and one or two sons).

Table VIII-7. Percentage Distribution by Acceptance Intentions, by Demographic and Social Characteristics for Wives Who Were Not Already Using Satisfactory Contraception[a/]

Characteristics	Total	Intended to accept: Sub-total	Intended to accept: Soon	Intended to accept: Eventually	Did not intend to accept: Sub-total	Did not intend to accept: Ambi-valent	Did not intend to accept: Other reasons	Percentage choosing IUD among those intending soon	Percentage soon among those intending to accept
All wives	100	86	23	63	14	8	6	84	27
Number of living children and sons									
No children	100	89	0	89	11	1	10	0	0
One child									
No son	100	92	4	88	8	4	4	75	4
One son	100	92	4	88	8	3	5	75	5
Two children									
No son	100	94	6	88	6	2	4	83	7
One or two sons	100	88	14	74	12	6	6	83	16
Three or four children									
No son	100	88	9	79	12	6	6	88	10
One son	100	86	18	68	14	7	7	87	21
Two or more sons	100	81	43	38	19	12	7	90	53
Five or more children	100	79	49	30	21	14	7	88	61
Number of additional children and sons wife wants									
No more	100	76	55	21	24	16	8	89	73
One more, any sex	100	90	9	81	10	4	6	75	10
One more son	100	92	6	86	8	4	4	83	7
Two or more, any sex	100	91	5	86	9	1	8	100	6
Two or more, at least one a son	100	91	3	88	9	3	6	67	3
Prior birth control experience									
Contraception									
Now using, no abortion	100	100	100	0	*	*	*	89	100
Now using, had abortion	100	100	100	0	0	0	0	93	100
Past use, no abortion	100	86	36	50	14	8	6	86	42
Past use, had abortion	100	89	44	45	11	4	7	89	49
Abortion only	100	82	49	33	18	11	7	86	60
Never used anything	100	85	20	65	15	8	7	85	24
Wife's education									
Primary school not completed	100	84	24	60	16	9	7	86	29
Primary school grad.	100	86	24	62	14	8	6	84	28
Junior high school	100	88	25	63	12	6	6	88	28
Senior high school	100	88	27	61	12	5	7	85	31

[a/] Excluding women already sterile, women who accepted at or before first home visit, and women whose characteristics were unknown.

3. 30 to 42 per cent of those who had previously used contraception and/or abortion intended to act soon (as compared with 19 per cent of those who never had used anything).

Generally similar differences could be cited for the proportion answering "soon" among those intending to accept soon or later. The proportion choosing the IUD among those saying "soon" follows a similar pattern, although the differences are smaller and more erratic as a result of the small base to which we have now narrowed the comparisons.

Neither wife's education nor any of the other social characteristics (considered in unpublished tabulations) produce the systematic differences found for the demographic variables.

Some women gave ambivalent responses when asked their reasons for not accepting family planning. They did not express unreserved opposition, but said that they were undecided or that they wanted to talk it over with their husbands. The group that explicitly expressed ambivalence may represent a much larger group that felt considerable ambivalence although expressing an intention to accept soon or later. This probably helps to account for some contradictions between stated attitudes and behavior. In a society where fertility has traditionally had a high value, a change to explicit ideas of family limitation involves cross-pressures of opposing ideas and pressures, balancing now on one side and now on the other over a period of time for any individual.

Explicit ambivalence is most common precisely in those groups which have the highest proportions intending to accept soon and actually doing so, although we might have expected to find it among groups expressing either opposition or intention to accept only eventually, at an undefined future time. But these are not the facts. Ambivalent responses were most frequent where the situation made the decision about family planning highly salient—that is, in the same situations of demographic pressure associated with intention to accept soon.[14] For example, among those wanting no more children, 16 per cent gave an ambiguous response as compared with 1 to 4 per cent of those wanting more children. An ambiguous response does not mean avoidance of action, since by the end of the observation period acceptance rates for this group were about at the average and substantially above the rates of those intending eventual acceptance. The acceptance rates for the ambivalent were low during the first month following the home visit; presumably they were debating with themselves or with their husbands and others, etc. But over the long run, the demographic situation that occasioned the ambiguity led them to accept in substantial numbers.

[14] Ambivalence in intentions was also somewhat higher among those with little education than for the better educated, but these differences were much smaller than those having a demographic basis.

HOW THE BACKGROUND CHARACTERISTICS AFFECT WHETHER INTENTIONS ARE CARRIED OUT

Does knowing of the intention to accept soon or later help in predicting actual acceptance, or can we do as well by considering only the background characteristics of the couple? Actual acceptance rates, the proportion intending to accept soon, and preference for the IUD were all found to be higher in the later demographic stages of family life. It is therefore quite possible that statements of intention add very little, simply reflecting the respondent's family life-cycle position. This is a possibility, but it does not fit the facts (Table VIII-8).

Those intending to accept soon had higher acceptance rates than those with any other intentions. This is true for every category of every social or demographic characteristic considered, usually by a very wide margin.

Table VIII-8. Cumulative Acceptance Rate to July 31, 1965, by Initial Acceptance Intention, by Demographic and Social Characteristics[a]

		Intended to accept		Did not intend to accept		
Characteristics	All wives[a]	Soon	Eventually	Already using	Ambivalent	Opposed and other reasons
All wives	22	44	15	19	23	11
Number of living children and sons						
No children	3	--	4	*	*	0
One child						
No son	6	19	6	*	4	0
One son	10	30	9	17	*	0
Two children						
No son	8	29	6	25	*	*
One or two sons	18	34	15	19	26	14
Three or four children						
No son	19	52	13	38	*	*
One son	21	32	19	20	24	11
Two or more sons	29	48	25	19	24	17
Five or more children	30	46	29	17	26	14
Additional children and sons wife wants						
No more	31	45	35	18	25	16
One more any sex	20	42	19	21	21	4
One more son	18	30	16	29	20	11
Two or more any sex	16	*	13	*	*	*
Two or more, at least one a son	8	27	7	14	12	7
Prior birth control experience						
Contraception						
Now using, no abortion	21	50	--	18	*	*
Now using, had abortion	24	55	--	19	--	--
Past use, no abortion	35	56	25	--	*	*
Past use, had abortion	36	50	21	--	*	*
Abortion only	35	50	19	--	33	*
Never used anything	20	40	14	--	22	11

Table VIII-8 (continued).

Characteristics	All wives[a/]	Intended to accept: Soon	Intended to accept: Eventually	Did not intend to accept: Already using	Did not intend to accept: Ambivalent	Did not intend to accept: Opposed and other reasons
Age of wife						
20-24	14	41	11	18	21	7
25-29	22	44	16	21	24	18
30-34	25	46	18	19	24	7
35-39	24	42	21	17	21	12
Years since wife's first marriage						
Under 5	14	40	10	21	20	10
5-9	23	44	18	19	25	13
10-14	26	46	19	19	23	11
15 or more	25	42	23	17	24	11
Wife's education						
Primary school not completed	21	44	14	16	25	13
Primary school grad.	21	43	16	16	19	11
Junior high school	24	46	17	23	24	9
Senior high school	25	44	14	27	*	8
Husband's education						
Primary school not completed	19	39	13	14	26	19
Primary school grad.	21	44	16	15	20	10
Junior high school	22	45	15	14	28	15
Senior high school	24	47	15	25	29	6
Husband's occupation						
Farmer	22	43	14	20	25	18
Nonfarm manual worker	20	43	15	15	21	11
Proprietor	19	41	14	13	24	7
White collar worker	25	48	17	24	26	10

[a/] Excludes those already sterile or believing self to be sterile, those accepting on or before the first home visit, and indeterminate cases.

* Base is less than 20.

Whether those intending to accept soon followed through with action is affected by some of the demographic characteristics, e.g., by the number of living children and sons or by the number and sex of additional children wanted. However, even in the demographic situation least favorable to acceptance (e.g., among couples with only one child and that one a daughter), the acceptance rate for those who said they would act soon was very much above that for couples in that same demographic situation stating any other intention, although much lower than the rate for those answering "soon" who were in the later stages of family growth. Such demographic variables as wife's age and duration of marriage have very little effect on acceptance rates among those who said "soon." The demographic variables having an effect are those directly indicating life-cycle stages.

So the stated intention and the family life-cycle stage each help to predict acceptance, but both together still leave much unexplained.

Even if the wife said that she intended to accept soon, the proportion accepting soon was no more than 56 per cent in any of the demographic subgroups considered. While far above the average acceptance rate of 19 per cent, this result may be disappointing if we remember that one element here is a direct prediction of possible action by the individual involved.

Demographic variables have their most powerful effect on performance among those who said that they would accept eventually but not soon. For example, the proportion fulfilling this long-run intention within the thirty months of observation was only 4 per cent among those who initially had no children, increasing monotonically to 29 per cent among those with five or more living children. Among those with any specific number of children, the probability of action to fulfill intention is further increased substantially with the number of sons. Those who want no more children have the highest acceptance rate—35 per cent—and the proportion accepting decreases substantially both with the number of additional children wanted and if at least one additional son is wanted. Since "eventually" is a long time, all of the long-run intentions may be fulfilled in time, but this seems unlikely in view of the performance of those who intended action soon.

In general, the acceptance rates among those who originally said that they would not accept does not vary in any systematic way with the background characteristics. Among those initially saying that they were opposed to the whole idea, acceptances increased with number of living sons (plausible), but decreased with social status measures (perhaps this means that the higher status groups had a firmer basis for their opposition?). Among those not accepting because already using satisfactory contraception, the proportion that switched to a program acceptance increased with wife's education and decreased with number of living sons. For these patterns we have no ready interpretation.

The independent usefulness of the statements of intention can be evaluated, finally, by considering how much variation remains in the acceptance rates for different intention categories after adjusting for the effects of other demographic and social categories. If the effect of the intentions simply reflects the demographic and social categories with which they are correlated, then after adjustment all the differences should disappear and all intention categories would have the average acceptance rate. The preceding analysis has prepared us for the fact that this is unlikely.

In Table VIII-9 we show how the acceptance rates for intention categories are affected by adjusting first for wife's education and then for four demographic categories: number of children and sons; number of additional children and sons wife wants; prior use of birth control; and wife's age.

Table VIII-9. Cumulative Acceptance Rates to July 31, 1965, by Initial Acceptance Intention, Unadjusted Rates and Rates Adjusted for Wife's Education and for Four Demographic Variables[a]

	Acceptance rates		
		Adjusted for:	
Initial acceptance intention	Unadjusted	wife's education	demographic variables and wife's education
Stated intention to accept:			
soon	44	44	38
eventually	15	15	23
Stated intention never to accept because:			
already using contraception	19	18	5
ambivalent or undecided	23	20	22
opposed to general idea and others	11	12	15
Total[b]	22		

[a] The demographic variables are: wife's age, number of living children and sons, number of additional children and sons wife wants, and prior birth control experience. (See Table VIII-8 for the categories defining these variables.)

[b] This analysis excluded the sterilized, those accepting before or at the first home visit, and the indeterminate cases.

First of all, note that the acceptance rates are affected very little by adjusting for the effects of wife's education. This only confirms preceding analyses in another way.

When we adjust additionally for the effects of the four demographic variables, the basic pattern of variations by intention categories remains, although there are some changes. The high acceptance rate for those intending to accept soon is not simply a function of the advanced life-cycle status of this group, since this rate is reduced only modestly by the adjustment. For those intending to accept eventually the acceptance rate is actually increased by the adjustment, reflecting the fact that this group was concentrated to a greater extent in the earlier family life-cycle stages. This suggests that when the members of this group are at more advanced family life-cycle stages, more of them will accept. Those already using contraception before the program began would have had a much lower rate were it not for their demographic characteristics. In part, this simply reflects the fact that one of the control variables is prior birth control experience, but it also results from the fact that this group was already at an advanced family life-cycle stage. The ambivalent category is little affected by the demographic adjustment, although the ambivalent tended to be in advanced family life-cycle stages. This may mean that ambivalence is really associated with a predisposition to act that is independent of the life-cycle stage.

THE INTERACTION OF GROUP MEETINGS AND INTENTIONS

Effective group meetings, the intention to accept soon, and preference for the IUD each contributed independently to higher acceptance rates (Table VIII-10). The result is that acceptance rates

Table VIII-10. Cumulative Acceptance Rates to July 31, 1965, by Initial Acceptance Intention, by Group Meeting Effectiveness

Effectiveness of group meetings	All wives	Intended to accept soon: IUD	Intended to accept soon: Other methods	Intended to accept soon: Total	Intended to accept eventually	Never intended to accept: Already using	Never intended to accept: Ambi- valent	Never intended to accept: Opposed and other reasons
All wives	22	45	33	44	15	19	23	12
Wives living in lins with:								
Effective meetings	25	50	34	48	17	22	28	11
Ineffective meetings	18	38	36	38	12	20	9	3
No meetings	19	41	32	39	12	16	21	15

were highest (50 per cent) for women intending to accept an IUD soon and living in lins where an effective meeting was held. The preference for a particular method and the effectiveness of the meetings is less important than intention to accept soon, since the maximum differences in the table are between those intending early acceptance and the other intention categories. Nevertheless, there was a sizable additional influence in most intention categories from the effective meetings, which apparently helped to move those intending early acceptance to act. Ineffective meetings did not have this influence, since the acceptance rates in lins with ineffective meetings do not systematically differ from those for the lins without any meetings at all.

IX. Perceptions of Contraceptive Practice by Others: Effects on Acceptance

*BY J. A. PALMORE AND R. FREEDMAN**

THE PROBLEM

THERE has been considerable evidence in preceding chapters that word-of-mouth diffusion of information about family planning played an important part in the Taichung program. This is consistent with evidence that such informal communications have been vital to organized family planning programs in many other places. The early Puerto Rico study by Hill, Stycos, and Back[1] stressed the relevance of the interpersonal factor for a family planning program. In economically deprived areas of Chicago an informational campaign started in 1962 stimulated a large volume of informal communication, and Palmore[2] demonstrated that information spread to a much larger population than was reached directly. In a Kentucky project, preliminary data indicated that one-third of the clients for birth control had heard about the program through friends, relatives, and neighbors.[3] Such sources were also reported by 46 per cent of those who came to the clinics in the Sundong Gu project of Seoul, Korea.[4] Reports from Thailand[5] indicate the major role played by in-

* We acknowledge special assistance by Beverly Beers, Christopher Langford, and Charles Kindermann in the work on this chapter.

1 R. Hill, J. Stycos, and K. Back, *The Family and Population Control,* Chapel Hill: University of North Carolina Press, 1959, pp. 350-64.

2 J. Palmore, "The Chicago Snowball: A Study of the Flow of Influence and Diffusion of Family Planning Information," *Sociological Contributions to Family Planning Research*, pp. 272-363. Also see J. A. Palmore, Jr., "Hypotheses for Family Planning Among the Urban Disadvantaged: U. S. A.," *Proceedings of the World Population Conference, 1965,* New York: United Nations, 1967, II, 297-300.

3 J. A. Palmore and D. M. Monsees, "The Eastern Kentucky Private Physician-Plus-Education Program: First Evaluation of Results," in D. J. Bogue, ed., *The Rural South Fertility Experiments*, Report No. 1, Community and Family Study Center, University of Chicago, February 1966, Part II, pp. 11-26.

4 E. Hyock Kwon, "Sungdong Gu Action-Research Project on Family Planning: A Progress Report (for period 10 July—31 December, 1964)," The School of Public Health, Seoul National University, Seoul, Korea, April 1965, pp. 24-26. For data on the rural Koyang study in Korea, see Jae Mo Yang, Sook Bang, Myung Ho

formal communication patterns there. The series of surveys carried out by the Mainichi Press in Japan also indicates the importance of informal communication channels which carry information derived from the mass media.[6]

In Taichung, as elsewhere, the organized program represented an attempt to intervene in an ongoing system of relationships and behavior. Before any organized program existed, there must have been a substantial amount of information about this subject circulating by means of the informal communication network of that city. Therefore, we begin by considering the early situation. Long before the action program began, some women had used contraception. They were asked in the first Taichung survey for retrospective reports on who first suggested the methods they used. These reports are probably distorted by the biasing effects of intervening events on memory. However, the general categories of their responses are so distinctive that these answers probably represent in broad terms the proper magnitudes. About one-third of the women, reporting on the period before the program, said that adopting contraception was their own idea and not the result of a "suggestion" by anyone else (Table IX-1). Undoubtedly many of these women were affected by diffuse informal communications with others, since the necessary ideas and information came to them through some channel of communication. Such underlying informal communications may not have been perceived as an explicit "suggestion" that could be reported in the interview.

About two-thirds of the women did report that a specific person suggested the method used. Among these, informal associates (friends, relatives, or neighbors) were clearly the sources most frequently remembered, with the network of health services (especially doctors) as an important secondary source. If we consider only respondents

---

Kim, and Man Gap Lee, "Fertility and Family Planning in Rural Korea," *Population Studies*, 18, No. 3, March 1965, 243-44.

[5] J. Y. Peng, "Thailand: Family Growth in Protharam District," *Studies in Family Planning*, No. 8, The Population Council, New York, October 1965, 1-10. Note especially Table 10, p. 5. Also see the report on an IUD clinic in Bangkok: J. T. Fawcett, Aree Somboonsuk, and Sumol Khaisang, *Diffusion of Family Planning Information by Word of Mouth Communication*, Family Planning Research Unit, Chulalongkorn Hospital, Thailand, November 1966.

[6] For example, see The Population Problems Research Council, Mainichi Newspapers, *Summary of Eighth National Survey on Family Planning*, Tokyo, 1965.

Table IX-1. Kinds of People Who Suggested Contraceptive Methods Used Before and After the Action Program: Percentage Distributions

Sources of information	Percentage distributions based on all sources of information: Before program, First method used	Before program, Second method used	During the program's first year	Percentage distributions based on specific other sources mentioned: Before program, First method used	Before program, Second method used	During the program's first year
Health personnel						
Doctors	14	17	5	23	26	6
Program staff	--	--	32	--	--	42
Other health workers	4	6	8	6	9	11
Informal associates						
Friends	15	15	8	25	22	11
Neighbors	9	12	11	14	22	14
Husband	13	9	7	21	14	9
Other relatives	4	4	3	6	6	4
Other persons	3	1	2	5	1	3
Nobody else[a]	33	30	18	--	--	--
Not ascertained	4	6	5	--	--	--
Total per cent	100	100	100	100	100	100
Number	429	138	411	270	87	316
Summary categories						
Program personnel	--	--	32	--	--	42
Other health workers	18	23	13	29	35	17
Informal associates	41	40	29	66	64	38
Other people	3	1	2	5	1	3
Own self	33	30	18	--	--	--

[a] Respondent says she started on own initiative.

mentioning a specific source of suggestion, about two-thirds cited primary associations and the rest mainly health personnel.

The Taichung program was designed to take advantage of this situation. The goal was to introduce the influence of a large number of family planning health workers who could suggest directly the adoption of family planning. This would be a change. It was hoped that such an approach would have much greater effect than the less numerous suggestions previously coming from the existing network of health services. It was anticipated that the direct effect of this major new formal intervention would be multiplied by diffusion through the same informal network that had done most of the work before the program was established.

These expectations appear to have been realized (Table IX-1). Among those reporting the adoption of a new contraceptive method during the year of the program[7] (between the surveys carried out

[7] This includes women accepting a method either under the program or in other ways, and therefore represents a larger group than just the acceptors in the formal program.

before and after): (1) the proportion reporting spontaneous adoption (without a personal suggestion) decreased greatly; (2) among those indicating a source of suggestion, about equal numbers reported the official program personnel and informal associations as the source of the suggestion; (3) there was a sharp decline in the percentage reporting a doctor as the source of influence, but this was to be expected since private doctors were not participants in the Taichung IUD program. The larger influence of the doctors before the program began was cumulative, involving many years of experience reported on by many respondents. Their influence in a single year would predictably be less.

As partial evidence that the people who were recommending methods between the two surveys were actually "influential" and really had some impact on decisions to adopt family planning, we asked the women whether this first person's suggestion was the most important influence in their final decision to use the contraceptive in question. Eighty-eight per cent of the women who answered this question said that this first person was the most important influence. An additional 7 per cent claimed that the most important influence was the second or third person who suggested the use of that method.

Obviously, the formal intervention of the program had a major effect, but this direct effect was greatly multiplied by the diffusion of influence through the existing primary[8] network of friends, relatives, and neighbors. Although the data in Table IX-1 shows the formal program sources as slightly more important than the informal associations, we suspect that this order would be reversed with more adequate measurement. The informal interpersonal influence is likely to be diffuse and cumulative over a long period of time. Therefore, it is more likely to be taken for granted and less likely to be reported as a specific source of suggestion than are the clearly defined and specialized contacts with the program agent. The very process of being interviewed and the questions asked were likely to be reminders of the formal program contact. We are not likely to be in

[8] Enduring, non-specialized informal associations are often referred to as primary groups in sociological literature. While we cannot claim that all the informal contacts reported in this chapter are of this character, it is likely that most of them are. Hence, we will use the terms primary associates and informal associates or contacts interchangeably. We assume that many, if not most, of these informal interactions involved powerful emotional ties and sanctions, which control or modify behavior according to a normative structure.

error if we conclude that the stimulus of the formal program was at least matched and probably exceeded by the resulting indirect influence of the informal diffusion. This speculation is supported by the fact that about half of the acceptances in Taichung came from outside of the Everything lins, and even some of the acceptances in the Everything lins probably resulted from informal contacts.

We shall deal directly here with only two specific aspects of the process of diffusion which the Taichung program aimed to change: discussion in the population about family planning and perceptions of how many others were practicing it. First of all, it was hoped to increase the amount of discussion about family planning in the population. Secondly, it was hoped that this increased discussion, along with other influences, would increase also the number of people perceiving that others approved of family planning and were practicing it. This was believed to be one way of legitimizing family planning.

The program should have increased the amount of discussion on the subject in at least two ways. In the first place, many husbands and wives were involved directly in discussions with program personnel and with each other by the home visits made to more than 11,000 families in the Everything lins. These visits were expected to increase directly in this third of the population of childbearing age the awareness of and information about family planning, and perhaps also the readiness to practice it. Secondly, these direct program contacts were expected to stimulate other discussions with friends, neighbors, and relatives. Presumably, discussion chains might also be activated by the hundreds of group meetings, by the thousands of letters and posters, and by the comings and goings of the large program staff.

Increasing the amount of discussion was not an objective in itself. It was hoped that this would lead to intermediate changes in attitude and information and ultimately, through such changes, to the adoption of family planning. One of the important intermediate objectives was to change perceptions about what other people who were trusted believed and did about family planning. Before the program began there appeared to be considerable pluralistic ignorance about general attitudes toward family planning. It was our impression that while large numbers of both the leaders and the common people approved of family planning and used it, a very large number believed that others did not share such a modern position. Such misconceptions about the attitudes of others might have been the basis for ambivalence and for the ineffective and intermittent practice of contraception described in previous chapters.

A number of pilot surveys in Taiwan and Taichung had already convinced those planning the Taichung program that approval and practice of family planning were at much higher levels than was generally perceived by the population. One purpose of the first pre-program survey was to check these preliminary findings against data from a large representative sample, so that the results could be incorporated as facts into the program. Both the pre-test results and the confirming findings of the larger survey were communicated to the fieldworkers as rapidly as possible. The standard message of the fieldworkers, liberally paraphrased, was something like this:

> If you are interested in family planning you are not alone or deviant. A large majority of Taichung couples with three or four children want no more. Almost all couples approve of the idea of family planning. Many of them—your friends, neighbors, and relatives—have already begun to do something to limit family size either before or in the program. We are prepared to help you and them to use family planning safely and by convenient, inexpensive methods.

A message of this type was, of course, only one of the program stimuli which might influence the communication process and affect the levels of discussion and the content of perceptions about family planning. So far as perceptions of the practice of family planning by others are concerned, the fact that a rather large minority of women did become acceptors in the program was undoubtedly a most important stimulus. This minority was drawn from an even larger number who debated becoming acceptors and must have discussed their plans and doubts with their informal associates.

A SUMMARY OF RESULTS

What were the results? The answer depends somewhat on the measures used, but the following summary provides a quick overview of the conclusions which we will document in some detail.

1. The levels of discussion probably did not change very much during the program; but perceptions definitely did. There was an increase in the number of respondents who believed that their friends, relatives, and neighbors were practicing contraception.

2. Adoption of contraception was higher among those who believed that an increasing number of their primary associates were practicing contraception.
3. Those who rarely discussed family planning had very low acceptance rates; but beyond a certain minimum level of discussion, it made little difference whether discussion was more frequent or took place with a wider range of primary associates.
4. What people believed to be the practice of their associates was more important than how often they talked about family planning with them.

CHANGES IN DISCUSSION AND PERCEPTION OF FAMILY PLANNING

The conclusions that we reach about the changes in the level of discussion depend on the measures used. The respondent was asked in both pre-program and post-program surveys how often she discussed family planning with friends, neighbors, husband, and other relatives. From these independent "before" and "after" responses, we calculated measures of change in amount of discussion for each type of primary associate. We refer to these as "calculated changes." The respondent was asked also at the second interview for a retrospective estimate of whether the amount of discussion about family planning with each type of informal associate had increased, decreased, or remained the same. This was in effect asking the respondent herself to calculate the change retrospectively. Obviously, the "retrospective change" report is suspect as a measure to correlate with changed contraceptive practice, because it will often be influenced by whether the respondent herself has adopted contraception. The calculated change measure, however, is based on two independent responses and is anchored in an initial response that precedes the program entirely. It is very unlikely that a respondent would remember her first response a year later and adjust her second response to it.

The calculated level of informal discussion did not show a net rise during the year of the program (Table IX-2). For each type of primary relationship there was, in fact, a small net decrease in the balance between those reporting more and less discussion over the period extending from before to after the program. By contrast, the effect of the program personnel is evident in the fact that 41 per cent of the respondents reported higher frequency of contact with such

Table IX-2. Change in Frequency of Discussion about Contraception with Several Kinds of People (Based on Comparison of Independent Reports by Same Respondents at First and Second Surveys)[a]

Type of change	Changes in frequency of discussion of birth control with: Relatives	Neighbors	Friends	Husband	Health personnel
Up (more people)	20	28	21	26	41
Same high level in both surveys	4	8	4	14	1
Same low level in both surveys	51	32	49	28	43
Down (fewer people)	25	31	26	32	15
N.A.	0	0	0	0	0
Total per cent	100	100	100	100	100
Number	1227	1227	1227	2443	1227

[a] Changes were classified by comparing answers to the same question asked once in the first survey and once in the second survey. For all items except the discussion with the husband, information on the first survey is not available for the supplementary sample since the question was not asked on the first survey.

workers in the second report than they had in the first, representing a net gain of 26 per cent in the calculated increases (as compared with the decreases).

Given the extensive program stimuli, it is hard to believe that there was not at least some increase in the amount of discussion at the informal level. It is possible that the calculated change measure of discussion was distorted by the fact that the "after" measurement was made when there was considerably more family planning activity in the city. Under these circumstances, the respondent may have adjusted her answer downward in relation to the increased level of activity and discussion. That is, a respondent answering that she discusses family planning "sometimes" or "often" may set higher standards for defining these terms in a situation where family planning is more salient and is discussed more freely. What appears to be no change or no downward change in our calculations may really be an increase hidden by a change in the yardstick used by the respondent. This interpretation is necessarily speculative, but it gains some support from the fact that there was a substantial increase in discussion with every kind of group in the retrospective changes reported by the respondent in the second interview (Table IX-3).

In spite of the measurement problem, it seems probable to us that if the increase in the discussion level had been substantial it would have appeared even in the calculated change measures. In any case, since the more rigorous calculated change data show no increase in the level of discussion as measured, we feel bound to accept this as a tentative conclusion at least. We doubt that we would have rejected

Table IX-3. Frequency of Discussion of Contraception with Several Kinds of People: Changes from Just Before to Just After Intensive Program (Based on Retrospective Change Reports at Second Survey)

	Discussions with:				
Frequency of discussion as compared to last year	Husband	Relatives	Neighbors (not relatives)	Friends (not relatives or neighbors)	Midwives, doctors, druggists, and others
More now	28	20	32	21	29
About the same	21	21	22	18	13
Less now	13	7	7	6	20
Never discussed	39	52	39	54	38
N.A.	0	0	0	0	0
Total per cent	100	100	100	100	100
Number	2443	2443	2443	2443	2443

a finding of "more discussion" on the grounds of measurement error, so we do not feel justified in rejecting the conclusion that there was no change.

There was clearly a net gain in the proportion of respondents who believed that contraception was being practiced by larger numbers of couples in each of the four reference groups considered (Table IX-4). This is a calculated change, measured by comparing independent responses before and after the program, so it is not simply a result of retrospective bias in reporting. The fact that there was an increase in contraceptive practice in the aggregate means that what was perceived actually did happen. We have no outside confirmation of this kind against which to test changes in the discussion level.

HOW CHANGES IN PERCEPTION AFFECTED ACCEPTANCE

For our purpose, changes in amount of discussion and in perception are not important in themselves. Our primary interest is in how discussion or perception affected the acceptance of contraception. Changes in discussion levels or perception might not be followed by changes in contraceptive behavior. On the other hand, it is quite possible that individual changes in contraceptive behavior might be associated with changes in amount of discussion or in perception, without any aggregate net shift in discussion or perception levels. What did happen?

In at least two of the three primary groups considered, perception of a change toward more practice of contraception was associated with the highest acceptance rates[9] (Table IX-5). The lowest rate was that of

[9] In Tables IX-5 to IX-10, acceptances through the second survey include both

Table IX-4. Changes in the Perception of How Many Others Were Practicing Contraception, by Group of Reference[a]

Type of change in perception of number practicing	Perception of contraceptive practice among: Relatives	Neighbors	Friends	Taiwanese generally
		Panel A		
Determinate answers				
Up (more people)	40	41	30	25
Same high level in both surveys	10	21	17	60
Same low level in both surveys	30	15	28	1
Down (fewer people)	20	24	25	14
Total per cent	100	100	100	100
Number of women who gave determinate answers (=100% for Panel A)	1339	1297	1197	1306
		Panel B		
Don't know and N.A. responses				
Don't know on first survey and high level on second survey	7	13	10	20
Other don't know or N.A. responses[b]	38	34	41	27
Total per cent	45	47	51	47
Total number of women (= 100% for Panel B)	2443	2443	2443	2443

[a] Changes were classified by comparing answers to the same question asked once in the first survey and once in the second survey.

[b] This includes those who were (a) "don't know" before and at a low level on second survey, (b) all those who were "don't know" at the second survey, (c) those who were N.A. at either survey (a very small number), and (d) those who were "don't know" at both surveys. Categories (c) and (d) are roughly 11% of the total (2443) for each of the groups: relatives, neighbors, friends, Taiwanese generally.

the large residual group of couples who either said that they didn't know what others were doing or did not report some continuing practice for at least one kind of group. In short, believing that contraceptive practice was increasing among trusted associates led to higher acceptance rates and the absence of such beliefs led to lower rates.

We feel justified in making such causal inferences, because the higher rates of acceptance associated with perception of practice by others continued even *after* the perception increase was measured. So the higher perception not only accompanied but preceded high acceptance rates. The higher acceptance rates continued in an eighteen-

---

those within the official program and the adoption of contraception in other ways. Unfortunately, data on acceptances outside the program were not available for the period after the second survey, so the additional acceptances reported for the following eighteen months are all in the program. These later acceptances are almost all of the IUD.

Table IX-5. Acceptance Rates, by Changes in Perception of Practice of Contraception in Several Reference Groups, for Wives Not Already Practicing Contraception[a] or Sterilized[b]

Changes in perception of contraceptive use among three groups: friends, relatives, and neighbors[c]	Number	Acceptance rates at two dates: Second survey	Acceptance rates at two dates: July 31, 1965	Difference: (acceptance rate July 31, 1965)--(second survey rate)
Perceives more practice in 2 or 3 reference groups	241	15	29	+14
Perceives more practice in one of three reference groups	352	13	22	+ 9
Perceives no increase but reports some practice at both interviews for at least one reference group	114	11	22	+11
All others: report no changes or no practice or doesn't know[d]	854	5	12	+ 7
Total, all categories	1561	9	17	+ 8

[a] As of the first survey.

[b] Sterilized by date of second interview.

[c] The changes in perception were measured by comparing answers to the same questions asked once before and once after the action program.

[d] See note b on this category in Table IX-4. Women we could classify on at least one but not all the groups (relatives, friends, neighbors) were classified on the basis of partial information. They were not automatically placed in the one residual category.

month period following the "after" measurements of the second survey. At the extremes the differences in acceptance rates are very substantial: two to one. Further, the data we have been discussing are particularly relevant because they refer to an eligible population: fecund women who had not begun the practice of contraception by the first interview nor been sterilized as of the second. The rather strong pattern of differences found in Table IX-5 is less clear in a comparable unpublished table for all women in which relationships are obscured by problems of eligibility.

The summary data on perceptions just discussed groups together the three types of primary associations—those with friends, neighbors, and relatives. The data about each of these kinds of informal associations and also about Taiwanese in general are contained in Table IX-6, with more detail regarding both the levels of and the changes in perception. By and large, in the case of each type of association, the women who perceived that the number practicing contraception had increased or remained at a high level were more likely to have adopted contraception than those who believed that the number had decreased or stayed at the same level throughout the year. This is true whether the informal group considered is friends, neighbors, or

Table IX-6. Acceptance Rates, by Changes in Perception of the Numbers of Others Practicing Contraception, by Groups of Reference, for Wives Not Already Practicing Contraception[a] or Sterilized[b]

Type of change in perception of number practicing contraception[c]	Relatives: Number	Relatives: Second survey	Relatives: July 31, 1965	Neighbors: Number	Neighbors: Second survey	Neighbors: July 31, 1965
Up (more people)	311	12	24	374	14	25
Same high level in both surveys	62	16	27	112	11	22
"Don't know" on the first survey and high level on second survey	100	8	22	190	5	16
Same low level in both surveys	272	7	13	138	8	16
Down (fewer people)	138	9	20	152	7	15
Other "don't know" and N.A.[d]	678	7	14	595	7	13
Total	1561	9	17	1561	9	17

Type of change in perception of number practicing contraception[c]	Friends: Number	Friends: Second survey	Friends: July 31, 1965	Taiwanese generally: Number	Taiwanese generally: Second survey	Taiwanese generally: July 31, 1965
Up (more people)	211	18	31	218	10	23
Same high level in both surveys	60	18	22	395	9	18
"Don't know" on first survey and high level on second survey	129	12	26	358	8	15
Same low level in both surveys	277	6	13	4	*	*
Down (fewer people)	129	10	16	106	10	19
Other "don't know" and N.A.	755	6	13	480	8	16
Total	1561	9	17	1561	9	17

(Acceptance rates at two dates by group whose contraceptive practice was perceived to change)

[a] As of the first survey.

[b] Sterilized by date of second interview.

[c] The changes in perception were measured by comparing answers to the same questions asked once before and once after the action program.

[d] See the note on this category on Table IX-5.

* Base is less than 20.

relatives. It is true whether we consider the acceptance rate at the time of the second survey or eighteen months after this second measure of perception.

One perhaps surprising observation, based on Table IX-6, is that women whose perceptions led them to believe that the number of people practicing birth control had decreased were more likely to be acceptors than women who believed that this number had stayed at the same low level through the one-year period. One possible explanation for this phenomenon is the crudity of the calculated change measurement. Those who perceived practice to be at a high level at the time of the first survey could only repeat this opinion or lower their estimate. For example, a woman classified as revising her estimate downward might still be at a relatively high level at the second interview. We do not have enough cases to take such distinctions into account.

Some further evidence of the effect of perception on acceptance is provided by the fact that women who moved from "not knowing" about others on the first survey to a perception of a high level of contraception at the second survey had high acceptance rates when compared with the women who began "not knowing" about others and ended either in the same indeterminate category or believing that there was little practice of contraception (compare lines 3 and 6 of Table IX-6).

Perceptions about the behavior of Taiwanese in general were not related to acceptance rates in the consistent manner found to be true of the perceptions about informal associates. This is significant, because it confirms the view that behavior is affected more by the influence of trusted informal associates than by such a vague reference group as "Taiwanese in general." On the basis of these detailed findings, the data for perceptions about "Taiwanese generally" were not used in constructing the summary measures found in Table IX-5.

THE EFFECTS OF CHANGES IN DISCUSSION LEVELS

Acceptance rates were higher for women who reported at both surveys that they engaged in some minimum of discussion than for those who did not have such a continuing minimum level of discussion (Table IX-7). However, it seemed to make little difference whether the amount of discussion increased beyond this minimum level, or whether the discussion took place with several types of primary associates or only one. In fact, the highest acceptance rates were among those who reported some discussion but did not report an increase. Clearly, discussion does not appear to be as important for acceptance as perceptions of the behavior of others.

These rather negative findings about the effects of discussion are based on the "calculated changes." We have already indicated our a priori methodological preference for this measure rather than the retrospective change report in considering changes in the level of discussion. However, since results are different depending on the measure used, we present in Table IX-8 the relationship between acceptance rates and the "retrospective" change measure. With this set of data the results are quite different. For each type of association and for each date of reference, the following consistent results appear:

1. Those reporting "more" discussion have the highest rate of acceptance.

able IX-7. Acceptance Rates by Changes in Frequency of Discussion about Contraception with Several Kinds of People[a/]

anges in level of discussion th three groups: friends, elatives, and neighbors[b/]	Number	Acceptance rates at two dates: Second survey	Acceptance rates at two dates: July 31, 1965	Difference: (acceptance rate July 31, 1965)--(second survey rate)
equency of discussion increased with two or three groups	215	12	21	+ 9
equency of discussion increased ith one group	262	11	20	+ 9
increase, but discussed contra- ception at least sometimes with ne or more groups both before nd after program	66	20	35	+15
btotal, women who were high in iscussion level by second survey	543	12	22	+10
l others: mainly those who never iscussed it at one of the inter- iews or women who did not answer his question[c/]	54	7	14	+ 7
tal, all categories	1090	9	18	+ 9

[a/] Only wives in the original sample.

[b/] The changes in discussion levels were measured by comparing answers to the same questions asked once before and once after the action program.

[c/] This category includes a few women (three) who could not be categorized on their discussion.

able IX-8. Acceptance Rates, by Retrospective Self-Reported Changes in Discussion Levels with Different Associates; for Fecund Wives; Rates as of Second Survey and as of July 1965

requency of iscussion s compared o last year	Husband: Number	Husband: Second survey	Husband: July 31, 1965	Husband: Change[a/]	Other relatives: Number	Other relatives: Second survey	Other relatives: July 31 1965	Other relatives: Change[a/]
ore now	659	18	33	+15	460	17	31	+14
bout the same	478	12	20	+ 8	443	11	19	+ 8
ess now	172	5	10	+ 5	124	6	17	+11
ever discussed	867	4	10	+ 6	1148	7	15	+ 8
.A.	1*	--	--	--	2*	--	--	--
otal	2177	10	19	+ 9	2177	10	19	+ 9

requency of iscussion s compared o last year	Neighbors (not relatives): Number	Neighbors (not relatives): Second survey	Neighbors (not relatives): July 31, 1965	Neighbors (not relatives): Change[a/]	Friends (not relatives or neighbors): Number	Friends (not relatives or neighbors): Second survey	Friends (not relatives or neighbors): July 31, 1965	Friends (not relatives or neighbors): Change[a/]	Midwives, doctors, druggists, and others: Number	Midwives, doctors, druggists, and others: Second survey	Midwives, doctors, druggists, and others: July 31, 1965	Midwives, doctors, druggists, and others: Change[a/]
ore now	726	14	26	+12	469	17	30	+13	678	18	31	+13
bout the same	468	9	18	+ 9	387	10	18	+ 8	280	15	26	+11
ess now	137	5	11	+ 6	114	5	13	+ 8	363	8	15	+ 7
ever discussed	845	7	14	+ 7	1206	8	16	+ 8	850	2	9	+ 7
.A.	1*	--	--	--	1*	--	--	--	6*	--	--	--
tal	2177	10	19	+ 9	2177	10	19	+ 9	2177	10	19	+ 9

[a/] Increase in acceptance rates between second survey and July 1965.

* Acceptance rates are not shown when the number is less than 20.

2. Those reporting "about the same" level of discussion have higher rates of acceptance than those reporting less discussion or "never" discussing this topic.
3. Acceptance rates do not differ consistently between those discussing the topic less and those never discussing it.

We are skeptical about these findings based on retrospective self-ratings, because many of those who accepted family planning are likely to have projected their own interest onto their recollection of changes in their own behavior. It is true that acceptance rates in the eighteen months *after* this self-rating continued to be highest for every type of association for those who reported "more" discussion. However, those who reported discussion as "about the same" no longer have consistently higher acceptance rates for this post-rating period than those reporting "less" or "no" discussion.

These contradictory findings from two types of measurement are of some importance, because informal discussion in primary groups is a critical variable in almost any conceptualization of how influence moves through a communication-social organization network to affect family planning (or any other) behavior. Our primitive measurements of changes in discussion are obviously deficient. Even so, we have presented them in some detail because they appear to be more pertinent to the issues in an experimental sense than any other systematic empirical observations of which we know.

THE JOINT EFFECT OF DISCUSSION AND PERCEPTION

Since there is only a modest association between the changes in levels of discussion and of perception (Table IX-9), it is quite possible that the joint effect of these changes may be different from the effects found by considering them separately. Therefore, in Table IX-10 the acceptance rates are related to simultaneous classification of changes in discussion and perception. Perception is clearly much more important than discussion, although each has some independent influence. When both have increased during the program period, acceptance is at its highest level. When neither has increased or both are at a low level, the acceptance rate is at its lowest level. Between these two extremes, however, perception is more important than discussion in every comparison. Increasing perception alone has more effect on

Table IX-9. Indices of Predictive Association[a] (λ_A, λ_B, λ_{AB}) Between a Woman's (a) Change in Perception of the Number of Women Practicing Contraception in Certain Groups, and (b) Change in Discussion Level with the Same Groups Using the Categories of Tables IX-8 and IX-10, Omitting all "Don't Know" Responses

Change in perception of number of women practicing contraception vs. change in level of discussions of birth control for:	λ_B	λ_A	λ_{AB}
Friends	8%	10%	9%
Relatives	4%	8%	6%
Neighbors	6%	6%	6%

[a] For an elementary discussion of this statistic, see William L. Hays, Statistics for Psychologists, Holt, Rinehart, and Winston, New York, 1963, p. 606 ff.

Table IX-10. Acceptance Rates by Changes in Perceptions and Change in Discussion of Contraception[a]

Type of change in perceived support and contact with the informal communications system[b]	Number	Acceptance rates at two dates: Second survey	Acceptance rates at two dates: July 31, 1965	Difference: (acceptance rate July 31, 1965)--(second survey rate)
Perception and discussion both at high level for both interview for at least one group or increase in perceived practice and discussion of it for at least one group	222	15	25	+10
Perception of practice at high level for both surveys for at least one group, or increase in perception for at least one group, but no similar change for discussion	213	11	23	+12
Level of discussion high or increasing for at least one group but no similar change for perception	289	9	17	+ 8
All others: includes those with no upward changes in perception or discussion or those who didn't know about practice by others or couldn't answer the questions	366	6	12	+ 6
Total, all categories	1090	9	18	+ 9

[a] Only wives in original sample.

[b] Changes were measured by comparing answers to the same question asked once before and once after the action program.

acceptances than increasing discussion alone, from the lowest level of both on up. If there has been a maximum change in perception, only little more is added when the amount of discussion has also moved to a high level. All of these generalizations are valid whether the acceptances are measured at the time of the second survey or eighteen months afterward. These data, again, refer to the most pertinent part of the population: those who are fecund and not already using family limitation. The greater importance of perception stands out also when we consider the change in acceptance rates between the second survey and July 1965, and this is the most rigorous test.

In this comparison of the effects of perception and of discussion, both are measured in terms of "calculated" changes. If we use the retrospective changes of discussion, the role of discussion becomes more important. We have not taken this direction in our analysis because of the doubts already expressed about the retrospective measure, and also because we would then have to mix a "retrospective" discussion measure with a "calculated" perception measure.

X. Effectiveness of Intrauterine Contraception: Termination Levels and Correlates*

BY R. G. POTTER, JR., L. P. CHOW, A. K. JAIN, AND C. H. LEE

THE PROBLEM

HIGH acceptance rates in a family planning program have little value unless the acceptors continue to use the methods adopted for a reasonable period of time. At the time the Taichung experiment was begun, almost all family planning programs concentrated their efforts on influencing large numbers of couples to begin contraception. Little attention was given to problems of continuation and termination. The tacit assumption, only occasionally made explicit, was that continuation rates would not be a great problem with the IUD, since theoretically it could remain in place for years and its use required no recurrent decision. Only discontinuing use required a decision.

It soon became apparent in Taiwan and elsewhere that despite its many advantages, the IUD was not a perfect contraceptive and that many couples were terminating use. Only a small proportion of terminations resulted from pregnancies with an IUD in place; a larger minority resulted from involuntary expulsion of the device; but the major cause of terminations turned out to be voluntary removal of the device for medical or other reasons. Such voluntary removals were made mainly at the request of the woman, because of minor side effects such as some excess bleeding, headaches, or backaches. In the large majority of cases these side effects were diagnosed as not serious

* This chapter is based on a manuscript prepared by these authors in multilith form in February 1967 as a publication of the University of Michigan Population Center, under the title "Expanded Report on Social and Demographic Correlates of IUD Effectiveness: The Taichung IUD Medical Follow-Up Study." An earlier version of this paper appeared in the *Proceedings of the Social Statistics Section, 1966,* American Statistical Association, Washington, D.C., 1966, pp. 272-77. The present chapter was revised by R. Freedman to include the material on reinsertions and on life table rates for all segments, and to include reference to some recent developments.

from a medical point of view, and an unknown but substantial proportion were believed to be of psychological origin. Of course, whatever the physical basis of the complaint, the symptoms were very real to the women involved.

In Taichung, 34 per cent of the women who had an IUD inserted had terminated the use of this first device within one year after the initial insertion, and 51 per cent within two years. Where adequate data exist, the results in other countries are not grossly dissimilar.[1] These results were disappointing to those who expected the IUD to be the perfect contraceptive and that it would, once inserted, prevent any further pregnancies for all users. In retrospect, such expectations were unrealistic. So far as we know, no other contraceptive has even as good a record as the IUD for continued use over a period of a year or two in a mass program in a developing country. Preliminary reports from experiments underway with the pill in Taiwan and Korea indicate lower continuation rates than those for the IUD.[2] It

[1] Some roughly comparable total termination rates are as follows:

	Cumulative total termination rates for 1st insertions at 12 months:
Present Taichung study	34
Taiwan island-wide study 1965	38
1966	38
Korea national IUD study 1965	35
1966	39
India: New Delhi Clinics	22
Thailand (rural Prothoram)	39
United States	27

Some of the variation shown results from differences in the type of IUD used. For example, the relatively high Taichung rate is due in large part to the early use of the small loop, which has high pregnancy rates associated with it.

[2] The trial pill programs have so far concentrated mainly on women giving up the IUD, so this is not an adequate test of what the situation would be in an unselected general population. Former IUD users may be a group selected against persistence, but they are also likely to be a motivated and experienced group. Singapore and Malaysia, where substantial programs are now concentrating on the pill, should provide more pertinent evidence. In Taiwan, where a follow-up survey was carried out in June 1967 on the experimental pill program in twenty-one townships, the termination rate was 46 per cent at the end of six months as compared with the rate of 26 per cent for the same period for the island-wide IUD program. One problem in evaluating the pill programs is that the test of pregnancy and birth rates becomes much more important, since continuous use of the pill is much more difficult to establish, while only a physical examination is required to determine whether the IUD is in place.

well may be that the contraceptive pill or some method not yet in use or some combination of methods may eventually result in much higher continuation rates, but this is not yet the case as this is written late in 1967. A rational program in most places would probably be one that offered a choice of several or all of the safe and reliable methods. Different methods will appeal to different couples, and a choice of methods would maximize the probability that a couple giving up one method would turn to another rather than ending contraceptive practice entirely.

The level and correlates of the IUD termination rates have been studied more scientifically, with better data and samples, and in more detail in Taiwan and Taichung than in any other mass family planning program as of 1967.[3] It is ironic that this careful evaluation at first produced some unjustified criticism both of the Taiwan program and of the IUD, since the standard of comparison was perfection —the unrealistic 100 per cent continuation. Only as data and experience have accumulated has it become clear that IUD continuation rates even in such places as the United States are not substantially higher than those in Taiwan. It has also become clear that so far no contraceptive method has a better record for continued use in a mass program than the IUD.

None of this should minimize the very real problems posed by the high termination rates. We believe that it is the judgment of most qualified observers that no program should rely on this or any other single method. However, while the IUD is far from perfect, it is one of the important resources for any mass program in a developing country.

THE DATA AND THE METHODOLOGY

The method for evaluating termination-continuation rates, their correlates, and their effects on fertility have developed, in Taiwan as elsewhere, step by step, in response to program problems. The methods initially evolved out of studies concentrating on the history of the first device inserted; these studies have then moved slowly toward becoming studies of the complete contraceptive and fertility history of the couples who had an insertion. The broader perspective now be-

[3] The Korean data are rather comparable to those for Taiwan, but the analysis has lagged for various reasons. However, the material published on Korea has resulted in the same kind of unfounded pessimism on the part of outside observers as that roused by the Taiwan material.

gins with the insertion of the first device but extends to include also data on what is done about birth control following any termination and with what results.[4]

The first follow-up studies of IUD users were designed mainly for the important purposes of keeping a check on medical problems and particularly of monitoring any potentially harmful side effects. The development, in the course of these studies, of statistics and methods for measuring termination rates and their correlates was an incidental by-product, whose importance only became clear as the programs moved from concentration on insertions to a necessary concern with long-run use.

In the case of Taichung, the data necessary for studying terminations were collected as an incidental by-product of the Taichung IUD Medical Follow-Up Study.[5] The objective was to follow every woman who received an IUD insertion in the Taichung program, including those who accepted between July 1962 and February 1963 in a small-scale pre-program trial. The present analysis is based primarily on the data collected for the period up to December 1964, the cutoff date for the first set of data analysed.

This analysis concentrates mainly on the first segments of experience—that is, on the period from first insertion to first termination or to the cutoff date, whichever comes first. Such an emphasis on the first insertion was virtually universal at the time the data were first collected, because the concern was a clinical interest in what happened to the first device inserted. As emphasis has shifted from the history of the device to the experience of the couples, methods have been devised to take into account IUD reinsertions.[6] Some of our

[4] For some preliminary results based on this broader perspective, see Chaps. XII and XIII. Also see L. P. Chow, R. Freedman, R. G. Potter, and A. K. Jain, "Correlates of IUD Termination in a Mass Family Planning Program: The First Taiwan IUD Follow-Up Survey," Milbank Memorial Fund *Quarterly*, 46, No. 2, Part 1, April 1968, 215-35.

[5] This continuing study, supported by grants from the Population Council, was under the supervision of Dr. C. H. Lee of the provincial Taiwan Health Department during the phase of data collection described in this chapter. After 1965 the follow-up field work and coding procedures were revised and transferred to the Taiwan Population Studies Center, under the direction of Dr. L. P. Chow. The follow-up of both current users and terminated cases is continuing, and an analysis of the experience through December 1966 is now in preparation.

[6] Dr. C. Tietze of the Population Council has been the leader in developing methodology for IUD follow-up studies and is carrying out in the United States the largest of such follow-up studies. His reports appear in a series of mimeo-

analyses will include such later segments of use. It is now clear that to complete the picture we must also have data on contraceptive practice following any final termination of IUD use. Such more complete data for the present sample will be available later.[7]

The sample consists of 7,295 women, three-fifths of them residents of Taichung and the other two-fifths from outside Taichung. The latter, who heard about IUD indirectly, had to travel greater distances to reach the clinic and therefore have a rather different relationship to the Taichung family planning program. During most of the calendar period under study a small size of the Lippes loop was favored, about two-thirds of the devices inserted being of this type. Later a shift was made to larger sizes of the Lippes loop. As a result, the composition of the sample is mixed with respect to both choice of device and relationship to family planning program. Nevertheless, the sample may still be viewed as representative of the total group responding to the whole Taichung program during the period from July 1962 to December 1964. The follow-up procedures were strong enough, according to evidence reviewed below, to ensure that biases from incomplete follow-up were not large.

The plan was to reinterview each woman six and twelve months after insertion and once a year thereafter. A postcard was mailed to each woman to remind her of the scheduled visit to the clinic. At the clinic, an interview and an examination determined whether the device was still in place and covered a checklist of possible problems and symptoms. If the woman did not come to the clinic in re-

---

graphed progress reports of The Cooperative Statistical Program for the Evaluation of the Intra-Uterine Devices. See also, among his many other publications, the following: C. Tietze, "Effectiveness and Acceptability of Intra-Uterine Contraceptive Devices," *American Journal of Public Health*, 55, No. 12, December 1965, 1874-79; C. Tietze, "Intra-Uterine Contraception: A Research Report," *Studies in Family Planning*, No. 18, April 1967, 20-24, and in the same issue, C. Tietze, "Intra-Uterine Contraception: Recommended Procedures for Data Analysis," pp. 1-6. See also in this issue an important review of experience in many places: W. P. Mauldin, D. Nortman, and F. F. Stephan, "Retention of IUD's: An International Comparison," pp. 1-12.

[7] Data for almost all of the cases considered in the present chapter and for all of the new Taichung IUD cases have been collected and coded for the period up to December 1966. These new data cover both continuing users of the IUD and terminated cases. The data include information on contraceptive practices, abortion and sterilization following terminations, and fertility rates both before and after insertion. These analyses should be available in detail sometime in 1968. Preliminary results are reported in Chapter XII.

sponse to the postcard, a fieldworker went to her home, interviewed her, and asked her to return to the clinic if the device might still be in place. If she had terminated use of the IUD, an attempt was made to ascertain the circumstance and time of the termination.

Some of the women returned to the clinic even before the scheduled dates because they had been told to come back at once if they experienced any problems. Roughly 30 per cent of the women came to the clinic without a home visit. For the rest, home visits were necessary. Because of the heavy and uneven load of work, these visits were not always made on schedule.

Out of a total sample of 7,295 women, only 650 were not visited at least once, nearly half of these because of the short interval between insertion and cutoff date of the study. These 650 women are necessarily excluded from the analysis. Another 388 women were visited one or more times, but their last scheduled visit was overdue and this part of the data is missing. It is believed that these missed visits are more a reflection of staff limitations than of patient resistance. Indeed, only 54 cases were reported in which a woman actually failed to respond to a follow-up visit, indicating a high level of respondent cooperation. Information on these 442 women (388 plus 54) is included in the analysis up to the time of the latest follow-up visit. No important differences were found between the social and demographic characteristics of women adequately followed up and those of the women for whom one or more scheduled visits were missing (see Appendix X-1). It is believed, therefore, that bias from inadequacies of follow-up is small.

Attention is restricted mainly to first segments, by which is meant the period of use from first insertion of an IUD to first interruption of its use or to the end of the period of observation, whichever was earlier. The lengths of these first segments have been defined conservatively. Months of use by any woman classified as a continuing user are counted only up to her last clinic visit, when it was verified that the device was still in place.

As the length of time since insertion increases, the number of women exposed rapidly decreases. In the present analysis, sample size is large enough to yield fairly stable rates for the first two years. For the third year the number of cases becomes too small for stability.

In any follow-up study of users of IUD in an ongoing program, observations are made of women for whom the length of time since first insertion varies. Some of the women will already have terminated their use by the time of observation. Other women, usually comprising a majority of the sample, will be classified as continuing users at time of last observation even though their histories are truncated. Naturally, one wants to be able to use these incomplete histories as well as the more complete ones to derive an unbiased picture of retention and loss of IUD as a function of length of time since insertion. The life table method is designed to cope with precisely this problem.

The useful wearing of an intrauterine device may terminate for any of several reasons—pregnancy, expulsion, or removal, which reasons themselves may be subdivided. To be satisfactory, then, the life table methodology must provide for competing risks of termination. The University of Michigan Population Studies Center, in collaboration with Dr. Christopher Tietze of the Population Council, has participated in developing such a procedure. More precisely, the multiple-decrement life table was adapted to the analysis of IUD effectiveness.[8] Assistance with respect to sampling error calculations was received from Dr. Norman Johnson, Mr. W. Kenneth Poole, and Dr. Bernard Greenberg of the University of North Carolina.

Two types of termination rates will be used. What Tietze has called "net rates" allow for the presence of competing risks. For example, a net cumulative rate of expulsion allows for, and is slightly reduced by, some women becoming pregnant or removing the device before they have had a chance to expel it. Net cumulative rates are additive. The net rates of pregnancy, expulsion, and removal add up to the exact rate of termination for the three reasons combined. Because of this additive nature, net cumulative rates are appropriate for studying the relative frequency of different types of termination in a single sample.

However, a problem arises when net cumulative rates are used in comparing the relative frequency of a particular type of termination, such as expulsion, in two different samples or in subgroups within a sample. For example, suppose that the monthly rates of expulsion —that is, the probabilities of expelling during the first month after insertion, the second, and so on—are lower in sample B than in sample A for those retaining the device up to the beginning of that

[8] Dr. Robert G. Potter of Brown University, a Visiting Research Associate of the Michigan Center, has directed the technical development and testing at the University of Michigan.

month. Now, if the levels of competing risks are also lower in B than in A, so that fewer women in B are lost to pregnancy and removal and therefore more women are exposed on the average longer to the risk of expulsion than is the case in A, then it is possible for sample B to show a higher net cumulative rate of expulsion despite its lower monthly rates of expulsion.

To handle this problem one may use what Tietze calls "gross rates." A gross cumulative rate is the hypothetical proportion of women that would have been observed to lose the device from one type of risk had it been possible to eliminate all competing risks, leaving just the one risk operative in the population, and if the monthly probabilities of loss from this one risk were unaffected by the elimination of the competing risks. As a practical matter it is necessary to assume this absence of effect, but in fact this condition will not obtain unless the women losing the device for any of the competing risks are unselected with respect to the single risk under review. As it is calculated, a gross cumulative rate is a pure function of the corresponding monthly rates, and subject to the qualification just noted will be independent of the level of competing risks. Hence, in the example above, the gross cumulative rate of expulsion in sample B with its lower monthly rates of expulsion is necessarily lower than that in A, and in this manner leads to a comparison of samples that is more easily interpreted. Gross rates will be used in dealing with differentials between major subgroups of the sample.

It is important to recognize that the cumulative life table termination rates, like those in a mortality life table, are synthetic constructs, based on merging the experience of different cohorts. The numbers of women shown in Table X-6, for example, are all those contributing at least one month of experience. The number still wearing the device decreases with length of time since insertion. Thus, in some subgroups only a small number of the women are left with the IUD in place at the end of twelve months. However, this does not necessarily mean that cumulative rates have a high sampling error, because they are built up from the individual monthly termination rates for months one through twelve, based on the experience of larger numbers of women. The standard errors shown take into account the attrition in sample size over time.

This brief summary of methodology may suffice for those primarily interested in substantive aspects. For those having methodological interests, a more complete exposition is furnished in Appendix A-2.

TERMINATION RATES BY TYPE IN THE TOTAL SAMPLE

Table X-1 gives net cumulative termination rates per hundred first insertions at the end of twelve and twenty-four months by type of termination. Looking at the bottom row, one sees that about one-third of the first segments terminate by the end of one year and about one-half by the end of two years. Returns from a follow-up study covering all of Taiwan indicate that termination rates in this more general sample are somewhat higher, with 38 instead of 34 per cent of first segments terminating within a year.[9]

Table X-1. Cumulative Net Termination Rates and Standard Errors per 100 First Insertions, at End of 12 Months and 24 Months of Use, by Detailed Type of Termination

	12 months after insertion		24 months after insertion	
Type of termination	Rate	Standard error	Rate	Standard error
Pregnancy				
Device in situ	3.3	.2	5.9	.4
Device undetermined	1.2	.1	2.3	.2
Total	4.5	.3	8.2	.4
Expulsion	12.2	.4	14.9	.5
Removal				
Medical reasons	15.1	.5	22.0	.6
Personal reasons	.7	.1	1.2	.2
Nonrelevant reasons	1.9	.2	5.0	.4
Total	17.7	.5	28.2	.7
Total terminations	34.4	.6	51.3	.8

The termination rates presented in Table X-1 are of the same general order of magnitude as those reported by Tietze for the United States. He calculates two-year termination rates ranging from 34 to 60 per cent for different types of IUD. However, for the small Lippes loop mainly used in the Taichung study, Tietze reports a termination rate of 54 per cent—very close to the Taichung rate of 50 per cent for the small loops, and 51 per cent for all loops.

Table X-2 shows the termination rates in broader type categories, but in month by month detail regarding period of use. Also, it presents both gross and net rates for each cause, so that the difference between the two types of rates can be easily seen. Total termination rates (designated in the table as the "correct" total) are the sum of the

[9] For a more complete report on the first Taiwan island-wide IUD follow-up study, see L. P. Chow, R. Freedman, R. G. Potter and A. K. Jain, *op.cit.* "Correlates of IUD Termination."

Table X-2. Cumulative Gross and Net Termination Rates per 100 First IUD Insertions and the Difference Between the Two Rates, by Months Since First Insertion, by Type of Termination

	Type of termination										
	Pregnancy			Expulsion			Removal			Total	
Months of use	Gross rate	Net rate	Diff.	Gross rate	Net rate	Diff.	Gross rate	Net rate	Diff.	Correct sum of net rates	Incorrect excess over correct
1	.2	.2	.0	2.6	2.5	.1	3.5	3.5	.0	6.3	0.1
2	.6	.6	.0	4.3	4.2	.1	5.2	5.0	.2	10.1	0.3
3	1.1	1.0	.1	5.9	5.7	.2	7.0	6.8	.2	13.9	0.5
4	1.6	1.4	.2	7.4	7.0	.4	8.9	8.5	.4	17.9	1.0
5	2.3	2.0	.3	8.4	7.9	.5	10.3	9.8	.5	21.0	1.3
6	2.6	2.3	.3	9.2	8.6	.6	11.5	10.9	.6	23.3	1.5
7	3.3	2.8	.5	10.1	9.4	.7	13.1	12.3	.8	26.5	2.0
8	3.8	3.2	.6	11.0	10.1	.9	14.5	13.5	1.0	29.3	2.5
9	4.2	3.5	.7	11.9	10.9	1.0	15.7	14.5	1.2	31.8	2.9
10	4.8	3.9	.9	12.6	11.4	1.2	16.9	15.5	1.4	34.3	3.5
11	5.2	4.2	1.0	13.2	11.9	1.3	18.2	16.6	1.6	36.6	3.9
12	5.6	4.5	1.1	13.6	12.2	1.4	19.6	17.7	1.9	38.8	4.4
13	6.0	4.8	1.2	14.1	12.6	1.5	21.1	18.9	2.2	41.2	4.9
14	6.2	4.9	1.3	14.6	12.9	1.7	22.0	19.7	2.3	42.8	5.3
15	6.8	5.3	1.5	15.1	13.3	1.8	23.5	20.9	2.6	45.4	5.9
16	7.5	5.8	1.7	15.6	13.6	2.0	24.5	21.6	2.9	47.6	6.6
17	8.0	6.1	1.9	15.8	13.8	2.0	25.4	22.4	3.0	49.2	6.9
18	8.7	6.5	2.2	15.9	13.9	2.0	26.5	23.2	3.3	51.1	7.5
19	9.2	6.8	2.4	16.4	14.2	2.2	27.6	24.1	3.5	53.2	8.1
20	10.1	7.3	2.8	16.4	14.2	2.2	28.9	25.0	3.9	55.4	8.9
21	10.6	7.6	3.0	16.6	14.3	2.3	29.8	25.7	4.1	57.0	9.4
22	10.9	7.8	3.1	16.8	14.4	2.4	30.5	26.2	4.3	58.2	9.8
23	11.1	8.0	3.1	17.0	14.6	2.4	31.9	27.3	4.6	60.0	10.1
24	11.5	8.2	3.3	17.5	14.9	2.6	33.2	28.2	5.0	62.2	10.9

net rates, and are equal to the rate obtained if type of termination is ignored in calculating the life table. If, on the other hand, the gross rates by type are added, an incorrect total is obtained, because this procedure assumes that women can terminate due to more than one of the competing causes. The result, for example, is that the discrepancy between the correct and incorrect total termination rates is 11 per cent of the initial cohort by the end of two years.

During the early part of 1967, in at least three different developing countries, greatly exaggerated termination rates were being reported (and possibly influencing policy). They had been obtained by adding gross rates in this incorrect way. The ultimate logical absurdity of this incorrect procedure can be illustrated with an example[10] from the island-wide study carried out in Taiwan in 1965, where adding the gross rates for very young women would yield a termina-

[10] For women under 25 years of age the correct total termination rate in the Taiwan island-wide study was 76 at eighteen months. If the total had been obtained by adding gross rates, the total would have been 104!

tion rate of more than 100 per cent! The higher the termination rates of each type, the greater the discrepancy produced.

The data in Tables X-1 and X-2 indicate that removal is the predominant cause of IUD loss.[11] Expulsion and pregnancy are next, in order of importance. Over three-quarters of all removals are alleged to be for medical reasons (bleeding, pain, menstrual irregularity, and the like). Removals for "non-relevant reasons," mainly because of plans for another baby, account for less than a fifth of all removals. Contributing a still smaller share are removals for "personal reasons"; half of these are connected with shifts to another device or to another technique of family planning.

As the second most common cause of IUD loss, expulsions are confined almost entirely to the first year.

Slightly less than 10 per cent of the Taichung women become pregnant (usually with the device in situ) during the initial twenty-four months prior to termination for other reasons. As will be shown later, this rather high pregnancy rate reflects a primary reliance at first on the small loop. Because of the high pregnancy rate associated with it, the small loop was later abandoned for larger sizes of loop.

AN EXTRAPOLATION

The above results cover only the first two years following insertion. For a long-range picture of protection received from IUD, one would like to be able to extrapolate cumulative retention and termination rates beyond the two years covered by the present study. Here it is useful to think of two extremes between which the proportion of women retaining the device would be likely to fall. First, if monthly probabilities of loss progressively decline, reaching very low levels by the end of the second year, then there will be few losses thereafter and one may predict that the five- and ten-year retention rates will not be much different from the two-year rate of approximately 0.5.

[11] Comparisons between studies or countries as to the distribution of removals among medical causes, personal reasons, and so forth are not likely to be very valid, because the classification will depend greatly on the philosophy, knowledge, and practice of the medical personnel involved. Attitudes about whether minor symptoms or psychological complaints are medical problems may make a considerable difference. In some places, even the classification as expulsion or removal may be suspect, since a woman may remove the device herself or have it removed by a private practitioner but then report the loss as an involuntary expulsion in order to give a more pleasing response to a fieldworker or interviewer.

Alternatively, if monthly probabilities of pregnancy, expulsion, and removal are independent of time elapsed since insertion, then to derive five- and ten-year retention rates one would simply raise the two-year rate of 0.5 by powers of 5/2 and 5 respectively and in this manner estimate that only about one-sixth of the women would retain the device for as long as five years and only 2 to 3 per cent as long as ten years.

Thus a more assured extrapolation becomes possible if one knows the manner in which the monthly probability of loss is varying as a function of time elapsed since insertion. Net monthly rates of loss are given in Figure 3 for three types of termination. Net probabilities of

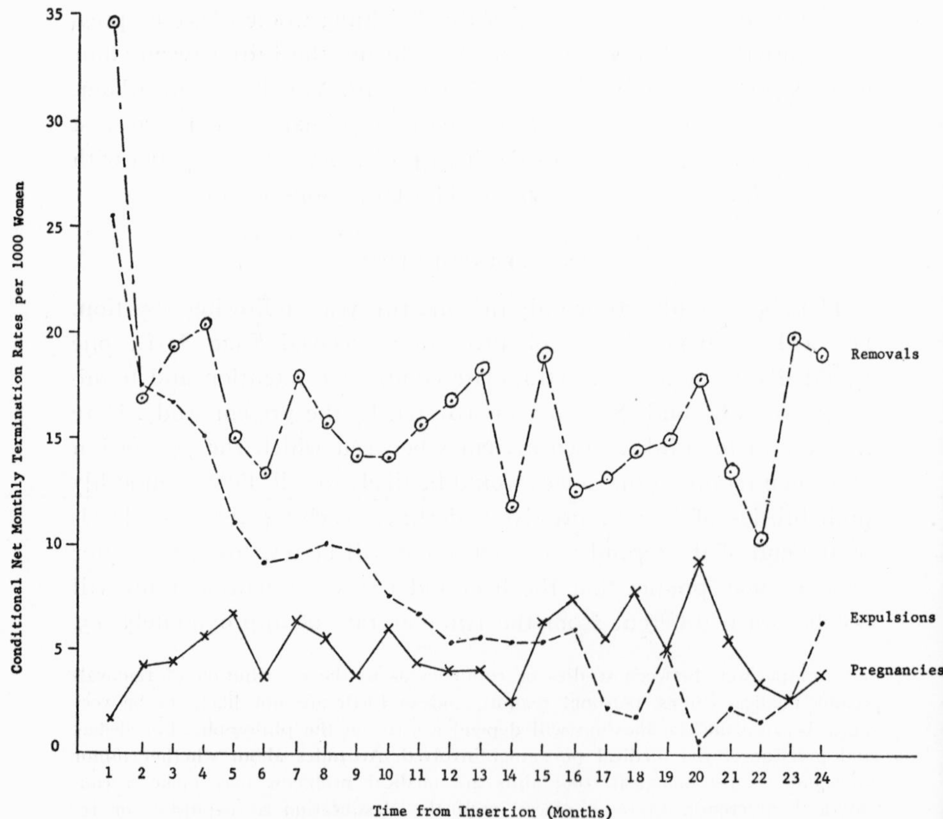

Figure 3. Conditional Net Monthly Probabilities of Termination per 100 Women by Type of Termination and Time from Insertion

terminating IUD within the next six months conditional to retaining it zero, six, twelve, and eighteen months are given in Table X-3 for a more detailed classification of termination types. It is plain from both graph and table that there is some decline in loss rates during the first year, but very little decline during the second year.

Table X-3. Net Probabilities of Terminating Within Six Months Given Retention to Start of Interval, by Duration from Insertion and Type of Termination

	Six-month interval (from time of insertion)			
Type of termination	1-6	7-12	13-18	19-24
Pregnancy				
Device in situ	.017	.020	.022	.021
Device undetermined	.006	.008	.009	.008
Total	.023	.028	.031	.029
Expulsion	.086	.046	.025	.018
Removal				
Medical reasons	.099	.067	.058	.055
Personal reasons	.004	.003	.004	.005
Nonrelevant reasons	.005	.018	.021	.030
Total	.109	.088	.084	.089
Total terminations	.218	.161	.140	.135

The monthly rate of removal declines for two months but then levels off at a surprisingly high level with little further decline. The rate of removals for non-relevant reasons (mainly plans for another baby) increases slightly during the twenty-four-month interval, while the rate of removals for medical reasons barely declines. That women who have worn the device for twelve or eighteen months should continue to show such high rates of removal for medical reasons is puzzling, since one would expect physical side effects to subside after the first few months.

The curve for expulsions follows a more expected course: starting high and declining to a low level by the end of the first year. This is the pattern one would expect to find if a minority of women had uteri intolerant of the device and if these women prone to expulsion were progressively eliminated from the sample, leaving behind a subsample characterized by relatively lower risks of expulsion.

As in the case of removals, the monthly rate of pregnancy shows little tendency toward decline. The presence of postpartum amenorrhea presumably operated to keep the rate of pregnancy relatively low during the first few months after insertion.[12]

It appears, then, that during the first months after insertion the monthly risks of removal and expulsion decline, but that during the second year, when losses from expulsion have already become low, there is little trend. Longer observation may reveal gradual declines for the monthly probabilities of pregnancy as well as for removals due to medical reasons. Nevertheless, the empirical results fit best a model of termination rates unaffected by elapsed time after the first few months. Therefore, as a rough approximation, we assume a constant monthly risk of loss after the first two years. That is, for purposes of a five- or ten-year extrapolation we accept the experience of the first two years as observed. Then we project the next three or eight years on the basis of the monthly retention rate derived by averaging the monthly rates of the second half of the second year. This exercise leads to an expectation that about one-fifth of the women will still be wearing the device after five years and only about 5 per cent after ten years. Under the same assumptions, the average length of first segments is estimated to be around 3.3 years.

Naturally these assumptions will prove pessimistic if subsequent observation reveals an appreciable decline of monthly termination rates commencing after the second year. However, barring such a decline, the above estimates dramatize the brevity of protection being obtained by the present sample from *first* insertions of IUD as a consequence of relatively high removal rates.

PROTECTION FROM IUD REINSERTIONS

The preceding discussion underestimates the protection period of the IUD, because it is based only on the data for the first device inserted. It does not take into account the additional months of protection for those who had one or more additional insertions.[13] In the Taichung sample such reinsertions usually occurred after only a relatively brief period without protection. Twenty-nine per cent of those who terminated the first segment had at least one reinsertion. The probability of a reinsertion was much higher if the termination resulted from an expulsion rather than if it was due to pregnancy or

12 See the section on differentials, below.

13 See Appendix X-3 for an analysis of the incidence of reinsertions in relation to social and demographic characteristics.

removal, but reinsertion rates were rather high even when a completed pregnancy terminated the first segment, especially if the pregnancy was ended by an induced abortion.

Type of termination	*% of terminated cases with at least one reinsertion*
Expulsion	65
All other causes	12
All pregnancies	19
pregnancies ending in:	
live birth	9
spontaneous abortion	19
induced abortion	31
pregnancies in progress	0
Voluntary removals	9
All cases terminating first segment	29

The reinsertion rates were low for those whose pregnancies ended in live births, since these births were recent and many of the women believed that they were protected by lactation. Fifty-three per cent of all those pregnant after a first insertion and 73 per cent of those with a completed pregnancy terminated it with an induced abortion. These women are obviously highly motivated, so it is not surprising that more than 30 per cent had a device reinserted. Nor is it surprising that reinsertion rates are much higher after an involuntary expulsion than after a voluntary removal. The woman who has the device removed because of a complaint is less likely to have another device inserted than the woman who loses the device involuntarily.

Table X-4 provides a comparison of the termination rates for first insertions and those for all insertions. Taking reinsertions into account reduces the termination rates from 34 to 27 per cent at twelve months and from 51 to 42 per cent at twenty-four months. Considering all insertions rather than just the first makes the most substantial difference in the case of expulsion rate, since reinsertions are most frequent after this type of termination. The effect on the distribution of terminations by type at successive time periods is shown in Table X-5. For example, twelve months after the first insertion the percentage

Table X-4. Cumulative Net Termination Rates, by Type of Termination, for First Insertions and for All[a] Insertions, for Selected Periods after First Insertion

Number of months after first insertion	Pregnancy		Expulsion		Removal		Total terminations	
	1st segment	All segments	1st segment	All segments	1st segment	All segments	1st seg ment	All segments
1	0.2	0.1	2.5	0.8	3.5	3.0	6.2	3.9
3	1.0	0.8	5.7	2.1	6.8	6.0	13.5	8.9
6	2.3	1.9	8.6	4.0	10.9	9.9	21.8	15.8
12	4.5	3.9	12.2	6.2	17.7	16.7	34.4	26.8
18	6.5	5.6	13.9	7.7	23.2	22.1	43.6	35.4
24	8.2	6.9	14.9	8.7	28.2	26.9	51.3	42.5

[a] For those cases with more than one insertion, the period between insertions are omitted and periods with device in situ are added for the "all segments" classifications. For example, consider a woman who has the device removed after six months, then after an interim period of 3 months has a second device inserted which she retains for 6 months. She is considered as having a device in place for 12 months. The entire experience for "all segments" is classified by the type of the last termination, if the last device inserted is no longer in place. However, in the few cases in which the first termination cause was a pregnancy, only the first segment is considered.

Table X-5. Percentage Distribution of Terminations by Type (Net Rates), for First and All[a] Insertions, for Selected Periods After First Insertion

Number of months after first insertion and whether first or all insertions	Pregnancy	Expulsion	Removal	Total
1 month				
1st	3.2	40.3	56.5	100
All	2.6	20.5	76.9	100
3 months				
1st	7.4	42.2	50.4	100
All	9.0	23.6	67.4	100
6 months				
1st	10.6	39.4	50.0	100
All	12.0	25.3	62.7	100
12 months				
1st	13.1	35.5	51.4	100
All	14.6	23.1	62.3	100
18 months				
1st	14.9	31.9	53.2	100
All	15.8	21.8	62.4	100
24 months				
1st	16.0	29.0	55.0	100
All	16.2	20.5	63.3	100

[a] See footnote in Table X-4.

of terminations which are removals is 51 per cent for first segments but 62 per cent for all segments. The increase in terminations by removal comes mainly from a decrease in the proportion of terminations which are expulsions. These data reinforce further the important conclusion that the major cause of termination is removal.

HOW DEMOGRAPHIC AND SOCIAL CHARACTERISTICS AFFECT IUD TERMINATION RATES

It is reasonable to expect that some groups in a population will derive longer spans of protection from IUD than others, either because of the physical factors that figure in pregnancy and expulsion risks or because of the mixture of motivational and physical factors that govern risks. Obtaining results for an entire cross-sectional sample is no more than a first step; an equally important part of the analysis is an examination of differences amongst IUD wearers classified according to social and demographic characteristics.

Tables X-6 and X-7 present differentials between various categories measured in terms of gross rates, each gross rate representing a cumulative proportion of women terminating IUD for a specific cause under the assumption that this particular cause is the only one operative and that all competing risks are eliminated. Table X-6 offers cumulative gross rates and corresponding standard errors for twelve months after insertion; Table X-7 furnishes the same estimates for twenty-four months after insertion. A number of very significant differentials appear in the data in Tables X-6 and X-7:

1. The two strongest discriminators for termination rate are wife's age and the number of her births (including stillbirths) preceding first insertion.[14] By the end of twenty-four months the difference in relation to parity is truly remarkable. Termination rates are 91 per cent for women below second parity and only 37 per cent for sixth or higher parity, with a regular monotonic decrease in the intervening parities. Correspondingly, at the end of twenty-four months the youngest and oldest age groups show termination rates of 76 and 35 per cent respectively.

   While all types of termination decrease monotonically with advancing age or parity, the changes are small for pregnancy rates,

[14] The termination rates by number of pregnancies preceding first insertion are not shown, since results are essentially the same as those for the number of live births.

Table X-6. Cumulative Gross Rates and Standard Errors[a] per 100 First Insertions, at End of 12 Months, by Type of Termination, by Social and Demographic Characteristics

Characteristics	Number of wives	Cumulative gross rates at end of 12 months: Pregnancy	Expulsion	Removal	Total termination
Age of wife at first insertion					
13-24	895	6.6 ± 1.1	26.0 ± 1.8	34.8 ± 2.0	54.9 ± 1.9
25-29	2112	6.7 ± .7	17.0 ± .9	22.6 ± 1.1	40.1 ± 1.2
30-34	2109	5.7 ± .6	10.3 ± .7	15.6 ± .9	28.6 ± 1.1
35 and over	1521	3.7 ± .5	7.3 ± .7	14.1 ± 1.0	23.3 ± 1.1
Number of live births and stillbirths preceding first insertion					
0-1	201	5.4 ± 2.5	28.0 ± 3.7	51.3 ± 4.6	66.8 ± 3.6
2	772	7.0 ± 1.2	25.6 ± 1.9	32.5 ± 2.1	53.3 ± 2.0
3	1287	6.6 ± .9	17.9 ± 1.2	23.4 ± 1.4	41.3 ± 1.5
4	1388	6.1 ± .8	12.5 ± 1.0	18.3 ± 1.2	32.9 ± 1.4
5	1131	5.4 ± .8	9.7 ± 1.0	16.4 ± 1.2	28.6 ± 1.4
6-17	1857	4.2 ± .5	8.3 ± .7	12.9 ± .8	23.5 ± 1.0
Areal location					
Taichung, urban	2769	6.4 ± .6	15.2 ± .8	23.3 ± .9	39.2 ± 1.0
Taichung, rural	1331	5.3 ± .7	13.3 ± 1.0	20.3 ± 1.2	34.6 ± 1.4
Outside Taichung	2456	5.1 ± .5	11.9 ± .7	14.6 ± .8	28.6 ± .9
Husband's education					
No formal education	784	6.1 ± 1.0	11.8 ± 1.3	11.3 ± 1.9	26.5 ± 1.7
Primary school	3213	5.3 ± .5	12.9 ± .7	17.7 ± .8	32.1 ± .9
Junior high school	748	5.9 ± 1.1	15.0 ± 1.5	23.1 ± 1.8	38.6 ± 1.9
Senior high school or more	1816	5.7 ± .7	15.6 ± 1.0	25.0 ± 1.2	40.3 ± 1.3
Wife's education					
No formal education	2300	5.3 ± .6	12.0 ± .7	15.6 ± .9	29.7 ± 1.1
Primary school	3077	6.0 ± .5	14.4 ± .7	20.9 ± .8	36.4 ± .9
Junior high school	701	6.4 ± 1.2	13.7 ± 1.5	23.2 ± 1.9	37.9 ± 2.0
Senior high school or more	527	3.4 ± 1.0	16.7 ± 1.8	24.9 ± 2.2	39.6 ± 2.3
Type of device at first insertion					
Loop 1	4351	6.8 ± .5	12.9 ± .6	18.1 ± .7	33.5 ± .8
Loop 2-4	922	1.9 ± .5	11.5 ± 1.5	25.1 ± 3.0	35.0 ± 2.8
Coil	1372	3.4 ± .6	17.2 ± 1.1	23.6 ± 1.2	38.9 ± 1.3
Contraceptive methods used prior to first insertion					
None	4422	5.6 ± .4	15.0 ± .6	19.4 ± .7	35.4 ± .8
Ota ring	685	5.0 ± 1.0	8.5 ± 1.2	14.5 ± 1.5	25.6 ± 1.8
Other	1364	5.3 ± .7	11.6 ± 1.0	22.5 ± 1.3	35.2 ± 1.4

[a] In this and succeeding tables the standard errors are shown ± immediately following the rates.

Table X-6 (continued).

Characteristics	Number of wives	Cumulative gross rates at end of 12 months			
		Pregnancy	Expulsion	Removal	Total termination
Number of induced abortions prior to first insertion					
0	4797	5.7 ± .4	15.7 ± .6	19.7 ± .7	36.1 ± .7
1	1136	5.9 ± .8	9.7 ± 1.0	19.0 ± 1.3	31.2 ± 1.5
2	441	5.6 ± 1.3	5.9 ± 1.3	21.6 ± 2.2	30.4 ± 2.3
3-8	267	2.8 ± 1.1	6.3 ± 1.7	16.9 ± 2.5	24.4 ± 2.8
Outcome of pregnancy preceding first insertion					
Live birth	4994.	5.6 ± .4	15.2 ± .6	19.7 ± .6	35.7 ± .7
Induced abortion	1271	5.5 ± .7	8.3 ± .9	18.9 ± 1.2	29.7 ± 1.4
Other	253	6.6 ± 1.9	11.9 ± 2.2	21.6 ± 3.0	35.5 ± 3.2
Interval between last preceding live birth and first insertion[b/]					
0-3 months	592	2.8 ± .9	14.1 ± 1.7	19.6 ± 1.9	32.8 ± 2.1
3-6 months	856	3.2 ± .8	14.3 ± 1.4	23.4 ± 1.6	36.5 ± 1.8
6-12 months	1349	7.5 ± .9	16.4 ± 1.2	20.3 ± 1.3	38.3 ± 1.5
12 or more months	2154	6.1 ± .6	15.1 ± .9	18.0 ± 1.0	34.6 ± 1.1
Interval between end of last preceding pregnancy and first insertion					
0-3 months	1327	4.6 ± .7	11.7 ± 1.0	18.8 ± 1.2	31.6 ± 1.4
3-6 months	1090	4.1 ± .7	13.1 ± 1.2	22.7 ± 1.4	35.7 ± 1.6
6-9 months	786	7.4 ± 1.2	14.9 ± 1.5	22.0 ± 1.7	38.5 ± 1.9
9-12 months	734	7.4 ± 1.3	16.5 ± 1.6	19.9 ± 1.7	38.1 ± 2.0
12 or more months	2508	5.7 ± .6	14.0 ± .8	17.8 ± .9	33.3 ± 1.0
Total sample	6583	5.6 ± .3	13.6 ± .5	19.6 ± .6	34.4 ± .6

[b/] For wives whose last preceding pregnancy ended in a live birth.

larger for expulsion rates, and largest for removal rates. For example, according to the gross rates of Table X-7, in the absence of competing causes of loss, 83 per cent of women of less than second parity would have had the device removed within twenty-four months, as compared to only 22 per cent for women of parity six or higher.

Perhaps the physical systems of young or low-parity women tolerate the device less well and physical effects are more severe. Possibly, too, they are less willing, being at an early stage of their fam-

Table X-7. Cumulative Gross Rates and Standard Errors per 100 First Insertions, at End of 24 Months, by Type of Termination, by Social and Demographic Characteristics

Characteristics	Number of wives	Cumulative gross rates at end of 24 months			
		Pregnancy	Expulsion	Removal	Total termination
Age of wife at first insertion					
13-24	895	14.9 ± 3.1	32.0 ± 2.4	58.1 ± 3.0	75.8 ± 2.2
25-29	2112	15.0 ± 1.5	22.5 ± 1.3	40.1 ± 1.8	60.5 ± 1.5
30-34	2109	12.3 ± 1.2	13.9 ± 1.1	26.5 ± 1.4	44.6 ± 1.5
35 and over	1521	6.2 ± .8	9.5 ± 1.0	23.9 ± 1.6	35.4 ± 1.6
Number of live births and still-births preceding first insertion					
0-1	201	15.3 ± 9.7	36.8 ± 5.3	82.8 ± 6.0	90.8 ± 3.5
2	772	13.5 ± 2.9	30.5 ± 2.5	54.1 ± 3.3	72.4 ± 2.4
3	1287	14.7 ± 1.9	22.7 ± 1.6	41.9 ± 2.4	61.7 ± 2.0
4	1388	13.2 ± 1.5	16.9 ± 1.5	33.4 ± 2.0	51.9 ± 1.9
5	1131	11.0 ± 1.5	13.3 ± 1.4	27.2 ± 1.9	43.8 ± 2.0
6-17	1857	8.7 ± 1.0	11.2 ± 1.0	21.7 ± 1.4	36.5 ± 1.5
Areal location					
Taichung, urban	2769	12.4 ± 1.0	17.5 ± .9	38.9 ± 1.4	55.9 ± 1.2
Taichung, rural	1331	13.0 ± 1.5	17.9 ± 1.4	33.4 ± 1.8	52.4 ± 1.7
Outside Taichung	2456	8.4 ± .9	18.0 ± 1.4	24.2 ± 1.6	43.1 ± 1.6
Husband's education					
No formal education	784	8.4 ± 1.4	15.0 ± 1.6	22.8 ± 2.5	39.9 ± 2.4
Primary school	3213	12.2 ± 1.0	17.8 ± 1.0	29.8 ± 1.2	49.3 ± 1.2
Junior high school	748	11.3 ± 1.9	16.5 ± 1.6	38.3 ± 2.8	54.3 ± 2.4
Senior high school or more	1816	11.9 ± 1.4	18.2 ± 1.2	41.4 ± 1.9	57.8 ± 1.6
Wife's education					
No formal education	2300	9.7 ± 1.0	15.8 ± 1.0	27.0 ± 1.4	44.5 ± 1.4
Primary school	3077	13.1 ± 1.0	18.6 ± 1.0	34.3 ± 1.3	53.5 ± 1.2
Junior high school	701	11.2 ± 2.4	15.8 ± 1.8	43.3 ± 3.1	57.6 ± 2.8
Senior high school or more	527	11.3 ± 2.6	21.9 ± 2.7	40.9 ± 3.5	59.0 ± 3.1
Type of device at first insertion					
Loop 1	4351	13.4 ± .8	16.7 ± .8	31.4 ± 1.0	50.5 ± 1.0
Loop 2-4	922	1.9 ± .5	14.1 ± 2.9	43.4 ± 7.8	52.3 ± 6.8
Coil	1372	7.0 ± 1.1	21.2 ± 1.4	37.5 ± 1.8	54.2 ± 1.6
Contraceptive methods used prior to first insertion					
None	4422	12.1 ± .9	19.2 ± .8	33.3 ± 1.1	52.7 ± 1.1
Ota ring	685	8.8 ± 1.7	10.6 ± 1.5	28.4 ± 2.8	41.6 ± 2.7
Other	1364	10.9 ± 1.3	15.0 ± 1.3	35.2 ± 1.8	51.0 ± 1.1

Table X-7 (continued).

Characteristics	Number of wives	Cumulative gross rates at end of 24 months: Pregnancy	Expulsion	Removal	Total termination
Number of induced abortions prior to first insertion					
0	4794	12.4 ± .8	20.0 ± .8	34.0 ± 1.1	53.8 ± 1.0
1	1136	10.6 ± 1.5	13.4 ± 1.3	33.4 ± 2.2	48.5 ± 2.1
2	441	9.3 ± 1.9	7.8 ± 1.7	30.1 ± 2.8	41.6 ± 2.9
3-8	267	3.7 ± 1.5	6.3 ± 1.7	25.5 ± 3.9	32.9 ± 3.8
Outcome of pregnancy preceding first insertion					
Live birth	4994	12.5 ± .8	19.7 ± .8	34.4 ± 1.1	53.9 ± 1.0
Induced abortion	1271	8.4 ± 1.1	10.5 ± 1.1	29.6 ± 1.8	42.3 ± 1.8
Other	253	7.5 ± 2.1	14.9 ± 2.7	33.1 ± 4.5	47.4 ± 4.1
Interval between last preceding live birth and first insertion[a]					
0-3 months	592	18.6 ± 3.8	20.0 ± 2.6	39.6 ± 3.6	60.7 ± 3.2
3-6 months	856	12.2 ± 2.1	21.0 ± 2.1	38.3 ± 2.5	57.2 ± 2.3
6-12 months	1349	11.5 ± 1.4	21.1 ± 1.6	34.7 ± 2.1	54.3 ± 1.9
12 or more months	2154	11.7 ± 1.1	18.6 ± 1.1	31.5 ± 1.5	50.8 ± 1.4
Interval between end of last preceding pregnancy and first insertion					
0-3 months	1327	12.6 ± 1.7	15.3 ± 1.4	34.7 ± 2.1	51.7 ± 2.0
3-6 months	1090	11.2 ± 1.7	18.8 ± 1.8	36.2 ± 2.1	54.0 ± 2.0
6-9 months	786	11.6 ± 1.9	19.9 ± 2.1	36.7 ± 2.8	55.2 ± 2.5
9-12 months	734	11.6 ± 1.9	20.9 ± 2.1	31.5 ± 2.6	52.1 ± 2.4
12 or more months	2508	10.8 ± 1.0	17.3 ± 1.0	30.4 ± 1.4	48.6 ± 1.3
Total sample	6583	11.5 ± .7	17.5 ± .6	33.2 ± .9	51.3 ± .8

[a] For wives whose last preceding pregnancy ended in a live birth.

ily-building, to accept temporary discomfort from the IUD. Evidence from other aspects of the Taichung study supports the idea that motivational as well as physical factors are contributing to the wide variation in removal rates. Those women having insertions at low parities or young ages are very much in the minority among women like themselves. It is also clear that there is a strong consensus in Taiwan that three or four children and one or two sons is the desirable family composition. Among low-parity women a very small proportion said initially that they intended to have an IUD inserted, and among those who did, a smaller than average proportion actually carried out their expressed intentions. These results are consistent with the following interpretation: many women in Taiwan, and especially those of lower parity, are ambivalent about the use of contraception. Those of lower parity get minimum reinforcement of their interest in contraception from demographic pressure or from acquaintances in a similar situation. Therefore, they are most likely to yield to the counterpressures of their ambivalent situation. Low-parity women are least likely to have used contraception previously, to have expressed interest in adopting the IUD, or to carry through on an expressed intention to try it. Therefore, it is hardly surprising that they are also subject to very high removal rates.

2. Women coming from outside Taichung have pregnancy and expulsion rates barely lower but removal rates appreciably lower than do Taichung residents. The relatively greater distance that women from outside Taichung had to travel to reach the clinic may select for higher motivation, which expresses itself in a greater toleration of side effects.
3. Wives of highly educated husbands show slightly higher pregnancy and expulsion rates but substantially higher removal rates than wives of less-educated husbands. The same result in attenuated form obtains when classification is by wife's education. A first interpretation placed on this rather surprising result is that well-educated persons, having a wider range of family planning alternatives available to them, are less disposed to persist with IUD in the face of side effects. Results from the follow-up study covering the whole island indicate that the well educated more often turn to other methods after discontinuing IUD than do the less educated. It is shown later, however, that some of the tendency on the part of wives of educated husbands to have relatively high expulsion and removal rates depends on the fact that they are relatively young.
4. Users of loop 1 (small size) have lower removal rates than users of loops 2-4 (larger sizes). Unfortunately, users of the small loop also have appreciably higher pregnancy rates than the other group. This finding, anticipated in American work, prompted the eventual shift from the smaller size of loop to the larger sizes.

5. Those who have previously used the Ota ring display lower expulsion rates and lower removal rates than do women who have either practiced no previous contraception or some form of contraception other than the Ota ring. However, as will be demonstrated below, an important part of this differential depends on the fact that wearers of the Ota ring tend to be older. The Ota ring is an older form of IUD which was available from private practitioners before the official program began, so former users of this method had already had experience with this general class of contraception. The Ota ring was the most widely used type of contraception in Taiwan before the program, and it continues to be the method most often used outside of the official program.
6. The greater the number of previous induced abortions at time of insertion, the lower are rates of expulsion, removal, or pregnancy with the device in situ. For women having two or more induced abortions, the rate of expulsion is distinctively low. The persistence of this difference within age classes raises the possibility that repeated induced abortion affects the uterus in such a way as to make it more tolerant of an IUD.
7. This result is supported by the fact that women whose last pregnancy preceding first insertion ended in induced abortion have a lower expulsion rate than women whose preceding pregnancies ended either in a live birth or in an unintended pregnancy loss.
8. When the interval between the last preceding live birth and first insertion is short, the pregnancy rate after twelve months is relatively low, but after twenty-four months this contrast disappears. Presumably, postpartum amenorrhea holds down the pregnancy rate during the first few months following a live birth. This constraint on pregnancy is less noticeable when classification is by length of interval between preceding pregnancy and first insertion, as expected, since postpartum amenorrhea is shorter after a pregnancy that does not end in a live birth than after one that does.

   There is also a tendency for the pregnancy rate to decline as the interval between previous birth and insertion lengthens. This tendency can be shown to depend partly on age ties.
9. Not shown in Tables X-6 and X-7 are results obtained by classifying women into six-month groupings according to the calendar date of their first insertion. Here the basic issue is whether rates

of loss for women at the same interval after insertion change during the course of the thirty-month observation period. A reduction of the pregnancy rate is caused by the shift from the small loop 1 to larger sizes of loop. The analysis has therefore been restricted to users of loop 1. Essentially, no important differentials emerge. A small, if statistically significant, tendency is found on the part of women with recent insertions to have slightly lower pregnancy and expulsion rates than the majority with earlier insertions. Such an outcome is reasonable if pregnancies and expulsions are typically discovered after a delay, so that an insertion close to the cutoff date automatically reduces chances of detecting these events. It was originally theorized that rates of expulsion and removal would prove highest among the women having the most recent insertions. The reasoning was that these women would not be scheduled for a first visit before the end of the study, and therefore would not become part of the follow-up system at all unless they heeded the advice to come back to the clinic right away if they experienced a problem. Since they were selected on this basis, their rate of termination would naturally tend to be high. Perhaps this bias did operate, but involved so few women that it was offset by the suggested opposing bias.

10. In data not shown in the published tables it was found that the experimental program variables did not affect termination rates. For couples in the intensive cross-sectional sample survey only, there were no significant differences in cumulative gross twelve-month termination rates between the couples living in the lins receiving the following categories of treatment (see Chapter VI for definitions):

    a. Ehw with effective group meetings
    b. Other Ehw lins
    c. Ew with effective group meetings
    d. Ew lins
    e. Mail and Nothing lins

THE INTERACTION OF AGE AND PARITY

Attention is now turned to the interaction of the two strongest differentiators, age of wife and her parity (including stillbirths) at time of first insertion. In Tietze's analysis (see Table X-8), wife's age

Table X-8. Cumulative Rates at End of First Year, by Age Group by Parity, for Pregnancies, Expulsions, Removals for Bleeding and/or Pain: Loop D, First Insertion Three Months Post Partum or Later[a/]

	Age group			
Termination and parity	15-24	25-29	30-34	35-39
Number of insertions				
Parity 1 and 2	913	464	268	260
Parity 3 and 4	476	580	356	315
Parity 5 or more	66	272	310	259
Total	1455	1316	934	834
Pregnancy rate				
Parity 1 and 2	3.3 ± 0.7	2.6 ± 1.0	0.9 ± 0.7	0.0
Parity 3 and 4	3.6 ± 1.0	2.6 ± 0.8	1.3 ± 0.7	0.0
Parity 5 or more	*	3.7 ± 1.3	1.6 ± 0.8	2.3 ± 1.0
Expulsion rate**				
Parity 1 and 2	16.6 + 1.4	11.5 ± 1.7	5.6 ± 1.5	3.5 ± 1.3
Parity 3 and 4	15.0 ± 1.8	8.5 ± 1.3	5.6 ± 1.3	2.6 ± 1.0
Parity 5 or more	*	6.5 ± 1.6	4.9 ± 1.3	5.1 ± 1.5
Rate of removal for bleeding/pain				
Parity 1 and 2	15.3 ± 1.4	12.9 ± 1.9	13.3 ± 2.5	10.9 ± 2.5
Parity 3 and 4	9.0 ± 1.5	12.7 ± 1.6	10.3 ± 1.9	9.6 ± 1.9
Parity 5 or more	*	8.9 ± 1.9	6.6 ± 1.6	7.8 ± 1.9

[a/] Reproduced from C. Tietze, "Cooperative Statistical Program for the Evaluation of Intra-Uterine Devices: Sixth Progress Report," National Committee on Maternal Health, Inc., December 1965, Part II, Table 18.

* Not shown for less than 100 cases.

**Includes expulsions associated with pregnancies with device undetermined.

and parity (exclusive of stillbirths) are correlated moderately enough so that he could cross-classify women into twelve age-by-parity groups and still obtain adequate frequencies in most subclasses. In the Taichung sample, age and parity are more closely correlated, so that more of the same subclasses lack sufficient cases to produce rates stable enough to be useful. Nevertheless, for the sake of comparison, Tietze's classification is retained in Table X-9 and the data are restricted to one type of loop and to removals for medical reasons only.

The main findings of the American experience (Table X-8) are that: (1) pregnancy rates are lower for those combinations of age and parity that are associated with lower average fecundity; (2) expulsion rates decline with advancing age, and within age classes are relatively insensitive to parity level; (3) in contrast, removal rates decline as parity increases but within parity classes exhibit little relationship to age.

Table X-9. Gross Cumulative Termination Rates and Standard Errors per 100 First Insertions, at the End of 12 Months, by Type of Termination, by Wife's Age and Parity at Time of First Insertion, for Users of Loop 1 Only

Termination and parity[a]	Age group 13-24	25-29	30-34	35 and over
Pregnancy				
0-2	11.0 ± 2.5	9.0 ± 3.0	(8.4 ± 5.7)[c]	[b]
3-4	7.8 ± 2.4	8.4 ± 1.2	9.3 ± 1.6	3.7 ± 1.8
5 or more	[b]	7.0 ± 1.9	6.9 ± 1.0	4.0 ± .8
Expulsion				
0-2	35.3 ± 3.2	28.7 ± 4.1	(14.2 ± 7.7)[c]	[b]
3-4	24.1 ± 3.8	17.0 ± 1.4	10.8 ± 1.6	5.4 ± 2.1
5 or more	[b]	7.5 ± 1.8	9.3 ± 1.1	6.5 ± .9
Removal for medical reasons				
0-2	28.9 ± 3.3	26.9 ± 4.1	(17.2 ± 7.9)[c]	[b]
3-4	22.2 ± 3.6	18.6 ± 1.5	13.1 ± 1.7	19.5 ± 3.6
5 or more	[b]	12.4 ± 2.3	12.9 ± 1.2	10.9 ± 1.2
Total terminations				
0-2	59.1 ± 3.0	52.6 ± 4.1	(34.9 ± 9.4)[c]	[b]
3-4	45.5 ± 4.0	38.1 ± 1.8	29.7 ± 2.3	26.6 ± 3.9
5 or more	[b]	24.6 ± 2.9	26.4 ± 1.6	20.0 ± 1.5

[a] The measure of parity includes still births as well as births.

[b] Under 25 wives belonging to this class.

[c] Only 30 wives belonging to this class.

The Taichung results (Table X-9) are less consistent, but conform in general to the American conclusions (Table X-8). Agreement between the two sets of results is poorest for pregnancy rates. For Taichung, pregnancy rates are somewhat lower for the oldest group, while changes over the first three age classes are slight. Nor is there any tendency for pregnancy rates to increase with higher parity within age classes, as is the case in the American data.

In the case of removals, Taichung results are more consistent with American experience. Rates of removal for medical reasons decline primarily as a function of parity and show little response to age within parity classes. Expulsion rates in Taichung tend to decline with advancing age within parity groups. Expulsion rates also decline with increasing parity in the two younger age classes but not in the two older age classes. Overall, the total termination rates decrease substantially with increasing parity within every age class. Among women of less than fifth parity, there is also a substantial decline in termination rates with increasing age, within two parity classes.

PARITY AND THE DESIRE FOR ADDITIONAL CHILDREN

For those couples in the intensive cross-sectional sample survey, it was possible to consider whether their desire for additional children had an effect on termination rates independent of parity, although the small number of cases required grouping into the following broad categories:

Cumulative Gross Total Termination Rates at 12 Months:

Did wife want more children at end of 1962?	*No. of children already born by end of 1962*		
	Less than three	*Three or four*	*Five or more*
No	51	39	28
Yes	61	43	28

Parity continues to be very important whether or not additional children were wanted at that point, just before the program began. Wanting more children made a substantial difference at very low parities. Apparently demographic pressures were dominant, overriding preferences about children when the number exceeded the number considered ideal in Taichung.

HOW AGE AFFECTS OTHER TERMINATION DIFFERENTIALS

Since age and parity at first insertion are such strong discriminators, the possibility exists that other variables yield differentials entirely or partially on the basis of associations with age or parity. To check this possibility, each independent variable has been cross-tabulated with age and number of pregnancies at time of first insertion. Examples of two independent variables whose correlations with age and parity are not close enough to affect termination patterns are place of residence (inside or outside Taichung) and type of device first inserted.

When a sizable association was found with age, as was the case for education of husband, a procedure of indirect standardization was applied to see how much of the original differentiation remained after age differences were taken into account. As an example, consider removal rates as differentiated by education of husband. For each class based on husband's education, an expected cumulative rate of removals was calculated on the assumption that class members share the same age-specific removal rates as the entire sample.[15] This expected rate is then subtracted from the observed removal rate of the class as a measure of the effect of husband's education when the effect of wife's age is eliminated.

The results of applying this procedure to pregnancy, expulsion, removal, and total termination rates, taken at durations of twelve and twenty-four months, are given in Table X-10 for two variables: education of husband and type of contraceptive used prior to first insertion. After eliminating the effects of age in this way, the differentials for husband's education and prior contraceptive practice are considerably less than is the case without such adjustment (compare the results in Table X-10 with those in Tables X-6 and X-7). For example, with respect to total terminations, the reduction amounts to about 50 per cent. Thus the differentials generated by previous contracep-

Table X-10. Differences Between Observed and Age-standardized Gross Cumulative Termination Rates per 100 First Insertions, at End of 12 and 24 Months, by Type of Termination, for Two Characteristics

	12 months of use				24 months of use			
Characteristics	P	E	R	T	P	E	R	T
Contraceptive methods used prior to first insertion								
None	.3	.6	-1.3	- .2	- .2	.4	-2.2	- .4
Ota ring	.1	-2.7	-2.8	-4.4	-1.8	-4.2	-1.3	-4.1
Other	-.1	-1.6	3.3	1.7	- .9	-2.2	2.0	.7
Husband's education								
No formal education	.9	.2	-6.6	-4.2	-2.2	- .2	-7.7	-6.6
Primary school	-.2	- .3	-1.6	-1.3	.3	.7	-3.3	- .8
Junior high school	.1	- .4	1.2	1.3	-1.4	-3.4	1.0	- .7
Senior high school or more	-.2	.2	3.4	3.3	- .8	-1.6	4.2	2.9

P = pregnancy; E = expulsion; R = removal; T = total termination

15 More specifically, an expected ratio is calculated by using the age composition of the education of husband class as a set of weights for the age-specific removal rates observed in the entire sample.

tive experience and husband's education can be accounted for in part, though certainly not entirely, by their association with wife's age. Similarly, it can be shown that age ties contribute to the lower pregnancy rates found among women for whom the interval between last previous pregnancy (or birth) and first insertion is longer than twelve months.

The independent effect of number of previous abortions beyond its obvious association with age is shown in Table X-11. Here rates of loss

Table X-11. Gross Cumulative Termination Rates and Standard Errors per 100 First Insertions, at End of 12 Months, by Type of Termination, by Wife's Age and Number of Induced Abortions Prior to First Insertion

Type of termination and number of induced abortions	Age group		
	29 or less	30-34	35 or more
Pregnancy			
0	6.7 ± .7	5.5 ± .7	3.9 ± .7
1	6.1 ± 1.4	7.4 ± 1.6	3.6 ± 1.2
2-8	8.9 ± 2.9	3.8 ± 1.3	3.3 ± 1.1
Expulsion			
0	21.4 ± 1.0	11.6 ± .9	7.9 ± 1.0
1	12.7 ± 1.9	8.7 ± 1.5	7.2 ± 1.6
2-8	8.1 ± 2.6	5.3 ± 1.6	5.8 ± 1.5
Removal			
0	25.8 ± 1.1	15.1 ± 1.0	12.4 ± 1.2
1	27.5 ± 2.6	15.7 ± 2.0	13.6 ± 2.0
2-8	23.8 ± 3.9	18.2 ± 2.7	19.3 ± 2.4
Total termination			
0	45.5 ± 1.1	29.1 ± 1.3	22.5 ± 1.5
1	40.6 ± 2.7	28.8 ± 2.4	22.6 ± 2.4
2-8	36.2 ± 4.2	25.5 ± 3.0	26.5 ± 2.6

for women with varying numbers of prior induced abortions are examined within three age classes. Modest differentials persist with respect to expulsion, though not in the case of pregnancy or removals.

The discussion of differentials has so far been based entirely on data for the first segment. If all segments are considered (Tables X-12 and X-13), the very marked relationship of the termination rates to parity and age persists and tends to be somewhat strengthened, although the levels of the rates are lower. The differences between relationships and the rates for first segment only and those for all segments are especially marked in the case of expulsions, which are most likely to be followed by reinsertions. Expulsion rates are

Table X-12. Cumulative 12 Month Gross Termination Rates, by Type of Terminations, for First Insertions and for All Insertions[a/] by Age of Wife, and by Number of Live Births and Still Births Preceding First Insertion

	Pregnancy		Expulsion		Removal		Total terminations	
Characteristics	1st segment	All segments	1st segment	All segments	1st segment	All segments	1st segment	All segments
Age of wife at first insertion								
Under 25	6.6	5.3	26.0	15.3	34.8	30.9	54.9	44.6
25-29	6.7	5.4	17.0	8.9	22.6	20.5	40.1	31.5
30-34	5.7	4.5	10.3	4.4	15.6	14.0	28.6	21.5
35 and over	3.7	3.1	7.3	3.4	14.1	12.3	23.3	17.9
Number of live births and still births preceding first insertion								
0-1	(5.4)[b/]	(4.9)	(28.0)	(22.2)	(51.3)	(46.8)	(66.8)	(60.7)
2	7.0	5.1	25.6	15.9	32.5	28.5	53.3	43.0
3	6.6	5.4	17.9	9.6	23.4	21.2	41.3	32.7
4	6.1	4.8	12.5	4.8	18.3	16.5	32.9	24.3
5	5.4	4.2	9.7	4.7	16.4	14.4	28.6	21.8
6 or more	4.2	3.7	8.3	3.4	12.9	11.6	23.5	17.8
Total	5.6	4.5	13.6	6.9	19.6	17.6	34.4	26.8

[a/] See the footnote in Table X-4.

[b/] Rates in parentheses are based on less than 100 wives exposed at the beginning of 12 months.

highest and reinsertion rates lowest for the young and low-parity women. The result is that the ratio between the expulsion rates for the youngest and oldest women at twelve months is five to one for all segments, but less than four to one for the first segments.

TIME TRENDS IN TYPES OF TERMINATION

With the analysis of the differentials in hand, it is useful to return to a more general consideration of the distinctively different curves of monthly risk shown for pregnancy, expulsion, and removal in Figure 3. It is worthwhile to speculate on the kind of processes that must be generating these curves. Only the expulsion rate starts high and progressively decreases, and therefore fits a model of widely varying expulsion risk and progressive elimination of the women prone to expulsion. Further evidence for this view comes from American experience, which shows that the risk of expulsion is much

Table X-13. Cumulative 24 Month Gross Termination Rates, by Type of Termination, for First Insertion and All Insertions,[a] by Wife's Age and by Number of Live Births and Still Births at First Insertion

Characteristics	Pregnancy 1st segment	Pregnancy All segments	Expulsion 1st segment	Expulsion All segments	Removal 1st segment	Removal All segments	Total terminations 1st segment	Total terminations All segments
Age of wife at first insertion								
Under 25	(14.9)[b]	(12.2)	(32.0)	(25.4)	(58.1)	(51.2)	(75.8)	(68.1)
25-29	15.0	10.9	22.5	13.2	40.1	35.8	60.5	50.3
30-34	12.3	9.4	13.9	6.9	26.5	23.9	44.6	35.8
35 and over	6.2	4.9	9.5	5.2	23.9	21.0	35.4	28.8
Number of live births and still births preceding first insertion								
0-1	(15.3)	(14.9)	(36.8)	(34.3)	(82.8)	(77.9)	(90.8)	(87.7)
2	(13.5)	(9.7)	(30.5)	(22.2)	(54.1)	(48.2)	(72.4)	(63.6)
3	14.7	10.8	22.7	15.8	41.9	37.9	61.7	53.3
4	13.2	9.5	16.9	8.2	33.4	29.3	51.9	41.3
5	11.0	8.9	13.3	6.2	27.2	24.2	43.8	35.2
6 or more	8.7	6.9	11.2	5.7	21.7	19.3	36.5	29.2
Total	11.5	8.8	17.5	10.4	33.2	30.0	51.3	42.5

[a] See the footnote in Table X-4.

[b] Rates in parentheses based on less than 100 cases exposed at the beginning of 24 months.

higher after a reinsertion.[16] Presumably physical factors are dominant in determining expulsion risk, since the very different behavior exhibited by expulsion and removal rates as a function of length of time since insertion casts doubt upon the hypothesis that many of the expulsions are merely disguised removals.

The monthly pregnancy rate, which is relatively low and only declines very gradually, fits the idea of a set of uniformly low pregnancy risks among IUD wearers. If nearly all wearers have fixed low monthly risks of pregnancy, then variation with respect to pregnancy risk among women is small at any time. This necessarily means that change in risk composition is slow, with the result that a very gradual decline in the monthly pregnancy rate is observed. If this view is correct, it means that gross monthly pregnancy rates are relatively insensitive to competing levels of expulsion and removal. The frequencies

[16] C. Tietze, "History and Statistical Evaluation of the Intra-Uterine Contraceptive Device," *American Journal of Public Health*, 55, No. 12, December 1965, 447.

of pregnancies and expulsions, or pregnancies and removals, show only modest positive correlations in association with age or parity. Otherwise, study of Tables X-6 and X-7 reveals no conspicuous tendency for the cumulative pregnancy rate to vary with the size of either the cumulative expulsion or the removal rates.

The monthly rate of removals for medical reasons is relatively high and only declines very slowly. It is hardly plausible to assume that most women share removal risks close to the monthly rates observed for the whole sample, inasmuch as the marked differentials in removal rates by age and parity indicate a wide variation of monthly risks. The gradual decline in monthly rates, coupled with the inferred wide variation of risk among women, means that for some women at least the monthly risk of removal for medical reasons is rising as the length of time since insertion increases. This maintains the monthly average nearly at a level, even though disproportionately many of the younger women prone to removal have already been eliminated.

Presumably, motivational as well as physical factors figure in the determination of removal risks. One conjectures that a woman whose system is intolerant of IUD would experience relatively more severe symptoms and thereby would be predisposed to greater than average risks of both expulsion and removal. That is, risks of removal and expulsion are positively correlated. Tables X-6 and X-7 make it clear that in association with age and parity such a positive correlation does exist. Hence one cannot assume that the competing risks of removal and expulsion are independent. As a consequence, slightly lower gross monthly rates of removal will be calculated when the competing level of expulsion is higher; and conversely, slightly lower gross monthly rates of expulsion will be calculated when competing levels of removal are higher. However, the fact that expulsions are not the chief source of loss reduces the effects of competing levels of expulsion upon gross rates of removal. The fact that most expulsions occur in the early months, before a large number of removals have cumulated, reduces the effects of competing levels of removal upon calculated gross expulsion rates.

COMPARISON OF THE IUD AND TRADITIONAL METHODS

In the Taichung study a significant minority of women accepted traditional[17] methods of contraception rather than the IUD. A com-

[17] For a definition of traditional methods, see Chapter III.

parison of these two types of acceptors after six months of use clearly indicates that IUD acceptors had much higher rates of continuation and much lower pregnancy rates. Nevertheless, those accepting traditional methods had pregnancy rates significantly below the level to be expected without such protection. Moreover, many of those giving up the traditional methods switched to other, more reliable methods.

The 921 couples who accepted traditional methods in the intensive phase of the Taichung program (February-October, 1963) were contacted after six months. In Table X-14 we show the results of this follow-up, with percentages based on both the total number of cases and the total minus the cases not found for the follow-up. Unfortunately, those who accepted traditional methods were not followed up as persistently as the IUD acceptors. The loss to follow-up of approximately 17 per cent of those choosing traditional methods is regrettable, although not excessive for studies of this type. In the following discussion we cite in most cases two percentages: the lower one is based on all the cases, and the higher on the cases actually followed up.

Between 48 and 58 per cent of the wives reported "continuing" use of the traditional method, with an additional 5 per cent reporting current use with previous periods of interruption. Since it is difficult to know just what is meant by "continuous" or "regular" use of traditional methods, the most we can say is that after six months about one-half to two-thirds of the couples reported current use of the method, with most indicating that they had used the method regularly.

A significant minority of the couples—13 to 16 per cent—had switched to a more effective, "continuous" method during this period. Between 11 and 13 per cent switched to IUD under the formal program. About 2 per cent obtained Ota rings from private practitioners. One per cent were sterilized.

A small number of women—about 2 per cent—discontinued use of the method in order to have another child. In addition, 8 to 10 per cent discontinued for various other reasons. Approximately 2 per cent of the women reported that they had never used the contraceptive they accepted.

Between 5 and 6 per cent of the couples discontinued because of an unintended pregnancy. We do not know whether the pregnancy occurred while the contraception was being used regularly. It is likely that there were a significant number of pregnancies among those who could not be followed up for various reasons. Women who became pregnant may have avoided the interviewer. It is likely that some of the fourteen women who reported discontinuing use to have a planned pregnancy were rationalizing an unintended pregnancy after the fact, so we have calculated pregnancy rates both including and excluding those pregnancies.

The pregnancy rate per hundred woman-years of exposure is between 14.8 and 21.8, depending on the assumptions made.[18] This is far below the rate expected, if the women were completely unprotected. Between 6 and 8 per cent of the women followed up reported a pregnancy during this six-month period. The net cumulative pregnancy rate for the IUD at six months is about 2 per cent. The IUD rate makes no allowance for pregnancies after a final IUD termination, but this is not likely to be a substantial omission since at six months the number of IUD cases that had been subject to the risk of post-termination pregnancy is small.

A very rough comparison of the continuation and pregnancy rates at the end of six months is as follows:

	Traditional Method	*IUD*
Cumulative % pregnant at 6 months	7	2
% terminating use of the original method[19]	36-42	16-21

Clearly, the IUD had the better record as to either pregnancies or terminations. As Table X-14 indicates, however, many of those giving up the traditional methods took up other birth control practices. If we add to those continuing at least irregular use of a traditional method those who adopted another contraceptive method or were sterilized, about 80 per cent of all the couples were currently protected,

[18] The low value is derived by excluding pregnancies reported as intended and by including in the denominator as part of the risk period all of the months from initial insertion to the date of follow-up. The high value counts all pregnancies, whether or not reported as intended ones, and for cases of pregnancy and termination it counts in the risk period only half of the time between initial acceptance and the follow-up date. Data were not obtained on the exact dates at which pregnancies or other terminations occurred within the six-month period covered.

[19] For traditional methods the range depends on including or excluding intermittent use. For the IUD the range depends on whether first or all insertions are considered.

Table X-14. Contraceptive Status at Six Months Follow-Up of Acceptors of "Traditional" Methods in Taichung, February-October 1963, Percentage Distributions

Contraceptive status at six months follow-up	Percentage Distribution	
	All cases	All cases, excluding those with "no information"
Still using the method, regular use	48.3	58.0
Still using the method, irregular use	4.6	5.5
Changed to the IUD	10.9	13.0
Changed to the Ota Ring	1.5	1.8
Was sterilized	1.2	1.4
Discontinued, unintended pregnancy	5.2	6.3
Discontinued, planned pregnancy	1.5	1.8
Discontinued for other reasons	8.1	9.8
Never used the method, although "accepted"	2.0	2.4
No information, no follow-up attempted	5.2	--
No information, other reasons	11.5	--
Total per cent	100.0	100.0
Number	921	767

at least to some degree, at six months, and 16 per cent of the original group were practicing more reliable methods than those first adopted. Chapter XII contains preliminary data showing that six months after insertion 75 per cent or more of the Taichung IUD cases were currently protected by contraception or abortion, the exact proportion varying with the definition used. Clearly, those who begin to use either traditional or newer methods in Taiwan and Taichung include many highly motivated and highly fecundable women for whom termination of one method does not mean an end to family planning practice.

SOME IMPORTANT IMPLICATIONS FOR POLICY

The reader who has followed us through a somewhat technical discussion may find some reward in the fact that the substantive results include some rather startling differentials which may have important implications both for social policy and for further scientific study of reproduction.

First of all, the contrast between the relatively low termination rates for the older women of higher parity and the very high termination rates for the younger women of lower parity constitutes a serious challenge to the view that reaching the older women in a family planning program has little value. This is a view often advanced with respect to sterilization as well as the IUD, on the grounds, for example, that women in their thirties or in the sixth parity are unlikely to have many more children, so that their participation in a family planning program is of little consequence. Of course, it is obviously true that a family planning program will have the most effect if it reaches young women before they have many children and if they persist in effective contraceptive practice once they begin.

However, in Taichung the termination rates for the younger and low-parity women are so much greater than those for the older women of higher parity that the effects of insertions for the older women could be much greater, even if their fecundability was substantially lower than that of the younger women. Reaching highly fecundable younger women does little good if they do not persist in their contraceptive practice.

The significance of the high continuation rates for the older women may be even greater if another often-neglected fact is taken into account: those older women of higher parity who accept an IUD or other contraceptive service in a family planning program are very likely to be a selected group with much higher fecundability than the average women of their age class: that is precisely why they are likely to be accepting contraception. Therefore, they are capable of producing quite a few additional children. The implication of some writing on this subject is that a woman of 30 who has six children has somehow used up her fixed quota. Since she has reached the sixth parity so quickly because she is highly fecundable, and since she is likely to have demonstrated her continuing fecundity only recently, she may be quite capable of adding another six children or more to her family and to the nation's population.

The significance of contraceptive practice for older women is indicated by the fact that almost all of the 21 per cent decline in the birth rate of Taiwan between 1959 and 1965 was a result of declines at these older ages.

Of course, it is true that there is a definite upper limit to the possible effect of declines at older ages and higher parities on total fertility trends. The point is, however, that there is a considerable range for influence in these older ages and higher parities where the beginning of a decline is likely to occur, since these are the women who are likely to feel the demographic pressure which motivates action. It is less likely that action will begin with the younger women, who must project themselves into a future situation in which the problem will exist for them. It seems more likely that they will initiate action at an early stage of the family life-cycle if they have the example of the older women as a model. Of course, there must be some trend before too long toward the acceptance of contraception at earlier ages and parities. There is some evidence that such a downward shift has already begun in Taiwan:

	IUD acceptances for:	
% of all acceptors in period who:	*January-June 1964*	*July-December 1966*
Were under 30 years old	27	39
Had fewer than four children	30	40

These observations on the significance of the termination rates by age and parity gain added importance from the fact that the general patterns observed in Taichung are repeated not only for Taiwan as a whole, but also, so far as comparable data exist, in Korea, India, Thailand, and the United States.

Another finding with major implications for policy is the fact that the chief cause for IUD loss in the present sample is removal for medical reasons, the rate of which continues high even after twelve or eighteen months of use. In contrast, the expulsion rate has dropped to a low level by the end of the first year, while the pregnancy rate is relatively low as compared to the removal rate, especially when the larger sizes of loop are employed. Obviously, then, to achieve any substantial improvement in the retention rate for the IUD, ways must be found to lower rates of removal for medical reasons.

The fact that termination rates depend so much on removals also suggests that it will not be easy to generalize the results of the IUD follow-up studies from one population or country to another. If the biological phenomena represented by pregnancy and expulsion were the dominant factors in terminations, the argument might be made that the cultural variations would be minimal, permitting generalizations from almost any reasonable sample of one population to another population, although even such biological events may have cultural correlates and associated genetic differences. Nevertheless, voluntary removals much more obviously involve a complex of cultural variables, including the readiness of women to accept discomfort, the doctor's medical philosophy and knowledge, and the availability of alternative forms of birth control.

The fact that the rates for removal, the dominant cause of termination, are highly correlated with age and parity further means that total termination rates will depend on the present stage of fertility decline and of spread of family planning in a society, which in turn will affect the age and parity of those available to enter a program. All of this suggests that IUD termination rates cannot be extrapolated from one population to another without very careful study. Even within a single society the extrapolation from one particular population stratum to the whole society is very risky if the sample studied is different in pertinent ways from the total population. If the goal is to describe the termination and continuation pattern of a heterogeneous population, the only safe procedure is to do this on the basis of a good probability sample of the population of IUD cases to be described. The frequent practice of basing IUD studies on special clinic samples or on the population of experimental health areas or other special populations of this type is especially suspect as a basis for generalizing to a whole population. These special clinic or "model area" populations frequently receive a quality of medical care and other attention that is not generally available and that potentially may affect termination rates considerably. For example, intensive clinic sample studies in Korea have much lower termination rates than probability samples of all of the Korean women ever accepting an IUD.[20] The Taichung Medical Follow-Up study has the merit of

[20] The Seoul National University Medical School has had under its supervision a special cooperative clinical study of the IUD. The cumulative termination rate for first insertions after twelve months was 22.5 for a group of 5,771 women who had insertions at five medical school hospitals and one private maternity hospital and were observed from January 1963 through June 1967. For details, see H. S. Shin and S. W. Kim, "Extended Clinical Trial with IUD in Korea: Fourth Progress Report, June 20, 1967," Department of Obstetrics and Gynecology, Seoul National University Medical School, mimeographed. The Yonsei University College of Medicine has had under its supervision a special field study of the IUD, in which extensive follow-up visits by fieldworkers have been maintained. The cumulative termination rate for first insertions after twelve months was 33.2 for a group of 2,283 women who had their insertions between January 1964 and December 1966. For details of this study, see J. M. Yang, S. Bang, and S. W. Song, "Progress Report of the Koyang Family Planning Action-Cum-Research Project (April 1962-March 1967)," Department Preventive Medicine and Public Health, Yonsei University College of Medicine, mimeographed. The corresponding termination rate for a

representing all of the IUD insertions in a large scale program for a whole city. However, since the program for the whole city had unusual medical supervision and follow-up, it is not surprising that the Taichung retention rates are higher than those for Taiwan as a whole.

If it is difficult to generalize termination rates from one population to another, it is even more risky to attempt to develop some universal coefficient that will translate number of IUD insertions made to "number of births averted," as is often done. The number of births that will be averted depends in the first place on the termination rate, which is not a constant. It also depends on other factors which are not constant: on the fertility of the couples prior to the insertion, on what they would do if there were no insertion, and on what they do about alternate methods of birth control when the use of the IUD is terminated. All of these factors depend on the situation in the population. For example, even with fixed termination rate these other variables will depend on the proportion of the IUD acceptors who were already limiting their fertility in other ways and the proportion of those terminating who adopt alternate methods of limitation. Administrators who impatiently demand a fixed universal number that translates acceptances into births averted without research on the local situation can be given an answer, of course, by making an arbitrary set of assumptions. The results are unlikely to be realistic.

---

probability sample of 4,796 women representing the 329,508 women who had their first insertions in Korea in 1964 and 1965 was 37.6. See *National Intra-Uterine Contraception Report*, Ministry of Health and Social Affairs, Republic of Korea, June 1967.

XI. The Pre-Program Fertility of Acceptors

AN INITIAL OVERVIEW

If the couples who accept the services of a family planning program are of above average fecundability, the potential effect of the program on birth rates is obviously enhanced. Many of those who accept in the Taichung program and elsewhere are women over 30 and of relatively high parity. Since women over 30 have on the average, much lower fertility than younger women, this has led many observers to a pessimistic view of the extent to which family planning programs can succeed in reducing fertility. However, the Taichung acceptors, whether over or under 30, were a selected high-fertility group. A greater concentration of acceptances among younger women would undoubtedly increase the potential effect of the program, and acceptances from older women can be only the first stage in any program to reduce fertility. However, the relatively high fertility of acceptors in Taichung, whatever their age, makes the possible consequence of the present acceptance pattern much greater than most observers had supposed.

The following summary of substantive results is presented as a background for the more detailed discussion below:

1. Acceptors had much higher recent fertility rates than non-acceptors.
2. Among acceptors, recent fertility rates were much higher for those who had not previously used birth control than for those who had. For acceptors without prior birth control experience, recent fertility rates at ages 30-39 were 70 to 90 per cent above the average rate for their age group and 50 to 80 per cent above the rates for acceptors with prior experience.
3. This means that the distribution of the acceptors between these two categories—those with and those without previous family limitation experience—has an important effect on any comparison of fertility rates for acceptors and non-acceptors.
4. Among those with prior birth control experience, the acceptors had much higher recent fertility than the non-acceptors. Apparent-

ly many non-acceptors among the prior users were successful in limiting their fertility without the assistance of the formal program, perhaps partly through luck.

5. While all of these generalizations apply to both the 20-29 and 30-39 age groups, the differentials and relationships are very much greater at older ages than at younger.
6. For acceptors without prior family limitation experience, the recent fertility rates at ages 30-39 were as high as the average rate for the whole 20-29 age group.
7. The higher fertility of the acceptors is not only evident in the recent past; it goes back many years. If the higher fertility were only a recent phenomenon it would have little significance for the future, because it might be a temporary, chance trend not necessarily continuing into the future. That this higher fertility has persisted over a considerable period makes it plausible that the acceptors may have relatively high fecundability that would be likely to affect future fertility as well.

THE DATA

We have seen in earlier analyses that the more recent the last birth, the higher the acceptance rate. But reliance on the last birth alone provides too limited a perspective in terms of time. In the first place, chance will play too great a part in the timing of any single birth and in determining whether any particular birth interval is long or short. Secondly, to estimate the effect of any given number of acceptances on future fertility, it is desirable to have comparable fertility rates for specific periods of prior years for non-acceptors and for various types of acceptors. This permits both comparison with other data and projection to future years. We have arbitrarily chosen for initial examination the three years and five years preceding the program, as periods that a priori seem long enough to average out some of the chance effects and short enough to represent the experience likely to motivate most strongly any current action on family limitation.

Table XI-1 shows the average annual fertility rates, for the three-year and five-year periods preceding the first interview of the Intensive Survey, of women married throughout the periods in question. The couples are classified as "acceptors" or "non-acceptors" as of July 1, 1965—approximately two and a half years after the start of the program.

Table XI-1. Fertility Rates per Annum in Three Years[a] and Five Years[a] Preceding the First Intensive Interview, by Whether Acceptor in Program by July 1965, by Prior Use of Contraception or Abortion, by Age of Wif

Acceptance status and prior use of contraception	Fertility rates for previous: 3 years	Fertility rates for previous: 5 years	Relative fertility rates[b] for previous: 3 years	Relative fertility rates[b] for previous: 5 years	Number of couples in base for 3-year rates	Number of couples in base for 5-year rates
			Current age: 20-29			
Sterilized by second interview	297	340	71	84	46	43
All acceptors	475	452	114	111	155	112
Prior users[c]	421	429	101	106	53	35
Prior non-users[c]	503	462	121	114	102	77
Non-acceptors: prior users	380	413	91	102	187	142
Non-acceptors: prior non-users	424	396	102	98	477	303
Total	417	406	100	100	865	600
			Current age: 30-39			
Sterilized by second interview	113	152	50	61	204	202
All acceptors	338	358	150	143	214	212
Prior users	243	282	108	113	103	103
Prior non-users	426	429	189	172	111	109
Non-acceptors: prior users	189	224	84	90	369	363
Non-acceptors: prior non-users	251	262	112	105	480	471
Total	225	250	100	100	1267	1248
			All ages			
Sterilized by second interview	147	185	49	62	250	245
All acceptors	396	390	131	130	369	324
Prior users	303	319	100	106	156	138
Prior non-users	463	443	153	148	213	186
Non-acceptors: prior users	253	277	83	92	556	505
Non-acceptors: prior non-users	338	315	112	105	957	774
Total	303	300	100	100	2132	1848

[a] Calculated only for women married throughout the period.

[b] Ratio of fertility rates to total for age group.

[c] Prior users had used contraception and/or abortion prior to the first intensive survey.

It is important that the reference dates for the fertility rates all end at a common point, just before the program began. If, instead, we had measured fertility back from the varying acceptance dates, we would have maximized the influence of very recent births and the chance component in fecundability. This would have made the relative fertility of the acceptors even higher than it is in our tabulations.

Those couples sterilized by the time of the second interview (October-December 1963) are shown separately, since they were obviously ineligible to become acceptors during the entire period or most of it. The acceptors are not only considered as a single group, but are subclassified according to whether or not they had previously used a birth control method (i.e., abortion and/or contraception). Those non-acceptors who were prior users are also treated separately, since both their recent fertility and their status as non-acceptors may be affected by prior practice of family limitation.

The data are shown separately for women 20-29 and those 30-39, as well as for the total sample. In Table XI-1 the fertility rates are shown not only in absolute terms, but also as indices relative to the fertility rate for all women of the same age group and period of observation.

FERTILITY RATES FOR THE FIVE-YEAR PERIOD, BY ACCEPTANCE STATUS

The recent fertility rate for acceptors is much higher than the average rate for the total sample (Table XI-1). The relative fertility of the acceptors as compared with non-acceptors is much higher for women in their thirties than for those in their twenties. This is consistent with earlier findings that the correlation between demographic variables and acceptances is much greater for older women than for younger. It is also consistent with the view that at this stage of demographic development in Taiwan interest in family limitation develops only after the presence of the three or four children almost universally desired begins to generate pressures on daily life and on aspirations. In Taiwan most women reach this stage in their early thirties rather than in their twenties.

In the case of women in their thirties, the fertility rates for all acceptors were 50 per cent higher than the average at that age for the three-year period and 43 per cent higher for the five-year period. For women in their twenties, fertility rates for all acceptors are higher than the average by a much smaller margin.

The amount by which the fertility of the acceptors over the three-year period exceeds the average depends on whether the acceptors had used some form of family limitation before the program began. Prior use of family planning methods, even if not too effective, should and does reduce fertility in the aggregate, at least to some extent. Among acceptors in their thirties, fertility rates were only 8 per cent above average for prior users, but 89 per cent above average for those who were not prior users. At ages 20-29, the fertility rates for acceptors were 1 per cent and 21 per cent above average for prior users and non-users respectively. This difference in the rates of acceptors with and without prior family limitation experience is much greater for older women than for younger. Under current Taiwan conditions, the women in their twenties who have used family limitation have usually begun late—that is, very recently—so that the effect of their use on fertility rates for the preceding three or five years will be relatively small. These results are important for assessing IUD programs, because they mean that the projection of recent differential fertility trends into the future will depend on the previous level of use of family limitation outside the program, among both the acceptors and non-acceptors.

Obviously, then, the proportional mix between prior users and non-users among the acceptors will greatly affect the relative fertility of the acceptors taken as a single group. For example, in the case of women 30-39 let us assume that the specific fertility rates of prior users and non-users were fixed as in Table XI-1, but allow the proportion of acceptors who are prior users to vary. Then the overall fertility of the acceptors (for the preceding three years) would change as follows under the indicated assumptions about the proportions of prior users:

	Actual	*Alternate Assumptions*		
% of acceptors who were prior users	48%	10%	75%	90%
		Calculated resulting rates:		
Three-year fertility rates for all acceptors	338	408	289	261

In developing countries, the proportion of the population already using contraception at the start of official family planning programs has been found to vary considerably. This factor will affect any calculations of the relative fertility of acceptors and non-acceptors in both IUD programs and those emphasizing other methods of family limitation. It will also affect comparisons of the rates for acceptors or non-acceptors with the average rates for their age groups, since as more women use birth control the "average" fertility levels will be lower.

Of those who were not prior users, the minority that became acceptors in Taichung also had much higher fertility rates than those who did not: for the three-year period, about 70 per cent higher at ages 30-39 and about 20 per cent higher at ages 20-29.

It is also true that among prior users, those who became acceptors had higher recent fertility than those who did not. Apparently, those prior users who came into the program either were less effective in their practice of family limitation or began later. This result is consistent with our earlier finding that acceptance rates were especially high among those who had used only abortion or whose contraceptive practice was not current, that is, among couples not currently protected against pregnancy just prior to the interview.

Those prior users who did not become acceptors were apparently quite successful in keeping fertility at low levels in the most recent period, so the program was less relevant for them. Their three-year fertility rates were lower than their five-year fertility rates by a wider margin than was the case for any other group except those sterilized at ages 30-39:

	Previous 3-year fertility rates as % of previous 5-year fertility rates for wives of current age:	
	20-29	*30-39*
Sterilized by 2nd interview	87	74
All acceptors— (total)	105	94
Prior users	98	86
Not prior users	109	99
Non-acceptors		
Prior users	92	84
Not prior users	107	96
All couples	103	90

Note, also, that the ratio is highest of all for those who were acceptors but not prior users. Not only was their fertility level the highest, but it had increased recently in comparison with the trend for the whole age group. In either age group, the ratio of the most recent (three-year) period to the whole period is highest for this category.

The three-year fertility rates for those who are neither prior users nor acceptors are slightly higher than average at ages 20-29 and 12 per cent higher at ages 30-39 (See Table XI-1). This results from the fact that the sterilized and the successful prior users of contraception (the non-acceptors) bring the general average down, especially by ages 30-39, when these two groups comprise 45 per cent of those married at least three years (as compared with 27 per cent at ages 20-29). Those never using birth control had quite low fertility during the early years of marriage. But their recent fertility rates appear to be high as compared with the average. This is the case because for all women in their thirties, fertility is lowered later in marriage by the family limitation activities of those in the group who were initially more fertile. All of this should remind us that in a situation where a significant proportion of acceptors or non-acceptors have already used family limitation, the recent fertility of those who have never practiced it will appear to be higher in relative terms than we might otherwise expect, because the general fertility level, which is the standard of comparison, is already depressed by the action taken by the others.

Acceptors in their thirties had recent fertility rates not much below the high average fertility levels of women in their twenties. This is important, since not a few observers believe that acceptances by women past 30 are less important than those of younger women, not only because the younger women have a longer period of potential fertility, but also because their current fertility rates are so much higher. At least for the Taichung acceptors, the latter argument does not appear valid.

The three-year fertility rates for women 30-39 were below the total fertility rate for all women at ages 20-29 by the following percentages:

	% by which 3-year fertility rates for women 30-39 differ from the average rate for all women 20-29
Sterilized by 2nd interview	—73
All acceptors (total)	—19
Prior users	—42
Not prior users	+ 2
Non-acceptors	
Prior users	—55
Not prior users	—40
All couples	—46

The acceptors in the 30-39 age group who were not prior users actually had fertility rates slightly higher than the average for all women 20-29. All other categories were below this level, but by amounts consistent with status regarding prior use and acceptance.

Those who were prior users may be assumed to have demonstrated that they were strongly motivated to limit family size. Of the members of this motivated group, those who did not become acceptors were sufficiently successful or lucky so that their fertility fell below the average level for the 20-29 age group by 55 per cent. The rate for those who became acceptors differed by less—40 per cent—and was close to the average for ages 30-39. For this motivated group such an average decline was apparently unsatisfactory, so they became acceptors. In the 30-39 age bracket, when family growth has reached the desired limit for a large number of Taiwanese families, a moderate decline in fertility still leave unsatisfied those families that want very much to limit further family growth, as indicated by their independent use of contraception earlier.

It is important that fertility differences between acceptors and non-acceptors are much greater for women in their thirties than for those in their twenties.[1] We believe that this results from the fact that acceptance selects for a relatively recent birth, and in so doing selects against sterility. When wives are in their twenties, only a small proportion of couples are sterile. Only after the wife reaches thirty does the proportion of sterile couples become large enough to have the potentiality of affecting fertility rates significantly. In this connection, note (Table XI-1) that between ages 20-29 and 30-39 the fertility rates of acceptors who are not prior users decline only from 503 to 426 (a 15 per cent decline), whereas the corresponding decline for non-acceptors who are not prior users is from 424 to 251 (a 41 per cent decline). All of this means that the error made in assigning to acceptors the average fertility of their age group is much greater in the case of older women than for younger ones.

FERTILITY RATES BY ACCEPTANCE STATUS: THE LONGER RETROSPECTIVE VIEW

The higher fertility of the acceptors in the three or five years preceding the program need not necessarily reflect a higher basic fecundability likely to persist into future years. Fecundability is a probability concept, and involves a considerable chance component. We have probably minimized the importance of this circumstance by going back as far as five years. However, it is theoretically possible that many

[1] We are especially indebted to Dr. Robert G. Potter for suggestions on which this paragraph is based.

of the acceptors were couples who only by chance had one or more children during the three- or five-year period rather than just before or after these intervals. To the extent that this is true, the high recent fertility is not predictive of the future level.

However, a look backwards over a longer period (Table XI-2) indicates that the acceptors among women in their thirties have had higher fertility for a long time.[2] If we go back beyond the five-year

Table XI-2. Duration-Specific Annual Birth Rates per 1000 Women for Periods of Months Counted Backwards from Time of First Intensive Survey Interview for Women 30-39 Years Old, Married at Least 10 Years

Acceptance status and prior use of contraception		Periods of months preceding first interview							Number of women married at least 10 years
		0-11	12-23	24-35	36-47	48-59	60-119	120-179*	
All wives		184	196	241	262	283	350	388	1100
Sterilized by second interview		104	93	124	212	197	353	459	193
Acceptors by July 1965?	Use of contraception or abortion before first interview?								
yes	yes	187	242	242	286	352	365	389	91
yes	no	523	364	364	443	409	402	411	88
no	yes	76	170	261	242	289	363	429	318
no	no	234	217	254	256	276	323	320	410

*In this column the rates are shown for women married at least 15 years.

Table XI-3. Duration-Specific Annual Birth Rates per 1000 Women for Periods of Months Counted Backwards from Time of First Intensive Survey Interview for Women 20-29 Years Old, Married at Least 5 Years

Acceptance status and prior use of contraception		Periods of months preceding first interview					Number of women married at least 5 years
		0-11	12-23	24-35	36-47	48-59	
All wives		372	385	405	427	443	600
Sterilized by second interview		186	419	209	419	465	43
Acceptors by July 1965?	Use of contraception or abortion before first interview?						
yes	yes	400	429	371	371	571	35
yes	no	442	480	468	442	480	77
no	yes	261	366	394	507	535	142
no	no	429	360	426	393	373	303

period, it is clear that those who used birth control before the program began or accepted it within the program had much higher than average fertility even that far back. Those acceptors who were using

[2] Table XI-3 shows similar trends for the younger women. There are many more deviations from the trend, because the number of cases is smaller.

birth control for the first time had very high fertility in the preceding three years, but they also had high fertility rates for as far back as 15 years.

Those practicing birth control before the program began, whether acceptors or not, also had high fertility rates going back many years. Presumably, it was this higher fertility that brought many of them to use birth control on their own. Of this group, those who did not become acceptors had very high fertility five or ten years or more before the program, but their fertility has declined steadily, so that just before the program it was quite low. The successful use of birth control, combined with some luck, has reduced their fertility so rapidly that it is not surprising that the program did not interest them.

Those former users of birth control who became acceptors also had high fertility rates much earlier in married life. Their fertility also declined over the years, but not so rapidly as that of the users who did not become acceptors. The prior users whose fertility fell only moderately presumably became acceptors because their success in limiting their families was insufficient to match their high motivation.

Anrudh K. Jain has provided an independent test of the results just considered by estimating the fecundability of the sample of couples in another way and relating this fecundability to their status regarding acceptance and prior use.[3] Jain's test essentially depends on the number of months required for a first conception after marriage for the couples not using birth control prior to their first conception. The results, illustrated in Table XI-4, indicate that acceptors and prior users have relatively high fecundability. For either younger or older women, fecundability was highest among those who were both acceptors and prior users. It is least among those who were neither acceptors nor prior users. The importance of these calculations is that they indicate that the acceptors and prior users were distinguished by high fecundability according to a measure taken at the beginning of marriage as well as according to the measure of recent fertility, on which we have largely relied.

[3] The general methodology and its significance is treated in Jain's Ph.D. dissertation in sociology at the University of Michigan: "Fecundity Components in Taiwan: Application of a Stochastic Model of Human Reproduction." The specific analysis summarized in the present paragraph is discussed in detail in Anrudh K. Jain, "The Relative Fecundability of Users and Non-Users of Contraception Measured Early in Marriage," *Social Biology* (in press).

Table XI-4. Average[a] Fecundabilities for All Wives Including Those Without Any Pregnancy Prior to Interview by Whether Acceptor in the Program by July 1965 by Prior Use of Contraception or Abortion, by Wife's Age at First Intensive Survey[b]

Acceptance status and prior use of contraception		20-29 Absolute fecund-ability	20-29 Relative fecund-ability	20-29 Number of wives	30-39 Absolute fecund-ability	30-39 Relative fecund-ability	30-39 Number of wives	20-39 Absolute fecund-ability	20-39 Relative fecund-ability	20-39 Number of wives
All wives		202	100	1066	130	100	1190	158	100	2256
Sterilized by second interview		217	108	40	140	108	193	151	96	233
Acceptors by July 1965?	Use of contraception or abortion before first interview?									
yes	yes	241	120	51	151	116	99	177	112	150
yes	no	215	107	128	118	91	102	163	103	230
no	yes	219	109	173	147	113	336	168	106	509
no	no	189	94	674	99	76	460	143	91	1134

[a] Averages are shown in units of 1,000 women.

[b] Wives who were premaritally pregnant (158) or used contraception during first pregnancy interval (29) are excluded.

From these results we draw the conclusion that in a situation like that of Taichung, acceptors have a fertility rate much higher than average not only just prior to acceptance but for many years before that. Without effective birth control, it is likely that they would continue to have much higher than average fertility for some years to come. Therefore, estimates of the potential effect of acceptances based on average age-specific fertility rates are probably in error, especially for older women. This error will be compounded if older acceptors retain the IUD for longer periods than the younger, as we saw in Chapter X is the case. Of course, it is necessary to hold up against these considerations the fact that the older acceptors will have diminishing fertility with each succeeding year, so that there is definitely an upper limit to the reduction of the birth rate where many acceptors are in the older age groups.

The evidence and the line of reasoning followed above indicate that there is a considerable potential for reduction of fertility among the acceptors. Whether that potential is realized with the aid of the IUD depends on whether this device is used continuously or replaced by adequate substitutes in a sufficient number of cases. However, even if birth control were used continuously up to the menopause by every acceptor and if it prevented all additional births, we could not necessarily argue that this was all a result of the program. Given the motivation necessary to enter the program, an unknown proportion of the couples would probably have taken some more or less effective action on their own, without the program. The program may have been a substitute for other alternatives for some couples. We shall examine this line of argument in the next chapters. At this point we can surely say, however, that there does exist a definite possibility that the program can affect the fertility levels of those it reached. If that were not the case, there would be no need to try to decide whether the program accomplished anything.

XII. How the Program Affected Fertility and the Practice of Birth Control

As of the first interview, in late 1962, 36 per cent of the Taichung couples had already used some form of birth control (contraception, abortion, or sterilization). By July 1965, this proportion had increased to at least 51 per cent and was probably closer to 60 per cent. The proportion of those who had ever used contraception increased from about 28 per cent at the first interview to at least 37 per cent and probably to at least 40 per cent by July 1965.

Unfortunately the estimates for July 1965 are minimal, because while they include substantially all of the acceptances in the program up to that date, new birth control practice outside of the program is included only for the first year of the program, that is, up to the second Intensive Survey at the end of 1963. It is likely that there were also a significant number of additional new users outside the program between the end of 1963 and July 1965. We can summarize the known cases as shown on page 293.

During the intensive first year of the program (that is, between the two Intensive Surveys), the proportion of new users inside the program was slightly greater than the proportion of those starting use outside the program. It seems likely that some of those newly practicing birth control on their own were encouraged to do so by the information, stimulus, and legitimation provided by the program. The absolute increase of new birth control practice during the first year of the program—10.3 per cent—means a 28 per cent increase in the proportion ever practicing, apart from the effect of the program in reinforcing the practice of those who had started before the program began or in persuading those who had earlier given up birth control to reinstate their practice. While we have no comparative annual figures for earlier years, it is likely that the previous annual rate of adoption was very much lower than that for 1963, since the cumulative figure of 36.1 per cent at the time of the first survey would otherwise have been attained in a little over three years—a most unlikely possibility.

To arrive at a more realistic estimate of total birth control practice by the end of July 1965, we have made two assumptions about the practice of birth control outside the program after the second

	% of all couples	*% of those not ever practicing before the program*
a. Couples who had practiced some form of birth control before the program (abortion, contraception, or sterilization) as of the first Intensive Survey at end of 1962	36.1	—
b. First used abortion, contraception, or sterilized in first year of program and didn't become acceptors by July 1965 (these are new users in period between first and second surveys)	4.8	7.5
c. Program acceptors during first year of program who had not previously practiced any form of birth control	5.6	8.8
d. Additional acceptors by July 1965, who had not previously practiced birth control at end of first year of program (accepted between time of second survey at end of 1963 and July 1965)	4.7	7.4
Total of known new users of birth control by July 1965 (b+c+d)	15.1	23.6
Total known ever to have used birth control by July 1965 (a + b + c + d)	51.2	—

Intensive Survey: (1) that new practice of birth control continued to increase by the same absolute percentage of the total number of couples as it did in the first year of the program, and (2) that the ratio of new practice outside and inside the program was the same for the period to July 1965 as it was for the first year of the program.

To the known total of 51.2 per cent for July 1965 we can add between 4.0 (assumption 2) and 7.2 (assumption 1). This yields a total range of 55.2 to 58.4 per cent. Since, in addition, some of the acceptors are missing in our accounting,[1] probably between 55 and 60

[1] As we indicated in Chapter VII, those acceptors who moved out of their initial lin of residence would not appear in the count of respondents in the Intensive

per cent of the couples had used birth control by July 1965—an absolute increase of 19 to 24 per cent and a relative increase of 53 to 66 per cent from the start of the program. It is possible, but implausible, that there would have been an increase of this size in such a limited period of time without the program.

For a small and special subsample of three hundred couples[2] from the Intensive Survey we do have data on the increase in certain birth control practices between the time of the second Intensive Survey interview and May 1966. In this sample, 60 per cent had ever used contraception by May 1966 as compared with about 36 per cent at the end of 1963. The percentage of sterilized cases in this subsample increased from 10 to 16 per cent during the same period. These figures from the subsample cannot be generalized, because of the character of the sample selection, but the size of the increases enhances the plausibility of an estimate that at least 60 per cent of the larger sample had practiced some form of birth control by July 1965.

In preceding chapters we have looked intensively at the characteristics of the acceptors only. It may be useful now to consider briefly the characteristics of all those ever practicing birth control by July 1965, whether inside or outside the program, as compared with the situation at the time of the first survey, considered in some detail in Chapters III and V. In Table XII-1 we show the following data for couples classified by several selected social and demographic characteristics:

1. the per cent ever practicing birth control before the program (that is, as of the first survey).
2. the per cent taking up birth control practice for the first time outside of the program during its first year (that is, between the first and second surveys).
3. the known per cent accepting birth control for the first time in the program up to July 1965.
4. the total per cent *known* ever to have practiced birth control by July 1965.

Survey who became acceptors after the end of 1963. This means the loss of perhaps 15 per cent of the acceptors from this accounting.

[2] A subsample of three hundred of the husbands from the couples in the Intensive Survey sample were reinterviewed in May 1966 in a study of consumption patterns by Deborah S. Freedman. The sample was selected to meet special needs of the economic study and is not a random cross section, but it does represent all major strata of the city.

Table XII-1. Percentage of Couples Ever Using Any Form of Family Limitation in 1962 and 1965 and Percentage of New Birth Control Users Outside and Inside the Program, by Selected Social and Demographic Characteristics

Social and demographic characteristics of the couples at time of first survey (late 1962)	Number of couples	Percentage ever using any form of family limitation: at first survey (late 1962)	by July 1965	Percentage of total group who had not used any form of family limitation at first survey who began practice: outside of the program by second survey	as acceptors in the program by July 1965	either as acceptors or outside the program
All couples	2443	36	51	5	10	15
Family type						
Living in extended unit	1263	31	47	5	12	17
Living in nuclear unit						
Once in extended unit	658	40	54	4	10	14
Always nuclear	522	45	57	5	8	13
Wife's education						
None	767	19	35	4	13	16
Primary school, not grad.	303	30	45	5	10	15
Primary school grad.	842	38	54	5	12	17
Junior high school	320	57	68	5	7	12
Senior high school grad. or higher	211	72	83	4	7	11
Husband's employment status						
Farmer	448	17	36	2	16	19
Other traditional employment	641	34	48	6	9	15
Employed by non-relative	1199	41	56	5	10	15
Professional	155	63	72	4	5	9
Number of modern objects owned						
0 or 1	191	17	42	3	23	26
2 or 3	572	22	38	5	12	16
4	375	26	39	6	9	14
5	380	36	50	6	8	14
6	537	46	62	5	12	16
7 or more	388	63	73	4	6	10
Number of living children and sons						
No children	143	7	15	4	4	8
One child						
No son	154	12	22	5	6	10
One son	176	15	28	1	13	14
Two children						
No son	96	11	17	3	2	5
One or two sons	320	28	44	4	12	16
Three or four children						
No son	71	23	31	3	6	8
One son	217	34	52	5	14	18
Two or more sons	619	51	68	6	12	17
Five children or more	647	49	66	6	12	17
Comparison of children alive and number wife wanted at first interview						
Wife wanted at least 2 more	597	10	22	3	9	12
Wife wanted 1 more	640	28	46	5	14	18
Had number wanted	664	54	68	6	9	14
Had more than wanted	452	60	77	5	12	17
NA, up to God, Fate, etc.	90	13	27	2	11	13

These data indicate that in July 1965, as in late 1962, the total known practice of birth control was substantially correlated to measures both of modernization and of demographic pressure. However, the socio-modernization differentials had decreased during the period because: (1) new practice of birth control in the program was correlated inversely to modernization variables, and (2) new practice of birth control outside of the program had no significant relationship to modernization variables.

These results are of some importance because they reinforce the interpretation offered earlier, that the program had the effect of bringing to the practice of birth control significant numbers of the traditional and lower status couples who initially were not proportionately represented among those practicing birth control. So far as those never practicing any form of birth control are concerned, the direct effect of the program is greatest for the traditional and lower status groups. That those initiating birth control outside of the program were drawn about proportionately from the more and less modern strata may be equally important, because it may be that the program had enough indirect influence to help in producing this effect.

THE EFFECT OF THE PROGRAM ON FERTILITY

Did the Taichung program reduce the birth rate of the Taichung acceptors and of Taichung as a whole? This seemingly straightforward question is not easy to answer in any simple way. We can demonstrate that:

1. the Taichung acceptors were a group whose prior fertility had been very high (see Chapter XI).
2. after they entered the program, their fertility fell far below its former high levels and far below the level of the average Taichung woman of the same age.
3. even those women who gave up the intrauterine device, which was the method of choice, managed in various ways to keep their fertility very low.

This is certainly a necessary starting point for an assessment of the possible effects of the program. It indicates that those coming into the program had fertility high enough so that its control might be significant for population change, and that this fertility was substantially reduced following their participation in the program. We shall deal with this issue presently, but we begin here with a demonstration of what happened to those who entered the program, because if their fertility had remained unchanged the questions of causality and of historical alternatives would not arise.

THE REDUCTION OF THE FERTILITY OF ACCEPTORS

The fertility of acceptors fell substantially during the several years after the program began. There is no doubt of that. However, to measure the amount of the decline and to compare this decline with the one that occurred in the fertility of non-acceptors is a more complicated matter, and requires some estimation and technical discussion. We present approximate answers based on several different sets of data. These data were just being processed as this book was completed, so we must be content with rough approximations and with inelegant treatments of some problems. However, the preliminary results are sufficiently consistent and striking as to make it likely that the final results, after more careful work, will not be greatly different.

One measurement is based on following by means of the population register the fertility history of everyone interviewed in the Taichung Intensive Survey, a cross section of the married couples who were 20-39 years old at the end of 1962 and who still lived in Taichung in early 1967.[3] By following the reproductive performance of this sample, we can make at least rough comparisons between the fertility of acceptors and non-acceptors after the program began. We can also divide the non-acceptors into those already using contraception and those not doing so, and thus get some idea of how the fertility history of the

[3] The register was checked for all of the women who were interviewed in both the first and second Intensive Surveys. In this preliminary analysis we have omitted women for whom we were unable to obtain from the register complete fertility records up to the time of the check, carried out mainly in April-June 1967. Most of the omitted cases are women who moved out of Taichung. We have their fertility histories up to the time of their moves, and we will consider these in later analysis. It was not possible to include this material here without delaying inordinately the publication of this book. Even if the migrant couples and those whose records could not be matched in the register differ fairly significantly from the couples considered, they are not sufficiently numerous to affect the overall results very much. Only a part of the 1967 record was covered in the check, but since the portion of the year covered did not differ systematically for the different groups, the results are presented. The 1967 data, however, should be used only for a comparison of the relative position of the groups in that year, not for any evaluation of absolute changes from earlier periods.

acceptors compares with that of persons using contraception outside the program.

Before examining the substantive results, we must call attention to several limitations of the data. Since we were only able to identify individual acceptors through July 1965, those who became acceptors after that date are included with the non-acceptors. This makes our comparison conservative, since this classification will tend to lower the fertility of non-acceptor groups for 1966 and 1967.

Our data on prior use of contraception by non-acceptors only extends to the date of the first survey (end of 1962). We are certain that quite a few couples began using contraception outside of the program after the first survey. This will affect the fertility rates of couples we have classified as both non-acceptors and non-users, and this undoubtedly accounts for some part of the fertility decline in this group. Also, since we did not interview the women in this sample again after 1963, we do not know about sterilizations after 1963. Such sterilized cases might appear in any of the other categories and lower their fertility rates. Another problem is that we are following the history of a group of couples 20-39 years old and married as of the end of 1962, and we therefore do not represent the couples who migrated into the city during the years in question. These are likely to be rural couples with higher than average fertility. This does not necessarily detract from our examination of what happened to our initial panel. However, it does affect any comparisons with trends for the city as a whole.

The register has certain limitations which also affect the results. There is probably some under-registration of births, particularly if the infant dies soon after birth. There are delays in birth registration. These problems will have a small influence on the absolute level of the rates, but are unlikely to change differentials. The registration process was influenced by a census that was taken at the end of 1966, so that more than the usual number of births were registered at the end of 1966 with a corresponding deficit early in 1967. Again, it is unlikely that these technical problems will affect differentially the groups we are comparing.

Table XII-2 shows the fertility rates of the various groups in the intensive sample for the period preceding the survey and the program and also for selected years after the program. These rates are also shown as ratios to the total for the given year. Table XII-3 shows the

Table XII-2. Actual and Relative Fertility Rates for Taichung Intensive Survey Sample, by Acceptance and Contraception Status, for 3 Years Prior to First Interview and for 1964-67

	Fertility rates per annum					Relative fertility rates[b]				
Contraception acceptance status	3 years prior to first interview[a]	1964	1965	1966	1967	3 years prior to first interview	1964	1965	1966	1967
						All ages: 20-39				
Sterilized by second interview[c]	147	0	0	0	0	49	0	0	0	0
Acceptors by July 1965	396	144	92	78	61	131	70	60	58	68
Non-acceptors: prior users[c]	253	133	83	55	51	83	65	54	41	57
Non-acceptors: prior non-users	338	308	239	222	155	112	150	157	164	172
Total	303	206	152	135	90	100	100	100	100	100
						Age at first interview: 20-29				
Sterilized by second interview	297	0	0	0	0	71	0	0	0	0
Acceptors by July 1965	475	192	158	136	106	114	58	62	61	64
Non-acceptors: prior users	380	260	167	83	72	91	78	66	37	43
Non-acceptors: prior non-users	424	414	322	302	223	102	125	127	135	134
Total	417	333	254	223	167	100	100	100	100	100
						Age at second interview: 30-39				
Sterilized by second interview	113	0	0	0	0	50	0	0	0	0
Acceptors by July 1965	338	102	34	29	23	150	109	55	51	62
Non-acceptors: prior users	189	63	37	40	40	84	67	60	70	108
Non-acceptors: prior non-users	251	155	119	106	57	112	165	192	186	154
Total	225	94	62	57	37	100	100	100	100	100

[a] Since the first interview was taken in October-December of 1962, this would be approximately the period of November 1959 to November 1962.

[b] Ratio of the fertility rates to total for the age group.

[c] The user classification is as of the first interview late in 1962. The sterilization classification is as of the second interview late in 1963.

percentage decline from the period before the program to various years after the program began.

The results clearly indicate that those groups classified as acceptors or users in the early part of the period have substantially larger fertility declines than the large residual group of couples who were neither acceptors nor otherwise users at that time. The declines for acceptors are not substantially different from those for the users who were not acceptors. This is neither surprising nor contrary to the objectives of the program. We have previously noted that those users who did not become acceptors were presumably practicing contraception relatively effectively, since their fertility had been declining rapidly in the years before the program. The ultimate aim is a situation in which the program will no longer be needed, because all the couples who need contraceptive supplies will be getting them routinely from regular sources rather than from a special organization.

Table XII-3. Percentage Change in Annual General Fertility Rates for Taichung Intensive Survey Sample, by Acceptance and Contraception Status, for Period from Three Years Prior to First Interview and for 1965-67

	Percentage decline in annual general fertility rate from 3 years prior to first interview								
	1965			1966			1967		
	Age at first interview			Age at first interview			Age at first interview		
Contraception acceptance status	20-39	20-29	30-39	20-39	20-29	30-39	20-39	20-29	30-39
Sterilized by second interview[b/]	-100	-100	-100	-100	-100	-100	-100	-100	-100
Acceptors by July 1965	- 77	- 66	- 90	- 80	- 71	- 91	- 85	- 78	- 93
Non-acceptors: prior users[b/]	- 67	- 56	- 80	- 78	- 78	- 79	- 80	- 82	- 79
Non-acceptors: prior non-users	- 29	- 24	- 52	- 34	- 29	- 58	- 54	- 47	- 77
Total	- 50	- 39	- 72	- 55	- 46	- 75	- 70	- 60	- 84
Decline for all Taichung married women of same age distribution as the acceptors[c/]	- 39	- 9	- 44	- 46	- 11	- 48			

[a/] Since the first interview was taken in October-December of 1962, this would be approximately the period of November 1959-November 1962.

[b/] The user classification is as of the first interview late in 1962. The sterilization classification is as of the second interview in late 1963.

[c/] Calculated by applying the age-specific birth rates for all married women in Taichung to the age distribution of the acceptors in the given year.

Our classification of the couples as users, sterilized, or acceptors is for a time relatively early in the period considered, and some changed their status later on in this period. We have examined the subsequent fertility of a group of couples classified initially as users and/or acceptors. The unknown later changes and crossovers in user status probably minimize the difference we have shown. If all of the facts were known, the relative fertility of acceptors and of users would be even lower when compared with that of the general population of non-users.

The bottom row of Table XII-3 shows, for comparative purposes, the amount of decline in fertility that might have been expected for the total Taichung sample on the basis of the age-specific fertility rates for all married women of the age groups in question for each year. This is an independent measure of the effect of aging and of the secular trend in fertility. The decline for both acceptors and other prior users was substantially higher in both age groups than the decline attributable to the aging and secular effects. This comparison is conservative, since the overall secular decline base includes the declines of the acceptors. Even some of the decline of the other users may be due to the indirect influence of the program. The proper comparison for the acceptors and other users may be with the non-user who did not accept, and this makes the differences considered much larger.

The relative advantage of the acceptors and other users is much greater at younger ages than at older. This is not surprising, because fertility rates are much higher at younger ages and because the secular decline for the age group 20-29 during this period was almost nil. Note that the actual percentage decline was greater for the older acceptors than for the younger acceptors and other users. The *relative* advantage of the young acceptors is only in contrast with young non-users and non-acceptors, whose fertility didn't decline very much because neither the aging effect nor the secular decline was very large for them.

We have another, independent source to consult in assessing the fertility decline of the Taichung IUD acceptors. This is the detailed follow-up study made of 7,020 IUD acceptors, covering their fertility histories before the acceptance of the IUD and during the period up to December 31, 1966.[4] These data are in the initial stages of analysis as this chapter is being written. However, it is possible to draw from the preliminary results some approximations which are probably adequate for assessing broad trends and comparisons.

On the basis of the detailed interviews with these women, their birth rates per annum were as follows in the years preceding the program:

1960	412
1961	383
1962	402
Average for 1960-62	399

For the period after IUD insertion, the birth rate was 90 per thousand (after allowing for nine months of non-exposure for all the IUD

[4] Not all of the women in this Taichung Medical Follow-Up study were residents of Taichung. About 10 per cent of the sample are women who lived in townships immediately surrounding Taichung. This set of data is from the second Taichung Medical Follow-Up study of IUD acceptors. The first Taichung Medical Follow-Up study yielded the data reported in Chapter X. The second study covered all of the women included in the first study, except a small number living in townships not immediately surrounding Taichung and excluded because of the problem of transportation for follow-up. The second study also includes, in addition, new cases accepting the IUD between January 1965 and December 1966. However, the new cases after April 1965 are only those inserted in the central Maternal and Child Health Association clinic. They do not include those inserted by private practitioners or in the nine smaller health station clinics of Taichung.

acceptors). This is a decline of approximately 77 per cent from the average level of fertility in the three years preceding the program. Of course, some of this decline would have occurred anyway as a result of two factors: (1) the women were getting older, and (2) there was a general decline in fertility for Taichung as a whole.

If the fertility of the IUD acceptors in 1965 had matched that of all Taichung married women of their own age group as of 1965, the fertility rate of the acceptors would have been 215 instead of 90. Using this as our standard, we can say that the decline from 399 to 215 was the effect of aging and of the general secular decline in fertility. The additional decline from 215 to 90 was a result of something associated with being an IUD acceptor. Approximately 60 per cent of the decline in the fertility of the IUD acceptors was the expected result of the secular trend and of normal aging effects, but 40 per cent represented something else distinctive to this group.

Although these calculations and those based on the Intensive Survey are necessarily preliminary ones at this writing, it is comforting to see that the approximate levels of decline for acceptors yielded by these two quite different sources are similar. In one case we are relying on the register, and in the other on responses to the surveys. Further, in the Intensive Survey we are dealing with a sample of all acceptors as of July 1965. In the IUD follow-up study we have a larger number of respondents for a longer period of observation (through the end of 1966), but we are concerned with only the IUD cases.

Some particulars will change when we have been able to analyze all the data more carefully, but the preliminary results all point in the same direction. The acceptors in the program who initially had much higher than average fertility have much lower than average fertility in the post-insertion period. There is a decline in fertility for the period of observation of about 77 per cent. This is about twice as large a decline as might be expected on the basis of the normal aging effects and the secular trend in fertility for the general population.

BIRTHS AVERTED BY AN INITIAL IUD INSERTION

The decline in the birth rates of the IUD acceptors cannot be attributed entirely to the immediate protection of the IUD itself. We have just seen that perhaps half of the fertility decline may be the result of the aging and of the general secular trends in fertility. Even the remaining portion of the decline is not necessarily a result of the IUD, since many of the IUD cases were terminated during the period of observation.

Robert Potter has made elsewhere a careful estimate of the number of births averted by each initial IUD insertion for women of different age groups.[5] Table XII-4, taken from his work, illustrates the results.

Table XII-4. Births Averted Per First Segment of IUD, by Age of Wife and Assumption Respecting Potential Fertility[a]

Assumption concerning fertility in absence of IUD	Births averted per first segment of IUD				
	Age group				All ages
	20-24	25-29	30-34	35-39	
Maximal (no family planning)	.54	.80	1.12	1.10	.94
Medium	.54	.68	.72	.54	.64
Conservative (everybody substituting)	.47	.51	.46	.24	.43

[a] Source: R.G. Potter, "Estimating Births Averted in a Family Planning Program," S.J. Behrman, L. Corsa, and R. Freedman (eds.), Fertility and Family Planning: A World View, Ann Arbor: University of Michigan Press, in press.

Under the most reasonable (medium) assumptions, the initial IUD insertion prevents fewer births for the younger women than for the older. This is a surprising but understandable outcome when we remember that younger women retain the first IUD for a much shorter period of time than older women. Under a plausible medium assumption, the initial IUD is estimated by Potter to avert about 0.9 births per case.

While these calculations by Potter are both important and elegant, they do not indicate the total effect of the program on the fertility of the acceptors. He is studying the history of the first IUDs inserted rather than of the acceptors. Our calculations in the last section, imperfect though they may be, relate to the fertility histories of the couples rather than to the histories of the initial IUDs. The fertility decline which occurred beyond the aging and secular trend is due partly to the births averted by the first IUDs inserted, but it also depends on the effects of reinserted IUDs and of the various alternative methods adopted by acceptors who gave up the IUD entirely:

[5] Robert G. Potter, "Estimating Births Averted in a Family Planning Program," in S. J. Behrman, L. Corsa, and R. Freedman, eds., *Fertility and Family Planning: A World View.*

sterilization, abortion, and other methods of contraception. In this context the relatively "high" termination rates for the IUD and the relatively "small" number of births averted by the initial device inserted are less serious than critics have supposed. Those who became acceptors in the program are sufficiently interested in controlling family size to manage to keep their fertility relatively low whether or not they retain the initial IUD device.

WHAT HAPPENS AFTER IUD TERMINATION

A large majority of the IUD users succeeded in avoiding having additional live births either with or without the IUD they had accepted originally. Table XII-5 shows in detail the birth control status

Table XII-5. Birth Control Status in December 1966 of 6726 Wives Having an IUD Insertion in Taichung Between July 1962 and December 1966, by Months Between First Insertion and Last Contact[a/]

Birth control status at interview	Months between first insertion and last contact							
	0-5	6-11	12-17	18-23	24-35	36-47	48-53	Total
IUD in situ: total	78.6	67.5	58.9	57.8	50.7	49.2	42.9	55.3
original device	75.6	64.0	53.2	48.9	42.5	38.6	33.4	47.4
reinserted device	3.0	3.5	5.7	8.9	8.2	10.6	9.5	7.9
IUD not in situ: total	21.4	32.5	41.1	42.2	49.3	50.8	57.1	44.7
Currently using other contraception or sterilized	1.4	6.4	13.8	13.7	19.6	24.8	35.7	17.7
Not currently protected by contraception or sterilization: total	20.0	26.1	27.3	28.5	29.8	26.0	21.4	27.0
But all pregnancies aborted	0.9	2.4	3.1	4.6	4.3	5.0	3.6	4.0
Never pregnant	17.0	16.4	13.5	12.4	10.5	9.8	9.5	11.8
Had at least one live birth	0.0	0.2	2.7	6.0	9.5	9.0	3.6	6.6
Currently pregnant	2.1	7.1	8.0	5.5	5.5	2.2	4.7	4.6
Total per cent	100.0	100.0	100.0	100.0	100.0	100.0	100.0	100.0
Number of couples	575	452	878	548	2118	2071	84	6726
Per cent having a live birth after first insertion[b/]	0.0	0.5	4.0	10.8	16.2	19.9	16.1	12.8

[a/] Excludes 79 cases never contacted after first insertion and 215 for whom details of birth control practice was incomplete. The schedule of contacts is explained in Chapter X.

[b/] Women who at last contact had not terminated their only pregnancy since first insertion are excluded.

of 6,726 Taichung cases at various periods following first insertion.[6] Consider, for example, the more than 2,000 women with three to four years of experience observed after first insertion of the IUD. Approximately 49 per cent were still wearing an IUD at that time, and an additional 25 per cent were either sterilized or currently using other contraception. This means that, in all, 74 per cent were currently protected by sterilization or contraception. An additional 5

[6] We have excluded 79 women not followed up after first insertion as well as 211 women whose contraceptive status after termination was unknown.

per cent, not currently protected by contraception or sterilization, had aborted all their pregnancies after first insertion, so 79 per cent can be classified as protected by some form of birth control. An additional 10 per cent were not practicing birth control but had never been pregnant since their IUD insertion. This leaves only 11 per cent unprotected and unsuccessful—that is, these women were not practicing birth control and either had had a live birth (9 per cent) or were currently pregnant (2 per cent). Some of these currently pregnant women will have either an induced or a spontaneous abortion.

We would be exaggerating the continuity and success of the birth control practice if we did not note that some of those currently practicing birth control had a live birth between the time of their first insertion and their resumption of contraception or sterilization. About 11 per cent of all the cases for the three to four year period are of this type. This means that, altogether, 21 per cent of the women at risk for three to four years had a live birth during this period. This is far less than the expected proportion, especially since some of these births were planned. If we consider only the women who had terminated the use of the first IUD, we find that after three to four years:

17 per cent were wearing another IUD
58 per cent were protected currently by another IUD, by sterilization, or by other contraception
66 per cent were currently protected in one of these ways or had intentionally aborted all pregnancies
82 per cent were either protected in one of these ways or had not faced the problem because never pregnant since first insertion

Only 18 per cent were not currently protected *and* either had had a live birth since first insertion or were currently pregnant.

Again, to avoid giving an over-optimistic picture we note that a larger percentage—almost one-third of the cases ever terminating—did subsequently have a live birth. A minority of these intentionally stopped the use of contraception in order to have a child. Perhaps more important is the fact that a majority (55 per cent) of those who had had a live birth since termination were already using contraception again or had been sterilized. At least 25 per cent of those who had had a live birth had terminated another post-termination pregnancy by an induced abortion.

These Taichung data are consistent with those presented in the next chapter for Taiwan as a whole. Both sets of data indicate that a large majority of the IUD acceptors either continued to be protected by the IUD itself or managed to use other means to avoid having a live birth in the period after IUD termination. For both Taiwan and Taichung, the data on contraceptive status following insertion are consistent with the sharp decline in fertility for the IUD acceptors. It is significant that the general fertility rate after insertion for Taichung (90) is similar to that for all of Taiwan (80). It may not be a coincidence that the post-insertion fertility rate for the Korean national IUD sample (82) was also at approximately the same level.[7]

THE CHANGE IN FERTILITY FOR ALL TAICHUNG COUPLES

Our discussion of the fertility declines has so far been concerned only with changes in the fertility of the acceptors. We now turn to the more general question of what happened to the fertility and birth rates for all the couples of Taichung. For this more general analysis we can rely on the data from the population register in comparing Taichung, the four other large cities, and Taiwan as a whole. These are shown in Table XII-6.

During the first year following the program, the birth rate and various fertility measures fell more sharply in Taichung than in Taiwan as a whole or in the four other major cities. The rate of decline for most fertility measures during that year was about twice as great in Taichung as in the other four major cities of Taiwan. The birth rates fell more rapidly in Taichung than in the other cities or in the province in every age group, except the extremely low or high parts of the age range (15-19 and 45-49), where the program is known to have had little effect. The declines in Taichung were particularly distinct in the 35-44 age group.

In the years 1964 and 1965, Taichung's fertility decline was not higher than that of the other cities or of the island as a whole; it was in fact somewhat less. We had expected that the Taichung decline would continue to pace the rest of the island, but this has not been the case. This probably results partly from the fact that the program was quickly expanded to cover the whole island, begin-

[7] Data from *Family Planning Studies in Korea*, No. 1, December 1967, mimeographed release from Seoul, Korea.

Table XII-6. Percentage Changes in Crude Birth Rates, General Fertility Rates, Total Fertility Rates, and Age-Specific Birth Rates in 1962-63, 1963-64, 1964-65, and 1963-65, for Taichung, Other Cities, and the Province as a Whole

	1962-1963			1963-1964		
Type of fertility rate	Taichung	Other cities[a]	Province	Taichung	Other cities	Province
Crude birth rate	- 2.6	- 3.9	- 2.9	- 5.4	- 2.6	- 4.7
General fertility rate	- 1.9	- 2.5	- 2.3	- 7.1	- 3.3	- 4.7
Total fertility rate	- 0.7	- 2.5	- 2.1	- 6.4	- 3.1	- 4.7
Age-specific birth rates for women in ages:						
15-19	-29.3	- 8.3	- 8.9	- 6.9	- 9.1	-10.0
20-24	- 4.5	- 5.7	- 1.2	- 3.0	+ 3.9	+ 0.8
25-29	+ 0.3	- 1.0	- 0.3	- 0.9	- 1.0	- 0.6
30-34	+ 4.7	- 2.5	- 1.7	- 7.9	- 6.6	- 7.4
35-39	+10.3	+ 3.8	- 4.1	-22.4	-13.9	-13.7
40-44	- 4.3	- 7.0	- 7.7	-20.5	- 7.5	-13.3
45-49	-28.6	+14.3	0.0	0.0	0.0	-20.0

	1964-1965			1963-1965		
Type of fertility rate	Taichung	Other cities	Province	Taichung	Other cities	Province
Crude birth rate	- 5.7	- 8.1	- 5.5	-10.7	-10.5	- 9.9
General fertility rate	- 6.3	- 8.8	- 6.2	-13.0	-11.8	-10.6
Total fertility rate	- 6.1	- 8.0	- 5.5	-12.1	-10.9	- 9.9
Age-specific birth rates for women in ages:						
15-19	+18.5	+ 2.5	0.0	+10.3	- 6.8	- 9.8
20-24	0.0	+ 1.2	+ 2.8	- 2.5	+ 5.2	+ 3.6
25-29	- 5.3	- 8.1	- 3.3	- 6.1	- 9.0	- 3.9
30-34	-10.8	-10.3	- 8.9	-16.8	-16.2	-15.6
35-39	-18.1	-22.6	-16.7	-36.4	-33.3	-28.1
40-44	-28.6	-27.0	-21.2	-43.2	-32.5	-31.7
45-49	0.0	-25.0	-25.0	0.0	-25.0	-40.0

[a] Taipei, Kaohsiung, Tainan, and Keelung.

ning in 1964 (see Chapter XIII). Further, the island-wide survey carried out by the Taiwan Population Studies Center in 1965 produced evidence that the use of contraception, abortion, and sterilization was increasingly widespread throughout the island. Given the excellent transportation and communication network of the island, it is to be expected that ideas and practices that meet widely felt needs will spread fairly rapidly.

DID THE PROGRAM LOWER TAICHUNG'S BIRTH RATE?

We will never know conclusively whether the program reduced Taichung's birth rate. It is difficult at best to know what would have happened if some part of a general historical situation had been different from what it was. In dealing with a single unit like Taichung the problems of inference are much more difficult, because we cannot use the statistical analysis of many units to separate out various factors (an illustrative attempt in this direction, using the local areas of Taiwan, is developed briefly in Chapter XIII). The fact that the changes were already underway in birth control, fertility, and other aspects of development makes the situation much more complicated. We have to demonstrate that the program accelerated changes already begun.

The fact that the birth rate for 1963-64 fell faster in Taichung than it did in other places in Taiwan can plausibly be related to the program. In 1963 Taichung was the object of a large program that did not exist elsewhere on the island, but after 1963 the effort concentrated on Taichung was not distinctive. However, even for 1963-64 we cannot conclusively demonstrate that the acceleration might not have occurred without the program. But then, it is also impossible to demonstrate the reverse: that the change would have occurred without the program.

Since Taichung's total acceptance rate up through 1967 was somewhat higher than that for other cities, we had expected that its fertility rate would continue to fall faster than was the case in other places, even after 1964. Although a faster decline would have made the case for a relationship between program and accelerated decline more plausible, even this would not have been conclusive. It still would not have been possible to demonstrate that the program made the difference. Of course, if it is logical to argue that the accelerated decline in 1963-64 would have occurred without a program, we could also argue that without a program the 1964-65 Taichung decline would have been less than it was. The question "what would have happened in history if . . ." is a sharp sword in an argument, but it has two cutting edges.

There is little doubt that those who entered the program reduced their fertility very considerably in this period and that this fact is probably responsible for Taichung's general fertility decline. The unanswerable question is whether this decline would have taken place without the program. Obviously, those who entered the program were motivated to take up birth control. Given the increasing general use of sterilization, abortion, and contraception, certainly some—and possibly all—of the acceptors might have taken equally effective steps anyway.

We think it is quite unlikely that the program made no difference. In the first place, the size of the decline in the fertility of the acceptors seems too large to have occurred spontaneously. We would expect more failures and less of a decline in a group adopting birth control without any support from a program.

A more important argument for the program's effect is the radical change in the characteristics of those accepting contraception within the program. Our previous analysis has indicated that a strong positive correlation between birth control practice and modernization or social status existed before the program began. This relationship disappears for those who are acceptors or for new birth control users outside the program. Apparently the program is effective in reaching low-status and traditional couples as well as the more advanced strata when the degree of demographic pressure is similar. We have argued in earlier chapters that the program provided legitimation, services, and support to groups which felt the need for birth control but were ambivalent or otherwise not equipped to begin effective practice on their own. If this is correct, then many of the more traditional and lower status couples would not have begun or continued birth control practice without the encouragement and services provided by the program. Again, we can't demonstrate that all of this would not have happened anyway, but it seems unlikely that without the program's influence there would have been in any short period such a rapid shift in the character of those accepting birth control. Admittedly, our argument would be much stronger if we had data on the full range of birth control practice in the general population for the whole period of time. We have to reason from incomplete data.

Dudley Kirk has advanced the view that much of the effect of programs like those of Taiwan and Korea may be indirect.[8] Quite

[8] "Fertility Trends in the Developing Countries—Recent Trends and Prospects," in S. J. Behrman, L. Corsa, and R. Freedman, eds., *Fertility and Family Planning: A World View.*

apart from direct services to acceptors, the program may increase the use of alternate methods of birth control by increasing the amount of information and discussion about birth control and by legitimizing the general ideas. This seems very plausible. We have already indicated that many acceptors kept their fertility low after giving up the method originally accepted by using "non-program" methods. It seems likely that many of these persons would not have continued any birth control practice, or perhaps would not have started at all, without the initial program influence. It is also plausible that many people who never became acceptors took up the practice of birth control on their own because they were influenced by the program more or less directly; but it is even more likely that they did so because they were influenced indirectly by the general diffusion of information and legitimation induced by the program.

PART 4. NEXT STEPS

XIII. The Family Planning Program for All of Taiwan[1]

BY R. FREEDMAN, L. P. CHOW, A. HERMALIN, AND J. Y. TAKESHITA

THE DEVELOPMENT OF THE TAIWAN PROGRAM

PERHAPS the most important consequence of the Taichung experiment was that it set the stage for a renewed effort to bring family planning to all of Taiwan. There had been earlier efforts to bring traditional contraceptives to parts of Taiwan,[2] but it was not until after the Taichung experiment that the machinery to bring the IUD to all parts of Taiwan was set up. The modest results of the previous efforts with traditional contraceptives had been interpreted by some as reflecting the relative unpreparedness of the population for family planning. When the ambitious effort in Taichung was being planned, there had been warnings by some observers that a large part of the population was too illiterate to understand the message; that the Chinese family tradition was inconsistent with a massive use of birth control; that even if young people were interested, the older generation would be outraged; that the IUD would not have mass appeal. To be sure, dissenting voices were occasionally heard in the course of the Taichung program, and the traditional values probably did contribute to the ambivalence toward family planning already discussed. But on the whole, the program received a cordial reception. The gloomy forecasts were incorrect, and the Taichung experience suggested that the earlier doubts about the readiness of the population may have been unfounded. The eligible married couples in Taichung responded by adopting family planning in large numbers; the IUD appeared to be acceptable and safe; and no

[1] This chapter draws freely on the following papers: L. P. Chow, "Studies on the Demographic Impact of the Intrauterine Contraceptive Device," mimeographed paper, 1967; L. P. Chow and T. C. Hsu, "Experiences with the Lippes Loop in Taiwan, Republic of China," a paper presented to the Regional Seminar of the Western Pacific Region of the International Planned Parenthood Federation, Hong Kong, November 1967. It also draws on the Interim Reports of the Taiwan Population Studies Center and their monthly reports.

[2] See Chapter I for a brief description of this earlier program.

significant political issues or other problems that might have prevented further extension of the program developed.

Reassured by the Taichung experience, the Taiwan Provincial Health Department began a new program early in 1964 to bring family planning services to all of Taiwan. The program was available at first in only a limited number of Taiwan's 361 local administrative units. Although the program reached many of the local units only after several years and some not at all, 380,000 women had received IUD insertions under the program's auspices by the end of December 1967.[3] This represents about 22 per cent of the married women of childbearing age.

Table XIII-1 shows how the cumulative number of acceptors varied from quarter to quarter. It also shows how the number of units with at least one participating doctor and at least one family planning worker grew. The number of acceptors grew fairly rapidly until early 1965. After that time the number of insertions averaged, with seasonal and other variations, about 8,000 to 9,000 a month or about 100,000 per annum. These figures come to an annual insertion rate that equals about 6 per cent of the married women of childbearing age. This rate is raised to about 7 per cent for 1967 if the number of women already served in the program by then are removed from the denominator as ineligible.

To describe and analyze in detail the history of the island-wide program would require a separate book. Here we can only touch on some aspects of the program, emphasizing major points of continuity with the Taichung experience and important ways in which the two programs differed.

The basic service plan of the island-wide program differs in some significant respects from that of the Taichung program. The IUD has been offered almost exclusively until recently. This policy followed not only from the overwhelming preference for the IUD in Taichung, but also from the obvious administrative advantages of

[3] This accounting, based on the doctors' submission of coupons for payment, needs to be deflated somewhat to take into consideration reinsertions. However, it is believed that the number of reinsertions for which coupons are submitted is relatively small. Due to terminations, the number of women with the IUD in situ as of December 1967 was much lower than 380,000. By the end of 1968, the number of women who had received an initial IUD insertion from the official program had passed 500,000. In addition, a contraceptive pill program conducted on a smaller scale had reached more than 60,000 women, some of them former uses of the IUD.

Table XIII-1. Time Progress of the IUD Program: Number of Insertions per Quarter and Cumulative to End of Each Quarter; Number of Worker-Months of Each Type in Each Quarter; Number of Townships in Each Quarter with Some Input of Each Type; and Input of Months of Work of Each Type per 1,000 Women in Child-bearing Years

		Number of insertions		Number of worker-months in each quarter			Number of town-ships in each quarter with some input of:		Input of months of work per 1,000 married women in childbearing years[b]			
Year	Quarter	In quarter	Cumulative to end of quarter	PPH workers	VHEN's	Doctors[a]	PPH workers or VHEN's	Doctors	PPH workers	VHEN's	PPH workers or VHEN's	Doctors
1963	Total	3,650	3,650	--	--	--	--	--	--	--	--	--
1964	First	2,529	6,179	85	56	123	47	28	.06	.04	.10	.08
	Second	9,844	16,023	263	90	474	122	80	.17	.06	.23	.31
	Third	15,445	31,468	333	133	763	160	108	.22	.09	.31	.50
	Fourth	18,782	50,250	413	108	948	210	123	.27	.07	.34	.62
1965	First	24,425	74,675	562	97	1,224	238	142	.36	.06	.42	.78
	Second	29,437	104,112	666	42	1,352	237	155	.42	.03	.45	.86
	Third	20,771	124,883	662	50	1,576	225	204	.42	.03	.45	1.00
	Fourth	24,620	149,503	652	107	1,727	258	216	.41	.07	.48	1.10
1966	First	28,176	177,679	662	106	1,759	257	229	.41	.07	.48	1.09
	Second	28,636	206,315	639	92	1,826	256	246	.40	.06	.46	1.14
	Third	24,462	230,777	600	95	1,883	267	255	.37	.06	.43	1.17
	Fourth	29,968	260,745	664	90	1,911	252	246	.41	.06	.47	1.19
1967	First	25,944	286,689	694	63	1,926						
	Second	30,064	316,753	815	40	1,944						
	Third	24,059	340,812									
	Fourth											

[a] The availability of doctors simply means that the doctor took a short training course and was certified as qualified to make insertions. Many of such doctors made very few insertions.

[b] Rates represent worker-months in quarter to 1,000 married women 20-44 years of age as of mid-year.

setting up a single supply line, record-keeping system, and training, evaluation, and follow-up service. Insertions are made for a fee by private medical practitioners authorized to provide the service following a short training course. The doctor receives a fee of 60 Taiwan Dollars ($1.50 U.S.) for each insertion, half of it from the client and half as subsidy from the Maternal and Child Health Association, under whose jurisdiction the whole program falls. The doctor's claim for a subsidy payment is established by sending into a central office a portion of a coupon which contains essential information about the client, as well as identification of the doctor, the address of the client, and the name of the referring fieldworker. The coupons are given out by the fieldworkers, by private referral agents,[4] by doctors themselves, or, in some cases, through a mailing to special groups of women.

The fieldworkers are the mainstay of the program. Information is brought to eligible women in their homes by personal visits from (1)

[4] Such as practicing midwives, beauty parlor operators, traveling salesmen, etc.

Family Planning Workers, more commonly known under their original name of Pre-Pregnancy Workers (PPH), who live in the local areas, or (2) traveling teams of Village Health Education Nurses (VHEN), who cover an area intensively in a short period and then move on to another area. The VHEN combine their work on family planning with more general work on village sanitation improvement.

The fieldworkers can make up priority lists of potential local acceptors from the register of married women of childbearing age who already have several children. The criteria for priority have varied over the course of the program. For example, in 1966 the fieldworkers were asked to give priority to women with a recent birth, since such women were very responsive.

The fieldworkers have a variety of supporting techniques, in addition to the house to house visits with the aid of pamphlets and visual aids, to help them reach potential acceptors. For example, the group meetings found effective in Taichung were used in some areas and in a carefully monitored experiment were found to be more effective per dollar spent than the individual home visits alone.[5] Other aids used by the fieldworkers included: (1) mailings to recent mothers and to other special groups, (2) offers of a free insertion for a limited time only, (3) the use of widely distributed "handbill flyers," mainly in connection with the free offer, and (4) the assistance of lay workers encouraged by a special incentive system to recruit cases.

The locally based PPH worker is undoubtedly the major agent in recruiting acceptors for the program, but there are other important sources. The extensive health care network centered on the private medical practitioners is potentially an important channel through which a large part of the eligible population can be reached. One way of assessing the sources is by counting how many persons of a given category are listed as official referral agents on the coupons sent in after insertions (Table XIII-2). During 1964, the first year of the island-wide program, a significant proportion of the cases were apparently recruited directly by the doctors authorized to make the insertions. While this may still be the case, the coupon data on referral agents have increasingly lost their validity, because as the program developed the doctor has come increasingly to give the local field-

[5] L. P. Lu, H. C. Chen and L. P. Chow, "An Experimental Study of the Effect of Group Meetings on the Acceptance of Family Planning in Taiwan," *Journal of Social Issues*, 23, No. 4, October 1967, 171-79.

Table XIII-2. Official Sources of Referral Listed on Coupons for 1964-67: Percentage Distribution

Source of referral	1964	1965	1966	1967[b]
Doctors	30	21	9	7
Family Planning Workers (PPH)	36	48	64	67
Village Health Education Nurses	7	6	6	4
Health station personnel	17	10	7	1
Mailings	--	1	4	7
Others[a]	10	14	10	14
Total	100	100	100	100

[a] Includes midwives, public and military hospital personnel, Family Planning Association of China, and miscellaneous other sources.

[b] January through October.

worker "credit" for some of the cases he may recruit from his own practice. Apparently, he does this to help the fieldworker attain her assigned quota. This is illustrative of the perils of a statistical system based on a field arrangement where the status and pay of a large number of workers are at stake. Table XIII-2, showing the official sources of referral reported on the IUD acceptance coupon, indicates a steady decline in the percentage of referrals by doctors and an increase in the proportion credited to PPH workers. There apparently has been a similar shift of credit to the PPH workers from the general health station workers, who have no personal quotas to meet. Since the health station workers are associates of the PPH workers, they would have some motivation to help their friends make a good showing and little to lose by doing so.

Fortunately, an independent report on sources of information is available from an island-wide survey of the sample of all the women who had an IUD insertion up to July 1966[6] (see Table XIII-3). Apart from the fact that this set of data is free from the kind of distortion just described, it has the advantage of including the original source of information, which might not be any of the formal agents usually cited on the coupon. In fact, the most important single source of information reported in the survey was persons in the informal

[6] This was the second follow-up survey of a sample of all those ever having an IUD insertion in Taiwan. The first such survey was carried out in 1965, and some results of that survey appear in L. P. Chow, R. Freedman, R. G. Potter, Jr., and A. K. Jain, "Correlates of IUD Termination in a Mass Family Planning Program: The First Taiwan IUD Follow-up Survey," 215-35.

Table XIII-3. Sources of Information about IUD Reported in the Second Island-Wide IUD Follow-up Survey for a Sample of the 206,315 Wives Having an Insertion Up to July 1966[a]

Sources of information mentioned[b]	Percentage of all sources mentioned
Neighbors, friends, and relatives who had used IUD	32
Husband	3
Family Planning Workers (PPH)	23
Doctors	7
Village Health Education Nurses (VHEN)	3
Health workers	14
Midwives	5
Newspapers, magazines, etx.	4
Other sources	8
No source mentioned	1
Total percentage	100
Total informal sources[c]	35
Total direct program sources[d]	33
Total other health sources[e]	19

[a] The weighted sample size for this survey was 4648.

[b] Includes sources mentioned first or second. 38 per cent of all respondents mentioned two sources and 99 per cent mentioned at least one.

[c] Friends, neighbors, husband, and other relatives.

[d] PPH workers, VHEN's, and doctors. We assume that almost all mentions of doctors refer to those qualified for the program. Mass media references not included in this group may have originated with the program.

[e] Health workers and midwives.

network of friends, neighbors, and relatives, confirming once again the importance and power of diffusion. Obviously, such an informal network does not generate the information spontaneously; it must be connected to focal points of a formally established network. In this formal network of the program, the PPH workers clearly played a key role.

The direct effect of the program may not be fully appreciated from Table XIII-3, since different elements of the program are listed separately. If we assume that most of the referrals by doctors were from those authorized to make insertions, then around 33 per cent of the reported referrals were from direct program sources—probably about the same number of referrals as those from word-of-mouth communication.[7]

The variety of approaches tried in Taiwan cannot be discussed here in detail, but a few of the special activities which may be pertinent for other countries as well are discussed in the sections that follow.

THE POSTPARTUM MAILING PROGRAM

The Taichung experiment indicated that a recent birth was an important stimulus to acceptance. This is consistent with evidence from other countries, including the results of a large international program especially organized to make family planning available during the immediate postpartum period.[8]

Building on some of this experience, the Taiwan program has been mailing information about the IUD with an offer of a free insertion to new mothers shortly after the new baby is registered. In the year beginning on April 1, 1966 the program sent out 139,755 such letters. The acceptance rate resulting directly from these mailings is estimated at 5.3 per cent. The direct cost per acceptance for this program is only 61 U.S. cents, much below the estimated cost of $2.70 per case for the program as a whole.

Specially marked free coupons are distributed with the letters, and the direct response to the mailing is measured by counting the number of these subsequently returned to the central office. It is possible, of course, that some of these acceptances would have occurred through regular program channels; but on the other hand, it is also possible that some women who were interested by the mailings accepted through the regular program channels, with the credit going to the doctor or to the family planning worker.

There is some independent evidence of the value of the postpartum mailings from another study, in which 67,399 letters were sent out to all women of childbearing age in townships without a family planning

[7] In a retrospective reporting on source of referral it is likely that the informal sources would be under-reported as compared with the official program personnel, since contacts with the latter would be more clearly differentiated than those with informal associates. For example, casual conversation with a relative or neighbor continued over months on many topics might include incidental reference to the IUD, and this might be the first source of information.

[8] See "International Postpartum Family Planning Program: Report on the First Year," *Studies in Family Planning*, No. 22, August 1967, 1-23.

worker. The acceptance rate in this study varied with the period since the last birth, as follows:

Period since last birth	*Acceptance rate*
Less than 6 months	6.0%
6-11 months	2.0%
12-23 months	0.9%
24 months or longer	0.4%

The acceptance rate for the postpartum women (those whose last birth had taken place less than six months ago) in this special study is very similar to that in the regular postpartum mailings to areas with a worker. The very rapid decline of the acceptance rate with the increasing length of the open birth interval is a powerful demonstration of the significance of a recent birth in motivating acceptance. The evidence also suggests that the ineffectiveness of the earlier general mailings in the Taichung and Korean programs may have been due to the diffuseness of their target, which included all women of childbearing age.

THE "FREE OFFER" FOR A LIMITED TIME

Insertions have been offered "free" for a limited period of three months to groups of thirty townships chosen on a rotating basis. During the period of the free offer there has always been a large increase in the number of acceptances, usually an increase of 100 to 175 per cent as compared with the preceding three-month period. One recurrent question has been whether this increase was only a borrowing of cases from the future, so that a subsequent decline in acceptance would erase these gains. It has even been argued that the free offer program might result in a lower average acceptance rate over the course of nine to twelve months, because women might wait for a free offer and become pregnant in the meantime.

These fears appear to be unfounded. The acceptance rate does decline in the first three months after the free offer period ends, but then there is a recovery to levels about as high as those prevailing before, so that the gains made during the free offer period are not dissipated. Data from six different groups of thirty townships validate this general statement (Table XIII-4). The acceptance rate in the

Table XIII-4. Insertions per Month in Sets of 30 Townships for Periods Before, During, and After Three Months "Free Offer" Program

Groups of 30 town-ships with free offer	Before offer	Free offer	First three months after free offer	Second three months after free offer	Six months after free offer	Free offer and six months after free offer
			Absolute number of insertions per month			
1st set	644	1,466	549	900	725	972
2nd set	862	2,400	1,065	884	975	1,450
3rd set	727	2,227	654	704	679	1,195
4th set	1,271	2,193	1,020	1,153	1,086	1,455
5th set	784	1,621	803	934	868	1,119
6th set	876	1,658	989	849	919	1,165
Average	865	1,927	847	904	875	1,226
			Relative number of insertions per month (Pre-insertion period = 100)			
1st set	100	228	85	140	113	151
2nd set	100	278	124	103	113	168
3rd set	100	306	90	97	93	164
4th set	100	173	80	91	85	114
5th set	100	207	102	119	111	143
6th set	100	189	113	97	105	133
Average	100	223	98	104	101	142

180 townships taken together more than doubled during the free offer period. Then, during the next three months, there was an average decline of about 2 per cent from the levels preceding the free offer. This was compensated for, however, by a rise of 4 per cent during the succeeding three months, so that, overall, the average rate during the six months following the free offer was slightly higher than the rate for the three months preceding the free offer. The end result was a 42 per cent increase in acceptances per month, if we add together acceptances for the three months of free offer and the six months that followed and compare this total with the earlier level. The insertion rate per month for the three months preceding the free offer is exceeded in the nine months that follow by 14 to 68 per cent in the six different trials (Table XIII-4).

PROGRAM INPUT, AREA CHARACTERISTICS, AND ACCEPTANCE RATES[9]

Acceptance rates in 1964 and 1965 were highest in the townships where program input by family planning workers and doctors was

[9] This section is based on an unpublished paper by Mary Speare.

greatest. After the fact, this may seem to be obvious. However, it was quite possible that the effort might have been ineffective or that after some minimum level of input further effort would fail to have any additional effect. So far as we know, this fundamental question of whether work input has the hoped-for effect on acceptances has not been investigated previously with the desirable multivariate controls. The question is not simply whether acceptances are correlated with work input but, more fundamentally, how much of the correlation, if any, can be attributed to work effort as distinguished from some other factors. The amount of input as well as the acceptance rate might be affected by such favorable factors as the educational level or the fertility decline already underway in the area.

Before presenting some detailed results, we can make the summary statement that in both urban and rural areas the acceptance rates were more strongly correlated with the input of effort by family planning workers than with any of the demographic or social characteristics investigated in the areas. The acceptance rate is more strongly related to program input than to any of the other variables, even when nine other relevant variables are taken into account simultaneously. The effect of the program input is not a spurious by-product of the allocation of effort to areas with a favorable potential for accepting family planning.

In the case of either urban or rural townships, the acceptance rates are more strongly correlated with the input of effort by family planning workers than with any of nine other demographic, program, or social variables (see the zero-order correlations in Table XIII-5). This is not to say that other variables are not also significantly related to acceptances. For the more numerous rural townships, for example, the acceptance rates are also higher: the higher the ratio of qualified doctors, the higher the proportion of women with at least a primary school education, the lower the crude death rate, and the shorter the distance to the nearest city of 50,000 or more population. In the urban townships, similar relationships hold between the acceptance rates and these variables, except that the magnitude of the relationship is much less for educational level and crude death rate.

There are lower correlations with other variables also, but the ten variables taken together explain a much higher proportion of the variance than the family planning worker ratio taken alone. (See bottom panel of Table XIII-5.) This is what raises the question of

Table XIII-5. Regression Values for Correlation Between Acceptance Rates (1963-65) and Program, Social, and Demographic Variables for 78 Urban Townships and 204 Rural Townships of Taiwan

	78 urban townships		204 rural townships[g]	
Program, social, and demographic variables	Zero order correlations	Partial beta coefficients	Zero order correlations	Partial beta coefficients
Family planning worker ratio, 1964-65[a]	+.62	+.76	+.42	+.36
Doctor ratio, 1964-65[b]	+.31	+.58	+.25	+.19
Percentage of females with at least primary education[c]	+.09	+.17	+.27	+.28
Total fertility rate, 1963	-.22	+.19	-.34	-.23
Change in total fertility rate, 1961-63	-.07	-.04	-.08	+.11
Percentage of male workers in agriculture and fisheries[d]	+.02	+.18	-.02	+.15
Net migration rate, 1961-63	±.00	-.02	-.13	-.03
Logarithm of population density in 1963[e]	+.14	+.14	+.07	+.06
Distance to nearest city of 50,000 population or more[f]	-.30	-.40	-.22	-.12
Crude death rate	-.14	+.01	-.29	-.12

Proportion of total variance in acceptance rates explained by:	78 urban townships	204 rural townships
1. family planning worker ratio	38	18
2. (1) plus doctor ratio	46	20
3. (1) plus total fertility rate, change in total fertility rate, and female education	49	37
4. All ten variables listed above	58	41

[a] Months of work in 1964 and 1965 per 100 married women 20-44 by PPH workers and VHEN's.

[b] Months of presence of trained doctors in 1964 and 1965 per 100 married women 20-44.

[c] Among females 12 years old or over.

[d] Among males in the labor force.

[e] Density measured as persons per square kilometer.

[f] Measured in miles.

[g] Excludes 30 townships with large aboriginal populations.

whether or not the influence of the family planning worker variable is simply the result of the placement of input in an area where conditions were favorable to begin with.

One answer to this question is given by a multivariate analysis which indicates that even when other variables are taken into account (see the partial beta values in Table XIII-5), the family planning worker ratio remains the variable most closely associated with acceptances. There are, to be sure, significant associations with other variables as well. In the rural areas, the most important of the non-program variables are the educational level of the women and the total fertility rate; in the urban areas, in addition to these two factors, the percentage of male workers in agriculture and fisheries and the distance to the nearest city of 50,000 or more are important variables. The relation of the availability of doctors qualified to make insertions to the acceptance rate is also significant, but this relationship is considerably weaker than the relationship of input by family planning workers to acceptance.

The latter relationship between acceptance rates and the family planning worker ratio is not diminished by holding constant the doctor ratio and the total fertility rate, as the following comparisons indicate:

	Correlation between acceptance rate and family planning indices:			
	worker ratio		*doctor ratio*	
	Urban	*Rural*	*Urban*	*Rural*
Zero-order correlation	.62	.42	.31	.25
Partial correlation holding constant:				
(a) the doctor ratio and the total fertility rate	.64	.40		
(b) the family planning worker ratio and the total fertility rate			.29	.17

While each has independent influence, the input of effort by family planning workers is clearly more important than the doctor ratio, and its importance is not diminished when the existing fertility level is further taken into account. As we have already demonstrated with the partial betas, even holding constant a whole array of other variables leaves the family planning worker's input more closely correlated to acceptance rates than any other single variable. The doctor ratio ranks second in the correlation measures in the rural areas and fourth in the urban areas.

On the whole, the results for the urban and the rural areas are roughly comparable, but in the urban areas the influence of the two program input variables is even greater than it is in the rural areas, both initially and after adjustment for the effect of other variables. We have no ready explanation for this. A major difference between the two kinds of areas is that being close to a city of 50,000 or more is much more important for the urban townships, while the mortality and educational levels are more important in the rural areas.

It is useful to see how the acceptance rates vary with the individual categories of the important variables (Tables XIII-6 and XIII-7). It is especially notable that there is a substantial number of acceptances even where there is no or very little input of effort by family planning workers or where there are no qualified doctors. Where no doctors are available, women must have sufficient motivation to travel to an adjacent township for an insertion.

In one group of thirty townships that have a large proportion of aborigines in their population neither doctors nor family planning workers are available, so this group provides an excellent further test of the power of diffusion of information from other areas. The acceptance rates up to August 1967 in these townships compare with the others as follows:

Cumulative acceptance rate to August 1967	*Aboriginal townships*		*Other townships*		*All townships*	
	Number	*Per cent*	*Number*	*Per cent*	*Number*	*Per cent*
30% or more	1	3	24	7	25	7
25-29%	1	3	57	17	58	16
20-24%	7	23	112	34	119	33
15-19%	5	17	85	26	90	25
10-14%	7	23	43	13	50	14
Less than 10%	9	31	10	3	19	5
Total	30	100	331	100	361	100

Table XIII-6. Mean Cumulative Acceptance Rate (1963-65) for 78 Urban Townships, by Selected Program, Social, and Demographic Characteristics

Program, demographic, and social characteristics	Mean acceptance rate	Number of townships	Program, demographic, and social characteristics	Mean acceptance rate	Number of townships
Family planning worker ratio, 1964-65			Crude death rate, 1963		
less than 0.05	6.7	8	less than 6	9.3	15
0.05-0.14	7.9	17	6.0-6.9	10.4	40
0.15-0.29	9.5	22	7.0-7.9	9.0	14
0.30-0.49	10.8	18	8.0 or more	8.9	9
0.50-1.99	13.1	13			
Doctor ratio, 1964-65			Log of density, 1963		
less than 0.20	7.7	10	4.5-5.9	9.0	13
0.20-0.49	9.1	22	6.0-6.4	9.7	16
0.50-0.99	10.3	30	6.5-6.9	9.6	23
1.00-2.50	11.0	16	7.0-9.4	10.4	26
Percentage females, primary graduates,			Net migration rate, 1961-63		
20-39	9.4	31	-10 or less	9.3	12
40-49	9.5	22	-6.0 to -9.9	10.4	16
50-69	10.5	25	-0.1 to -5.9	7.9	16
			0 to 9.9	11.9	18
			10 or more	9.0	16
Percentage male labor force in agriculture and fisheries, 1963			Distance in miles to nearest town of 50,000 or more, 1961		
less than 30	9.3	14	Less than 1	10.5	23
30-49	10.7	19	1.0-5.9	10.4	12
50-59	9.8	20	6.0-10.9	7.9	26
60-69	8.9	11	11.0-15.9	11.9	7
70-89	9.7	14	16.0 or more	9.0	10
Total fertility rate, 1963					
4000-4999	10.7	23			
5000-5499	9.6	25			
5500-5999	9.9	16			
6000-7499	8.5	14			

Although the rates are, of course, significantly lower in the aboriginal areas than in the rest of Taiwan, it is remarkable that nine aboriginal townships had acceptance rates of 20 per cent or more despite the complete absence of any direct program stimulus. Two-thirds of the aboriginal townships had acceptance rates of at least 10 per cent, even under such unfavorable conditions.

The reasons for the variation of input for the island as a whole have been largely administrative. Initially, limited budget and personnel restricted the number of areas served. Problems of recruitment and turnover have also affected the allocation of workers. As it turns out,

Table XIII-7. Mean Cumulative Acceptance Rate (1963-65) for 204 Rural Townships, by Selected Program, Demographic, and Social Characteristics

Program, demographic, and social characteristics	Mean acceptance rate	Number of townships
Family planning worker ratio, 1964-65		
less than .05	5.0	24
0.05-0.14	7.7	44
0.15-0.29	9.5	30
0.30-0.49	9.3	45
0.50-0.74	10.5	37
0.75-1.99	12.1	24
Doctor ratio, 1964-65		
0.00	8.2	99
0.01-0.19	8.6	34
0.20-0.49	9.9	52
0.50-2.20	11.6	19
Percentage females, primary graduates, 1963		
0-19	7.0	22
20-29	8.7	53
30-39	8.7	63
40-49	9.9	50
50-69	11.4	16
Percentage male labor force in agriculture and fisheries, 1963		
20-49	7.9	11
50-59	8.3	16
60-69	9.8	51
70-79	9.4	54
80-89	8.7	57
90-99	7.6	15
Total fertility rate, 1963		
4000-5499	10.2	50
5500-5999	10.1	67
6000-6499	8.5	40
6500-8400	6.8	47
Crude death rate, 1963		
less than 6.0	8.5	21
6.0-6.9	10.4	80
7.0-7.9	8.7	68
8.0-8.9	8.0	18
9.0 or more	5.1	17
Log of density, 1963		
less than 5.5	7.7	45
5.5 to 5.9	10.5	35
6.0 to 6.4	9.4	66
6.5 to 7.9	8.8	58
Net migration rate, 1961-63		
less than -10	9.2	45
-6 to 9.9	9.3	75
-1 to 5.9	9.4	36
0 to 9.9	8.5	26
10 or more	7.7	22
Distance in miles to nearest town of 50,000 or more, 1961		
1-5.9	9.0	61
6-10.9	9.1	79
11-15.9	10.2	31
16 or more	7.7	33

the resulting variation in input has not been correlated very highly to factors which bear on fertility or on acceptance rates. As is summarized in Table XIII-8, the two input variables are not very strongly correlated with the non-program variables related to acceptances. Both the program and the non-program variables have independent influence on acceptances. The proportion of the total variance in acceptance rates that can be explained by adding various other combinations of variables to the family planning worker ratio is shown in the bottom panel of Table XIII-5.

Table XIII-8. Correlation between Family Planning Worker Ratio or Doctor Ratio and Other Social and Demographic Characteristics for Urban and Rural Townships

Program, social, and demographic characteristics	Family planning worker ratio (1964-65)		Doctor ratio (1964-65)	
	Urban townships	Rural townships	Urban townships	Rural townships
Acceptance rate (1964-65)	+.62	+.42	+.31	+.25
Percentage of females over 12 with primary education	-.10	+.13	+.22	-.01
Total fertility rate, 1963	+.01	±.00	+.31	-.02
Change in total fertility rate, 1961-63	-.08	-.15	-.07	+.02
Percentage male labor force in agriculture and fisheries	+.26	±.00	-.28	-.08
Net migration rate, 1961-63	-.05	-.17	+.12	+.06
Logarithm population density, 1963	-.16	-.15	+.34	-.06
Distance to nearest city of 50,000 population or more	+.07	+.06	-.11	+.11
Crude death rate, 1963	+.06	±.00	-.17	+.10

While the significance of the program effort for local areas seems substantial in these data from the early years of the Taiwan program, obviously no conclusive generalizations about the long-run effect of the program can be made at this early stage. Only after some time will we be able to determine whether the program effort has a lasting effect on contraceptive practice that cannot be attributed to other factors. Even for the short run, there are puzzling aspects to the results. We do not know, for example, why the acceptance rates are more closely correlated to the program variables in urban areas than in rural. Finally, it is still too early to tell whether there will be significant permanent effects on the fertility decline that would not have occurred anyway, as a result of other social changes. These statements of caution should not, however, be taken to mean that the program has left no visible results. After all, in the short run the program has achieved just what was hoped. Where effort has been expended, there have been correlated acceptances of contraception which cannot be explained by the other factors considered. These new acceptances of contraception were the first, most immediate goal of the program.

The Program for All of Taiwan

AN AREA ANALYSIS OF THE EFFECT OF ACCEPTANCES ON FERTILITY

An obviously crucial criterion for evaluating a family planning program is its effect on fertility levels. A recurrent theme in such evaluations is that disassociating the impact of the program from other ongoing processes is difficult. No single set of measurements is likely to suffice for an adequate, overall appraisal. A sounder judgment should emerge if we make use of a battery of criteria which are relevant to the basic question, studying the characteristics of acceptors, comparing their fertility prior to and subsequent to acceptance, and estimating births averted per acceptance.

This section approaches the question of the program's impact by studying the relation of acceptance rates to fertility in the 282 urban and rural areas of Taiwan.[10] The use of local areas rather than individuals as the basic unit of analysis has some disadvantages. For example, from an area analysis alone one cannot be sure that it is the individual acceptors that account for most of the observed drop in fertility; the decrease in fertility may be due to a greater extent to the fertility behavior of the non-accepting couples.

On the other hand, a number of questions have been asked about the impact of a family planning program which do involve area characteristics. For example, the contention that decreases in fertility are due to increasing levels of education, decreasing death rates, and other modernizing trends rather than to a new program per se can be tested by seeing whether, among various areas of the country, there is a relation between levels of fertility and levels of acceptance rates, after taking into account the socio-economic characteristics related to fertility. The question is whether the family planning program is a direct contributor to the changes in fertility, rather than merely a passive recipient of gains brought about by the modernizing trends within the society.

[10] There are 361 township-level administrative divisions in Taiwan. Of these, 42 are precincts of the 5 major cities and 7 are small cities. In addition, there are 78 units classified as urban townships, which are less densely settled than the cities and are characterized by having at least one market center of an urban nature. There are 204 rural townships which are predominantly collections of agricultural villages. Lastly, there are 30 rural townships designated as aboriginal because the people there differ in a number of ways from the rest of the population. The analysis here utilizes only the 78 urban townships and the 204 rural townships.

Table XIII-9, which shows a tendency for those areas with higher acceptance rates to have larger decreases in fertility between 1963 and 1965, gives a first view of the situation. The next step is to determine whether this relationship can be accounted for by the socio-economic or demographic characteristics of the area. It might seem that the best procedure would be to use the change in fertility together with the acceptance rates and socio-economic variables for each area in a correlational analysis. This procedure, however, runs afoul of the problem that the correlation of a change variable with another variable is a function of the intercorrelations between the two elements making up the change variable and the third variable, as well as the coefficient of variation of each variable. Very often the sign or level of magnitude of a correlation involving a measure of change will be constrained because of the intercorrelations existing among the three variables. Though correlations using change variables make sense intuitively, failure to note what lies behind them often leads to errors of inference.[11]

[11] Some of the points in this paragraph may be illustrated as follows: The proportional change in total fertility is $\frac{Z-Y}{Y} = \frac{Z}{Y} - 1$ where Z is the total fertility at the more recent date and Y is the total fertility at an earlier date. For correlational analysis, the proportional change may be defined simply as $\frac{Z}{Y}$ since the value of a correlation is not affected by addition or subtraction of a constant. To a close approximation, the correlation of this change variable with another variable X may be represented as:

$$r_{\frac{Z}{Y}X} = \frac{r_{ZX}v_Z - r_{YX}v_Y}{\sqrt{v_Z^2 + v_Y^2 - 2r_{ZY}v_Zv_Y}}$$

where v_Z and v_Y are the coefficient of variation of Z and Y respectively.

For the change in total fertility between 1963 and 1965 for the 78 urban areas, substitution of the appropriate values gives:

$$r_{\frac{Z}{Y}X} = \frac{.1235r_{ZX} - .1210r_{YX}}{.053}$$

The correlation between total fertility 1965 and total fertility 1963 is (.91). A number of variables will show about the same correlation with total fertility 1965 as with total fertility 1963. If we call this value r', the above equation may be further simplified to:

$$r_{\frac{Z}{Y}X} = .047\ r'$$

In these cases, then, the correlation using the change variable will be a small fraction of the correlation existing between the third variable and each of the components of the change variable.

The problem discussed above may be viewed as part of a more general problem sometimes discussed in statistical literature under the heading of index cor-

Table XIII-9. Percentage Distribution of Areas by Per Cent Change in Total Fertility 1963 to 1965 and Cumulative Acceptance Rate to March 1965

Per cent change in total fertility 1963 to 1965	Cumulative acceptance rate to March 1965			
	0.0-2.9%	3.0-4.9%	5.0% or more	Total
		Urban areas		
-12 or less	27	32	42	36
-5 to -12	60	52	50	53
-1 to -5	13	12	8	10
More than -1	0	4	0	1
Total per cent	100	100	100	100
Number	15	25	38	78
		Rural areas		
-12 or less	18	30	47	32
-5 to -12	42	51	42	44
-1 to -5	23	14	7	15
More than -1	17	5	4	9
Total per cent	100	100	100	100
Number	72	59	73	204

For this reason we will adopt a more roundabout approach that appears to be methodologically safer. Our focus will be on determining the relative contribution of various factors to the recent level of fertility in the local area. The factors to be analyzed include the prior fertility of the area, the acceptance rate, the health worker and doctor ratios, and such socio-economic and demographic variables as educational level of the females, density, and crude death rate. There is a temporal ordering to the variables as defined and a presumed causal sequence which can be visualized in Figure 4.

In Figure 4, below, each variable occurs earlier in time than those variables to the right of it and later than those to the left of it. Moreover, each variable can be affected by all of the variables which precede it, i.e., which lie to the left of it, though for clarity only some of the possible connections are shown.[12]

relation. See, for example, Q. McNemar, *Psychological Statistics,* New York: John Wiley and Sons, 1955, pp. 161-63. For more specific discussions of the problems arising in the use of measures of change, see: O. D. Duncan, R. P. Cuzzort, and B. Duncan, *Statistical Geography,* Glencoe: The Free Press, 1961, pp. 162-66; and P. M. Blau and O. D. Duncan, *The American Occupational Structure,* New York: John Wiley and Sons, 1967, pp. 194-99.

[12] Though the ordering of the variables follows a chronological pattern in the main, there are a few departures which merit explanation. Though the data for density and female education of the area are measured as of 1963, they are shown as prior to the crude death rate and total fertility for 1963 since in both cases they

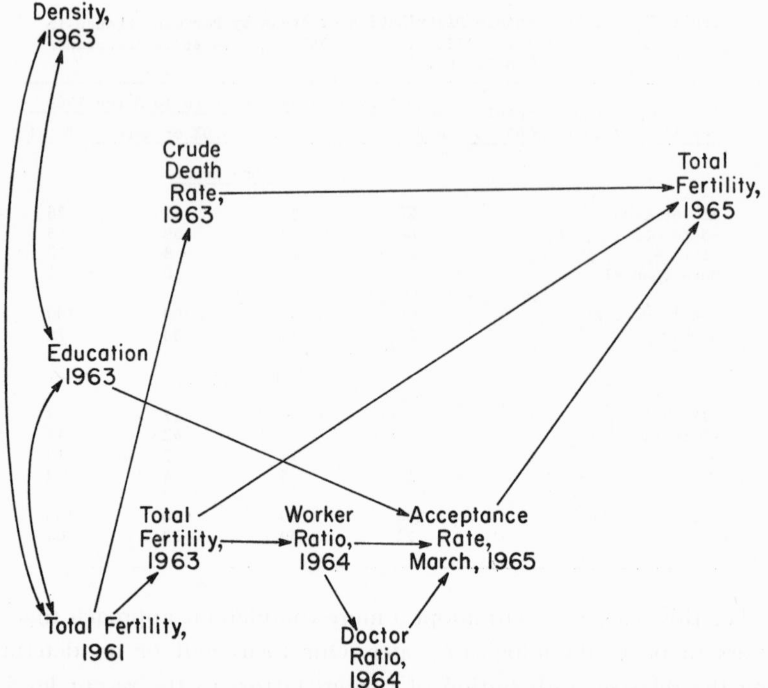

Figure 4. Basic Model of Factors Affecting 1965 Total Fertility

The sign and relative magnitude of the presumed causal connections can be determined by the use of path analysis, a multivariate technique with close affinities to conventional multiple regression analysis. Its main virtues are that it makes explicit the assumptions underlying the regression analysis and elucidates the indirect effects of the variables in the model.[13]

---

are characteristics which are cumulative resultants of long processes which change little in a one- or two-year period. Moreover, despite the fact that the measurement of all the variables pertains to the same period of time, the density and education may be considered logically prior, since, for example, a woman will typically have completed her education before bearing children.

The measurement of the doctor ratio for 1964 has as its numerator the number of doctors who took a short training course and became qualified to make insertions. The assumption is that doctors were prompted to qualify themselves by the health worker activity in their area and the demand thereby created, and for this reason the worker ratio for 1964 is shown as prior to the doctor ratio for 1964.

[13] For some detailed discussion of path analysis and various examples of its use, see O. D. Duncan, "Path Analysis: Sociological Examples," *American Journal of Sociology*, 72, No. 1, July 1966, 1-16; and Blau and Duncan, *op.cit.*, pp. 165-88. The abbreviated description given here draws heavily on these two sources.

In the model used here, the direct or net influences of one variable on another are represented by straight arrows. The sign and magnitude of these are given by the path coefficients which are the partial regression coefficients in standard form, the beta coefficients, obtained from the appropriate multiple regression. The path coefficients, then, measure the relative effect of one variable on another while controlling for the other variables in the model. For example, the path coefficients or direct influences on the health worker ratio are measured by the beta coefficients from a multiple regression in which the health worker ratio is the dependent variable and the independent variables are those antecedent to it in the causal scheme. A measure of the indirect influence of any variable on a subsequent variable is obtained by subtracting from the zero-order correlation between the two variables the value of the direct influence of the earlier variable on the later one.[14]

The zero-order correlations among the variables used in Figure 4 are shown in Tables XIII-10 and XIII-11. These tables show that the variable most closely associated with an area's 1965 total fertility is its prior fertility, represented here by total fertility in 1963 and 1961. The high correlations among these three fertility measures only mean, of course, that over this short period of time there has been little change in the relative rank of the areas regarding fertility, despite a general downward trend. From this not surprising persistence of relative fertility levels, our focus shifts to a consideration of the extent to which the other variables have any net influence on recent fertility.

To determine this, let us consider the multiple regressions set forth in Tables XIII-12 and XIII-13. These results are also shown in Figures 5 and 6. Consider first the paths to the 1965 total fertility rate in Figure 5 for urban areas. Aside from the expected strong influence of prior fertility, the most important direct influence is that of the IUD acceptance rate, the negative sign indicating that the higher the acceptance rate, the lower the fertility rate. There is also a direct influence on 1965 total fertility from another family planning variable, the worker ratio, but the sign here is positive. Despite the positive direct path coefficient, the indirect effect of the worker ratio is clearly negative. This can be seen by subtracting the direct path coefficient

[14] The measure so obtained reflects not only the influence of the variable transmitted indirectly through other variables, but also its joint effect with these variables.

Table XIII-10. Correlation Matrix of Variables in Path Analysis for 78 Urban Areas

	Total fertility 1965	Total fertility 1961	Total fertility 1963	Worker ratio, 1964	Doctor ratio, 1964	Cumulative acceptance rate to March 1965	Per cent women primary grads, 1963	Crude death rate, 1963	Mean	Standard deviation
Total fertility, 1965									4888	604
Total fertility, 1961	.80								5711	617
Total fertility, 1963	.91	.85							5423	656
Worker ratio, 1964[a]	-.21	-.10	-.19						.13	.11
Doctor ratio, 1964[b]	-.39	-.35	-.35	.26					.21	.20
Cumulative acceptance rate to March 1965[c]	-.34	-.13	-.21	.64	.45				5.1	2.3
Per cent women primary grads, 1963[d]	-.22	-.27	-.21	-.14	.23	-.01			43.6	10.0
Crude death rate, 1963	.56	.53	.51	-.05	-.15	.00	-.19		6.2	1.0
Log of density, 1963[e]	-.59	-.61	-.54	-.02	.37	.12	.22	-.48	6.64	.76

[a] Months of work in 1964 by PPH workers or VHEN's per 100 married women 20-44.

[b] Months of presence of trained doctors in 1964 per 100 married women 20-44.

[c] Rate of acceptance through March 1965 per 100 married women 20-44.

[d] Per cent of females 12 years old or more with at least a primary education.

[e] Density measured as persons per square kilometer.

Table XIII-11. Correlation Matrix of Variables in Path Analysis for 204 Rural Areas

	Total fertility 1965	Total fertility 1961	Total fertility 1963	Worker ratio, 1964	Doctor ratio, 1964	Cumulative acceptance rate to March 1965	Per cent women primary grads, 1963	Crude death rate, 1963	Mean	Standard deviation
Total fertility, 1965									5459	791
Total fertility, 1961	.75								6227	663
Total fertility, 1963	.88	.78							5971	740
Worker ratio, 1964[a]	-.40	-.22	-.32						.10	.12
Doctor ratio, 1964[b]	-.16	-.02	-.05	.31					.03	.09
Cumulative acceptance rate to March 1965[c]	-.45	-.34	-.35	.57	.29				4.3	2.7
Per cent women primary grads, 1963[d]	-.02	-.14	-.06	.04	-.02	.19			33.9	12.0
Crude death rate, 1963	.57	.50	.55	-.22	.13	-.21	-.07		6.7	1.2
Log of density, 1963[e]	-.46	-.44	-.47	.12	-.02	.13	-.26	-.31	5.98	.75

[a] Months of work in 1964 by PPH workers or VHEN's per 100 married women 20-44.

[b] Months of presence of trained doctors in 1964 per 100 married women 20-44.

[c] Rate of acceptances through March 1965 per 100 married women 20-44.

[d] Per cent of females 12 years old or more with at least a primary education.

[e] Density measured as persons per square kilometer.

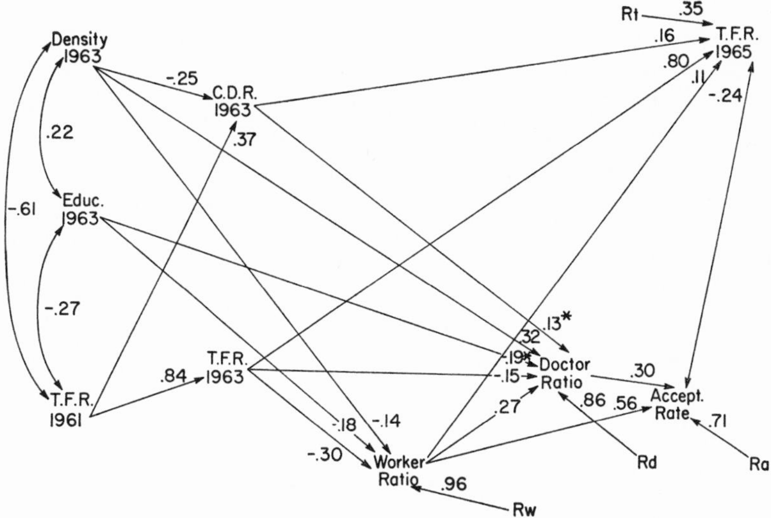

Figure 5. Path Diagram of Factors Affecting 1965 Total Fertility in 78 Urban Areas

Note: The paths Rw, Rd, Ra, and Rt represent residual paths, which encompass all other influences on the variable in question. The expression (1-square of the residual path) gives the proportion of variance accounted for by the variables with direct paths to the variable in question.

* Path coefficient is less than twice the standard error of the Beta coefficient.

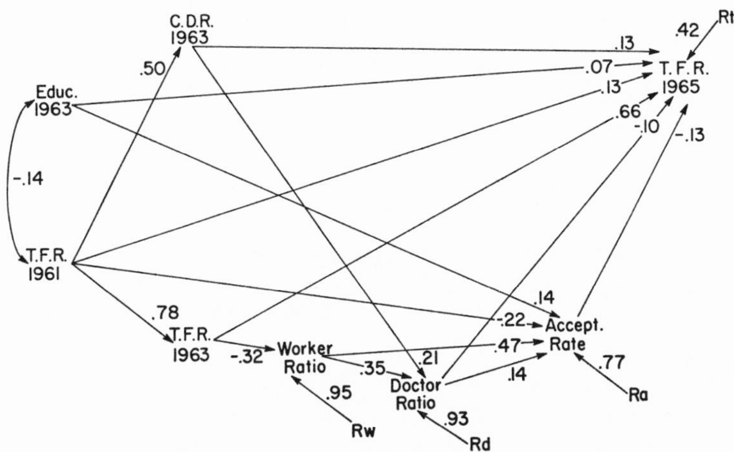

Figure 6. Path Diagram of Factors Affecting 1965 Total Fertility in 204 Rural Areas

Note: The variable density did not have any significant direct influence on 1965 total fertility or on any of the family planning variables and was therefore dropped from the model (see Table XIII-13). For explanation of paths Rw, Rd, Ra, and Rt see note to Figure 5.

Table XIII-12. Partial Regression Coefficients in Standard Form for Specified Combinations of Variables for 78 Urban Areas

Dependent variable	Independent variables								Coefficient of determination (R^2)
	Worker ratio	Doctor ratio	Acc. rate	TFR 1963	CDR 1963	Den. 1963	Educ. 1963	TFR 1961	
Worker ratio	--	--	--	-.36	.00	-.12	-.17	.08	.09
Worker ratio*	--	--	--	-.30	--	-.14	-.18	--	.09
Doctor ratio	.27	--	--	-.11	.14	.31	.18	-.06	.27
Doctor ratio*	.27	--	--	-.15	.13	.32	.19	--	.27
Acceptance rate	.57	.29	--	-.11	.11	.08	.01	.12	.52
Acceptance rate*	.56	.30	--	--	--	--	--	--	.49
Total fer. rate, 1965	.09	.01	-.23	.75	.13	-.08	-.01	.03	.88
Total fer. rate, 1965*	.11	--	-.24	.80	.16	--	--	--	.88

*Beta coefficients in this row used as estimates of path coefficients in Figure 5. Beta coefficients in the preceding row represent the path coefficients to this variable from all the variables antecedent to it in the basic model, Figure 4.

Table XIII-13. Partial Regression Coefficients in Standard Form for Specified Combinations of Variables for 204 Rural Areas

Dependent variable	Independent variables								Coefficient of determination (R^2)
	Worker ratio	Doctor ratio	Acc. rate	TFR 1963	CDR 1963	Den. 1963	Educ. 1963	TFR 1961	
Worker ratio	--	--	--	-.36	-.07	-.04	.02	.08	.11
Worker ratio*	--	--	--	-.32	--	--	--	--	.10
Doctor ratio	.34	--	--	-.06	.24	-.04	-.03	-.04	.14
Doctor ratio*	.35	--	--	--	.21	--	--	--	.14
Acceptance rate	.46	.15	--	-.04	-.01	.02	.15	-.17	.41
Acceptance rate*	.47	.14	--	--	--	--	.14	-.22	.41
Total fer. rate, 1965	-.04	-.10	-.11	.64	.12	-.03	.05	.13	.88
Total fer. rate, 1965*	--	-.10	-.13	.66	.13	--	.07	.13	.83

*Beta coefficients in this row used as estimates of path coefficients in Figure 6. Beta coefficients in the preceding row represent the path coefficients to this variable from all the variables antecedent to it in the basic model, Figure 4.

(+.11) from the zero-order correlation between worker ratio and 1965 total fertility (—.21) to obtain a total indirect effect of (—.32).

Aside from 1963 total fertility, the only non-program variable with a direct influence on 1965 total fertility is the 1963 crude death rate. The other variables have only joint and indirect effects, as does the crude death rate in addition to its direct influence. The question then arises of the extent to which these joint and indirect effects are operating through the family planning program variables, as against effects operating through the other socio-economic or demographic variables. By decomposing the correlation between 1965 total fertility and each of the socio-economic variables, it is possible to arrive at an answer to this question. For example, the correlation between the crude death rate and the 1965 total fertility rate may be expressed as follows:

$$r_{tc} = P_{tc} + P_{ts} \cdot r_{sc} + P_{tw} \cdot r_{wc} + P_{ta} \cdot r_{ac}$$

where $t = 1965$ total fertility; $c = 1963$ crude death rate; $s = 1963$ total fertility; $w =$ worker ratio; $a =$ acceptance rate; P is the path coefficient from the variable designated by the second subscript to the variable designated by the first subscript, and r is the zero-order correlation of the two variables indicated by its subscript.

The first term on the right of the equation represents the direct effect of the crude death rate, the other three terms constitute the joint and indirect effects. The second term on the right gives the joint and indirect effect of the crude death rate arising from its relation to the 1963 total fertility rate. This effect, which is independent of the family planning variables, turns out to account for almost all of the non-direct effects, as can be seen by substituting the values from the correlation matrix and Figure 5 into the above equation:

$$.56 = .16 + .80\,(.51) + .11\,(-.05) + (-.24)\,(.00)$$
$$.56 = .16 + .41 \quad - .01 \quad \pm .00$$

Similar results are obtained when the other socio-economic variables are analyzed.

The analysis of indirect effects also shows that most of the influence of the acceptance rate on 1965 total fertility is direct, since the correlation between these two variables is (—.34) and the path coefficient from acceptance rates to 1965 total fertility is (—.24). This leaves only (—.10) to be accounted for by the relationship of acceptance rates to the variables antecedent to it in the model.

Figure 6 for rural areas shows again that two of the family planning program variables have a direct effect on 1965 total fertility. In this case, the acceptance rate, with a path coefficient of (—.13), has as much direct influence as any of the socio-economic or demographic variables aside from prior fertility, though the coefficient is less in magnitude here than in the urban areas. In addition, the doctor ratio has a significant negative influence almost equal in magnitude to that of the acceptance rate. Unlike the situation in the urban areas, in rural areas most of the relation between acceptance rate and 1965 total fertility, as reflected in the correlation of (—.45), is indirect in nature, since the path coefficient is only (—.13). Most of these indirect effects are accounted for by the relation of acceptance rates to the earlier fertility levels, that is, to total fertility in 1961 and 1963.

The model used in this analysis is, of course, only one of a number of possible models. Addition or deletion of variables can be expected to affect the magnitude of the paths of the other variables to 1965 total fertility. How sensitive are the observed effects of the program variables to such changes? As one test of the extent of this sensitivity, a similar analysis was carried out which omitted the prior fertility variables, 1961 total fertility and 1963 total fertility. This model resulted in much higher direct effects on 1965 fertility rates for some of the remaining socio-economic and demographic variables. The reason for this is that in the earlier model much of their relationship with 1965 total fertility had appeared as joint and indirect effects transmitted through the prior fertility variables, with which they are highly intercorrelated. With the prior fertility variables removed from the model, more of their relationship to 1965 total fertility appears as a direct effect. Nevertheless, the effects of the family planning variables in this model remain as large as in the model given earlier, as can be seen from the table on page 339.

We can interpret this second model to mean that the social and economic variables were already affecting the level and trend of fertility, and that therefore the model which explicitly used the 1963 fertility levels largely took care of this influence on 1965 fertility. The program effect is a new and added intervention whose influence goes beyond that of the socio-economic variables. In other words, it appears to be true that the social and economic factors do indeed play a part in the fertility decline, as we expected, but it is also true that the program has a significant additional effect even where the socio-economic factors are operating.

It may be noted in passing that both Figures 5 and 6 confirm the conclusion of the previous section that the most important influence on acceptance rate is the family planning worker ratio. The doctor ratio also has a significant direct influence; in the urban areas it is the only other variable with such effect, and in the rural areas it is about as important as the two non-program variables with significant path coefficients.

In summary, the mode of analysis used here indicates that IUD acceptances do have a noticeable effect on subsequent fertility. This effect is not due simply to the relationship of the family planning pro-

Model 2 — Prior Fertility Variables Omitted

Beta Coefficients Between 1965 Total Fertility Rates and Program, Social, and Demographic Variables

	Urban Areas	*Rural Areas*
Acceptance rate to 3/65	—.26	—.22
Worker ratio, 1964	—.01	—.11
Doctor ratio, 1964	—.08	—.12
Density, 1963	—.33	—.30
Crude death rate, 1963	.38	.42
Education of women, 1963	—.07	—.03

gram to modernizing trends in Taiwan, but rather appears to represent a net contribution to fertility control beyond that of these other factors. These findings may be considered encouraging when it is remembered that the analysis is based only on the worker and doctor inputs in the first year of the program and on the acceptances of the first fifteen months, a period in which the program was barely underway. On the other hand, some analysts have claimed that a program has its major effect in its early phase and that after this the results are less pronounced. Detailed analysis focusing on the fertility of specific age groups and utilizing more recent data is now underway and will reveal the extent of impact of the program in its broader phase.

WHO ACCEPTS IN THE ISLAND-WIDE PROGRAM?

From the beginning, acceptance rates in the island-wide program have been correlated with such indications of demographic pressure as the number of living children and the wife's age. In 1964, the highest acceptance rates were among women with four or more children and among women 30-34 years of age. Over the next two years, however, there has been a gradual shift downward in both the parity and the age of acceptors, so that by 1966 the proportion of acceptors among women with three children or fewer as well as the proportion of the acceptors under 30 had risen from 31 to 37 per cent. Even in 1966, acceptance rates were still relatively low among those with fewer than two children and among the youngest wives, but over a period as short as two years, the trend shown in Table XIII-14 is clearly

Table XIII-14. Percentage Distribution of Acceptors, by Wife's Age, Number of Living Children, and Education, 1964-67

Characteristics of acceptors	1964	1965	1966	Jan.-June, 1967
All acceptors (per cent)	100	100	100	100
Wife's age				
20-24	6	7	9	9
25-29	25	26	28	29
30-34	34	33	32	32
35-39	25	23	21	20
40-44	8	9	8	8
45-49	1	1	1	1
Unknown	1	1	1	1
Number of living children at time of acceptance				
0	*	*	*	*
1	2	2	3	3
2	9	10	12	13
3	20	20	22	23
4	24	24	24	24
5	19	18	16	16
6 or more	22	21	18	17
Unknown	4	5	5	4
Wife's education				
None	40	42	40	40
Primary school	45	45	48	48
Junior high school	9	8	7	7
Senior high school or more	6	5	5	5

* Less than 1 per cent

toward relatively more acceptances from the demographic strata believed to be difficult to reach.

In the first year of the island-wide program, the wife's education was somewhat more closely correlated to acceptance rates than was the case in the Taichung program (Table XIII-15). The highest acceptance rates were for women with at least a junior high school education. However, in each of the two succeeding years the selective effect of education decreased, as acceptance rates rose most quickly among women with a primary education. This reflects in small part the slower growth in the size of this educational stratum as compared with the growth rate of higher educational strata, and consequent changes in the average age of the various educational strata.

The better-educated women wanted and had fewer children and began to use contraception earlier than the less-educated women, both before and during the program (Tables XIII-16 and XIII-17). Conse-

Table XIII-15. Rate of Acceptance of the IUD in Taiwan, by Wife's Age, Number of Living Children, and Education, 1964, 1965, and 1966 and Changes, 1964-1966[a/]

Characteristics of acceptors	1964	1965	1966	Percentage change 1964-66
Wife's age				
20-24	1.0	2.6	4.6	360.0
25-29	3.1	6.8	7.7	148.4
30-34	4.6	9.2	9.4	104.3
35-39	3.9	7.6	6.8	74.4
40-44	1.7	3.6	4.4	158.8
Number of living children				
0	0.1	0.3	0.3	200.0
1	0.5	1.4	2.1	320.0
2	1.8	4.4	5.7	216.7
3	3.7	8.0	9.5	156.8
4	4.2	8.4	9.3	121.4
5 or more	3.8	7.5	7.5	97.4
Wife's education				
None	2.4	5.2	5.5	129.2
Primary school	3.4	7.2	8.5	150.0
Junior high school	4.8	8.5	8.7	81.2
Senior high school or more	4.6	7.9	8.3	80.4
Total	3.0	6.3	7.0	133.3

[a/] Data from L.P. Chow and T.C. Hsu, "Experiences with the Lippes Loop in Taiwan, Republic of China," mimeographed paper prepared for the Regional Seminar of the Western Pacific Region of the International Planned Parenthood Federation, November 1967, Hong Kong.

quently, more education goes with higher acceptance rates at lower parities and younger ages. These findings for Taiwan parallel those already described for Taichung. Even in 1966, when some differentials had been diminished, acceptance rates increased markedly with education for those women with fewer than three children or for women in their twenties. For older women or for those with four or more children acceptance rates tend to be relatively low among the best educated, presumably because they are already protected by alternate birth control methods. Some confirmation of this last explanation is found in Table XIII-17, which shows the proportion of all married women already protected by contraception or sterilization in 1965 (including a small percentage who were using the IUD). Note, for example, the sharp increase with parity in the proportion already protected among women with a junior or senior high school education. So many better-educated, higher-parity women were already practicing

Table XIII-16. Acceptance Rate, by Wife's Education, by Number of Living Children, 1966

Wife's education	Number of living children									
	0	1	2	3	4	5	6	7	8 or more	Total
None	0.1	0.5	2.6	6.2	8.1	7.3	6.1	6.1	6.6	5.5
Primary school	0.4	2.1	6.7	12.9	10.8	10.1	8.8	7.8	13.3	8.5
Junior high school	0.5	5.7	13.6	11.8	9.3	6.6	4.4	4.5	5.1	8.7
Senior high school or more	0.8	9.5	11.8	12.5	6.6	3.9	4.6	3.7	7.5	8.3
Total	0.3	2.1	5.7	9.5	9.2	8.1	6.8	6.7	8.0	7.0

Table XIII-17. Percentage of Married Women Sterilized or Currently Using Contraception, by Wife's Education, by Number of Living Children, 1965[a]

Number of living children	Wife's education				Total
	None	Primary	high	Junior high or more	
Less than 2	3	1	4	23	3
2	5	11	15	51	11
3	11	28	55	49	22
4	21	40	75	75	35
5 or more	22	39	70	73	31
Total	16	26	46	53	23

[a] Based on data from the 1965 survey by the Taiwan Population Studies Center of an island-wide sample of married women under the age of 45. The survey covered a range of topics in the area of knowledge, attitudes, and practice of birth control as well as fertility histories.

family planning that it is not too surprising that they failed to become acceptors in larger numbers.

One of the most important characteristics of the acceptors is very high fertility in the three years preceding the insertion. This is important, first of all, because it indicates that the women with a problem of recent high fertility are motivated to accept family planning. Perhaps more important, it means that the potential effects of the acceptance on fertility are much greater than might be expected if it were assumed that the acceptors would have the average fertility of their age group. We present below the average annual fertility rates of the IUD acceptors for the three years preceding the first insertion and, as a point of comparison, the fertility rates of all married women in Taiwan for about the same period of time.

The Program for All of Taiwan

Age group	*IUD acceptors in 3 years preceding insertion*	*All married women in Taiwan (average for 1963-64)*	*Ratio of rates for IUD cases to rates for all married women*
20-24	580	430	135
25-29	493	379	130
30-34	343	241	142
35-39	259	143	181
40-44	159	65	245
Average	379	243	156

The IUD acceptors have much higher than average fertility in every age group, but it is significant that the ratio by which the fertility of the acceptors exceeds that of the general population increases rapidly with age. The fertility of acceptors 30-34 years of age is only slightly lower than that of the average married women 25-29 years of age. The acceptances of women in their thirties and even forties, if their fertility is at these high levels, can have a significant effect on the island's birth rate.

IUD TERMINATION RATES IN THE ISLAND-WIDE PROGRAM

The IUD termination rates in the island-wide program are somewhat higher than those for Taichung presented in Chapter X. This is not surprising, since the island-wide program could not match the control and the intensive medical follow-up of the Taichung program. The island-wide rates are roughly similar to those for Korea's national program.[15] The termination rates shown in Tables XIII-18 and XIII-19 are based on the island-wide IUD follow-up survey at the close of 1966. These tables show how the termination rates varied with selected social and demographic characteristics.

The important demographic correlates of terminations and the great importance of removals as the most frequent type of termination, traits found to characterize Taichung, also apply to the island as a whole. Termination rates for the island decrease especially rapidly with

[15] See Chapter X.

Table XIII-18. Cumulative Total Termination Rates 12 Months and 24 Months After First Insertion, for First Segment and for All Segments, by Selected Demographic and Social Characteristics, for Second Island-Wide IUD Follow-Up Survey Representing the 206,315 Women Inserted by July 1966[a/]

	Total termination rates at the end of:			
	12 months		24 months	
Characteristics	1st segments	All segments	1st segments	All segments
Type of area				
Large city	42.7 (1.5)[b/]	37.5 (1.5)	65.7 (2.0)	54.4 (2.0)
Small city	42.5 (2.8)	37.2 (2.7)	58.3 (3.4)	50.5 (3.4)
Small town	39.3 (1.4)	34.4 (1.3)	56.9 (1.8)	50.2 (1.7)
Rural	32.7 (1.1)	28.7 (1.1)	50.7 (1.6)	44.1 (1.5)
Age of wife at first insertion				
16-24	53.8 (2.5)	47.7 (2.5)	73.2 (3.1)	65.9 (3.2)
25-29	45.7 (1.4)	40.6 (1.4)	68.5 (1.7)	58.8 (1.8)
30-34	35.3 (1.3)	29.4 (1.2)	55.1 (1.7)	46.3 (1.7)
35-39	28.2 (1.5)	25.7 (1.4)	42.9 (2.0)	38.1 (2.0)
40-47	21.2 (2.4)	19.8 (2.3)	31.1 (3.3)	26.6 (2.9)
Number of live births before first insertion				
2 or less	56.6 (2.4)	51.3 (2.4)	80.1 (2.7)	74.0 (2.9)
3	45.8 (1.7)	39.5 (1.7)	63.7 (2.1)	56.0 (2.2)
4	35.3 (1.5)	31.0 (1.5)	57.2 (2.2)	45.8 (2.0)
5 or more	31.6 (1.0)	27.6 (1.0)	48.9 (1.4)	42.3 (1.4)
Wife's education				
None	33.5 (1.0)	29.8 (1.0)	52.6 (1.5)	45.3 (1.4)
Primary school	40.8 (1.2)	35.2 (1.2)	59.9 (1.6)	51.3 (1.6)
Junior high or more	45.5 (2.1)	39.8 (2.1)	63.6 (2.4)	55.6 (2.5)
Purpose of using IUD				
Limiting	35.1 (0.8)	30.3 (0.7)	53.2 (1.1)	44.7 (1.0)
Spacing	56.5 (2.2)	52.8 (2.2)	85.3 (2.5)	82.2 (2.8)
Cost of IUD insertion				
Fee charged	38.1 (0.8)	33.3 (0.8)	56.8 (1.0)	48.9 (1.0)
Free	36.2 (2.2)	32.8 (2.1)	48.9 (5.7)	54.2 (10.0)
Comparison of children alive and wanted				
Has more than wants	29.8 (1.2)	26.0 (1.2)	46.4 (1.7)	40.1 (1.7)
Has wanted number	37.3 (1.0)	32.2 (1.0)	57.6 (1.4)	47.8 (1.3)
Wants more	53.6 (1.8)	48.8 (1.8)	74.0 (2.2)	69.2 (2.4)
All wives	37.8 (0.7)	33.1 (0.7)	56.7 (1.0)	48.9 (1.0)

[a/] The weighted sample size for this survey was 4,648.

[b/] Standard errors are shown in ( ).

Table XIII-19. Cumulative Gross Termination Rate for 12 Months After First Insertion, for All Segments, by Type of Termination, by Number of Living Children and by Area Type

Type of termination and area type	Number of living children: 0-2	3	4	5 or more
Pregnancy				
Large city	5.8	11.6	13.3	6.1
Small city	5.3	10.0	11.6	12.3
Small rown	10.7	9.1	9.6	7.5
Rural area	15.8	7.1	5.0	5.5
Expulsion				
Large city	12.7	5.5	3.1	5.0
Small city	10.7	3.5	7.0	1.0
Small town	12.3	9.0	3.3	5.4
Rural area	22.0	10.3	7.0	3.8
Removal				
Large city	28.6	28.5	28.5	24.5
Small city	40.2	28.9	23.4	21.4
Small town	37.7	24.1	27.4	15.8
Rural area	32.3	24.8	13.0	14.4
Total, all types				
Large city	41.4	40.3	39.9	32.7
Small city	49.4	38.2	37.0	31.8
Small town	51.3	37.2	36.5	26.3
Rural area	55.6	37.4	23.1	22.2

age and parity. However, the island-wide data supply information on some other important correlates of termination:

1. *Women who had free insertions do not have termination rates significantly different from those of the women who paid a fee.* Some had feared that free insertions would be less valued, or would be obtained under some pressure and therefore would be terminated more readily.

2. *The larger and the more urban the place of residence, the higher the termination rates. However, the termination rates vary by type in very interesting ways that require further investigation.* The larger the place, the less the termination rates depend on the number of living children the woman already has. For those with more than three children, removal rates and total termination rates increase rather sharply as size of place increases. We suspect that this may be because high-parity women in the cities are more likely to have readily available birth control alternatives. Also, there may

be greater tolerance of discomfort in rural places and less access to doctors who can remove the IUD. In small families (fewer than three children) termination rates decrease with size of city. This results from fewer terminations by pregnancy in the larger areas, fewer expulsions, and lower removal rates for the largest cities.

3. *Understandably, women who took the IUD to space their births rather than to limit the number have much higher termination rates, and especially higher removal rates.*

FAMILY LIMITATION AFTER IUD TERMINATION

The kind of termination rates we have just considered have led to concern about the apparently short period of protection offered by the IUD. But as already indicated in the discussion of Taichung in Chapter X, the important question is not what happens to the device but what happens to the fertility control practices of the couple, regardless of whether they stay with a particular method. High termination rates are much less serious for population growth or for the particular couples if further births are prevented by (1) reinsertion of the IUD, (2) adoption of other contraceptive methods (including sterilization), or (3) use of an abortion to end pregnancies that do occur.

A large proportion of the Taiwan women ever having an IUD inserted were still protected in one or more of these ways at the time of the second island-wide IUD follow-up survey at the end of 1966. We present in Tables XIII-20 and XIII-21 the detailed breakdown of their status regarding birth control at that time. Approximately 61 per cent still had an IUD in place, including about 8 per cent of the initial sample who had had a device reinserted after one or more terminations. Of those ever terminating, 17 per cent had had a reinsertion and still had the device in place.

About 14 per cent of the couples had given up the IUD but were currently practicing another method or had been sterilized. This is 37 per cent of the terminated cases—higher than the percentage (28 per cent) ever practicing contraception before entering the program.[16]

[16] The figure currently practicing just before insertion is not known, but it probably was no higher than 20 per cent, if only 28 per cent had ever practiced contraception.

Table XIII-20. Family Planning Status at Time of Second Island-Wide Follow-Up Survey of All Couples Ever Having an IUD Insertion by Number of Months Since First Insertion

Family planning status at interview	Months between first insertion and interview					
	6-11	12-17	18-23	24-29	30 or more	Total
IUD in situ: total	72.0	62.7	58.7	54.1	47.2	61.3
Original device	69.1	58.5	50.2	41.1	27.5	53.6
Reinserted device	2.9	4.2	8.5	13.0	19.7	7.7
IUD not in situ: total	28.1	37.2	41.4	45.9	52.8	38.7
Currently using other contraception or sterilized	9.0	10.2	15.9	19.7	25.6	14.2
Not currently protected by contraception or sterilization: total	19.1	27.0	25.5	26.2	27.2	24.5
But all pregnancies aborted	6.5	11.7	8.9	10.3	6.1	9.0
Never pregnant	12.3	12.5	9.8	9.2	13.6	11.2
Had at least one live birth	.3	2.8	6.8	6.7	7.5	4.3
Total	100.0	100.0	100.0	100.0	100.0	100.0
Percentage of couples with at least one live birth since first insertion[a]	.3	3.1	8.5	9.5	13.8	5.8

[a] Includes a small number of cases who terminated the IUD, had a live birth, but were protected at the time of interview.

An additional 9 per cent of all the couples had given up the IUD and were not currently using contraception, but they had aborted[17] all the pregnancies they had had after the first insertion. While abortion may be undesirable from several points of view, it is nonetheless a method of birth control. We can say that 85 per cent of the couples were either practicing contraception or had used abortion effectively to prevent further births. An additional group of terminating couples —11 per cent of the total sample—were not currently using contraception but reported no pregnancies since first insertion. These couples do not yet have a problem, but should it arise a substantial portion are likely to use abortion to avoid it. If we add these couples to the preceding group, we can say that 96 per cent of all the couples ever having an IUD inserted were either using abortion and contraception to prevent further births or had been successful in avoiding

[17] Includes all pregnancies ending in a fetal death, whether induced or spontaneous.

Table XIII-21. Family Planning Status at Time of Second Island-Wide Follow-Up Survey of Couples with IUD No Longer in Place by Number of Months Since First Insertion

Family planning status at interview	Months between first insertion and interview: 6-11	12-17	18-23	24-29	30 or more	Total
Currently using other contraception or sterilized	31.9	27.4	38.5	43.0	48.5	36.7
Not currently protected by contraception or sterilization: total	68.1	72.6	61.4	57.0	51.4	63.3
But all pregnancies aborted	23.1	31.5	21.4	22.5	11.6	23.3
Never pregnant	43.9	33.6	23.6	20.0	25.7	29.0
Had at least one live birth	1.1	7.5	16.4	14.5	14.1	11.0
Total	100.0	100.0	100.0	100.0	100.0	100.0
Percentage of couples with at least one live birth since first insertion[a]	1.1	8.2	7.5	18.9	21.7	13.4

[a] Includes a small number of cases who terminated the IUD, had a live birth, but were protected at the time of interview.

further births between their first insertion (sometime in the period 1963-66) and the end of 1966. This means that among all couples ever having an IUD insertion, only about 4 per cent were both currently unprotected and had had a pregnancy that came to term since the first insertion.

A small additional group had a live birth after terminating the IUD, but had taken up contraception again by the end of 1966. When this group, comprising about 2 per cent of the total sample, is added to the residual group just considered, the proportion of those having a live birth comes to 6 per cent.

Obviously, the numbers falling into these various family planning categories will vary with the length of time since first insertion. Tables XIII-20 and XIII-21 show the family planning status at the end of 1966 of couples varying in length of time since first insertion. Without going into the details of the tables, it seems fair to say that even after thirty months only a small proportion (7 per cent) were in the residual category of those who had no current protection and also had borne a child. A very large number of those who had an IUD inserted tend to practice some form of fertility control, whether or not the device remains in place. The question of whether the IUD program produced this result is difficult to answer. It can be argued (see Chapter XIV) that the couples accepting the IUD were a selected group who would have done something about birth control anyway, even without a program. While we will consider this point later, this issue could not arise at all were it not possible to demonstrate that those entering the IUD program do practice fertility control in some way for a substantial period afterwards.

Women who became pregnant after the insertion of an IUD are apparently sufficiently motivated to limit their families so that a large proportion of them abort their pregnancies. The 913 pregnancies reported as terminated up to the end of 1966 by the women participating in the IUD follow-up survey ended as follows:

	All pregnancies		*Pregnancies with IUD in situ*		*Pregnancies after IUD termination*	
Outcome	*No.*	%	*No.*	%	*No.*	%
Live birth	269	29	60	15	209	40
Induced abortion	547	60	296	74	251	49
Other fetal death	97	11	42	11	55	11
Total	913	100	398	100	515	100

The percentage of all their pregnancies aborted by these women before the program began was approximately 9 per cent, so that there was a very significant increase in the use of abortion to terminate both pregnancies with IUD in situ and those occurring after the IUD was given up.

The 5,026 women in the second IUD follow-up survey, carried out at the end of 1966, had 3,560 aggregate years of exposure to risk of birth after insertion (after deducting nine months of exposure time for each woman to allow for the fact that almost all were not pregnant at time of insertion). In the three years prior to insertion they had an average annual birth rate of 379 per thousand. Let us assume conservatively that without the IUD they would have had a birth rate of 324 per thousand during the period of exposure after first insertion (this allows both for the aging of the women and for the general decline in fertility during the period). In that case these women would have had 1,153 births instead of the 269 that occurred between the date of insertion and the end of 1966: a decline of 77 per cent. If we assume that the 547 pregnancies aborted would have produced 500 live births, then we can say that about 55 per cent of the births were prevented by abortion and the remainder by contraception. This probably overstates the long-run significance of abortion—over, say, a period of five years—because about half of the pregnancies aborted were those that occurred with an IUD in place. Obviously, it was impossible for these particular pregnancies to have been prevented by turning from the IUD to another contraceptive method. The use of abortion lessens substantially after the IUD is terminated, and the use of alternate contraceptive methods or sterilization increases, so that the relative importance of contraception should be greater over a longer period.

In any event, the evidence that there was substantial fertility decline among these women after their first insertion is incontrovertible. On the average, they were exposed to the risk of live birth for about ten months between the time of first insertion and the follow-up survey at the end of 1966 (after adjusting for the fact that they could not have had a live birth for nine months after entering the program). On the basis of either the average fertility for all women of their ages or their own fertility for the three years preceding their entry into the program, we might have expected 20 to 50 per cent of them to have had a live birth during this period. The actual figure is 6 per cent. Certainly, not all of the reduction can be attributed to the program, but we can, at a minimum, say that those who entered the program reduced their fertility substantially. If this were not true, it would not be necessary or possible to discuss later the question of what part of the decline, if any, can be attributed to the program.

XIV. The Program Setting, Results, and Implications: A Summary View

BEFORE THE PROGRAM: THE SETTING

THE Taichung Family Planning Program did not begin in a population characterized by uncontrolled fertility. Even in preceding decades, when birth rates were fairly stable at rather high levels, the Taiwanese were undoubtedly using many time-honored ways to keep their fertility below a still higher maximum physiological potential. Such actions, whether or not deliberate measures to restrict family size, are common in most preindustrial societies.

Taichung and Taiwan had gone beyond this preindustrial system of folk controls even before the program began in Taichung in 1963. Fertility had been falling from its previous high levels at least since 1957. At the same time, the forces of modernization had reduced child mortality and increased family aspirations. Couples approaching the age of 30 were likely already to have all the children they wanted, so an increasing number of parents were experimenting with methods of limiting further family growth. The results, especially evident after 1957, was a decline in birth rates for women over 30, bringing the birth rates by 1962 to levels rather low for a developing country.

Just before the program began in 1963, many Taiwanese were already willing to say, when asked in surveys, that they wanted a moderate number of children, usually three or four, providing that at least one was a son. They expressed abhorrence for childlessness or for having an only child, and very few couples had fewer than two children after a few years of marriage or had tried any form of birth control in this early phase of family life.

Many couples did exceed their stated moderate fertility ideal and had the large families enshrined in theory as traditionally Chinese.[1] However, many of even these couples said that they had more children than they wanted. This is a significant admission in a society whose traditions stress the value of large families.

[1] Whether the ideal of the large family was ever actually functional for the mass of the Chinese population is a controversial question. See, for example, Levy, *The Family Revolution in Modern China.*

Such stated desires for a moderate number of children are sometimes dismissed as polite fictions designed to please the interviewers. Even if correct, this interpretation assumes that the women knew what a modern fertility response should be, and this is one step toward its adoption. There is still more substantial evidence. The women who had at least a moderate number of children and sons were also much more likely than others to say that they wanted no more children and to have tried some form of birth control before the program began. These were also the women who were most likely to be acceptors in the program later.

Before the program was established, fertility declines and the practice of birth control were most common in the more modern strata of the population. Even in these modern strata, birth control practice began relatively late, often after the family already had more children than were wanted. Nevertheless, fertility was much lower, birth control practices much more prevalent, and the period since the last birth much longer among the families most modern by such criteria as education, ownership of modern consumption objects, urban background, or a secular employment relationship not based on kinship ties.

It is not surprising that the modern couples were the most likely to adopt birth control, because they found in their secular contacts in the larger society both the necessary technical resources and the social reinforcements for a new form of behavior. Nevertheless, the modern couples were not much more satisfied than the more traditional couples with the results. The modern couples were successful in having fewer children than others, but since they wanted fewer and since more of their children survived, the discrepancy between aspirations and achievement was about as great for the modern couples as for the traditional.

Before the program existed, then, the transition from high to low fertility was underway in Taiwan and Taichung, but far from complete. Fertility was falling, but mainly in the older ages. Birth control practices were being adopted, but the practice was often so late or so ineffective that many couples were still having more children than they wanted. Fertility declines and birth control practices began late in the childbearing period, as a response to demographic pressures, rather than as a result of early rational planning and spacing of births.

The timing of the action and the methods used indicate that for many couples these were acts of desperation rather than part of a rational family plan. It is understandable that there was a great deal of ambivalence about birth control, since for generations Chinese tradition and family structure had stressed high fertility to counter high child mortality.

As of late 1962, just before the organized program began, a large proportion of the Taichung couples of childbearing years wanted no more children. The great majority of those who still wanted more children hoped to stop at a moderate number. At least on a verbal level, there was an overwhelming consensus that the idea of family planning was good. A significant minority of couples had tried some form of birth control, but a large number, especially of the more traditional and lower status couples, were having more children than they wanted and not doing anything about it.

THE EXPERIMENT

The Taichung experiment was planned to help the thousands of couples who wanted no more children to achieve their desires and in this way to reduce the birth rate. The goal was to achieve this objective while learning as much as possible about how to organize an effective program. The pre-program survey had established the fact that many couples wanted such help. Providing such help did not involve the ethical and political problems that might have arisen if the primary aim had been to persuade these couples that they should want fewer children.

The experimental program should be evaluated as an intervention into the complex existing social system, already undergoing change, for the purpose of controlling reproduction. Given the change already underway, it is difficult to determine how much of what happened in Taichung might have occurred anyway, without the program. It is also difficult to assess how much of the Taichung experience can be repeated with good results in countries at different levels of development. But none of these difficult historical and comparative questions can be answered without careful documentation of a series of specific cases such as that of Taichung.

This entire volume concerns the history of Taichung, and the generalizations presented below are descriptions of what happened in that one case. The entire Taichung experience and that of Taiwan as a whole may be discounted by some as inapplicable to other places on the grounds that Taichung and Taiwan are distinctive in various ways: for example, in being Chinese, developed, already in the demographic transition, etc. These critical statements may or may not be true. Certainly, it is plausible that the level of development influenced what happened in the Taichung experiment and in the more general island-wide program. But the flat assertion, without empirical evidence, that the Taiwan experience is not transferable seems to us to be as wrong as would a bald statement that it is a faultless blueprint for the rest of the developing world. Detailed comparative observations and experience are necessary to answer the complex question of whether such experience is transferable. It cannot be definitely resolved through this single case. The question here is which of the many specific aspects of the Taichung experience are inextricably linked to its own historical context and which are more general. The first task is to know just what happened in Taichung, before trying to generalize the experience.

It seems to us that the following are reasonable, selected descriptions of the major elements of the Taichung experience:

1. A large program was carried out without any significant opposition arising from either the population or important leadership groups, although the government had no official policy on the subject of population or family planning.
2. An intensive, short campaign substantially increased the effective practice of contraception (a) by bringing many couples to their first practice of contraception, and (b) by helping many couples who had already tried birth control to adopt methods more effective and more satisfactory to them.
3. The social characteristics of the acceptors were quite different from what had been expected, and these differences are potentially very important:
   a. Before the program, birth control practice was positively correlated to indices of modernization; but acceptance in the program was not correlated to modernization and was proportionately as frequent in the traditional and lower status groups as in the general population.

b. Acceptors who were not previous users of birth control were drawn disproportionately from the more traditional and less modern strata of population.

c. Acceptance was powerfully influenced by demographic pressures, as expected. Before the program, such pressures led mainly to increased use of birth control for the higher status, modern couples, but after the program was established such demographic pressures led to acceptances in all strata, traditional and modern, lower and higher.

d. Since the traditional and lower status strata are by far the largest, the net result was that acceptances were concentrated in those sectors of the population generally believed to be hardest to reach and most important for population change.

4. Some specific results are pertinent to questions frequently raised regarding the detailed design of programs:

   a. Approaching wives only was as effective as the more difficult and expensive measure of approaching both husbands and wives.

   b. Letters were not effective in increasing the acceptance rate, although this may be because the letters did not focus on the most popular method and were not addressed to the couples most likely to respond—those with a recent birth.

   c. Effective group meetings were especially productive as compared with either home visits or other stimuli.

   d. Diffusion of influence from concentrated foci of effort played a major role in circulating the effects of the program. It was not necessary to contact every potential acceptor directly. The power of diffusion through informal channels was considerable.

5. A new contraceptive, the IUD, was a very important factor in the situation, being chosen by a large majority of the acceptors. Information about it diffused widely through the network of primary relationships in the community. The availability of this method appeared to make a difference in the number and characteristics of the acceptors.

6. Many acceptors gave up the IUD, but not many gave up the idea and practice of birth control. The detailed study of the termination rate for the IUD shows that over time a considerable number of couples gave it up for various reasons. Concentrating attention

on this "failure rate" for the IUD is a mistake. In the first place, we have no reason to believe that "failures" would have been fewer with any other available contraceptive. More importantly, those accepting the IUD managed in various ways to prevent most of the births they might normally have had, even if they gave up the IUD. Apparently they were either highly selected for strong motivation initially, or they became so strongly motivated after initial acceptance that they did whatever was necessary to prevent additional births.

7. The belief that other people who were trusted—friends, relatives, and neighbors—were accepting birth control in large numbers was important in encouraging acceptance. Legitimation in various ways appeared to be important in a situation of considerable ambivalence where the new birth control practices conflicted with traditional familial values.
8. The most important personal characteristics determining acceptance were such indications of demographic pressure as high fertility rates and a recent birth. Prior statements that no more children were wanted were associated with much higher than average acceptance rates.
9. The fact that acceptance came mainly with demographic pressure on the individual couple usually meant that it came fairly late in the reproductive cycle. But this does not mean that it came too late to avert a significant number of additional births. The acceptors, though older than the average and of relatively high parity, were a selected high-fertility group capable of having a large number of additional births. If there had been more acceptors earlier in the reproductive cycle the birth rate would have fallen more rapidly, to lower levels, and there would have been fewer unwanted children. Nevertheless, the Taichung data contradict the widely held view that acceptances by older and higher parity women cannot significantly affect fertility. In the first place, many of the acceptors were in the middle stages of the family-building cycle rather than at the end. Second, and more important, the acceptors were selected for high fecundability to such a degree that even if they were already in their thirties and already had many children, they had the potential for producing many more.

10. Both the intensity of intentions to accept family planning and the realization of those intentions were strongly affected by demographic pressures in the family. Nevertheless, the intentions had an independent predictive value for behavior beyond the influence of their demographic correlates.
11. However, there remains a wide discrepancy between stated desires or intentions and behavior. A large proportion of those who said that they intended to become acceptors did not do so. A small but significant number of those who said that they would not accept eventually did. Even if what people say accurately reflects their current values, it is likely that frequently other values and forces are powerful enough to prevent behavior consistent with the stated fertility values.
12. It is probable that a large number of the couples had ambivalent feelings about family planning. Explicit statements of ambivalence were most common among those groups under the kind of demographic pressures likely to lead to acceptance, but these explicit statements probably represented only the "tip of the iceberg." Ambivalence and doubt probably existed precisely because the couples under demographic pressure were in a problematic situation for which there were no appropriate traditional solutions. The net result was that after an initially low acceptance rate, the ambivalent couples later had the higher acceptance rates characteristic of others under demographic pressure.
13. During the first year after the program, fertility rates fell substantially. The decline was initially greater in Taichung than in the other large Taiwanese cities, but after that period the Taichung rate of decline was lower than the rates of the other cities. This probably resulted partly from the rapid extension of the program to the whole island and partly from the general diffusion of birth control practices outside of the program.
14. It is clear that the fertility of the Taichung acceptors fell after acceptance, to levels substantially below their own prior fertility and below what might have been expected on the basis of aging of the women or secular fertility trends. While it seems unlikely that the decline would have been so large without the program, we cannot demonstrate this conclusively.

In its time the Taichung experiment was a bold, large effort—in the size of the population it aimed to reach quickly, in the number of workers used, in the number of home visits and group meetings held per thousand population. Yet it was hampered by several serious limitations: (1) For political reasons there was no mass media support, although the mass media potentially were highly important in this population. (2) Since there was no official national population policy, the program operated under a permissive, generally benevolent neutrality which nevertheless meant that there was no official legitimation. (3) Because it was a new kind of effort, most of the personnel had no experience on which to draw and no successes elsewhere to bolster their hopes about the feasibility of what they were trying to do. (4) The resources going into the program, while relatively good, were not optimal.

IMPLICATIONS OF THE TAICHUNG EXPERIENCE FOR OTHER POPULATION PROGRAMS

Since the Taichung program began in 1963 there have been many other new programs in other countries, often on a much larger scale, but we have only fragmentary reports about them. We do not know of any other case in which the program specifics, the population data, and the results have been documented in the detail of this volume, even with its limitations. We have the temerity to ask whether such results as those summarized above may have relevance for other places precisely because our stock of detailed observation is so small that it is necessary to make all possible use of what we have.

There is a natural tendency to reject out of hand the experience of such places as Taiwan or Korea for programs in other places like India, Pakistan, Indonesia, or Egypt, for example. The argument is that Taiwan and Korea are so much more developed and so much farther along the road of demographic transition that their experience could not possibly be relevant to places where literacy, per capita income, availability of medical personnel, evidence of preexisting birth control practice, etc., are much less. The basic premise of this argument is that increasing birth control practice and declining birth rates occur only when a society has reached a minimal level of development and social change not yet found in many of these other countries.

We accept this premise, since we are committed to the general idea that values and behavior regarding family size and birth control are deeply rooted in the social structure, particularly in the family. We agree with the widely held belief that high mortality levels and a kinship-oriented social structure that rewards large families probably account in a general way historically for high fertility levels in pre-industrial societies. However, we do not know with even approximate accuracy what specific changes in mortality or in social structure are necessary preconditions for specific changes in birth control practice and fertility. Recent detailed studies of the history of demographic transition in Europe have cast some doubts even on the validity of the premises about the European fertility decline, on which much of the prediction and theorizing about the future fertility of developing countries is based.[2]

Apart from the fact that our verified knowledge of the socio-demographic relationships in the European demographic transition still is weak, many generalizations about the developing countries seem to be based on the dubious assumption that their social development stands at the point Europe's did before its fertility began to decline.

To assert categorically that India or Indonesia or any other country "is not ready" for family planning or a fertility decline seems to assume that these countries are no different than they were twenty-five or fifty or one hundred years ago, when their mortality levels and kinship-centered social structures probably strongly supported high fertility norms and behavior. But, of course, we know that they have changed in many ways. First of all, the lower mortality that is rapidly coming to most of these countries is changing profoundly the internal demographic pressures in villages and in families in ways that we do not fully understand. Secondly, the elite in these countries, as well as increasing numbers of the general population, have been linked to the outside world through the mass media and the marketplace, so that there are rapidly changing levels of aspirations for consumer goods, better health, and other advantages. More generally, a whole series of unsettling, distorted visions of what life can and should be is increasingly being incorporated into self-definitions. This has proceeded much farther in some urban and educated strata than in the general population, but it is hard to travel even to the remote villages of a country like India without seeing many signs of links with the wider

[2] For example, see Ansley Coale, "The Decline of Fertility in Europe from the French Revolution to World War II," in Behrman et al., *Fertility and Family Planning: A World View.*

national and world community in the midst of traditional practices and ideas.

These changes, which seem to be in progress almost everywhere to some extent, have occurred in ways almost unknown at the time of the western demographic transition. Nevertheless, it may well be that in specific places population programs cannot be successful without much more profound transformations in the social structure with respect to such matters as the role of women, industrialization, and social security outside the family.

But granting that this may be true, it is still plausible to argue that the transformations that have already occurred *may* be sufficient to support a reasonably successful family planning program, at least in the advanced sectors of most populations. If the urgency of the "population problem" is conceded, then it seems necessary to act on the basis of this possibility while pursuing with all available means the more general social, economic, and familial transformations that are desirable for many reasons besides that of population policy.

One argument in support of the position that such a country as India is not "ready" for a program like Taiwan's is that the Indian program, going back many years, has not been very successful to date. But until recently the Indian program was poorly staffed and not very well organized or implemented. Although lately there has been a very considerable increase in effort and expenditure and acceptance rates, the test of an "all-out" program in India has not yet been made, because a systematic program making full use of even the potentially available funds and personnel has not been carried out in any large unit of the country for a reasonable number of years. Our argument is not that such a program would necessarily meet with great success; this is exactly what needs to be tested. It is possible, of course, to argue that the past failure of a country like India to carry out systematically the programs that have been drawn up on paper is an endemic symptom of the lack of development. This may be true; but given what is at stake, the issue should be tested not by words but by an effort to put into the field a program utilizing all available resources and energy.

In our analysis of the general Taiwan program we saw that input of program effort was a powerful determinant of acceptance rates. It is relevant that the obvious increase in effort in India in the last three years, while still grossly inadequate, has had a marked effect on acceptance rates. Similarly, substantially greater and better organized effort in Pakistan in the last few years appears to have had a significant effect on the number of acceptances, although it is still too early to assess the results.

Such countries as India and Pakistan are unevenly developed. The areas and parts of the population which are most advanced would presumably respond most readily to a program. This is an argument for concentrating more effort in some areas and strata than in others, at least to test this plausible idea. For various reasons, quite a different policy is being followed in many important programs. Most programs spread available resources and effort rather thinly and uniformly throughout the countries they serve. Concentration of effort, when it occurs, is likely to be adventitious.

Our general view is that whether the experiences of Europe's demographic transition or of programs like Taiwan's or Korea's are applicable to such places as Indonesia or India or Pakistan involves empirical questions that can be answered only by experimental programs which systematically test elements of the programs of Taiwan and Korea (or other more intensive and extensive variants). We doubt that these questions can be settled on the basis of theory or arguments from history for several reasons: (1) It is no longer clear just how the European fertility transition was set off by the changes in literacy, mortality, female roles, etc. generally considered to explain the fertility decline. (2) The kinds of contraceptives now available were not in existence in the earlier European period. (3) We do not know what would have happened in Europe if there had been an organized, intensive family planning program before the "spontaneous" decline in the Western birth rates. (4) The developing countries differ from eighteenth- and nineteenth-century Europe in various ways, but most especially in the existence of transportation and communication links which make members of these populations aware of what happened in the West and what is happening now in the more advanced developing countries. (5) The mortality declines, which took a relatively long time in the West, have occurred very rapidly in the developing countries and have quickly created the demographic pressures which built up only very slowly in the West.

We are not supporting the position that all of the developing countries are ready for rapid fertility decline if only the proper contraceptives and programs are made available. If motivation were already that high, it is likely that even the apparently weak programs would have elicited an overwhelming response by now. After all, the fertility decline occurred in Europe without benefit of organized programs or modern contraceptives; they began largely with the use of coitus interruptus, because the social changes had made the general motivation for family planning so great.[3]

The real question appears to be whether the demographic changes that should occur in the long run, as a result of other social and economic changes, cannot be hastened by the introduction of a new element: a large-scale, organized family planning program which will shorten the time required for the fertility decline by increasing the available information, supplies, and services, and, perhaps more importantly, by providing social support for actions that millions are thinking about, but with considerable ambivalence.

Our view is that as mortality declines and as social structure evolves toward modern forms, demographic pressures build up in the family and the local community. Many millions of couples begin to think that they are having too many children, if they are to satisfy their aspirations for their children and themselves. Tradition provides no easy solution for this situation, particularly since many institutions still encourage couples to have more children, or at least to leave such matters in the hands of God and fate. In the transitional period the balance between the new pressures and traditional norms changes, so that there are strong feelings of ambivalence. Some of the more adventuresome couples, particularly the most modern, experiment with traditional or modern forms of abortion or contraception. In the history of the West such experimentation had its socially cumulative impact only after a considerable period of time. The harassed couples facing the problem of too many children had only limited resources available to them (mainly illegal abortions, coitus interruptus, and the condom). Whatever they did was generally accomplished despite the opposition of the health professions, the state, and the church.

Such situations of ambivalence and cross-pressure regarding fertility and family planning must be very common in many of the developing countries, at least in some sectors of the population. The available resources, however, are much greater in some ways than was the case

[3] For some discussion of the French historical experience see Bergues et al., *La prévention des naissances dans la famille*. For England, see Lewis-Fanning, *Report on an Inquiry into Family Limitation During the Past Fifty Years.*

in the West. The list of reasonably effective and available contraceptives is now much more extensive and the volume of public discussion and information much greater. For millions of couples that are at the stage of ambivalence and experimentation, organized family planning programs may provide both the technical services and the social support which may help the value of limiting family size to win out over competing values and pressures.

This argument applies to those developing countries in which there has been sufficient social change and mortality decline to produce a substantial minority of fecund couples who want no more children but are ambivalent about both goals and means. It also assumes that without organized help there will be a considerable time lag while millions of couples search out the technical solutions and the social legitimation that their new behavior requires. Even when couples decide that they don't want more children, there is no immediate automatic connection between having made this decision and the adoption of the means that may be available in the environment. The availability and legitimacy of the means are likely to affect the goals of such couples.

Even if these assumptions are correct and if the family planning programs help the couples who want no more children, this would not solve the "population problem" in such countries as India or Pakistan, or, for that matter, in Taiwan, Korea, or the United States.[4] However, we believe that in most of the developing countries, the number of couples wanting no more children is so large that serving them can absorb in the immediate future most of the available resources of the family planning programs. If these "ready" couples are given the help they need and want, birth rates should fall substantially and families should be substantially smaller.

However, even if families are reduced to the average size that sample surveys have shown to be the ideal held by the couples in such developing countries as Taiwan, families will still grow rapidly and the "population problem," as usually defined, will not be solved.

[4] Kingsley Davis presents a strong argument in support of the view that it is now necessary to consider the ultimate goal of zero-growth, that the main thrust of population policies should be to change values about family size rather than simply to meet existing demand, and that family planning programs, while desirable as means, may divert attention from the primary goal of changing the social situation which motivates high fertility. See Kingsley Davis, "Population Policy: Will Current Programs Succeed?", *Science,* 158, No. 3802, November 10, 1967, 730-39.

Starting from this incontrovertible truth, an argument is sometimes advanced that such programs as we have described in this volume are ineffectual or unimportant, if necessary. We do not agree, for the following reasons:

1. While it may be necessary to reduce the number of children in the family from six or seven to two in order to reach a final solution to the "population problem," it is necessary to move through the average size of four to attain the ultimate goal of two. A program which helps to move the population 50 or 60 per cent of the way toward an ultimate goal is not ineffectual.
2. Programs which help to legitimate the idea that birth control can stop family growth at three or four children will also spread the idea that birth control can be used to achieve any desired family size. This will surely hasten the adoption of still smaller family sizes as the necessary minimal changes in social conditions provide a basis for changing motivations. It seems plausible that once the idea of reducing family size by rational means becomes prevalent, the goal, too, may change. To expect a sudden change from six to two children demands an improbable discontinuity in social values.
3. The emphasis in current programs on reaching those who want no more children, rather than trying to change values about family size, seems correct for several reasons:
   a. The programs for providing family planning services are run by health personnel who are not qualified for the unusual kind of social engineering required to change values about family size. The health services show commendable self-restraint in limiting their efforts to the area of their competency.
   b. It is very unlikely that any verbal messages or education programs on the part of the family planning programs would be successful in changing values regarding family size. This requires structural changes in the roles of the family, of women, and of children that are desirable but are outside of the purview of the family planning programs in their health contexts.
   c. It is usually, although not always, possible to win a consensus of relevant groups to help couples have the number of children that they want. Despite traditional values of high fertility, it seems possible to carry through programs with this objective

without serious political or popular opposition. If it is possible to weld a coalition of forces that are in favor of family planning for those who want it, why not do so and avoid until later the conflict that will arise when policies intended to change basic family values by social engineering may be considered? In countries like the United States it is probably not possible to postpone this political battle, because desired and actual family size are close together and both are above the replacement level that many consider desirable. But in most of the developing countries this is not the case at present. It may be that by the time the intermediate goal of reducing families from six to four has been attained in the developing countries, the more difficult step of going from three or four or two will have been taken in the West and can furnish useful guidelines for other countries.[5]

d. Although we agree that vigorous attempts should be made to speed development and other changes which will induce more rapid fertility decline, we fail to see that a family planning program which aims at more limited objectives obstructs the larger enterprise. It is sometimes said that family planning programs divert attention from broader programs for social change or are put forward as substitutes for them. We doubt that this is true. If it is, then there should be vigorous efforts to make it clear that the family planning programs in themselves can accomplish limited, although crucial, objectives. Enthusiasts for the family planning movement may make claims for it that are too great: such overstatement is almost unavoidable in social movements. But this does not mean that the programs do not have a legitimate role of some importance.

[5] In many of the countries of Europe the net reproduction rate is not very much higher than replacement even now. In the overseas European population, net reproduction rates are still substantially higher than replacement levels. In the short run, few economists would argue that it is not possible to have increasing per capita incomes along with present growth rates. However, in any kind of world that we can now envision it appears to be true that limitations of space will require reproduction at only replacement levels. On other grounds it is possible to argue that any further growth in a country like the United States is undesirable even now. If this position is taken, then it is necessary to argue for programs to change values about family size, since in the West growth rates are above replacement, because parents want more than two children.

Whether the Taichung-Taiwan experience is relevant to other countries is an empirical question. This question can be answered only by testing the results of this experience in other developing countries, if they are indeed beginning development changes and if they have some substantial minority of couples now who want no more children but do not have the technical or social support to do anything about it. We are uncertain which aspects of the Taichung-Taiwan experience are associated with the specific time, place, and circumstances of that particular program. There is enough doubt about whether a high level of development is a necessary precondition for some of the specific results to make it worthwhile to test what has been learned in Taiwan elsewhere. Where documented experience is so rare, can we afford to throw it away on the grounds that it *may* be peculiar to its time and place?

With this background, we list below a series of specific recommendations for other programs (e.g., for those in countries like India or Pakistan or Turkey), based on the Taiwan experience. These recommendations should be treated with all the reservations implicit in the preceding discussion.

1. *The health-oriented family planning programs should be directed primarily toward the large number of couples who say they want no more children.* Acceptance rates will be highest among the couples in this demographic situation. While many of those who say they want no more children will not become acceptors, the proportion of those who do and the size of the total base group are likely to be large enough to produce significant results. Wherever possible, it is desirable to find out what countervailing forces lead many couples to say that they want no more children and yet fail to practice birth control. In India, for example, many of those who say that they want no more children do not adopt birth control. The birth rate would fall sharply if all those who said that they wanted no more children had no more. What is needed are programs which (a) test the validity of the statement by doing everything possible to provide adequate services and social legitimation, and (b) follow up the large numbers that still fail to act according to their stated intentions, in order to analyze the basis for the discrepancy.

2. *Programs should concentrate their efforts at a number of focal points, rather than spreading them thinly over the total population:*

a. The power of diffusion has been demonstrated not only in Taichung and Taiwan, but in many other places as well. Since resources are limited, at least in terms of personnel, the effort should be programmed in such a way that there are significant focal points from which information and influence can diffuse outward through the primary group network of communication. This means, for example, that systematically spaced efforts are to be preferred to blanket coverage. This spacing can be achieved by selecting as focal points groups of villages, neighborhoods within cities, or townships and districts within the country.

b. Everything possible, consistent with the truth, should be done to increase the perception in the population that birth control is accepted by the primary group members whom they trust. Such perception leads to higher acceptance rates. It reduces "pluralistic ignorance"—the situation in which many people are in favor of some idea or action but think that everyone else is against it. While this may be done partly by disseminating information from surveys about attitudes toward and practice of contraception, such verbal reinforcements are not likely to be very powerful. More convincing is the perception by the couples that others in their community are doing something about birth control and that there is a great deal of activity regarding birth control, so that eventually it comes to be accepted as part of the environment. Therefore, ten acceptors in each of ten villages may be better than one in each of one hundred villages. Reinforcement from others who are trusted is especially important, because there is likely to be much ambivalence toward birth control in populations in transition. While the respondents may say "yes" or "no" to the questions "Do you want more children?" or "Do you want birth control?" on a survey, it is clear that often they mean "maybe." The "yes" or the "no" are only indicators of a range of position on a normative scale of behavior.

3. *Primary attention should be given to those couples who feel themselves to be under demographic pressure.* These are likely to be the couples who say they want no more children, but they will also include substantial numbers of others who have had the moderate numbers of children and sons that people say they want in most of the developing countries. This is a controversial recommendation, because it conflicts with the obvious truth that birth rates will fall sooner and faster if younger women of lower parity are attracted to the program. The goal of reaching the younger or lower parity women is probably much more difficult to attain without substantial social changes. All of our previous analyses indicate that the couples who feel that they have a problem are not the young, low-parity couples, but those who are somewhat older and have more children. These couples are responsive to the program as acceptors, keep to the practice of contraception more faithfully, and are more likely to adopt alternative forms of contraception if they give up a program method.

   An important point emerging from both the Taiwan and Korea data is that the somewhat older and higher parity women who become acceptors are a select group who are still sufficiently young and fecundable so that practice of birth control by sizable numbers of them will have a considerable initial effect on the birth rate. None of this is to denigrate efforts to reach younger and lower parity women, but successes in reaching the somewhat older and higher parity women are too quickly dismissed as failures or of trivial consequence. A major part of the difference between the birth rates of the developed and underdeveloped countries lies in the difference of birth rates for women over thirty and for parities over four.[6]

4. *The programs should be organized so that primary attention is given to the continuing practice of birth control by acceptors rather than continuing use of any particular method in the program.* The evidence from Taichung, Taiwan, and Korea is that high termination rates for the IUD, for example, do not mean the end of the birth control practice. In one way or another, those who were acceptors managed to continue to keep their birth rates

[6] See Simon Kuznets, "Economic Aspects of Fertility Trends in the Less Developed Countries," in Behrman et al., *Fertility and Family Planning: A World View.*

low by the use, if necessary, of other methods of contraception, sterilization, or abortion.

One implication of this evidence is that high termination rates for one or all program methods should not necessarily be a source of discouragement, because the objective is not the success of the program or of a particular method but successful practice of birth control by those whom the program reaches directly or indirectly.

A second implication is that, so far as possible, there should be alternatives available in the community environment, both within and outside of the program. Abortion, although illegal, has been very important for this purpose in Taiwan and Korea. Other countries may want to review their policies in this respect. Sterilization is another alternative. There are various other possibilities in terms of traditional forms of contraception or abortion. Those who enter the program have demonstrated by that act their motivation. It is likely that many will find any particular program method unacceptable for various reasons. The availability of alternatives to which the terminating couples can turn is potentially of very great importance. This may be one respect in which the Korea and Taiwan experiences are not easily transferable, since such alternatives as abortion or condoms may be more readily available there than in some other countries. The situation with respect to alternatives, however, may not be completely hopeless even in countries like India or Pakistan, where birth rates are high. The limited access to modern contraceptives in the villages at present does not mean that alternatives are not potentially available. The fact that birth rates are generally below the potential physiological maximum suggests that coitus interruptus, abortion, and other folk methods must already be used by a significant minority whose number and practices are unknown. An initially successful program which gains a substantial, if limited, number of acceptors for the pill, the IUD, or other modern methods may very well stimulate a wider use of these indigenous methods that are now practiced by a small minority. After all, the birth rate decline in western Europe resulted from widespread adoption of methods that had been available for generations but practiced by only a minority.[7]

[7] E.g., see Bergues et al., *op.cit.* or N. E. Himes, *A Medical History of Contraception*, Baltimore: The Williams and Wilkins Co., 1936.

5. *Every major family planning program should have a well-organized evaluation program that can both guide the program and contribute to the basic understanding of reproductive institutions essential for progress in the population field over the long run.* The evaluation activities in Taichung and Taiwan had many inadequacies, but we believe that they have demonstrated the operational value of such studies. For example:

a. The initial surveys helped to alleviate administrative and staff anxieties about the feasibility of such a program and led to a program larger than was originally planned for Taichung.
b. The quick reporting of results from the Taichung experience helped to lay the foundation for rapid expansion of the island-wide program.
c. When the anecdotal reports of IUD terminations began to worry administrators, the IUD follow-up surveys and their analysis helped to define the magnitude of the problem and to reassure administrators that the program was still worthwhile. There was no panicky, unwarranted abandonment of existing programs.
d. Information indicating that the IUD terminated cases were finding other ways to limit their birth rates was relevant to questions about whether it was important to invest a great deal in programs to reduce termination rates (as compared with investing in efforts to get more new users).
e. Information about the fact that the older women and higher parity women who were acceptors still had high fecundability provided reassurance that the program was still reaching women whose actions could make a difference for their families and for the general population.
f. The fact that women with short open birth intervals had especially high acceptance rates contributed to the decision to invest in a large-scale mailing program for postpartum cases.

These instances are only illustrative. The perceptive reader who is interested in the operational aspects of family planning programs can find other examples in the preceding chapters.

There is obvious scientific value in a systematic body of data about the family planning programs as major new phenomena in the social systems which affect human reproduction and population growth. The case study we have presented will have more meaning

and its deficiencies will be much clearer when
studies of a variety of populations.

6. *Countries which have much lower birth rates as*
tive should consider policies to change the soci
conditions which affect birth control practices ar
in addition to instituting programs to provide birt
The evidence from Taiwan certainly indicates that birth control was being adopted by the more modern sectors of the population before the program began. While the program had an encouraging success in reaching the less modern masses, the fact remains that the practice of birth control and fertility is still strongly associated with modernization and development and that this is likely to continue to be the case. How successful organized family planning programs will be in reaching the rural, the illiterate, and the traditional masses in countries which do not have such large modern strata or centers of modern influence as Taiwan still remains an open question. We are more optimistic on this issue than some observers, because we do not believe that the issue is closed either on the basis of historical evidence or of recent experience.

The present volume has been an attempt to analyze one family planning program rather than to review all of the possible population policies which might be pursued even in Taiwan. Kingsley Davis and others have been discussing the larger question. On the basis of our more restricted data from Taiwan, it certainly appears to be true that certain kinds of social changes are likely to be of particular importance in reducing fertility. For example, there should be:

a. More education, especially for women.
b. Implication in markets that transcend the local self-sufficient economy. In particular our data indicates the possible importance of modern consumer durables.
c. Involvement in impersonal work relationships that are not based on kinship ties.
d. Ties with the outside world through such mass media as the newspaper.

This is obviously a very incomplete list. Broadly speaking, there are a large number of changes which will probably have an effect on fertility and on marriage. Serious studies need to be made in order to termine which social changes will affect fertility most, their costs, and their relative advantages. These broad, long-run changes may have more profound effects on population growth rates than the family planning programs, but we believe that the family planning programs have a legitimate and important place in the larger programs for population change.

APPENDICES

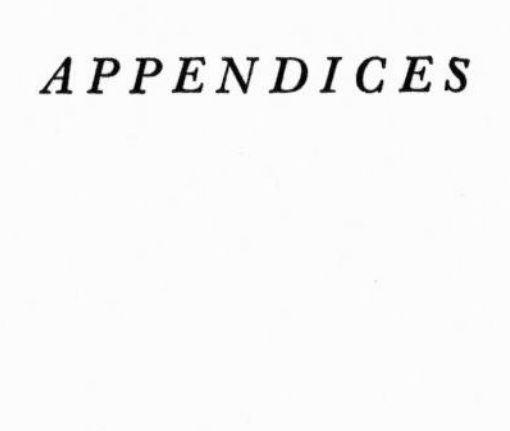

Appendix I-1. Sources of Data for Economic Indicators of Economic and Social Developments for Taiwan, 1952-64 (Table I-1)

Neil H. Jacoby, *U.S. Aid to Taiwan*, New York: F. A. Praeger, 1966 is the source for the basic data on all of the economic indicators (except labor force), for the data on intercity transportation, and for that on radio ownership. In some cases indices have been recomputed to give them a common base or to put them on a per capita basis. The education and labor force data and death rates are from the series *Household Registration Statistics of Taiwan*, published by the Taiwan Provincial Civil Affairs Department. Data on mail and telephone messages are from the *Taiwan Statistical Abstracts*, Bureau of Accounting and Statistics, Provincial Government of Taiwan. The number of inhabitants per doctor is from the *Taiwan Statistical Data Book*, 1964, Council of International Economic Cooperation and Development. Data on newspaper circulation are from the annual *United Nations Statistical Yearbook* and the *China Yearbook*.

Each of these statistical indicators involves problems of definition and validity which cannot be discussed in detail here. However, we believe that the character of the overall trends is not in question.

The demographic indicators deserve brief special mention. The registrations of births, deaths, and population are probably reasonably accurate except with respect to infant mortality and the death rate for children in the first two years of life. Infant mortality is underregistered by about 50 per cent and death rates in the second year of life are somewhat overstated. These errors affect the general crude death rate and the average life expectancy figure. It is likely that the true crude death rate is a point higher than the official figures. The life expectancy figures, correspondingly, are somewhat too high.

Appendix I-2. Sources of Data for Indicators of Social and Economic Development (Table I-2)

Data on Gross National Product are from the *United Nations Statistical Yearbook.*

Data on newspaper circulation, domestic mail, and number of inhabitants per doctor are from the *United Nations Statistical Yearbook,* with the exception of the inhabitants per doctor figure for Taiwan, which is from the *Taiwan Statistical Data Book,* 1964.

Data on percentage economically active in agriculture are from the *Production Yearbook* of the World Food and Agriculture Organization.

The data for Indonesia on inhabitants per doctor are excluded in calculating the ten country average, because they are so much higher than any other figure.

Each of the measures used has a variety of problems of definition, validity, and comparability. However, it is unlikely that any corrections could affect the general conclusion that Taiwan ranks well above the average and usually first or second among the developing Asian countries for which data were available. The countries and indicators used were those for which data could be assembled for any date since 1960. Data have been cited only for the period after 1960, with the exception of the literacy figure for Ceylon, which is included because it is high enough to make the comparison with Taiwan more conservative.

The figures on literacy are especially suspect, because this is a difficult concept to use in census operations, and the definitions used vary greatly. The figures on circulation of newspapers and domestic mail are probably better indicators of the functional literacy that might affect development levels.

The figures for Japan (the most developed country in Asia) and the United States are included to indicate that there is still a vast gulf between even the leading developing countries and the more developed countries in terms of any of the criteria used.

If the median rather than the arithmetic mean is used to compute the averages for the ten other Asian countries, it does not substantially affect the comparisons with Taiwan.

Appendix I-3. Methodology: Sources of Data, Sampling Design, and Other Methodological Problems[1]

A. Introduction: Chronology of the Study and List of Data Sources

B. The Area Units for the Experiment and Data Collection

C. The Intensive Survey
1. The sample design of the Intensive Survey
2. Sampling errors for the Intensive Survey
3. The questionnaire for the Intensive Survey
4. The interviewers for the Intensive Survey
5. Validity and reliability of responses

D. The Home Visits and the Household Survey

E. Group Meetings

F. The Acceptance Records

G. The IUD Medical Follow-up

H. The Household Registration Data

I. Schedule A

J. Home Visit Record.

1 This appendix is based on a set of much longer unpublished memoranda which includes the following:

A. K. Jain, "Memorandum on Sampling Errors for First Baseline Survey of the Taichung Study," 1964.

C. P. Chang, "An Analysis of Accuracy and Completeness of Birth and Death Registration in Taichung, Taiwan," 1966.

S. Chu, "Households with Several Eligible Respondents in the Taichung Survey No. 4: Effects of Interviewing Only One in Each Household," 1963.

———, "Comparison of Taichung Intensive Survey Respondents Reinterviewed and Not Reinterviewed in Second Interview," 1964.

R. Freedman, "Comparability of the Original and Supplementary Samples for the Taichung Intensive Survey," 1965.

T. H. Sun, "The Reliability of Survey Data on Fertility and the Use of Family Limitation Methods, and Its Relations with the Characteristics of the Respondents in the Taichung Survey," 1965.

J. Y. Takeshita, "Sources of Data and Some Methodological Notes," 1967 (a much longer version of the present appendix).

Appendices

A. INTRODUCTION: CHRONOLOGY OF THE STUDY AND LIST OF DATA SOURCES

The Taichung family planning program was started in February 1963, and the initial experimental phase continued into October of that year. The Intensive Survey of a sample of married women 20-39 years old was made before this program, the field work lasting from October 1962 through January 1963. This survey served as an initial bench mark against which we could measure changes associated with the organized program of family planning. During the early phases of the program a short Household Survey interview was conducted with each of the married women 20-39 living in the Everything lins—approximately 11,000 in number. In about half of the Everything neighborhoods in which home visits were scheduled, group meetings were held and brief records kept of them. Upon completion of the experimental phase in mid-October, the sample panel of the bench mark Intensive Survey was reinterviewed to measure changes that had taken place between the two surveys. From the beginning of the program through July 1965, records also were kept of all cases accepting contraception from the clinics in Taichung. These could be related to the interview records of the Intensive Survey sample and the Household Survey of women visited at home as part of the experimental effort, so that we could analyze in detail the characteristics of program acceptors. In addition, those who accepted the IUD in the program up to the end of 1964 were followed up periodically at intervals of six to twelve months, as described in Chapter X. Finally, an outside check on the impact of the Taichung program exists in the official household register data on births and population. We can summarize the chronology of the study and the various sources of data available to us in the following way:

Pre-survey
Experimental Program (Household Survey)
Post surv.
Acceptance Records
I.U.D. Follow-up Survey
1962 | 1963 | 1964 | 1965
10 11 12 1 2 3 4 5 6 7 8 9 10 11 12 1 2 3 4 5 6 7 8 9 10 11 12 1 2 3 4 5 6 7 8 9
Household register (birth rate trend)

The present study, then, draws its data from the following sources:

1. The Intensive Sample Survey interviews with a panel of married women in Taichung before and after the experimental family planning program.
2. Short interviews with all women who were visited at home in the Everything-lins during the experimental program.
3. Records of group meetings held in more than half of the neighborhoods (lins) in which home visits were made during the experimental program.
4. Records of acceptance of family planning in the clinics of Taichung from the start of the experimental program to July 31, 1965.
5. Records of medical follow-up visits made to all IUD acceptors in the Taichung program up to December 31, 1964.
6. Official birth statistics from the household registers.

Before discussing each of these data sources, we will describe basic area units which were the building blocks both for the experimental design and for the data collection program.

B. THE AREA UNITS FOR THE EXPERIMENT AND THE DATA COLLECTION

Administratively, Taichung is divided into 8 districts (or precincts). Of the 8 districts, 3 are rural in character, and while these rural districts are much larger than the 5 urban districts they surround, they contain only about one-third of the total population of the city. Each of the 8 districts is further subdivided into lis and lins. In 1962, there were 176 lis and 2,199 lins. The lins were the basic units for both the experiment and the data collection program. All the eligible couples in a lin were assigned to the same "experimental treatment." If the lin fell into one of the data collection samples, the goal was to interview all eligible women in the lin.

An average lin contained 25 households and about 12 women who were married and in the 20-39 age range. Some lins, however, were either very small or very large and adjustments in their boundaries were required to improve the efficiency of field work both for the survey and the family planning program. Seventeen per cent of the lins were combined with neighboring lins, and 27 per cent were subdivided to form reconstituted lins of about 15 eligible women (i.e., women married and of the ages 20-39).[2] The treatments were actually

[2] After these adjustments, 95 per cent of the lins had no fewer than ten and no more than twenty eligible couples.

allocated to the lins after these adjustments were made. These 2,389 "adjusted" lins (rather than the original official 2,199) are the units to which we refer throughout our discussion in this book.

The treatments were allocated randomly (at systematic intervals) to the 2,389 lins in different proportions, depending on the sector of the city in which they were located. For allocating the density of the treatments, the city was divided into 3 pie-shaped sectors which met at the city center and which were roughly equated initially on fertility, rural-urban distribution, occupational composition, and educational level, as the following data on the sectors indicate:[3]

	Sector		
	I	*II*	*III*
Ratio of children under 5 to 100 married women 15-49	115	115	108
Percentage male employees in:			
agriculture	27	30	31
commerce	16	17	16
Percentage 12 years old and over with more than primary school education:			
men	35	33	40
women	19	18	21

As explained in Chapter VI, in the experiment these sectors were differentiated by the proportion of lins that were assigned to the Everything treatment, which included the home visits either with both spouses or with just the wife: 50 per cent in Sector I, 33 per cent in Sector II, and 20 per cent in Sector III. They were designated Heavy, Medium, and Light density sectors in reference to the density of direct effort (that is, the percentage of Everything-lins) allocated to them. In each sector, the remaining lins (that is, those not assigned to Everything treatments) were allocated randomly (at systematic intervals) in equal proportions to the Mail and the Nothing treatments. The following table summarizes the treatment allocation of the 2,389 lins by sector and gives the estimated number of married women 20-39 (as of October 1962) in each cell of the experimental design:

[3] These data as of the end of 1961 were obtained from the registration offices of the eight districts in Taichung.

Treatment	*Density sector* Heavy	Medium	Light	Total
	Number of lins			
Everything: husband and wife	232	122	73	427
Everything: wife only	232	122	73	427
Mail	232	244	292	768
Nothing	232	243	292	767
Total	928	731	730	2,389
	Percentage distribution of lins			
Everything: husband and wife	25	17	10	18
Everything: wife only	25	17	10	18
Mail	25	33	40	32
Nothing	25	33	40	32
Total	100	100	100	100
	Number of married women 20-39			
Everything: husband and wife	3,454	1,844	1,138	6,436
Everything: wife only	3,469	1,834	1,169	6,472
Mail	3,480	3,745	4,508	11,733
Nothing	3,508	3,742	4,526	11,776
Total	13,911	11,165	11,341	36,417

C. THE INTENSIVE SURVEY

1. THE SAMPLE DESIGN OF THE INTENSIVE SURVEY[4]

The Intensive Survey sample was drawn on the basis of data from the continuous population registers in which all residents are required by law to be registered in household units. In order to minimize interviewer contamination, only one woman was interviewed from each household. If more than one eligible woman (i.e., married and of the ages 20-39) lived in a household, one was selected randomly for the interview. Just as the program treatments were allocated by lin units, so the sample for the survey was drawn by lin with no subselection of respondents within the sample lin (except that only one respondent

[4] A more extended discussion of the sampling design and sampling errors is found in the unpublished memorandum by A. K. Jain listed in note 1.

was interviewed per household). In short, the basic sampling design was a one-stage sampling of compact clusters (of relatively uniform size, as assured by the adjustments described above).

The sample for the Intensive Survey was composed of two subsamples:

a. A subsample of all married women 20-39, interviewed with the detailed interview schedule (Schedule A). This is known as the "original" sample.
b. A subsample of all married women 20-39 with at least two living children, interviewed with a shorter schedule of questions (Schedule B), all of which were included in the longer version. This is known as the "supplementary" sample.

The procedures and rates of sample selection were identical for the two subsamples. The only differences were that in the supplementary sample women with fewer than two living children were not interviewed and the interview was shorter. The objective of this design was to maximize the number of women interviewed on an essential core list of questions, and especially to maximize the number of respondents with enough children so that they would have a fertility history of some length and probable interest in the program. The pressures of time in getting the program underway made it difficult to maintain the sample size and use the longer interview for everyone. In retrospect, this rather complex design was a mistake, because it greatly complicated analysis. In any analysis where the data were available for both subsamples, the data were thrown together into a single sample with proper weights to adjust for the fact that women with fewer than two children were only represented in one of the two otherwise equal subsamples.

A total of 209 lins (105 for the original sample and 104 for the supplementary subsample) were selected on a systematic probability basis. The lins were selected in proportion to the estimated number of women in each district, by applying a predetermined selection interval to a list of all the lins in the district. The lins were listed to follow a serpentine ordering on the map in order, to provide a rough geographical stratification.

Once a lin was selected, all eligible women in it were part of the sample panel. A list of the women was obtained from the household register in order to include all currently married women 20-39 living with their husbands. For the supplementary sample there was the additional qualification that at least two living children must be listed in the register.

The size of the sample list was larger than the desired number of interviews to allow for expected losses due to errors in the register, discovery that listed couples were ineligible, migration out of the lin, refusals, and other non-response factors. We also took into account the fact that some eligible couples not listed in the register might be living in the area. This was done by having the interviewer visit *every* household in the sample lins to determine whether it contained an eligible respondent not on the list compiled from the register. In this way 215 women were added to the sample list. This was approximately balanced by the 243 women initially on the list of eligible women compiled from the register but found to have moved away when the interviewer visited the lin. There were, in addition, 84 women on the list from the household register who were found to be ineligible for various reasons (e.g., husband or woman herself had died, respondent was older or younger than eligibility limits, etc.).

After these various adjustments in the list, 2,515 women were found to be eligible for interviews. The overall response rate for the first interview was very high—97 per cent—as the following tabulation indicates:

	Number	*Per cent*
Completed interviews	2,432	96.7
Never found after at least 4 calls	52	2.1
Refused	21	0.8
Too ill or incompetent for interview	10	0.4
Total eligible for interview	2,515	100.0

This excellent rate of response among the eligible women was continued in the second interviews with this same panel at the end of 1963, when approximately 98 per cent of those still eligible and living in the city at a known address were interviewed. Of the 2,432 women interviewed in the pre-program survey, 2,207 responded the second time (90.8 per cent of the first panel). Only 1.1 per cent refused to be reinterviewed. The largest loss (6.2 per cent) was from the women who moved out of the city or moved to an unknown address within the city. Almost all of these losses were due to migration out of the city, since it was not difficult to find and follow those moving within the city and every effort was made to do so. The remaining losses (1.9 per cent) were a result of death, illness, change in marital status, or non-response other than refusal.

The remarkably high response rates on this survey are not unusual for carefully conducted surveys in developing countries. Response rates tend to be much higher than those regarded as acceptable or good in the United States and other industrialized countries. In part, this results from the higher response rates for interviews with women on the subject of fertility. But we believe that cultural factors and the quality and organization of the interviewing staff also make a difference.

The procedure for selecting the sample for the Intensive Survey raises a number of methodological questions. First, what bias was introduced by the fact that only one eligible respondent was interviewed in the 5 percent of all households which contained two or more eligible women? In these households one of the several eligible respondents was selected randomly for interview, because it was felt that it would be very difficult to obtain independent responses to the questions from several different women in a household. Privacy is neither highly valued nor possible in many households, so that all of the eligible women might well be present at the first interview. The 141 women chosen randomly for interview in the households with several eligible respondents represent in effect the 319 eligible women living in such households.

Women who live in such multiple-respondent households are likely to be living in joint families typical of traditional Chinese familial ideals, so we might expect them to differ from the rest of the sample on family and fertility values and behavior. There are two questions here: (1) Do the women in multiple-respondent households differ from others? (2) Are these differences large enough, considering the number of such cases, to bias the overall results, if we take only one woman from each multiple-respondent household?

The answers are that women in the multiple-respondent households are different but that the differences do not substantially affect our overall results, because the number of such women is small. As column 1 in Table I-1a indicates, there are substantial differences in some re-

Table I-1a. Index of Dissimilarity[a] Between Women in Households with Only One and with More than One Eligible Respondent and Between Samples Unweighted and Weighted for Subselection from Multiple-Respondent Households, by Selected Characteristics (First Survey)

Characteristics compared	Index of dissimilarity: Single- vs. multiple respondent households (1)	Index of dissimilarity: Unweighted vs. weighted sample (2)
Age of wife	7.6	0.4
Number of live births	7.1	1.4
Wife's ideal number of children	13.9	0.8
Attitude toward family planning	7.1	0.5
Use of birth control	17.9	0.9
Wife's education	5.3	0.5
Family type	86.7	5.0

[a] The index of dissimilarity is a measure of differences in two percentage distributions. It is obtained by taking the sum of the absolute differences in each category of the distributions and dividing by 2: $\frac{\sum |P_i - P'_i|}{2}$, where P_i is the percentage in category i for one distribution and P'_i is the percentage in category i for the other distribution. A high value for the index indicates greater difference in the distribution. Conversely, a low value indicates that the distributions are similar. The index value indicates in effect the percentage of each of the distributions that needs to be shifted in order to make them identical.

spects between single- and multiple-respondent households. However, these differences do not substantially affect our results as a whole. This last comparison was made by assuming that the 319 wives who might have been interviewed in multiple-respondent households had a distribution of characteristics resembling that of the random subsample of 141 who were actually interviewed. If we add the 205 potential additional respondents (and their simulated characteristics) to the sample actually interviewed, the weighted-up results differ very little from those of the original sample (see column 2 of Table I-1a).

A similar question arises from the fact that some women interviewed in the pre-program interview were not interviewed in the second, post-program survey. Most of these women lost to the second interview had left the city. Such mobile women might be expected to differ from others in being younger, having fewer children, and being more modern in various ways. This was true (see column 1 of Table I-2a). However, again, the number of such cases is sufficiently small so that

Table I-2a. Index of Dissimilarity[a/] for Cases Not Re-Interviewed, Cases Re-Interviewed, and Total Cases Originally Interviewed in the First Survey, by Selected Characteristics

	Index of dissimilarity	
Characteristics compared	Not re-interviewed cases compared with re-interviewed cases (1)	Total cases in first survey compared with re-interviewed cases (2)
Age of wife	17.6	1.9
Length of marriage	19.1	1.0
Wife's age at marriage	2.4	0.1
Number of live births	16.9	1.8
Wife's ideal number of children	18.5	1.9
Use of birth control	9.2	0.9
Pregnancy status	1.0	0.1
Wife's education	4.5	0.4
Husband's education	10.9	1.1
Couple's farm background	13.2	1.2
Wife's newspaper readership	9.2	1.0
Number of modern objects owned	11.2	1.1
Husband's employment status	15.6	1.6
Family type	13.3	1.3
Wife's attitude toward traditional family values	5.1	0.5

[a/] See footnote in Table I-1a for an explanation of this index.

there are only trivial differences (column 2, Table I-2a) between the initial sample and the somewhat smaller sample interviewed both times. The number of cases lost to the second interview is not large enough to affect the overall results even on the variables where those lost to reinterview were distinctive.

We conclude, then, that our results are not significantly affected either by the decision to interview only one respondent per household or by the fact that 10 per cent of the women were interviewed once rather than twice.

Because the lower parity women were excluded from the supplementary sample, it is necessary to inflate that sample in order to use it together with the original sample. The inflation involves the weighting up of the supplementary sample to make it represent the whole universe of married women 20-39 by duplicating the IBM cards for the 281 original sample respondents who had fewer than 2 living children and adding these to the supplementary sample. When this is done and the two subsamples are combined, the total inflated sample becomes 2,713 for the first survey (original sample: 1,367; supplementary sample: 1,065 + 281) and 2,443 for the second survey (original sample: 1,227; supplementary sample: 980 + 236).

For the pre-program characteristics for which there are common data for the two subsamples, the total inflated sample of 2,713 cases from the first survey is usually used. When the analysis involves those pre-program characteristics obtained for the supplementary sample only at the second survey, such as their detailed fertility characteristics, or when the analysis focuses on the changes between the two surveys or on post-program characteristics, then only the 2,443 cases, inflated from the 2,207 cases interviewed in both surveys, are used.

The use of different questionnaires for the two subsamples also raises methodological issues about the propriety of merging the samples. However, these are really questions about the validity of the response rather than the sample design, so we will deal with these problems when discussing the quality of the data.

2. SAMPLING ERRORS FOR THE INTENSIVE SURVEY

The survey results are, of course, subject to sampling error, since we are using a sample of about 2,500 women to represent the larger population of about 36,000 married women 20-39 years old. By the laws of chance, we might expect another sample of 2,500 to have produced somewhat different results, quite apart from any errors of validity in the study. Even if we had interviewed all 36,000 women there might have been errors resulting from the form of our questionnaire, the interview procedures, the lack of information of the respondents, or even intentional deception on confidential matters. Measures of sampling error do not encompass those sources of error. In fact, a well-selected sample will represent these errors as well as the true facts in the universe of responses, within the limits of sampling error. The object of measuring sampling error is simply to determine what the probability is that the results may vary by specific amounts, purely as a result of the fact that one selects a sample of a certain size and design rather than working with population values.

In Tables I-3a and I-4a we present measures of sampling errors for percentages. In these tables a range of figures is presented. The smaller number represents the estimate of sampling error on the assumption that a simple random sample had been used. Such a sample would have involved, for example, selecting the respondent completely randomly and independently from a list of the 36,000 eligible respond-

Table I-3a. Approximate Sampling Error[a/] of Percentages

Estimated percentages	Number of interviews 2,500	2,000	1,500	1,000	700	500	400	300	200	100
50	2.0-3.1	2.2-3.3	2.6-3.6	3.2-4.1	3.8-4.7	4.5-5.5	5.0-6.0	5.8-6.9	7.1-8.4	10.0-11.5
40 or 60	2.0-3.1	2.2-3.2	2.5-3.5	3.1-4.0	3.7-4.6	4.4-5.4	4.9-5.9	5.7-6.7	6.9-8.2	9.8-11.3
30 or 70	1.8-2.8	2.0-3.0	2.4-3.3	2.9-3.8	3.5-4.3	4.1-5.0	4.6-5.5	5.3-6.3	6.5-7.7	9.2-10.5
20 or 80	1.6-2.5	2.0-2.9	2.1-2.8	2.5-3.3	3.0-3.8	3.6-4.4	4.0-4.8	4.6-5.5	5.7-6.7	8.0- 9.2
10 or 90	1.2-1.8	1.3-1.9	1.5-2.1	1.9-2.5	2.3-2.9	2.7-3.3	3.0-3.6	3.5-4.1	4.2-5.0	6.0- 6.9
5 or 95	0.8-1.2	1.0-1.4	1.1-1.6	1.4-1.8	1.6-2.1	1.9-2.4	2.2-2.6	2.5-3.0	3.1-3.6	4.4- 5.0

[a/] The figures in this table represent two standard errors. Hence, for most items the chances are 95 in 100 that an interval equal to the estimated percentage plus or minus the sampling error would include the population value. Two sets of values are given for both this table and Table I-4a which shows the sampling errors of differences between percentages. The lower values are estimates of standard errors on the assumption of simple random sampling. The higher values are conservative estimates that take into account the sampling design effect on the following variables of the study: percentage ever used family limitation, percentage ever used contraception, percentage wives with at least primary school graduation, percentage wives with more than primary school graduation, percentage husbands with more than primary school graduation, percentage in nuclear family, and percentage wives read newspaper more than once a week.

Table I-4a. Approximate Sampling Error[a/] of Differences Between Percentages

Number of interviews	Number of interviews 2,500	2,000	1,500	1,000	700	500	400	300	200	100
				For percentages around 35 and 65						
2,500	2.8-4.3	3.0-4.5	3.3-4.7	3.6-5.1	4.3-5.6	4.9-6.3	5.4-6.7	6.1-7.5	7.3- 8.9	10.2-11.9
2,000		3.2-4.6	3.4-4.8	3.9-5.2	4.4-5.7	5.0-6.4	5.5-6.8	6.2-7.6	7.4- 8.9	10.2-11.9
1,500			3.7-5.0	4.1-5.4	4.6-6.0	5.2-6.5	5.6-7.0	6.3-7.7	7.5- 9.1	10.3-12.0
1,000				4.5-5.8	4.9-6.3	5.5-6.7	5.9-7.3	6.6-8.0	7.7- 9.3	10.5-12.2
700					5.3-6.7	5.9-7.2	6.3-7.6	6.9-8.3	8.0- 9.6	10.7-12.4
500						6.3-7.8	6.7-8.1	7.3-8.8	8.4-10.0	11.0-12.7
400							7.1-8.5	7.6-9.1	8.7-10.2	11.2-13.0
300								8.2-9.7	9.1-10.8	11.5-13.4
200									10.0-11.8	12.2-14.2
100										14.1-16.2
				For percentages around 20 and 80						
2,000		2.5-3.7	2.7-3.9	3.1-4.2	3.5-4.6	4.0-5.1	4.4-5.5	5.0-6.1	5.9-7.2	8.2- 9.5
1,500			2.9-4.0	3.3-4.3	3.7-4.7	4.1-5.2	4.5-5.6	5.1-6.2	6.0-7.3	8.3- 9.6
1,000				3.6-4.6	3.9-5.0	4.4-5.5	4.7-5.8	5.3-6.4	6.2-7.4	8.4- 9.8
700					4.3-5.3	4.7-5.8	5.0-6.1	5.5-6.7	6.4-7.7	8.6- 9.9
500						5.1-6.2	5.4-6.5	5.8-6.8	6.7-8.0	8.8-10.2
400							5.7-6.8	6.1-7.2	6.9-8.2	8.9-10.4
300								6.5-7.8	7.3-8.6	9.0-10.7
200									8.0-9.4	9.8-11.4
100										11.3-13.0

[a/] The figures shown are the differences required for significance at the 5 per cent level in comparisons of percentages derived from the different subgroups of the survey. As in Table I-3a, two sets of values are given: the lower values are based on simple random sampling, and the higher values are calculated for the study variables listed in that table, taking into account the sampling design effect.

ents. We did not do this. Instead, we used probability methods to select clusters of respondents in lins. Once a lin was selected, every eligible woman in it was in the sample. This procedure would give results identical to those of the simple random selection procedure if the lins were not internally homogeneous—that is, if the women in each lin did not resemble each other more closely than they resembled women in other lins or in the city as a whole. But this internal homo-

Table I-4a (continued).

Number of interviews	Number of interviews									
	2,500	2,000	1,500	1,000	700	500	400	300	200	100
					For percentages around 10 and 90					
2,000		1.9-2.8	2.0-2.9	2.3-3.1	2.6-3.4	3.0-3.8	3.3-4.1	3.7-4.6	4.5-5.4	6.1-7.2
1,500			2.2-3.0	2.4-3.3	2.7-3.5	3.1-3.9	3.4-4.1	3.8-4.6	4.5-5.4	6.2-7.2
1,000				2.7-3.5	3.0-3.8	3.3-4.1	3.5-4.2	3.9-4.8	4.6-5.6	6.3-7.3
700					3.2-4.0	3.5-4.3	3.8-4.6	4.1-5.0	4.8-5.8	6.4-7.5
500						3.8-4.7	4.0-4.9	4.4-5.3	5.0-6.0	6.6-7.6
400							4.2-5.1	4.6-5.5	5.2-6.2	6.7-7.8
300								4.9-5.8	5.5-6.5	6.9-8.0
200									6.0-7.1	7.3-8.5
100										8.5-9.7
					For percentages around 5 and 95					
2,000		1.4-2.0	1.4-2.1	1.7-2.3	1.9-2.5	2.2-2.8	2.4-3.0	2.7-3.3	3.2-3.9	
1,500			1.6-2.2	1.8-2.4	2.0-2.6	2.3-2.9	2.5-3.0	2.8-3.4	3.3-4.0	
1,000				2.0-2.5	2.2-2.7	2.4-3.0	2.6-3.2	2.9-3.5	3.4-4.1	
700					2.3-2.9	2.6-3.2	2.7-3.3	3.0-3.6	3.5-4.2	
500						2.8-3.4	2.9-3.5	3.2-3.8	3.6-4.4	
400							3.1-3.7	3.3-4.0	3.7-4.5	
300								3.6-4.2	4.0-4.7	
200									4.8-5.1	
100										

geneity does exist. In Taichung, as in other cities, neighborhoods tend to attract people with distinctive characteristics, that is, there is neighborhood segregation. To the extent that this is true for the characteristics being considered, the sampling error will exceed that of a simple random sampling procedure. How much the clustering effect increases the sampling errors will vary with the characteristic considered, since segregation is not the same for all characteristics.

The larger numbers in Tables I-3a and I-4a represent estimates of the sampling errors for percentages or differences between percentages, taking the clustering effect into account, in the case of the variables listed in the tables. The clustering effect, and therefore the sampling error, will vary for different variables. It is not possible to present an exhaustive list for all possible characteristics. However, the tables presented should give the reader an idea of how much sampling error may be expected. Unfortunately, most social science studies ignore the clustering effect, although there is such clustering in most sampling designs. If the reader chooses to ignore this effect, he can use the lower limits shown. The upper limits give him some idea of the error involved in such a simplifying assumption. Sometimes this error is not very substantial, but the tables provide some assurance of its probable dimensions.

Tables I-5a and I-6a present the sampling errors for means and differences between means for two of the important characteristics of the

Table I-5a. Approximate Sampling Errors[a/] of Averages and Differences Between Two Averages for Number of Live Births

Number of interviews	2500	2000	1500	1000	700	500	400	300	200	100
					Sampling error of averages[b/]					
	.14	.15	.17	.19	.22	.26	.28	.32	.40	.55
					Sampling error of differences between two averages[c/]					
2500	.19	.20	.22	.23	.26	.29	.31	.35	.42	.57
2000		.21	.23	.24	.27	.30	.32	.36	.42	.57
1500			.24	.26	.28	.31	.33	.37	.43	.58
1000				.27	.29	.32	.34	.38	.44	.58
700					.31	.34	.36	.39	.45	.59
500						.36	.38	.41	.47	.61
400							.40	.43	.49	.62
300								.46	.51	.64
200									.56	.68
100										.78

[a/] The figures in the table represent two standard errors.

[b/] The chances are 95 in 100 that the "true" average would be included within a range equal to the estimated averages plus or minus the sampling error.

[c/] The values shown are the differences required for significance at the 5 per cent level in comparisons of averages derived from the different subgroups of the survey.

Table I-6a. Approximate Sampling Errors[a/] of Averages and Differences Between Two Averages for Number of Children Wanted

Number of interviews	2500	2000	1500	1000	700	500	400	300	200	100
					Sampling error of averages[b/]					
	.07	.07	.08	.09	.11	.13	.14	.16	.20	.28
					Sampling error of differences between two averages[c/]					
2500	.09	.10	.10	.12	.13	.14	.16	.17	.21	.29
2000		.10	.11	.12	.13	.15	.16	.18	.21	.29
1500			.11	.13	.14	.15	.16	.18	.21	.29
1000				.14	.15	.16	.17	.19	.22	.29
700					.16	.17	.18	.20	.23	.30
500						.18	.19	.21	.24	.31
400							.20	.21	.24	.31
300								.23	.26	.32
200									.28	.34
100										.39

[a/] The figures in the table represent two standard errors.

[b/] The chances are 95 in 100 that the "true" average would be included within a range equal to the estimated averages plus or minus the sampling error.

[c/] The values shown are the differences required for significance at the 5 per cent level in comparisons of averages derived from two different subgroups of the survey.

study. In these tables the clustering effect has been built into the sampling error calculations. The sampling errors on the assumption of simple random sampling are not shown here, but for the two characteristics in these tables the clustering effect increases the sampling error by a factor of approximately 1.5.

The number of cases shown in the tables contained in the body of the text generally include the inflation factor required to weight in the supplementary sample. Therefore, they are somewhat higher than the actual number of interviewed cases. When the two samples are used together, it is necessary to deflate the number of cases by 8 per cent to arrive at an estimate of the sample size under which to enter the sampling error tables.

A few examples may illustrate the use of these tables:

a. Of the approximately 2,500 women interviewed, 36 per cent reported having practiced some form of birth control before the first interview. Entering Table I-3a under a sample size of 2,500 and interpolating between the entries for 30 and 40 per cent, we see that the error range is between 2 and 3 per cent. Therefore, we can say that the odds are 95 out of 100 that the sample is drawn from a population in which the true figure is between 33 and 39 per cent (36 ± 3). If we ignore the clustering effect, the range is 34 to 38 per cent (36 ± 2).

b. The average number of children wanted by the 856 women in the sample who had no education is reported as 4.25. From Table I-6a we conclude with a 95 per cent probability that this sample comes from a population in which the true figure is between 4.14 and 4.36 ($4.25 \pm .11$).

c. Consider the following data about the percentage of those who have used birth control:

   17 per cent of the 856 women with no education

   25 per cent of the 833 women who were primary school dropouts

   66 per cent of the 233 women who graduated from senior high schools

The differences between these percentages are statistically significant at the 5 per cent level. For example, the difference between the first two groups is 8 per cent, which is greater than the two standard errors of differences (4 to 5 per cent) between percentages around 20 per cent with about 800 cases in each of the subgroups under comparison (see Table I-3a). A difference as large as this could occur by chance only five out of one hundred times; hence, we conclude that the observed difference is significant at the 5 per cent level.

We must caution the readers that many of the statistics used in our analysis are based on rather small groups, and therefore the sampling errors involved are large. In particular, many of our comparisons between small subgroups do not always yield statistically significant results. However, when a number of such comparisons yield results that show a consistent pattern, we have regarded such results as significant, even where considerable sampling errors were involved in the individual comparisons.

3. THE QUESTIONNAIRES FOR THE INTENSIVE SURVEY

Four different interview schedules (A, B, C, and D) were used in the two surveys. Schedule A, with 321 questions, was used in the first survey of the original sample and took an average of 80 minutes to administer. Schedule B, an abbreviated version of Schedule A with 108 questions, was used in the first survey of the supplementary sample and took an average of 30 minutes to administer. Schedules C (with 213 questions) and D (with 257 questions) were used in the second survey of the original and supplementary samples, respectively, and took an average of 52 and 55 minutes to administer. In summary, the different forms were used in the following manner:

	First survey	*Second survey*
Original sample	A	C
Supplementary sample	B	D

Schedules C and D are identical for the most part, but the latter includes additional questions to supplement the abbreviated version (Schedule B) used for the supplementary sample in the first survey in order to have comparable pre-program data for both samples. The questions used in the surveys can be grouped into the following broad categories. Most of the questions in the second survey focus on changes in these areas since the first survey:

a. Household composition
b. Marital history, pregnancies, and births
c. Goals regarding family size

d. Fecundity status
e. Contact with action program (second survey only)
f. Knowledge, attitude, and practice of family limitation (including induced abortion)
g. Literacy and exposure to mass media
h. Attitudes toward traditional family system and actual family structure
i. Demographic, socio-economic, and migration characteristics of husband and wife

The second survey included, in addition, a check on any discrepancies between the marriage and birth data reported in the first survey and those recorded in the register.

Schedule A is reproduced in this appendix in translation from the Chinese to illustrate the type of questionnaire used. Readers interested in the other three forms may obtain copies by writing to the University of Michigan Population Studies Center (1225 S. University Avenue, Ann Arbor, Michigan 48104). We have reproduced this questionnaire because it is rather different from the type used by many survey organizations. It may also be of value because it has been used as a model in several other developing countries. It follows in general the form of questionnaires used on many studies at the University of Michigan Survey Research Center.

The questionnaire may seem rather long to the casual reader. The length arises partly from the fact that all of the questions are prepared in detail in advance for the interviewer, who is instructed to use these exact wordings and to deviate from them only if it is clear that the respondent does not understand the question. In many other investigations the wording of the question is left to the discretion of the interviewer. We do not follow this procedure, for four reasons: (1) this means that the stimulus presented to the respondent in the questions varies with the interviewer; (2) it places the investigator in the hands of the interviewer, who may change the meanings intended considerably; (3) the interviewers are not usually trained research investigators, but if they follow predetermined questions they can be given the advantage of the results of previous experience and pretesting with these questions; and (4) with the questions predetermined, the interviewer can concentrate on rapport with the respondents and on understanding their answers rather than on formulating the questions.

The questionnaire also seems long because different sets of questions are provided for different contingencies and kinds of respondents. No respondent answers all of the questions. For example, there are separate questions on some subjects for those who have fecundity problems, for those who are pregnant, for those who have or have not used contraception, and so on. The questionnaire is designed to make the interview as simple as possible for the interviewer. This is done at the cost of more paper and printing—a small cost, given the usual research budget.

4. THE INTERVIEWERS FOR THE INTENSIVE SURVEY

Thirty-four interviewers were used in the Intensive Survey. All of them had some combination of nursing and midwifery training. Eighteen were from the staff of the Taiwan Population Studies Center or such associated health units as the Maternal and Child Health Institute or the city's district health stations. The other sixteen were recruited from applicants with nursing or midwifery training. The interviewers always wore a public health nurse's uniform in the field, and were therefore easily identified by the public as health workers.

The interviewers were trained in the technique of survey interviewing by the senior staff of the Taiwan Population Studies Center. The training sessions before each survey lasted about a week. The curriculum consisted of: (1) general introduction to the research project, (2) general introduction to survey techniques, including elementary ideas about sampling, (3) detailed study of the questionnaire, with emphasis on wording and question objectives, (4) detailed instruction in the techniques of interviewing, (6) instruction in how to transcribe responses, (7) demonstration interviewing, followed by a critical review, (8) role-playing in interviewing under supervision, (9) practice interviewing in the field, (10) a critical review of the practice interviews on both an individual and a group basis, and (11) instructions on administrative routine of field work.

In addition to the training sessions, the interviewers were required to study and use as reference both a manual on interviewing translated and adapted from a similar manual prepared by the University of Michigan Survey Research Center for its professional interviewing staff and a booklet of specific instructions for each of the schedules of questions used. Finally, to ensure completeness and adequacy of responses vis-à-vis the question objectives, every returned interview was edited on a daily basis by the staff of the Taiwan Population Studies Center and problems were reviewed with the interviewers, insofar as this was practical, before they went into the field the following day. Interviewers were sent back for additional information if the initial returns were incomplete or inadequate.

5. VALIDITY AND RELIABILITY OF RESPONSES

In any survey the respondent's reports on their behavior and attitudes will include "errors," especially in the case of reports on the events of the past. The errors arise from a variety of sources: the respondents may not know the facts; their memories may be faulty; they may intentionally misreport on sensitive subjects, especially if others are present at the interview; the interviewer may bias the response in various ways; the form of the questionnaire, and especially the number of questions and their detail, may affect the nature of the response.

At least on factual matters, we believe that the Intensive Survey was done under such favorable circumstances as to maximize the probability of valid responses, although errors of unknown magnitude undoubtedly remain despite all the precautions taken. We shall first describe some of the favorable circumstances which probably helped to increase the validity of the data, and then present some approximate measures of error.

The factors which may have increased validity of the data include:

a. The quality, training, and supervision of the interviewers

The interviewers were carefully trained by methods already described. This is not unusual for good surveys, but there were certain special features of this situation which we believe were helpful. The interviewers were identified as public health workers, who have a good reputation and a favorable reception in the community. They worked full-time on the interviewing during the period of the survey, which increased both their commitment and their single-minded attention to this project. This intensity of work and training was reinforced by a dedication and an involvement which are not found in Western interviewing staffs, who are generally part-time employees with other major concerns.

The fact that the interviewing staff reported daily to a central office, when coupled with the fact that the interviews were edited daily, was very important. This made it possible to talk over with the interviewers any problems as they occurred. Obvious errors and discrepancies were noted, and if necessary the interviewers were sent back to the respondent to straighten these out. The fact that a detailed pregnancy, marriage, and birth control history was taken for each woman means that it is often possible to find internal inconsistencies in the course of such an editing process. Such on-the-spot editing and immediate field rechecking are only possible where labor costs are relatively low. Such procedures are extremely rare in Western countries.

b. The design of the questionnaire

An examination of the questionnaire will make it obvious that a great amount of detail was obtained on the fertility, marriage, and birth control experience of the couple. In some areas of questioning (e.g., abortion) questions were asked in several ways at different parts of the questionnaire. In general, in survey interviewing if the specific objectives of a questionnaire can be split up into component parts and questions asked about each part, the result will be more complete and accurate reporting than if a single global question is asked. For example, suppose the objective is to determine how many live births a woman has ever had. A beginning can be made by asking this question once in a straightforward manner. However, in a country like Taiwan, a woman who gives what she believes to be an honest report may be under-reporting the total number of births because, for example: (1) she has forgotten to report a child who died shortly after birth, (2) she has forgotten to report a child who is no longer living at home, (3) she has forgotten to report a child born in a former marriage, or (4) she has reported as a stillbirth what was really a live birth. We found that additional births were reported when each of these subareas was specifically probed with additional questions. Also, since each woman was interviewed twice, there was an additional opportunity for related questions to bring to the respondent's mind facts previously forgotten or to bring to the attention of the interviewer inconsistent facts that might lead, after some probing, to a more accurate total history. Obviously, we could not do such detailed work on all variables. For example, we know that income was under-reported on our survey, because we did not probe for the income of each member of the household from each possible source. We reserved this kind of accuracy check by detailed interviewing for the crucial fertility and birth control items. One question that was particularly helpful was a probe used by the interviewer where a respondent's fertility history showed a period of at least twenty-four months without a pregnancy. For any such periods the woman was, in effect, asked for an explanation—that is, she was asked whether contraception or abortion or the absence of her husband accounted for this "long period" without a pregnancy (see question B-30 in the questionnaire). This particular question improved the reporting of pregnancies, births, abortions, contraception, and periods of husband-wife separation.

c. Outside checks and reinterviews as means of improving the data

The final classification of the respondent with respect to such matters as birth and pregnancy history, use of birth control, education, and occupation was settled only after the second interview was completed. It was therefore possible to use not only the two interviews but also certain other outside sources of information to obtain classifications that we finally accepted as our closest approximation to valid data. The checks and corrections were carried out in this sequence:

(1) The first interview with each respondent was checked for internal errors. Obvious errors were corrected by sending the interviewer back to the respondent to obtain a consistent set of responses on factual items.

(2) Between the first and second interviews, the official household registration record was checked for each woman. If there was a discrepancy between the facts noted there and the first interview record, this discrepancy was checked with the respondent at the second interview and the answers reconciled in a consistent manner. The items that were checked in this way included the marriage history, births and deaths of children, the ages of the mother and the children, and the education of the wife and husband. The household registration was more often in error than the interview and was not taken as the final correct datum. Instead, it was the discrepancy between the two records that was taken as the resource for a checking operation. Usually, discrepancies were found to involve not intentional errors but forgetting or a failure to register on time.

(3) For 49 per cent of the respondents (all of those in the Everything lins) we had a completely independent short interview—the

Household Survey Interview—covering in a summary way the crucial fertility and family planning variables. These interviews were conducted by a separate staff of interviewer-fieldworkers who had no access to the Intensive Survey interviews. These shorter interviews were checked against the first Intensive Survey interviews. Discrepancies found were probed in the second Intensive Survey interview.

(4) After the second Intensive Survey interview, during the final coding process, the data from all of these diverse sources were checked again for inconsistencies and a final round of visits was made to respondents to reconcile the records.

This set of procedures was an unusual, and perhaps a unique, attempt to improve the validity of the responses on factual matters. If we regard the final classification on key items as our best approximation of valid responses, we can estimate error by comparing the responses on the first survey (when the outside checks were not available) to the final second survey responses. This is a procedure rather different from the usual post-survey reliability check, which involves comparing two independent responses to the same question. This more usual procedure is not really a validity check, because it is only a test of the variability of response in two independent question trials, each of which may be in error. We believe that our check is much more useful and meaningful, if difficult to carry out, because it tells us how far the original survey response differs from our best approximation of the truth (while recognizing that errors remain in our criterion, too). Also, the usual post-survey check with a subsample only serves as a measure of unreliability in response and rarely can be used to correct the data. In our procedure, the checking operation was of such a character as to improve the quality of the data.

It is necessary to present the measures of error separately for the original sample (the sample of all women) and for the supplementary sample (the sample of women with at least two live births), because the questionnaires, and therefore the errors, differed substantially for the two subsamples. In the case of the original sample, the first interview followed the schedule of questions reproduced in this book. (Schedule A). The supplementary sample was interviewed using a much shorter questionnaire on the first interview to save time; but the missing details were then obtained at the second interview. This means, for example, that we asked the supplementary sample on the first interview for the total number of births, pregnancies, abortions, etc., but did not obtain a detailed history of the dates and circumstances of these events. As would be expected from our earlier discussion, this resulted in a considerably larger number of errors of under-reporting on the first survey for the supplementary sample.

In Table I-7a we present a measure of the "gross error," that is, the percentage of respondents whose answers on certain key items were

Table I-7a. Rates of Gross Error[a] in Responses to Questions About Fertility and Family Planning for the Original and the Supplementary Sample

	Rate of gross error	
Variables	Original sample	Supplementary sample
Total number of pregnancies	5.5	19.7
Number of live births	1.3	9.0
Number of abortions	0.6	5.8
Experience of any abortion	0.6	4.3
Experience of sterilization	1.7	2.2
Experience of contraception	2.4	13.1
Timing of first use of contraception or sterilization	3.8	18.8

[a] Rate of gross error is simply the percentage of respondents who gave inconsistent responses between the first survey and other sources for the original sample and between the first and the second survey for the supplementary sample.

discrepant as between the first interview and the classification of the respondent after the second interview (which included consideration of all relevant checking materials). In general, the errors are rather few in number. The net errors (allowing for the compensation of errors in opposite directions) are even fewer (see Table I-8a), because on the first interview some respondents made over-reporting errors and others made compensating under-reporting errors, although on balance the errors were in the direction of under-reporting. The gross errors reported in Table I-7a tend to exaggerate the problems in the data, since they are based on people rather than events. The proportion of respondents misreporting a birth, for example, is much larger than the number of births under-reported or over-reported, since errors were usually of one birth on a base of several. Large errors (e.g., one birth rather than six) were rare. In Table I-9a we show the amount of error related to events as well as to reporting persons.

Table I-8a. Rates of Net Error[a] in Responses to Questions About Fertility and Family Planning for the Original and the Supplementary Sample

Variables	Rate of net error	
	Original sample	Supplementary sample
Total number of pregnancies	1.1	1.9
Number of live births	0.7	1.2
Number of abortions	0.4	2.5
Experience of any abortion	0.4	2.4
Experience of sterilization	0.6	0.7
Experience of contraception	2.2	7.6
Timing of first use of contraception or sterilization	3.0	6.0

[a] Rate of net error is simply the index of dissimilarity. It compares the percentage distributions of responses between the first survey before and after correction for the original sample and between the first and the second survey for the supplementary sample.

It is obvious from the data that the errors were much greater for the supplementary sample than for the original sample. In part, this is undoubtedly a result of the fact that the questionnaire for the original sample was much more detailed, so that errors could be eliminated during the interview process itself. We wish it were possible to assert that this is a quantitative demonstration of the effects of detailed questioning. Unfortunately, there also are other sources for the difference. In the first place, the supplementary sample was restricted to women with at least two living children, and higher parity means more opportunity for error in reporting fertility and birth control history. More important is the fact that for the supplementary sample we come closest to independent questioning on the two surveys, since the summary questioning about births, contraception, etc., on the first survey was followed by detailed and complete pregnancy and contraceptive histories on the second interview. In the case of the original sample the detailed information was obtained at the first interview, and there was therefore, no pressing need for the same complete replication of questions on the second survey. The check on the validity of the first interview for the original sample came from the household registration, the Household Survey, and the many related questions on the second survey.

The large amount of error in reporting abortions in the supplementary sample undoubtedly results mainly from the differences in the detail and wording of the questions. In the first interview in the supplementary sample there was not the detailed pregnancy history from which more accurate abortion reporting might come. We do not attribute this variability for the supplementary sample to the outside checks, since data on pregnancies or abortions were not available from the outside check and the corrections on the births were relatively small when compared to those on the pregnancies.

It has been known for some time that the Taiwan household register, while much more accurate than most vital registration systems in developing countries, incorporates errors.[5] In particular, the reporting of infant deaths is known to be much too low. The officially reported infant mortality rate of about 26 is about half what might be expected on the basis of mortality rates for the older ages. Furthermore, a number of careful independent checks[6] have confirmed the fact that perhaps half of the infant deaths are not registered. It is believed that such under-registration of infant deaths most frequently occurs when a child dies shortly after birth. In that case the household head may fail to register both the birth and the death. The effect, of course, is much greater on infant mortality than on the birth rate.

It is a source of some confidence in the results of the Intensive Survey that the infant mortality data from it produce a rate of about 50, which is consistent with other mortality rates. A painstaking household-by-household comparison of the register and the Intensive Survey indicates that reporting of both births and infant deaths was more accurate on the survey than in the register.[7] Further, a check of the discrepancies indicates that it is indeed true that about 75 per cent of the under-reporting of infant deaths was explained by the parents as occurring because the baby died soon after birth. Approximately half of the infant deaths reported by parents to the survey interviewer in the careful, detailed fertility and family history were not in the household register.

[5] See the section on the household register, below.

[6] For example, see L. P. Chow, "Studies on the Registration of Births and Infant Deaths in Taiwan," Unpublished Dissertation for the Doctor of Public Health Degree, Department of Maternal and Child Health, Johns Hopkins University School of Hygiene and Public Health, 1963.

[7] Analyzed in the unpublished memorandum by C. P. Chang listed in note 1.

The reliability checks and comparisons discussed so far relate to factual items rather than to questions about attitudes and values. What reliance can be placed on answers to questions about the desired number of children, whether any additional children were wanted, preference for sons, intentions to practice contraception, and so on? This is a much more difficult area for validation, and the meaning of a "valid" response is controversial. It does little good to repeat questions about attitudes on a second survey as a check, because attitudes change and it is impossible to separate unreliable responses from genuine changes. Even at one moment in time, it is likely that a response about an attitude represents a statement of a central tendency in an acceptable range of alternative responses. For example, suppose a woman with three children says that she wants no more. On being pressed she may indicate that if she were to have one more child, this would not be terribly serious, but that she would regard three more children as catastrophic. Whether she says that she would prefer three children or four may depend on her mood and circumstances on that day or month, although it would take most unusual changes to elicit the response that she wants six children.

All of this is to say that the answers to such questions in a good interview are likely to be more than random responses. But they should be regarded not as exact statements of fact but as central tendencies in an area of normative thinking. Deviations from the central tendency for different women are likely to be compensating in direction, so that the total picture obtained for the whole group may not be too far in error. Suppose that we have a reasonably accurate negative response to a question like "Do you want more children?" What does it mean? At most the response can be taken to mean that, other things being equal, the woman would prefer to have no more. But its meaning in terms of action depends on other attitudes and circumstances. For example, whether she will implement her desire to stop childbearing by coming to the clinic for an IUD may be influenced by her attitude toward the clinic and the method, her evaluation of the attitudes of her husband, mother-in-law, and friends, etc. In short, there is no reason to believe that this attitude will direct behavior without reference to other attitudes and circumstances.

This does not mean that there can be no check on the significance of the attitudes. For example, the data of the first Intensive Survey indicate that most respondents with at least three or four children and at least one son wanted no more children and that they were prepared to use some method of birth control for this purpose. Such responses have been obtained in many surveys in developing countries. One judgment is that such data are simply a reflection of what the respondent perceives to be the values of the interviewer and the modern world from which she comes. As already indicated, this at least means that the respondents have sufficiently internalized an appreciation of the modern small family norm to give a set of responses consistent with it. This, in itself, is an important social fact that is likely to influence behavior.

In the case of Taichung, however, there is more substantial evidence that the preference for three or four children (and for one or two sons) is affecting behavior substantially, because upon achieving this level:

(1) before the program began, substantial numbers of couples had tried to do something about limiting family size and had in fact slowed down their birth rate, as indicated by the length of the open birth interval.

(2) during the period of the program, the parity and number of sons was strongly correlated to

- (a) stated intentions to adopt contraception
- (b) probability of the insertion of an IUD or other birth control actions
- (c) persistence in retaining an IUD in place
- (d) reinsertion of an IUD or adoption of alternate methods after a first IUD termination

In short, there is a correlation between attitudes and behavior that is very substantial for human behavior studies. To expect a perfect correlation would be to hold the unrealistic view that this one attitude is so overriding as to eliminate all other considerations. Few attitudes have such dominance over behavior for any length of time.

None of this should be taken to mean that the attitudes expressed on the survey must be accepted as valid. They are fallibly measured and do not predict behavior infallibly. One of the most important items on the agenda for research in this field is to understand more completely the circumstances under which existence of certain attitudes will be followed by appropriate consistent behavior. However, we believe that, at least for the Taichung data, the attitudes expressed are an important datum, pertinent to behavior, and indicative, in the aggregate, of genuine motivations and tendencies to act under facilitating conditions.

For many purposes we have merged the original and supplementary subsamples into a single sample. So far as the sampling design is concerned this is perfectly proper, since they were selected in identical ways as samples from the same universe (except for the difference in parity, which can be taken into account by appropriate weights). However, we have just noted that differences in wording and in the detail of the questions make for a different rate of error in the two subsamples. This raises a question about the propriety of merging the samples. We feel justified in merging them for most purposes, because the samples do produce rather closely comparable distributions in the case of all but one of the nine items on which they were tested (after excluding respondents with less than two children from the original sample). As Table I-10a indicates, the index of dissimilarity is

Table I-9a. Comparison of Gross Errors in the Reporting of Births and Pregnancies with the Number of Respondents and the Number of Events as the Base for the Original and the Supplementary Sample

	Original sample		Supplementary sample	
Variables compared	Percentage of respondents reporting incorrect number	Percentage of events reported incorrectly[a]	Percentage of respondents reporting incorrect number	Percentage of events reported incorrectly[a]
Live births	5.5	1.5	19.7	4.9
Pregnancies	1.3	0.4	9.0	2.6
Abortions	0.6	5.9	5.8	24.7

[a] The sum of the number of events reported incorrectly is divided by the total number of events.

quite small on a range of nine important attitudinal and behavioral variables used in the study. The one variable for which there is a large difference is the attitude toward the general idea of family planning. This difference appears to arise from somewhat different ways of asking and coding the component questions which determine this attitude. The large resulting difference is mainly in the degree to which family planning was approved (whether with or without reservations and qualifications), rather than reflecting quite different attitudes.

Table I-10a. Index of Dissimilarity[a/] Between the Original[b/] and the Supplementary Samples by Selected Characteristics (First Survey)

Characteristics compared	Index of dissimilarity between original and supplementary samples
Age of wife	2.2
Number of live births	3.1
Wife's ideal number of children	3.6
Attitude toward family planning	31.2
Use of birth control	3.9
Wife's education	4.6
Family type	3.6
Couple's farm background	5.7
Wife's attitude toward traditional family values	6.1

[a/] See the footnote in Table I-1a for an explanation of this index.

[b/] Respondents with less than two children have been excluded from the original sample for comparability with the supplementary sample.

D. THE HOME VISITS AND THE HOUSEHOLD SURVEY

The family planning fieldworkers were supposed to visit all eligible women in the Everything lins to tell them about the new family planning program. As an incidental part of this visit, the fieldworker interviewed each woman, using the Household Questionnaire, a specimen of which is included in this appendix. Since this interview was only incidental to her basic educational task, the fieldworker was not asked to make the repeated visits used during the Intensive Survey to complete the interviews in cases where the women were not found at home easily. Nevertheless, 88 per cent of the approximately 13,000 eligible women in the Everything lins were interviewed successfully in the Household Survey.

The training and supervision of fieldworkers for this very large number of interviews could not be at the level of that for the Intensive Survey. Moreover, the brevity of these interviews makes it likely that they were of lower quality than those of the more intensive survey. Nevertheless, the frequency distributions obtained from the Household Survey compared quite closely with estimates made on the basis of the Intensive Survey and of the Household register. Since the Everything lins were a probability sample of all lins, the Household Survey sample is also a probability sample of all the women of childbearing years, so such comparisons are possible.

Wherever possible, preference is given to the data from the Intensive Survey, but we rely on the Household Survey where the large size of its sample permits detailed cross-tabulations or where its data are unique (e.g., intentions to accept).

The Household Questionnaire was also used for women who came to the clinics from outside the Everything lins. Therefore, we have the data of the Household Survey form for all acceptors regardless of their place of origin, and these are used at several places in our analysis.

The fieldworkers for the experimental family planning program who conducted the Household Interviews numbered twenty-seven in all: eighteen regular workers and nine supervisors. The supervisors, recruited from the professional nursing staff of the Provincial Maternal and Child Health Institute, had extensive public health experience. The team of eighteen fieldworkers included nine Pre-Pregnancy Health (PPH) workers, who had worked out of the city's health stations under the older family planning program, and nine additional workers who were recruited to assist them in the experimental program. Some of these also served as interviewers in the Intensive Survey. Nearly all had senior high school education and previous nursing or midwifery experience.

The twenty-seven fieldworkers were given a two-week training course under the supervision of a local health educator and an American advisor from the Population Council.[8] During the first week, they were given instructions on how to make home visits, conduct group meetings, use visual aid materials, keep records, and so forth, in addition to lectures on the physiology of reproduction and the techniques of contraception, including the new IUD and the pill. During the second week, they were sent to several health stations outside of Taichung, where they practiced making home visits, conducting group meetings, and keeping records under the supervision of the more experienced nurse-instructors.

The nine PPH workers with their assistants were stationed at the district health stations and were responsible for the home visits in the Everything lins in their districts and for assisting women who came to the health stations seeking family planning help. It was their responsibility to take the Household Survey at the time of the home

[8] Mr. Laurence Springfield, an experienced communications expert, was in residence in Taichung for about six months to assist the local personnel in training the fieldworkers and in planning the educational and service activities of the experimental program.

visits, to keep a record of each acceptor of family planning at the health stations, and to assist the supervisors in conducting group meetings.

E. GROUP MEETINGS

The experimental design provided that group meetings were to be held in each Everything lin before the fieldworkers made their home visits in that lin. A shortage of personnel and problems of timing made it impossible to hold more than 462 of the 860 scheduled meetings.

The meetings were usually held in the evenings, in order to maximize the possibility that both husbands and wives could attend. Nevertheless, about half of the meetings were attended only by women, and in the other half men were almost always in a small minority. In the central, urban part of the city the meetings were held indoors at the home of the neighborhood lin-leader, in a temple or other public building, or occasionally in the home of an eligible wife. In the outlying rural areas, the meetings were often held outdoors in a farmyard.

Flip-charts and slides were used extensively in the group meetings to supplement lectures. The audience was encouraged to raise questions and to express its own views. Although the formal presentation covered all of the medically accepted methods of birth control, the audience often became impatient if the speakers talked too long about the conventional methods. They often insisted that the speaker "get on" to the newer methods (the IUD especially) that they had already heard about by word of mouth. The average length of a meeting was two hours.

The supervisor was required to fill out a simple record immediately after the meeting and to bring it to the central office at the beginning of the following week. Three ratings on audience reaction were made by the supervisor at this time, before she knew the acceptance rate in the lin. The audience was rated on a five-point scale with respect to the number of questions raised, the amount of discussion, and the overall interest. A meeting was coded as being effective if it was scored as "1" or "2" (the two high points) on the five-point scale for each of these three characteristics. Seventy-nine per cent of all the meetings were coded in this way regarding their effectiveness. As we have already seen, the supervisor's perception of the effectiveness of the meetings was validated by the correlation of the acceptance rates over the succeeding months with these initial ratings.

F. ACCEPTANCE RECORDS

An acceptance record was filled out for each woman who either received instruction in contraception and/or supplies of contraceptives from the program personnel with intention to use them or was fitted with an IUD at the program clinics. The information obtained from each of the almost 11,000 acceptors was nearly identical with that obtained from the women in the Household Survey. One important additional question that was asked of each acceptor was the source of her knowledge about the experimental program.

If the acceptor had been visited at home and her home visit record was filed at the place where she accepted, her acceptance record was attached to it. Some women accepted at clinics other than those where their home visit records were on file. The matching of these acceptance records and the home visit records filed elsewhere was carried out by the public health nurses from the Taiwan Population Studies Center, who regularly visited all the health stations to code the information needed from the records.

The acceptance records of those in the Intensive Survey sample were also collated with their interview records.

From the acceptance records and the various interview records, then, we could calculate the acceptance rates in the different periods for (1) Taichung's married women 20-39 years of age, (2) the married women 20-39 years of age who lived in the Everything lins and were visited at home, and (3) the married women 20-39 years of age who were interviewed in the Intensive Survey. These rates could be calculated for the different density and treatment areas of Taichung, for different demographic and social strata of Taichung's general population of married women 20-39 years old, and especially for those in the Everything lins. For the sizable number of acceptors from outside Taichung we could not calculate acceptance rates, but could determine their demographic and social characteristics and compare them on this basis with those who accepted from the city.

G. MEDICAL FOLLOW-UP

All of the IUD acceptors were followed up at regular intervals by a special staff as part of a medical and demographic study of the IUD.

This study has been described in some detail in Chapter X. We need add here only that where desirable, it was possible to match the records of this medical follow-up with the other sources of data, provided that the acceptors fell into the samples in question.

H. REGISTRATION DATA

The household register[9] was an indispensable source of lists of persons and households for the sampling designs and also of tabulated data on the characteristics of the population throughout the study. These data, in their detail and accuracy and in the geographic units represented, are virtually unique for a developing country. In some respects they are superior to the data available for a developed country such as the United States.

The household registration system of Taiwan is based on the Household Registration Act, initially enacted in Mainland China in 1931 and amended in Taiwan most recently in 1954. The current Taiwan system is a modification of the system installed by the Japanese during the island's colonial period from 1895 to 1945. The system serves administrative, legal, and statistical purposes. It requires the registration of every person in household units and the possession at all times of an identification card by every person above fourteen years of age. The household head is required to report any change in the composition of the household and in the status of any member through marriage, birth, death, migration, etc., to the local registration office of the township.

The system is administered at the national level by the Interior Ministry, at the provincial level by the Civil Affairs Department, and at the municipal or county level by the local bureaus of civil affairs. Each of the 361 townships or city districts in Taiwan constitutes a household registration unit and is provided with a staff of clerks to handle the day-to-day operation of the system.

In addition to vital statistics about each registrant, his education and occupation are recorded. At the end of each year there is a prov-

[9] For a detailed description of the household registration system in Taiwan, see: *1964 Taiwan Demographic Fact Book*, Department of Civil Affairs, Taiwan Provincial Government, Republic of China, 1965. See also Paul K. C. Liu, "The Use of Household Registration Records in Measuring the Fertility Level of Taiwan," *Economic Papers of the Institute of Economics, Academia Sinica*, Selected English Series, No. 2, Republic of China, September 1967.

ince-wide check on the current status of the households on these items, but the adequacy of this check, especially with regard to the two social characteristics, is doubtful.

The population figures, the age and sex distributions, and the numbers of births, deaths, and marriages are reasonably accurate. The most serious under-reporting apparently occurs in the number of infant deaths and of births that result in infant deaths, as already discussed.

Many of the basic demographic data are quickly available for the province as a whole and for the major cities and the counties on either a monthly or a quarterly basis, and they are available on an annual basis within a year for the 361 townships that comprise the smallest administrative units in Taiwan. Since 1961, not only crude birth rates but also age-specific fertility rates, general fertility rates, and total fertility rates (among several other useful rates) for all administrative levels (province, city and/or county, and township) have been published very quickly. We list here the publications of the household registration system that have been most important and useful for the present study: *The Household Registration Statistics of Taiwan* for: 1946-58, 1959-61, 1962, 1963-64; *Taiwan Demographic Fact Book* for: 1961, 1963, 1964, 1965, 1966; *The Monthly Bulletin of Population Registration Statistics of Taiwan* (since January 1966).

In addition to these published data, many special tabulations were made available to us throughout the study by the Civil Affairs Department of the Provincial Government, the Bureau of Civil Affairs of the Taichung City Government, and the registration sections of Taichung's eight district offices.

I. SCHEDULE A

Taiwan Population Studies Center
Taichung, Taiwan

Study 4
October 1962

TAICHUNG CITY FAMILY AND FERTILITY SURVEY

Sample number:__________, Name of Head of Household:__________, Name of Respondent:__________

Address:___District___Li___Lin___Rd/St___Section___Lane___Alley___No.

[INTERVIEWER: IF THE REGISTERED FAMILY IS NOT LIVING AT THIS ADDRESS, ASK THE CURRENT RESIDENTS IF THEY ARE RELATED TO THE REGISTERED FAMILY AND IN WHAT WAY. AT THE SAME TIME, INQUIRE ABOUT THE HOUSEHOLD COMPOSITION AND IF THERE IS ONE OR MORE MARRIED WOMEN BETWEEN THE AGES 20-39 (THOSE BORN BETWEEN OCTOBER 2 IN THE 11th YEAR OF THE REPUBLIC AND OCTOBER 1 IN THE 31st YEAR OF THE REPUBLIC), CHOOSE ONE AND PROCEED WITH THE INTERVIEW]

☐ Different from the registered family

☐ Related to the registered family
Relationship: __________

☐ Unrelated to the registered family

Information about the registered family: __________
____
____

Record of Calls

Call No.	Date and hour	Interviewer	Outcome of call in detail
1			
2			
3			
4			
5			
6			

Time of interview: From___O'clock___minutes, To___O'clock___minutes
Total____hours____minutes.

Reason for non-interview (DESCRIBE IN DETAIL): __________
____
____

A. Household Composition

A1. First of all, we would like to know how many people live in this household with you and how they are related to your husband. Please tell me who they are.
(ENTER IN THE HOUSEHOLD RECORD FORM ON THE NEXT PAGE IN THE FOLLOWING GENERAL ORDER: R's HUSBAND, RESPONDENT(R), R's CHILDREN, HUSBAND's PARENTS, HUSBAND's BROTHERS AND SISTERS, OTHER RELATIVES AND NON-RELATIVES)

(FOR EACH PERSON LISTED, ASK)

A2. When was he (she) born? (ENTER IN HOUSEHOLD RECORD FORM UNDER "DATE OF BIRTH." ASK THE YEAR AND MONTH OF BIRTH FOR THE RESPONDENT, HER HUSBAND, AND THEIR CHILDREN, BUT ONLY THE YEAR OF BIRTH FOR THE OTHERS)

A3. Are any of these persons only temporarily here?

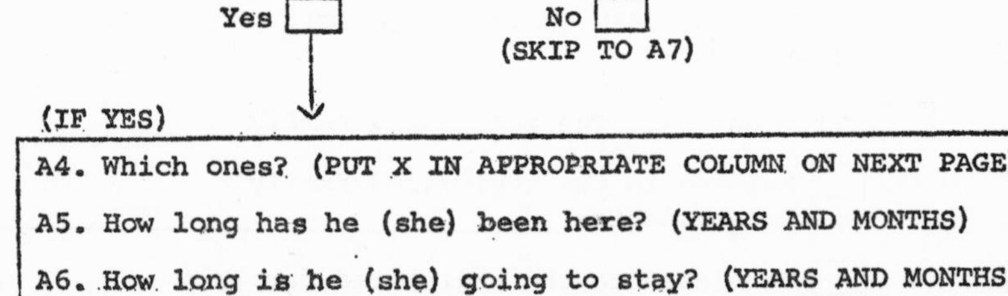

Yes ☐ No ☐
(SKIP TO A7)

(IF YES)

A4. Which ones? (PUT X IN APPROPRIATE COLUMN ON NEXT PAGE)

A5. How long has he (she) been here? (YEARS AND MONTHS)

A6. How long is he (she) going to stay? (YEARS AND MONTHS)

A7. Is there anyone from this household who is temporarily awa

Yes ☐ No ☐
(SKIP TO A14)

(IF YES)

A8. Who is it? (RECORD RELATIONSHIP TO R's HUSBAND)

A9. Anyone else?

(FOR EACH TEMPORARY ABSENTEE, ASK)

A10. When was he (she) born?

A11. Where is he (she) now?

A12. How long has he (she) been away? (YEARS & MONTHS)

A13. How long is he (she) going to be away? (YEARS & MONTH

RECORD RESPONSES TO ABOVE QUESTIONS IN THE HOUSEHOLD RECORD FORM ON THE NEXT PAGE →

Sample No.________

Household Record

		Sex		Birth Date		Temporary resident			Temporary absentee		
o.	Relation-ship to husband	M.	F.	Year	Month	Write X	How long has he been here?	How long is he going to stay?	Present address, name of the coun-ty/city	How long has he been away?	How long is he going to be away?
1	Husband										
2	Wife (R)										
3											
4											
5											
6											
7											
8											
9											
0											
1											
2											
3											
4											
5											
6											
7											
8											
9											
0											
1											
2											
3											
4											
5											

Household Record (Continued from previous page)

No.	Relationship to husband	Sex		Birth Date		Temporary resident			Temporary absentee		
		M.	F.	Year	Month	Write X	How long has he been here?	How long is he going to stay?	Present address, name of the county/city	How long has he been away?	How long is he going to be away?
26											
27											
28											
29											
30											
31											
32											
33											
34											
35											
36											
37											
38											
39											
40											
41											
42											
43											
44											
45											

A14. Who is the head of your household?

Husband ☐ (SKIP TO A16) (Someone else): ______________________ (SPECIFY RELATIONSHIP TO R'S HUSBAND)

A15. Is the head of your household the first son or what? ___s

A16. Is your husband the first son or what? ____son

B. Marriage, Pregnancies and Births

1. We are very much interested in learning where and by whom people generally like to have their babies delivered. If you were to have a baby now, where would you want to have it delivered? (READ OFF THE FOLLOWING ALTERNATIVES AND CHECK THE APPROPRIATE ANSWER OR SPECIFY)

   1. At home ☐
   2. Public hospital ☐
   3. Private obstetrician's clinic ☐
   4. Midwife's clinic ☐
   5. Other (SPECIFY): ______

2. By whom do you expect to have the baby delivered? (READ OFF THE ALTERNATIVES AND CHECK THE APPROPRIATE ANSWER)

   1. Midwife ☐
   2. Doctor ☐
   3. Husband ☐
   4. Mother-in-law ☐
   5. Other relative ☐
   6. Friend ☐
   7. Self ☐
   8. Other (SPECIFY): ______

3. When did you marry your husband? Republic _____year _____month

4. Is this your husband's first marriage?

   Yes ☐ (SKIP TO B6) No ☐

(IF NO)

B5. Did he have any children from his previous marriage?

   Yes ☐ No ☐

6. Is this your first marriage?

   Yes ☐ (SKIP TO B10) No ☐

(IF NO)

B7. How many times have you been married before? _______time(s)

(FOR EACH PREVIOUS MARRIAGE, ASK B8-B9)

	Record of Previous Marriage		
	First	Second	Third
B8. In what year and month did your (first, second, third) marriage begin?	______	______	______
B9. In what year and month did it end?	______	______	______

B10. Let's see, you now have here ____ children, right? (TRANSFER THE BIRTH DATE AND THE SEX OF R'S CHILDREN FROM HOUSEHOLD RECOR FORM TO PREGNANCY RECORD FORM WHILE SPEAKING)

B11. Do you have any other children besides these? For example, those not living with you or whose registration is transferred out from this household?

Yes [ ] No [ ] (SKIP TO B16)

(IF YES)

B12. How many children are there not living with you or not registered with this household? ________

(FOR EACH CHILD NOT LIVING TOGETHER, ASK B13-B15, AND ENTER IN THE PREGNANCY RECORD FORM ACCORDING TO THE ORDER OF PREGNANCY)

B13. When was he (or she) born?

B14. Is it a boy or a girl?

B15. When (YEAR AND MONTH) did he live apart from you?

B16. Do you have any children who are adopted out?

Yes [ ] No [ ] (SKIP TO B21)

(IF YES)

B17. How many children are there adopted out? ________

(FOR EACH CHILD ADOPTED OUT, ASK B18-B20, AND ENTER IN THE PREGNANCY RECORD FORM ACCORDING TO THE ORDER OF PREGNANCY)

B18. In what year and month was this child born?

B19. Is it a boy or a girl?

B20. When (YEAR AND MONTH) did you adopt him (her) out?

Pregnancy Record

Number of preg-nancy	Live birth									Non-live-birth		
	Birth date		Sex		Living apart	Adopt-ed out	Dece-ased	Date of separation, adoption, or death		Date of loss		Still birth miscar-riage, or abortion
	Year	Month	M.	F.				Year	Month	Year	Month	
0												
1												
2												
3												
4												
5												
6												
7												
8												
9												

(INTERVIEWER: AFTER COMPLETING THE PREGNANCY RECORD FORM, RENUMBER ACCORDING TO ORDER OF PREGNANCY IN SPACE PROVIDED TO THE RIGHT IN THE COL. SHOWING "NUMBER OF PREGNANCY." IF NECESSARY, ATTACH SUPPLEMENTARY FORM)

B21. Did any of your children die?

Yes ☐ → (IF ANY CHILD DECEASED)

No ☐ (SKIP TO B26)

(IF ANY CHILD DECEASED)

B22. How many? _________
(FOR EACH DECEASED CHILD, ASK B23-B25 AND ENTER IN THE PREGNANCY RECORD FORM ACCORDING TO ORDER OF PREGNANCY)
B23. In what year and month was this child born?
B24. Was it a boy or a girl?
B25. In what year and month did he (she) die?

B26. Some women, after becoming pregnant, have miscarriages, stillbirths or induced abortions. Apart from the children you told me about above, have you ever had any experience like these?

Yes ☐ → (IF YES)

No ☐ (SKIP TO B30)

(IF YES)

B27. Which pregnancy was it? __________(th) pregnancy
B28. When did it happen? That is, in what year and month?
(INTERVIEWER: ENTER THESE PREGNANCIES BY THEIR ORDER IN THE APPROPRIATE COLUMN BETWEEN LIVE BIRTHS)
B29. Was it a still birth, miscarriage or induced abortion? (SPECIFY IN THE LAST COLUMN)

(INTERVIEWER: GO OVER THE PREGNANCY RECORD. IF THERE IS AN INTERVAL OF TWO YEARS OR MORE BETWEEN THE DATES OF TWO PREGNANCIES, OR SINCE LAST PREGNANCY, ASK B30-B37)

B30. There was quite a long period without pregnancy (between your ___th and ___th pregnancies or since your last pregnancy), did we miss any that occurred in this period?

Yes ☐ → B31

No ☐ → B37

B31. Was it a live birth or what?
(ENTER IN PREGNANCY RECORD FORM)
(IF LIVE BIRTH)
B32. When was he (she) born?
B33. Is it a boy or girl?
B34. Is he (she) still alive
B34a. In what year and month did he (she) die?
(IF NON-LIVE BIRTH)
B35. When did it happen?
B36. Was it a still birth, miscarriage, or induced abortion? (SPECIFY IN THE LAST COLUMN)

B37. Why didn't you become pregnant for such a long period? Was it because your husband was away, you did somethin[g] to avoid getting pregnant, or what?
____
____
____

(IF R HAS HAD ONE OR MORE LONG INTERVALS, PLEASE REPEAT B30-B37 AND ENTER THE RESPONSES IN THE PREGNANCY RECORD FORM) (AFTER OBTAINING A COMPLETE HISTORY OF PREGNANCIES, YOU SHOULD RENUMBER EACH PREGNANCY ACCORDING TO ITS ORDER OF OCCURRENCE. THE NEW NUMBERS SHOULD BE ENTERED IN THE SPACE ON THE RIGHT IN THE COLUMN SHOWING "NUMBER OF PREGNANCY")

(ASK ALL RESPONDENTS)

B38. Are you pregnant now or not?

Yes ☐ No ☐ (SKIP TO B41) Uncertain ☐

(IF YES)

B39. When do you expect it?

________Year ________Month

B40. Why? ________________

____

B41. Has your husband ever been away from home continuously for three months or more? (INCLUDE PERIODS IN EVERY MARRIAGE)

Yes ☐ No ☐ (SKIP TO C1)

(IF YES)

B42. Between which pregnancies was it?
(PROBE) Any other time?

Between which two pregnancies?	Number of months absent?
Between ___(th) and ___(th)	_______ Months
Between ___(th) and ___(th)	_______ Months
Between ___(th) and ___(th)	_______ Months
Between ___(th) and ___(th)	_______ Months

B43. Between these two pregnancies, how many months did you not see each other due to his absence? (ASK FOR EACH PERIOD AND ENTER ABOVE)

C. Fecundity

(C1-C7 ARE ONLY FOR THOSE NOT CURRENTLY PREGNANT. IF PREGNANT, SKIP TO D1)

C1. Some couples cannot have more children because of an operation or physical reasons. How is it with you? Do you think you can have more children?

Cannot ☐ Can ☐ (SKIP TO D1) Not sure ☐ Don't know ☐

C2. Why do you think you can't have more children?

____

____

____

____

____

(IF R MENTIONS OPERATION, SKIP TO C4; IF MENTIONS INTRA-UTERINE RING, SKIP TO D1; OTHERWISE, ASK C3)

C3. Have you or your husband ever had any operation which makes another pregnancy impossible?

Yes ☐ No ☐ (SKIP TO D1)

C4. Who had the operation?

Wife ☐ Husband ☐

C5. When was it done?

________Year ________Month

C6. What kind of operation was it? ____________________

____

____

C7. Why are you not sure (don't know) whether or not you can have more children?

____

____

____

____

____

D. Family Size

(INTERVIEWER: INSPECT THE PREGNANCY RECORD AND COUNT THE NUMBER OF LIVING SONS AND DAUGHTERS. MEANWHILE, BASED ON THE HOUSEHOLD RECORD, COUNT THE NUMBER OF R'S ADOPTED SONS AND DAUGHTERS WHO ARE LIVING WITH HER, AND COMPARE THE TWO TABLES TO FIND OUT THE NUMBER OF SONS AND DAUGHTERS LEFT BY LATE (OR FORMER) WIFE. ENTER THESE NUMBERS IN THE TABLE BELOW)

	No. of living sons	No. of living daughters	Total
Own			
Adopted			
Former wife's			
Total			

D1. Let's see, you have ___ sons and ___ daughters, right? Do you want to have any (more) children?

Want more ☐ ↓

D2. How many (more children) do you want to have?

_____ (more) children

____

____

____

D3. Among these children, how many boys and girls do you want to have?

_____ (more) boys

_____ (more) girls

_____ either sex O.K.

D4. Why do you want ____ (more) children and not more or less?

____

____

____

____

____

Do not want any more ☐ ↓

D9. If you were just married, and you could have just the number of children you want, how many would you consider ideal?

_____ children (child)

____

D10. Among these children, how many boys and girls do you want to have?

_____ boy(s)

_____ girl(s)

_____ either sex O.K.

D11. Why do you want ____ children and not more or less?

____

____

____

____

____

D5. If you were just married and could have just the number of children you want, how many would you consider as ideal?

____ children (child)

D6. Among these children, how many boys and girls do you want to have?

____ boy(s)

____ girl(s)

____ either sex O.K.

D7. Have you ever thought about how frequently you would like to have your children?

Yes ☐ No ☐ (SKIP TO D19)

(IF YES)

D8. How long do you think the interval between each child should be (how many years and months)?

_____ Year(s)

_____ Month(s)

(FOR THOSE WHO HAS AS MANY OR MORE THAN THEIR IDEAL NUMBER OF CHILDREN, ASK D12-D16)

D12. When did you first feel you had enough children? After the birth of which child?

____

D13. After the birth of this child did you do anything to avoid having more children?

Yes ☐ (SKIP TO D15) No ☐

D14. Why didn't you?

____

____

____

____

D15. At the time, were you influenced by anyone to feel that you had enough children?

Yes ☐ No ☐ (SKIP TO D17)

D16. Who was it? (SPECIFY RELATIONSHIP TO RESPONDENT)

____

____

D17. Have you ever thought about how frequently you would like to have your children?

Yes ☐ No ☐ (SKIP TO D19)

(IF YES)

D18. How long do you think the interval between each child should be (how many years and months?

____Year(s) ____Month(s)

D19. Does your husband want to have any (more) children?

Want (more) ☐ — Doesn't want (any more) ☐ — Don't know ☐

D20. How many (more) children does he want?

_______ children (more)

D21. Among the (more) children he wants, how many boys and girls does he expect to have?

______ boy(s) more

______ girl(s) more

______ either sex O.K.

D22. If he could have just the number of children he wants, how many would he consider as ideal?

______ children

D23. Among these children, how many boys and girls would he want to have?

______ boy(s)

______ girl(s)

______ either sex O.K.

D24. Has your husband ever thought about how frequently he would like to have children?

Yes ☐ No ☐ (SKIP TO D31)

(IF YES)

D25. How long does he think the interval between each child should be (how many years and months)?

____Years ____Months

D26. If he could have just the number of children he wants, how many would he consider as ideal?

________ children

D27. Among these children, how many boys and girls would he want to have?

______ boy(s)

______ girl(s)

______ either sex O.K.

D28. Why doesn't he want (more than ____) children?

____

____

____

____

____

____

D29. Has your husband ever thought about how frequently he would like to have children?

Yes ☐ No ☐ (SKIP TO D31)

(IF YES)

D30. How long does he think the interval between each child should be (how many years and months)?

____Years ____Months

(ASK ALL RESPONDENTS)

D31. In general, how many children do you think would be most ideal for the average married couple in Taiwan?

______ children

D32. Among these children, how many should be boys and girls?

______ boy(s)

______ girl(s)

______ either

D33. In your opinion, more than how many children is too many for a couple to have?

More than _____ children   Other response ___________
(SKIP TO D35)

(IF A NUMBER IS GIVEN)

D34. Would ______ children be too many?

Yes ☐   No ☐

D35. In your opinion, fewer than how many children is too few for a couple to have?

Fewer than _____ children   Other response ___________
(SKIP TO D37)

(IF A NUMBER IS GIVEN)

D36. Would _____ children be too few?

Yes ☐   No ☐

D37. Nowadays, there are many people in Taiwan who say that it is not necessary to have as many children as possible, because almost every child now can survive to adulthood. Do you agree with this statement or not?

Agree ☐   Disagree ☐   Other: ________________

E. Attitude and Practice of Family Planning

E1. Nowadays, some married couples do something to keep from getting pregnant too often or having too many children (more than they want). Generally speaking, do you approve or disapprove of their doing this kind of thing?

Approve [ ] Depends [ ] (SKIP TO E6) Disapprove [ ] (SKIP TO E7)

(IF APPROVE)

E2. Do you strongly approve or moderately approve of this?

Strongly approve [ ] Moderately approve [ ]

E3. Why do you feel this way? ______________________

____

E4. Do you approve of young couples doing something to prevent having children right after being married?

Approve [ ] (SKIP TO E12) Depends [ ] (SKIP TO E5a) Disapprove [ ]

(IF DISAPPROVE)
E5. Why do you disapprove? ______________________

____

(IF DEPENDS)
E5a. How do you mean? ______________________

____

(IF DEPENDS)

E6. How do you mean? ______________________

____

(IF DISAPPROVE)

E7. Do you strongly disapprove or moderately disapprove of this?

Strongly disapprove [ ] Moderately disapprove [ ]

E8. Why do you feel this way? ______________________

____

E9. Are there any circumstances which would make you think that it is all right to do something to keep from getting pregnant too often or having too many children?

Yes [ ] No [ ]

(If Yes)	(If No)
E10. What would the circumstance be? ______________	E11. Do you think that every married woman should bear as many children as she can? ______________

E12. How does your husband feel about married couples doing something to keep from getting pregnant too often or having too many children (more than they want)? Does he disapprove or approve of this or what?

Disapprove ☐ Approve ☐ Other ______________ (SKIP TO E14)

E13. Is his feeling about this very strong, strong, or not so strong?

Very strong ☐ Strong ☐ Not so strong ☐

E14. Have you and your husband ever talked about doing something to keep from getting pregnant too often or having too many children (more than you want)?

Ever ☐ Never ☐ (SKIP TO E17)

(IF EVER)

E15. Would you say you talk about this very often, sometimes, or once in a while?

Very often ☐ Sometimes ☐ Once in a while ☐

E16. When was the last time you talked about this?

____

E17. Have you ever talked with your relatives about keeping from getting pregnant too often or having too many children (more than one wants)?

Yes ☐ No ☐ (SKIP TO E20)

(IF YES)

E18. Would you say that you talk about this very often, sometimes, or once in a while?

Very often ☐ Sometimes ☐ Once in a while ☐

E19. When was the last time you talked about this?

____

E20. Have you ever talked with your neighbors about keeping from getting pregnant too often or having too many children (more than one wants)?

Yes ☐ No ☐ (SKIP TO E23)

(IF YES)

E21. Would you say that you talk about this very often, sometimes, or once in a while?

Very often ☐ Sometimes ☐ Once in a while ☐

E22. When was the last time you talked about this? ______________

E23. Have you ever talked with your friends other than your neighbors about keeping from getting pregnant too often or having too many children?

Yes ☐ No ☐
(SKIP TO E26)

(IF YES)

E24. Would you say that you talk about this very often, sometimes, or once in a while?

Very often ☐ Sometimes ☐ Once in a while ☐

E25. When was the last time you talked about this?

____

E26. Have you ever talked about this matter with any other people -- such as health worker, midwife, doctor, druggist, or people of this kind?

Yes ☐ No ☐
(SKIP TO E30)

(IF YES)

E27. Whom have you talked with?

1. Health worker ☐
2. Midwife ☐
3. Doctor ☐
4. Druggist ☐
5. Others: ____

E28. Would you say that you talk about this very often, sometimes, or once in a while?

Very often ☐ Sometimes ☐ Once in a while ☐

E29. When was the last time you talked about this?

____

____

E30. Do you know any contraceptive methods that are used by married couples?

(INTERVIEWER: DO NOT SUGGEST ANY METHOD)

Know [ ] Don't know [ ] (SKIP TO E34)

(IF KNOW)

E31. What methods do you know? (CHECK THE FIRST COLUMN OF THE TABLE ON NEXT PAGE AND PROBE) Do you know of any other methods?

(FOR EACH METHOD KNOWN, REPEAT E32 - E33, AND ENTER IN THE TABLE ON NEXT PAGE)

E32. Where did you first learn about this method?

(PROBE FOR THE PLACE, PERSON, OR PERIODICAL FROM WHICH SHE LEARNED ABOUT THIS METHOD. RECORD IN DETAIL.)

E33. Do you actually know how to use this method or only know that there is such a method?

FOR ALL RESPONDENTS: BRIEFLY EXPLAIN THE CONTRACEPTIVE METHODS WHICH SHE DIDN'T MENTION IN E31. AND FOR EACH OF THESE METHODS, REPEAT E34-E36, AND ENTER IN THE TABLE ON NEXT PAGE. PUT A CHECK IN FIRST COLUMN FOR THOSE GIVEN VOLUNTARILY AND IN SECOND COLUMN FOR THOSE SUGGESTED BY INTERVIEWER IN E34.)

E34. Here are some other methods which married couples use to keep from having too many children (more than they want). Do you know ____________________ (method)?

(IF KNOWS, PUT A CHECK IN SECOND COLUMN ON THE TABLE ON NEXT PAGE, AND ASK E35 - E36.)

E35. From where or whom did you first learn about this method?

(PROBE FOR THE PLACE, PERSON, OR PERIODICAL FROM WHICH SHE LEARNED ABOUT THIS METHOD. RECORD IN DETAIL.)

E36. Do you actually know how to use this method or only know that there is such a method?

(IF THE RESPONDENT MENTIONS RING, COIL, OR PILL, PLEASE PROBE AS THE TABLE ON NEXT PAGE INDICATES. ENTER THE RESPONSES.)

Record of Knowledge on Contraception

Name of contraceptive methods	Yes to E31	Yes to E34	Source of first knowledge	Only heard about it	Know how to use it
1. Condom					
2. Foam tablet					
3. Jelly					
4. Diaphragm					
5. Rhythm					
6. Rhythm/Basal temp.					
7. Coitus interruptus					
8. Ring					
(IF KNOWS ABOUT THIS METHOD) A. When did you first learn about this method? (ASK FOR YEAR AND MONTH) ______ B. Does this kind of method appeal to you? Yes ☐ No ☐ Other ___ C. Why? ______					
9. Coil					
(IF KNOWS ABOUT THIS METHOD) A. When did you first learn about this method (ASK FOR YEAR AND MONTH) ______ B. Does this kind of method appeal to you? Yes ☐ No ☐ Other ___ C. Why? ______					
10. Pill					
(IF KNOWS ABOUT THIS METHOD) A. When did you first learn about this method? (ASK FOR YEAR AND MONTH) ______ B. Does this kind of method appeal to you? Yes ☐ No ☐ Other ___ C. Why? ______					
11. Vasectomy					
12. Ligation					
13. Others:*					

*Suggest to the respondent that others include douche, Chinese herb, etc.

E37. Have you ever used any of the methods I mentioned a moment ago?

Yes [ ] ↓ (IF YES)

No [ ] (SKIP TO E50)

	First method	Second method	Third method	Fourth method	Fifth method
E38. What was the first method you and your husband ever used? What was the second? And next? (PROBE) Is there any other method you have used (INCLUDING DOUCHE)					
E39. Are you currently using any method? (IF YES) What is it? Is there any other method you are using? (INCLUDING DOUCHE)					
E40. When did you first start using this method? Was it before 1st pregnancy or after which pregnancy was it? (FOR EACH METHOD USED, ASK THIS QUESTION)					
E41. Did someone suggest that you use this method? (IF YES) Who was it? (FOR EACH METHOD USED, ASK THIS QUESTION)					
E42. Were (are) you satisfied or dissatisfied with this method? Why? (FOR EACH METHOD USED, ASK THIS QUESTION)					
E43. (IF CURRENTLY USING) Do you and your husband use this method always, sometimes, or once in a while? (ASK FOR EACH METHOD CURRENTLY USING)					
E44. (IF APPLICABLE) Where do you usually get your supply? At a drug store, health station, or where?					

(IF YES TO E37)

E45. Have you ever become pregnant when you and your husband were using contraception?

Yes [ ] No [ ] (SKIP TO E50)

(IF YES)

E46. Which pregnancy occurred when you were trying to keep from becoming pregnant? (ENTER IN FOLLOWING TABLE, AND PROBE) Was there any other?

Order of preg-nancy	Method used	Conceived after use stopped	Conceived during use	Regularity of use

(FOR EACH PREGNANCY CONCEIVED DURING USE OF CONTRACEPTION, REPEAT E47 - E49 AND ENTER ABOVE).

E47. What was the method you were using then?

E48. Was it conceived after you stopped using it, or while you were using it?

(IF CONCEIVED DURING USE)

E49. Were you using it (1) all the time; (2) most of the time; (3) now and then; (4) just once in a while?

E50. For various reasons, some women have induced abortions. Do you disapprove or approve of this or what?

Disapprove [ ] Approve [ ] Other: ______

E51. Is your feeling very strong, strong, or not so strong?

Very strong [ ] Strong [ ]

Not so strong [ ]

(PROBE) ______

(IF APPROVE, SKIP TO E54, OTHERWISE ASK E52)

(IF DISAPPROVE OF ABORTION)

E52. Are there any special circumstances that would make you approve of some women having an induced abortion?

Yes [ ] No [ ] (SKIP TO E54)

(IF YES)
E53. What kind of circumstance would make you approve?

____

____

____

(IF THE RESPONDENT IS NOT CURRENTLY USING ANY CONTRACEPTIVE METHODS AND HAS NEVER HAD ANY OPERATION TO KEEP FROM GETTING PREGNANT)

E54. Do you expect to do something to keep from getting pregnant in the future?

Yes [ ] No [ ]

(IF YES)

E55. How many (more) children do you think you will have before you start using contraception?

____ (more) children

____ (more) boy(s)

____ (more) girl(s)

____ Begin right away

E56. Why don't you want to start earlier?

____

____

____

(IF USED ONCE, ASK: Why didn't you use it continuously?)

E57. Do you have any other reason? ____________

____

____

____

(IF NO)

E58. Many women who do not use contraception give birth once in 2 or 3 years until about 45. Do you expect to be the same way or what?

Yes [ ] No [ ] (SKIP TO E60)

E59. Do you think it's all right? Or do you think you might want to do something later on to prevent pregnancy?

All right [ ] (ASK E60)

Do something [ ] (GO BACK TO E55)

(IF NO TO E58, OR ALL RIGHT TO E59)

E60. Why? ____________

____

____

(IF SHE DID NOT MENTION ANYONE DISAPPROVING HER USING CONTRACEPTION IN E56 - E57 OR ANSWERED "NO" TO E54)

E61. Is there anyone who disapproves of your doing something to keep from getting pregnant too often or having too many children (more than you want) -- say, your parents-in-law or someone like that?

Yes ☐ No ☐ (SKIP TO E64)

(IF YES)

E62. Who is it? ______

E63. Why does he (she) disapprove?

______

(IF R OR HUSBAND HAS NOT BEEN STERILIZED, ASK E64 - E66)

E64. Are you interested in learning more about keeping from getting pregnant too often or having too many children (more than you want)?

Yes ☐ No ☐ (SKIP TO E67)

(IF YES)

E65. Do you know from where you can get information of this kind?

Yes ☐ No ☐ (SKIP TO E67)

(IF YES)

E66. Where? ______

(ASK ALL RESPONDENTS)

E67. Do you know how many days in a month a woman can conceive? Would you say several days, ten days, twenty days, every day of the month, or what?

Several days ☐ Ten days ☐

Twenty days ☐ All month ☐

Other: ______

E68. On which days do you think it is easiest to conceive -- a few days just before menstruation, a few days just after menstruation, days in between two menstruations, or what?

Just before ☐ Just after ☐ In between ☐

Other: ______________________________

E69. By the way, is there anyone among your relatives doing something to keep from getting pregnant too often or having too many children (more than they want)?

Yes ☐ No ☐ (SKIP TO E71) Don't know ☐ (SKIP TO E71)

(IF YES)

E70. Would you say that there are many, some, or a few such relatives?

Many ☐ Some ☐ Few ☐

E71. Is there anyone among your neighbors doing this kind of thing?

Yes ☐ No ☐ (SKIP TO E73) Don't know ☐ (SKIP TO E73)

(IF YES)

E72. Would you say that there are many, some, or a few such neighbors?

Many ☐ Some ☐ Few ☐

E73. Are any of your friends apart from your neighbors doing this kind of thing?

Yes ☐ No ☐ (SKIP TO E75) Don't know ☐ (SKIP TO E75)

(IF YES)

E74. Would you say that there are many, some, or a few such friends?

Many ☐ Some ☐ Few ☐

E75. How many people in Taiwan do you think are doing something to keep from getting pregnant too often or having too many children (more than they want)?

No one ☐ Few ☐ Some ☐

Many ☐ Don't know ☐

F. Channel of Communication

F1. Can you read Chinese -- say, a newspaper? Can [ ] Cannot [ ]

F2. Can you read Japanese? Would you say not at all, a little, somewhat, or very well?

Not at all [ ] A little [ ] Somewhat [ ] Very well [ ]

(IF THE RESPONDENT READS CHINESE OR JAPANESE)

F3. Some women have time and chance to read something, but some don't. Do you usually have a chance to read a newspaper? Would you say you read it every day, several times a week, once a week, or never?

Every day [ ] Several times a week [ ]

Once a week [ ] Less often [ ] Never [ ]

F4. In the past three months, did you have a chance to read any magazine?

Yes [ ] No [ ] (SKIP TO F6)

(IF YES)

F5. How many magazines did you read? ______________

F6. In the past six months, did you have a chance to read any book?

Yes [ ] No [ ] (SKIP TO F8)

(IF YES)

F7. How many books did you read? ___________

F8. Have you ever read any article or advertisement on ways to keep from getting pregnant too often or having too many children (more than one wants)?

Very often [ ] Often [ ] Never [ ] (SKIP TO F10)

(IF EVER)

F9. When was the last time? ____________________

F10. Do you usually have a chance to listen to the radio? Would you say every day, several times a week, once a week, less often, or never?

Every day [ ] Several times a week [ ]

Once a week [ ] Less often [ ] Never [ ] (SKIP TO F13)

F11. Have you ever heard any discussion or advertisement on the radio on ways to keep from getting pregnant too often or having too many children?

Very often [ ] Once in a while [ ] Never [ ]

(IF EVER)

F12. When was the last time? ____________________

F13. Some women have time and opportunity to attend meetings, lectures, training sessions, etc., but some don't. For instance, meetings like "Mothers' Meetings" held by health stations or "Lin Meetings." Do you usually attend most of these meetings, some, or not at all?

Most ☐ Some ☐ Not at all ☐ (SKIP TO F15)

(IF EVER)

F14. In the past six months, how many times have you attended this kind of meetings? ______

F15. The Farmers' Association has special classes for housewives like home economics improvement classes, etc. Do you usually attend most of these classes, some, or not at all?

Most ☐ Some ☐ Not at all ☐ (SKIP TO F17)

(IF EVER)

F16. In the past six months, how many times have you attended this kind of classes? ______

(IF EVER ATTENDED MEETINGS, LECTURES, ETC.)

F17. In the meetings you've attended, did you ever discuss the problem of keeping from getting pregnant too often or having too many children?

Very often ☐ Sometimes ☐ Never ☐ (SKIP TO F19)

(IF EVER DISCUSSED)

F18. When was the last time this was discussed? ______

F19. Can your husband read Chinese -- say, a newspaper?

Can ☐ Cannot ☐ (SKIP TO F21)

F20. Does he have any chance to read a newspaper? Would you say everyday, several times a week, once a week, less often, or never?

Everyday ☐ Several times a week ☐

Once a week ☐ Less often ☐ Never ☐

F21. Can your husband read Japanese? Would you say not at all, a little, somewhat, or very well?

Not at all ☐ A little ☐ Somewhat ☐ Very well ☐

G. Extended Family Relations

		Father	Mother
G1.	Are your parents still alive? (CHECK, IF ALIVE)	____	____
G2.	Are your husband's parents still alive?	____	____

(IF ANY OF THE PARENTS ALIVE)

G3. Is any living with you? Yes [ ] No [ ]

G4. Is any living in Taichung City? Yes [ ] No [ ]

G5. Is any living elsewhere in Taiwan? Yes [ ] No [ ]

(IF YES TO G4)

G6. How often do you or your husband visit them (any of them)?

Everyday [ ] Several times a week [ ]

Once a week [ ] Once a month [ ] Less often [ ]

(IF YES TO G5)

G7. How many times did you or your husband visit them (any of them) in the past year?

__________ times

G8. Do you consult with them (any of them) about your affairs?

Yes [ ] No [ ]

(IF YES) (SKIP TO G10)

G9. Do you consult all important things with them, some or only a few?

All [ ] Some [ ] Few [ ]

G10. In the past year, did you or your husband attend family gatherings with other relatives on the following occasions? (READ OFF THE FOLLOWING ITEMS AND CHECK THE APPLICABLE RESPONSES)

(1) Wedding [ ]
(2) Funeral [ ]
(3) Birthday [ ]
(4) Child birth [ ]
(5) Ancestral worship [ ]
(6) New Year [ ]
(7) Festival or worship of god [ ]
(8) Other: ______
______

G11. Taking everything into account, do you or your husband attend all these family gatherings, most of them, some, few, or not at all?

All [ ] Most [ ] Some [ ]

Few [ ] Not at all [ ]

G12. Do you expect to live with your children and grandchildren in your old age? Would you say definitely yes, probably yes, probably no, definitely no?

Definitely yes ☐ Probably yes ☐ Depends or uncertain ☐

Probably no ☐ Definitely no ☐

G13. Even if you do not expect to live with your children and grandchildren in your old age, do you want them to bear most of your living expenses? Would you say definitely yes, probably yes, probably no, or definitely no?

Definitely yes ☐ Probably yes ☐ Depends or uncertain ☐

Probably no ☐ Definitely no ☐

G14. If you have two or more grown sons, do you expect them to live with you in a large household after they are married? What would you say?

Definitely yes ☐ Probably yes ☐ Depends or uncertain ☐

Probably no ☐ Definitely no ☐

G15. In these days, is it very important to have a male heir in a family like yours? Would you say it's important?

Very important ☐ Important ☐ Depends or uncertain ☐

Not so important ☐ Not important at all ☐

G16. If your sons are able to pass examinations, what level of schooling do you expect them to receive?

(1) No need of schooling ☐ (2) ______________________ school

(IF MORE THAN PRIMARY SCHOOL)

G17. Would you want to send your sons to receive ____________ education even if it meant economic hardship or only when it is economically easy?

Regardless of economic hardship ☐

Only when economically easy ☐

G18. How about your daughters? What level of schooling do you expect them to receive?

(1) No need of schooling ☐ (2) ______________________ school

(IF MORE THAN PRIMARY SCHOOL)

G19. Would you want to send your daughters to receive ________ education even if it meant economic hardship, or only when it is economically easy?

Regardless of economic hardship ☐

Only when economically easy ☐

H. Wife's Background Characteristics

Now I would like to ask you something about your background.

H1. What schools have you ever attended? (CHECK ALL THE SCHOOLS ATTENDED)

		Graduated	Not graduated
00. No formal education	☐		
05. Tutored or private classes only	☐	☐	☐
1. Primary school	☐	☐	☐
2. Jr. vocational school	☐	☐	☐
3. Jr. middle school	☐	☐	☐
4. Sr. vocational school	☐	☐	☐
5. Sr. middle school	☐	☐	☐
6. College	☐	☐	☐
7. University	☐	☐	☐

(IF THE RESPONDENT HAD ANY SCHOOLING, ASK H2 AND ENTER ABOVE)

H2. Did you graduate or not? (FROM THE HIGHEST LEVEL OF SCHOOL ATTENDED)

H3. How long have you been living in Taichung City?

Since birth ☐ ↓ ______Year(s) ______Months (SKIP TO H9)

(IF THE RESPONDENT LIVED IN TAICHUNG ALL LIFE)

H4. Is this place a farm?

Yes ☐ ↓ (IF YES)

H5. Have you always lived on a farm?

Yes ☐ (SKIP TO H15) No ☐ ↓

H6. When were you living on a farm? (AGE)

From___to___ years old

From___to___ years old

(SKIP TO H15)

No ☐ ↓ (IF NO)

H7. Have you ever lived on a farm?

Yes ☐ ↓ No ☐ (SKIP TO H15)

H8. When were you living on a farm? (AGE)

From___to___ years old

From___to___ years old

(SKIP TO H15)

(IF THE RESPONDENT HAS NOT LIVED IN TAICHUNG ALL LIFE)

H9. Where were you born? In what province, hsien/city, and township?

_________ Province _________ Hsien/City _________ Township

H10. Was it a village, a small town, a city, or suburb?

Village ☐ Small town ☐ City ☐ Suburb ☐

H11. Where did you live longest before your marriage? Was it a village, a small town, a city, or suburb?

Village ☐ Small town ☐ City ☐ Suburb ☐

H12. Where have you lived longest after your marriage? Was it a village, a small town, a city, or suburb?

Village ☐ Small town ☐ City ☐ Suburb ☐

H13. Have you ever lived on a farm?

Ever ☐ Never ☐ (SKIP TO H15)

(IF EVER LIVED ON A FARM)

H14. When were you living on a farm (AGES)?

From ____ to ____ years old

From ____ to ____ years old

(IF THE RESPONDENT WAS BORN IN TAIWAN)

H15. Are you a Fukienese, Hakka, or what?

Fukienese ☐ Hakka ☐ Other: ____________________

(ASK ALL RESPONDENTS)

H16. Before you were married, did you ever work for someone away from your home?

Yes ☐ No ☐ (SKIP TO H18)

(IF YES)

H17. How many years did you work away from your home?

____________ year(s)

H18. How about it since you were married? Apart from housekeeping, have you ever worked on a farm, in a business, for a relative, or for other people?

Ever worked ☐ Never worked ☐ (SKIP TO H25)

(IF EVER WORKED)

H19. How long have you worked since your marriage? ____ year(s)

H20. When did you stop working?

To the present ☐ Till ____________________

H21. What was your last job?

____

H22. Was your last work your own business or were you working for someone else?

Own ☐ For others ☐

H23. Was this work at home or somewhere else?

At home ☐ Somewhere else ☐

H24. Married women work for various reasons, what has been your main reason for working? Would you say because you like to work, you want to get something extra for yourself or your family, your family really needs the income, or because your family needs helpers?

Like to work ☐ Get something extra ☐

Family needs income ☐ Family needs helper ☐

(IF NEVER WORKED)

H25. If you had a chance to work, do you think you would want to?

Yes ☐ Depends ☐ No ☐ (SKIP TO H27)

(IF YES OR DEPENDS)

H26. What would be your main reason for working? Would you say because you like to work, you want to get something extra for yourself or your family, your family really needs the income, or because your family needs helpers?

Like to work ☐ Get something extra ☐

Family needs income ☐ Family needs helper ☐

(ASK ALL RESPONDENTS)

H27. In general, if there is a proper person to take care of the children, do you think it is all right for a woman to go out to work or should she stay home?

Work outside ☐ Stay home ☐

I. Husband's Background Characteristics

Now, I would like to ask you something about your husband's background.

I1. What schools has your husband ever attended? (CHECK ALL SCHOOLS ATTENDED)

		Graduated	Not graduated
00. No formal education	☐		
05. Tutored or private classes only	☐	☐	☐
1. Primary school	☐	☐	☐
2. Jr. vocational school	☐	☐	☐
3. Jr. middle school	☐	☐	☐
4. Sr. vocational school	☐	☐	☐
5. Sr. middle school	☐	☐	☐
6. College	☐	☐	☐
7. University	☐	☐	☐

(IF HUSBAND HAS ANY SCHOOLING, ASK I2 AND ENTER ABOVE)

I2. Did he graduate (FROM THE HIGHEST LEVEL OF SCHOOL ATTENDED)?

I3. How long has your husband been living in Taichung City?

Since birth ☐ ______Year(s) ______Months
(SKIP TO I9)

(IF HUSBAND LIVED ALL LIFE IN TAICHUNG)

I4. Is this place a farm?

Yes ☐ No ☐

(IF YES)

I5. Has he always lived on a farm?

Yes ☐ (SKIP TO I15) No ☐

I6. When was he living on a farm? (AGE)

From ___to___ years old

From ___to___ years old

(SKIP TO I15)

(IF NO)

I7. Has he ever lived on a farm?

Yes ☐ No ☐ (SKIP TO I15)

I8. When was he living on a farm? (AGE)

From ___to___ years old

From ___to___ years old

(SKIP TO I15)

(IF HUSBAND HAS NOT LIVED ALL LIFE IN TAICHUNG)

I9. Where was he born? In what province, hsien/city, and district/township?

______Province ______Hsien/City ______District/Township

I10. Was it a village, a small town, a city or suburb?

Village ☐ Small town ☐ City ☐ Suburb ☐

I11. Where did he live longest before his marriage? Was it a village, a small town, a city, or suburb?

Village ☐ Small town ☐ City ☐ Suburb ☐

I12. Where has he lived longest after he was married? Was it a village, a small town, a city, or suburb?

Village ☐ Small town ☐ City ☐ Suburb ☐

I13. Has he ever lived on a farm?

Ever ☐ ↓ Never ☐ (SKIP TO I15)

(IF EVER LIVED ON A FARM)

I14. When was he living on a farm (AGES)?

From ____ to ____ years old

From ____ to ____ years old

(IF HUSBAND WAS BORN IN TAIWAN)

I15. Is your husband a Fukienese, Hakka, or what?

Fukienese ☐ Hakka ☐ Other: ____________________

(ASK ALL RESPONDENTS)

I16. What does your husband do to earn a living?

Employed ☐ (SKIP TO I19) Unemployed ☐ ↓

(IF UNEMPLOYED)

I17. How long has he been out of work? ____________________

I18. Has he been looking for work this past month? Yes ☐ No ☐

(ASK ALL RESPONDENTS. USE PAST TENSE WHEN ASKING THOSE UNEMPLOYED)

I19. What kind of work does (did) your husband usually do? Please tell me in as much details as you can. (IF NECESSARY) What does (did) he do on the job on a typical working day?

Title: ____________________ Farmer ☐ (SKIP TO I36)

Description of the job: ______________________________

____

I20. What kind of business is this job in? ________________

I21. How many days did he work in this past month? ________ days

I22. How many hours on the average does he work on a typical working day? On the average ________ hours per day

I23. Is he self-employed or working for someone else?

Self-employed ☐ Working for someone else ☐

I24. Does this business belong to your husband or to some one else in your family?

Husband's ☐ Family's ☐ (SKIP TO I31)

(IF HUSBAND'S)
I25. Is he is partnership with someone?

Yes ☐ No ☐ (SKIP TO I27)

I26. Does he work for someone in the family, for a relative, or someone else?

Family ☐ (SKIP TO I31)

Relative ☐ (SKIP TO I31)

Someone else ☐ (SKIP TO I35)

(IF SELF-EMPLOYED OR IN PARTNERSHIP WITH SOMEONE)

I27. Does he have anyone to help him? Yes ☐ No ☐ (SKIP TO I44)

(IF YES)
I28. How many of them are your family members? ______

I29. How many of them are your relatives? ______

I30. How many of them are hired from outside? ______

(SKIP TO I44) Total: ______

(IF WORKING IN FAMILY OR RELATIVE'S BUSINESS)

I31. Are there other helpers? Yes ☐ No ☐ (SKIP TO I44)

(IF YES)
I32. How many of the helpers are your family members? ______

I33. How many of them are relatives other than members of your family? ______

I34. How many of them are hired from outside? ______

(SKIP TO I44) Total: ______

(IF WORKING FOR SOMEONE ELSE)

I35. How many people usually work at the place (corporation) where your husband is employed?

__________ people (SKIP TO I44)

(IF HUSBAND IS A FULL-TIME OR PART-TIME FARMER)

I36. How much farm land does your family operate? How much of this is owned by your family, and how much is rented?

Size of farm land owned: ______ chia ______ fen

Size of farm land rented: ______ chia ______ fen

Total: ______ chia ______ fen

I37. Does your family own any of the following things or facilities? (READ OFF THE FOLLOWING ITEMS, AND CHECK THE THINGS OWNED)

(1) Cattle (buffalo, ox) ☐

(2) Buffalo cart ☐

(3) Hand tractor ☐

(4) "Rear-car" ☐

(5) Fertilizer bed ☐

(6) Irrigation pump ☐

(7) Space for drying grains, etc. ☐

(8) Granary ☐

(9) Room for drying tobacco leaves ☐

(10) Sprayer ☐

I38. How many of your family members work full-time on the farm?

____

I39. How many of your family members work part-time on the farm?

____

I40. Is there any busy period during the year that you feel short of hands?

Yes ☐ No ☐ (SKIP TO I42)

(IF YES)

I41. How many days are there like this in a year? ______

I42. Is there any lax period on farm during the year?

Yes ☐ No ☐ (SKIP TO I44)

(IF YES)

I43. How many lax months are there in a year?

______________ month(s)

(IF PART-TIME FARMER SKIP TO I49)

(ASK ALL RESPONDENTS)

I44. Apart from the main job mentioned above, does your husband do any other work?

Yes ☐ (ASK I45) No ☐ (SKIP TO I49)

(IF YES)

I45. What does he do? ____________________ Farmer ☐ (GO BACK TO I36)

I46. What kind of business is this in? ____________________

I47. How many days did he work on this job in this last month?

_______________ days

I48. On the day when he works on this job, how many hours a day does he work on the average?

__________ hours

I49. Besides you and your husband, does anyone else in your household have a job?

Yes ☐ No ☐ (SKIP TO I51)

(IF YES)

I50. Does every one share all that he makes with the rest of the household or each keeps his own but gives a certain amount, or what?

Share everything ☐ Support partly ☐

Other: ______________________________

I51. Considering your recent expenses, is your household income adequate? Would you say it's adequate, just balanced, or inadequate

Adequate ☐ Just balanced ☐ Inadequate ☐

I52. If you were to add up all your sources of income, how much would your total household income amount to in this last month? Please give a number on this card which represents your total household income in this last month. (SHOW INCOME CARD)

(1) Under NT$ 500 ☐
(2) NT$ 500-999 ☐
(3) NT$ 1,000-1,499 ☐
(4) NT$ 1,500-1,999 ☐
(5) NT$ 2,000-2,499 ☐
(6) NT$ 2,500-2,999 ☐
(7) NT$ 3,000-3,999 ☐
(8) NT$ 4,000-4,999 ☐
(9) NT$ 5,000 or more ☐

I53. How much was cash income from your husband's job? NT$ ________

(IF NEITHER SELF-EMPLOYED NOR FULL-TIME FARMER)

I54. Do you or your husband receive any other benefits like housing, provision, transportation, insurance, etc.?

Yes ☐ No ☐ (SKIP TO J1)

(IF YES)

I55. What do you receive?

____

J. Household Facilities

J1. Is this house your own?

Yes [ ] (IF YES) — No [ ] (SKIP TO J3)

J2. How much would it cost you per month to rent a house like this?

NT$ ____________

(SKIP TO J7)

(IF NO)

J3. Do you have to pay rent?

Yes [ ] — No [ ]

(If Yes)

J4. How much key money did you have to pay or rent per month you have to pay?

Key money: NT$ ________

Rent per month: ________

(SKIP TO J7)

(If No)

J5. How is that?

J6. How much a month would it cost you to rent a house like this?

NT$ ____________

J7. About how many pings of floor space does this house have?

____________ pings

J8. Do you own any of the following: (ASK FOR EACH ITEM ON THE LIST AND CHECK ITEMS OWNED)

(1) Bicycle [ ]

(2) Radio with record player [ ]

(3) Radio [ ]

(4) Electric fam [ ]

(5) Sewing machine [ ]

(6) Running water [ ]

(7) Electric iron [ ]

(8) Clock and/or watch [ ]

(9) Electric pan [ ]

(10) Motorcycle [ ]

(11) Newspaper subscription [ ]

(12) Private lavatory [ ]

J9. Do you think you might move within the next year or not?

Yes ☐ No ☐ Uncertain ☐

(IF YES)

J10. Where do you think you might move to? ________________

____

____

(IF NECESSARY)

J11. Will you move away from Taichung City or move to another place in Taichung City?

Away from Taichung ☐ Remain in Taichung ☐

J12. Can you give us the name of someone who might have your address after you move away? What is his (her) name? What is the address? (SPECIFIC ADDRESS)

Name: ________________________

Address: ________________________

Interviewer's Report

1. Persons other than the respondent present during interviewing (record as to their relationships to the respondent):

____________ ____________ ____________

____________ ____________ ____________

____________ ____________ ____________

2. Degree of cooperation: Very good ☐ Good ☐ Not so good ☐ Not good at all ☐

3. Reliability of responses: All reliable ☐ Partly reliable ☐ Unreliable ☐

Remarks: ________________________

4. Evaluation of socioeconomic status of the respondent's household:

Upper ☐ Upper middle ☐ Middle ☐ Lower middle ☐ Lower ☐

5. Other comments: ________________________

6. Description of the respondent and the location of the household for aid in re-interviewing. (If necessary, draw a map):

J. HOME VISIT RECORD

I-53

'aiwan Provincial MCHI 'PH Action Program

Sector: I II III Treatment: Ehw Ew Case ID [ ][ ][ ][ ][ ][ ]

Home Visit Record (I)

.. Registration Status:

a. Same household as register: Case is registered ( ) Case is not registered( )

b. Different household from register: Eligible women ( ); the case is one of ____ eligible women in this household
No eligible woman ( )

c. No one living at this address ( ): Explain____________

d. Case picked up in canvass ( ); the case is one of ____ eligible women

. Name of health station:________; 3. Home visitor:______________; 4. Case No.____

. Name of head of household:____________________

. Address:____District____Li____Lin____Rd/St____Section____Lane____Alley____No.

. Data on wife:

a. Name:______________; b. Birthplace:____Province____County/City____District/Township

c. Date of birth:________Year________Month________Day

d. Ethnic status: Mainlander ( ) Fukienese ( ) Hakka ( ) Other____________

e. Highest school attended:____________________ Graduated ( ) or not ( )

f. Can read -- say, a newspaper? Yes ( ) No ( )

g. Date of first marriage: ______Year ______Month ______Day

h. (If remarried) End of first marriage: ______Year ______Month ______Day

Date of second marriage: ______Year ______Month ______Day

. Data on husband:

a. Name:______________; b. Birthplace:____Province____County/City____District/Township

c. Date of birth:________Year________Month________Day

d. Ethnic status: Mainlander ( ) Fukienese ( ) Hakka ( ) Other____________

e. Highest school attended:____________________ Graduated ( ) or not ( )

f. Can read -- say, a newspaper? Yes ( ) No ( )

g. Occupation and position:____________________

. History of pregnancy:

a. Total no. of pregnancies:________ d. Total no. of induced abortions:________

b. Total no. of stillbirths:________ e. Total no. of live births:______ (M__F__)

c. Total no. of miscarriages:________ f. No. of deceased children:______ (M__F__)

. Past use of contraception:

(If ever used) 11. Method used*:____________________

12. After which pregnancy? ____________

Home Visit Record (II)

13. Date of home visit	Yr. Mo. Day	Yr. Mo. Day	Yr. Mo. Day	Yr. Mo. D
14. No. of additional children wife wants	M.:___ F.:___ Total:_______	M.:___ F.:___ Total:_______	M.:___ F.:___ Total:_______	M.:___ F.:_ Total:____
15. No. of additional children husband wants	M.:___ F.:___ Total:_______	M.:___ F.:___ Total_______	M.:___ F.:___ Total:_______	M.L___ F.:_ Total:____
16. Current use of contraception	Yes( ) No( )	Yes( ) No( )	Yes( ) No( )	Yes( ) No(
(If using) 17. Method(s)*				
18. Reaction: Satisfied				
Dissatisfied (Reasons)				
19. Current pregnancy Yes (date due)	Yr. Mo. Day	Yr. Mo. Day	Yr. Mo. Day	Yr. Mo. D
Maybe (date of onset of last menses)	Yr. Mo. Day	Yr. Mo. Day	Yr. Mo. Day	Yr. Mo. D
No (date of onset of last menses)	Yr. Mo. Day	Yr. Mo. Day	Yr. Mo. Day	Yr. Mo. D
20. Outcome of home visit Acceptance				
Currently using				
Sterile: Sterilized	H.( ) W.( )	H.( ) W.( )	H.( ) W.( )	H.( ) W.(
Other operation	H.( ) W.( )	H.( ) W.( )	H.( ) W.( )	H.( ) W.(
Others				
Currently pregnant Will use in future				
Will not use in future				
Irregular menstruation: Will use in future				
Will not use in future				
Want more children Will use in future				
Will not use in future				
Opposed (reasons)				
Others (specify)				
21. If Ehw: Contact with H. at same time				
Contact with H. at different time	Yr. Mo. Day	Yr. Mo. Day	Yr. Mo. Day	Yr. Mo. D
H. not contacted (explain)				

(If Acceptance on Home Visit)

22. Method(s) accepted:_______________ (If intrauterine device, fill out medical repo

(If applicable) 23. Amount of supply distributed:_______________

24. Amount charged: NT$_______________ Free of charge

25. Source of subsequent supplies: Home visitor( ), Health station

Drug store( ), Others_______

26. Date of first follow-up (after 15 days): ___Year ___Month ___

*Use the following abbreviations: CD (condom); FT (foam tablet); J (jelly); DP (diaphra
R (rhythm); BT (basal temperature); IC (coitus interruptus); UR (ring); UC (coil);
UL (loop); US (gut); L (ligation); V (vasectomy); OR (oral pills); DO (douche).

Appendix II-1. Differences Between Mainlanders and Native Taiwanese

A little over 10 per cent of the population of Taiwan are Mainlanders, most of whom came from Mainland China between 1945 and 1949 and settled principally in the cities. In the Intensive Survey sample of Taichung, 25 per cent of the husbands and 13 per cent of the wives were Mainlanders. The Mainlanders tend to be better educated and generally more modern in life style than the native Taiwanese. In the Taichung sample, for example, none of the Mainlander husbands but one in four Taiwanese husbands were farmers; most of the Mainlanders (88 per cent) were employed in non-traditional settings, as public servants or professionals (only 42 per cent of the Taiwanese were employed in similar settings); 61 per cent of the Mainlander husbands but only 16 per cent of the Taiwanese husbands had completed senior high school; and 75 per cent of the Mainlanders but only 13 per cent of the Taiwanese had always lived after marriage in a nuclear rather than the traditional extended family unit. The fertility behavior of the Mainlanders was more modern, too. Their past fertility and preferred family size were both lower than those of the Taiwanese, even after controlling for age and socio-economic differences between these groups. The wives of the Mainlanders were somewhat younger than the wives of the Taiwanese, but more of the former had already used some form of birth control before the program began (50 per cent vs. 31 per cent). Despite these differences between the two groups, the *patterns* of fertility and family planning before the program and of acceptances in the program within each group varied very little from the overall patterns described in this book. A detailed analysis of the pre-program patterns of fertility by ethnic status is available in T. H. Sun's doctoral dissertation: "Socio-Structural Analysis of Fertility Differentials in Taiwan," Department of Sociology, University of Michigan, 1968.

Appendix IV-1. Fecundability Differences

The relatively low fecundity of the less modern couples might possibly be a function of differential under-reporting of the pregnancies that occurred during the first part of married life—quite a long time ago for many couples. This possibility exists, because we know that in developing countries there is a marked tendency to fail to report on births if the child died before the interview date, and particularly if it died shortly after the birth. Mr. Anrudh Jain has concluded that differential under-reporting does not explain the differential fecundability, on the basis of a number of facts. The most important of these is that the differential does not appear to be a function of the age of the respondent, as we would expect would be the case if the memory factor were important.

There are additional reasons for believing that the data are reasonably valid. All the reports on births and deaths of children were checked against the population register, and where discrepancies were discovered the respondent was reinterviewed and a "corrected" birth-pregnancy history developed. The fact that the final survey results give an infant mortality rate much closer to the estimated correct result than does the register itself is further reassuring evidence. Most of the discrepancies between the register and the survey were found to be due to errors in the register.

Appendix VIII-1. Technical Notes for Chapter VIII

1. A respondent is classified as "intending to come soon" if she told the interviewer she would come to a clinic to have an IUD insertion or to obtain contraceptive supplies. In retrospect it might have been better to have tried to make specific appointments for each woman and to have classified as intending to come "soon" only those who made such an appointment. Those who gave various reasons for not coming to the clinic soon were classified as intending acceptance "eventually" if they answered "yes" to the question: "Will you practice family planning later?" It is not always clear that this practice would be within the organized program.
2. *Reasons Given for Intentions about Acceptance.* Strictly speaking, the "reasons" for intention recorded (most completely shown in Table VIII-4) were not always the respondent's explanation of why she stated a particular intention. In some cases we have classified as a "reason" the circumstance reported by the interviewer, even if not specifically stated as a reason by the respondent. For example, this happened regarding some of those who said they intended never to accept and were pregnant. Even some of the "reasons" explicitly given by respondents to explain their intentions should have been probed further, because logically they only explain the unwillingness to accept soon. For example, the women who were pregnant or wanted more children should have been asked whether they intended to use birth control eventually (after the end of the pregnancy) or when they had all the children wanted. One "logical" response that would have still kept women giving it in the "never intend" group would have been that regardless of current circumstances they wanted an unlimited number of children or were opposed to family planning on principle. Another limitation of our data is that we do not have information for all women on some of the circumstances given as an explanation. For example, we only know about lactation or menstruation for those women who gave this as a reason for postponing acceptance or never accepting. It would have been better to get these data for all women.

Appendix X-1. Sample Comparisons As a Check on Selection

Of 7,295 women in the total IUD Medical Follow-Up sample, 650 were not effectively followed up even once, and in the case of another 442, one or more follow-up visits were missing. These two subgroups are compared with the total sample on a number of characteristics. The comparisons, conducted in terms of percentage distributions, are each summarized by an "index of dissimilarity" which is simply one-half of the sum of absolute differences between corresponding percentages. These coefficients are collected in Table X-1a. On the whole,

Table X-1a. Wives Not Followed Up and Wives with One or More Follow-up Visits Missing Compared with All Women Included in the Taichung IUD Medical Follow-up Study

Characteristics	Index of dissimilarity[a/]	
	No follow-up (N=650)	One or more follow-up visits missing (N=442)
Age of wife at first insertion	1.3	2.3
Number of pregnancies at first insertion	1.1	3.6
Contraceptive method used prior to first insertion	7.0	5.3
Number of induced abortions prior to first insertion	2.5	1.1
Areal location	3.2	2.1
Wife's education	4.1	4.5
Husband's education	4.7	2.8
Interval between preceding pregnancy and first insertion	12.4	12.9
Type of device at first insertion	17.4	9.3
Outcome of pregnancy preceding first insertion	0.8	1.9
Calendar date of insertion	27.6	18.6

[a/] Index of dissimilarity equals $\frac{1}{2} \sum|A - B|$, where A is a percentage of wives for whom follow-up data are incomplete and B is the corresponding percentage of wives in the total sample (N = 7295).

agreement is excellent and includes the two most crucial variables, namely, wife's age and her number of pregnancies at time of first insertion. Agreement is poor with respect to type of device at first insertion and interval between preceding pregnancy and first insertion. The two subgroups also differ from the larger sample in their distribution of calendar dates of first insertion, but rates of loss of the device do not vary appreciably by date of insertion.

For the purposes of analysis, these measures of dissimilarity greatly exaggerate the important differences, because what is important is the difference between the figures we use in the main analysis and those we might have had if all women not properly followed up could have been included. Since these groups with missing data are a small part of the total and since they did not differ significantly from the main group that was analyzed on most characteristics, it is clear that their omission cannot significantly affect our conclusions.

Appendix X-2: Use-Effectiveness of Intrauterine Contraception As a Problem in Competing Risks

BY R. G. POTTER, JR.

A. INTRODUCTION

As was argued at the outset of Chapter X, to delineate adequately the protection being conferred by IUD it is necessary to know the proportion of acceptors still wearing the device at specified intervals after insertion, and, for those not still wearing it, the time and circumstance of loss. A problem arises because observation is complete, in the sense of ascertaining when and under what circumstance the device was lost, for only some of the women in any follow-up study of users of the IUD. Other women, usually comprising a majority of the sample, will be classified as continuing users at time of last visit. Naturally, one wants to be able to use these incomplete histories as well as the more complete ones to derive an unbiased picture of retention and loss of IUD as a function of time from first insertion. The "life table" or "actuarial" approach, as it is sometimes called, is designed to meet this problem. Because the useful wearing of an IUD may terminate for any of several reasons—for example, pregnancy, expulsion, or removal of the device—a satisfactory analysis must provide for competing risks. Phrasing it differently, a cohort of IUD acceptors is subject to multiple decrements.

While a great deal of literature exists on the multiple-decrement life table, no extensive account of its application to the problem of measuring contraceptive effectiveness has been published. A substantial part of this appendix is given over to qualitative discussion of basic concepts together with a step-by-step numerical illustration of procedure. Most of the mathematical detail is confined to two subsections (G1 and G2).

B. RELEVANT LITERATURE

During the last decade and a half, the life table approach has been applied to an increasing range of problems and has been the object of numerous theoretical studies as well. A classic introduction of the subject of competing risks is given by Neyman.[1] Three excellent general discussions are those of Berkson and Gage,[2] Dorn,[3] and Cornfield,[4] all of whom are able to cite earlier work. An advanced,

[1] J. Neyman, *First Course in Probability and Statistics*, New York: Henry Holt & Co., 1950, pp. 69-95.

[2] J. Berkson and R. P. Gage, "Calculation of Survival Rates for Cancer," *Proceedings of the Staff Meetings of the Mayo Clinic*, 25, May 1950, 270-86.

[3] H. F. Dorn, "Methods of Analysis for Follow-up Studies," *Human Biology*, 22, December 1950, 238-48.

[4] J. Cornfield, "The Estimation of the Probability of Developing a Disease in the Presence of Competing Risks," *American Journal of Public Health*, 47, May 1957, 601-7.

comprehensive treatment is that of Chiang.[5] Three other useful references are Littell,[6] Elveback,[7] and Kimball.[8]

All but one of the studies cited rest on the simplifying assumption that competing risks vary over time but are constant among individuals at any given point in time. For the sake of expedience, the same assumption is adopted in the present study. A few theoretical treatments feature varying risks among individuals but require that individual risks remain fixed through time.[9] Such a model is not useful in the present context, because there is no way to estimate the manner in which specific risks of loss vary among women as a function of length of time since first insertion.

Use of the actuarial approach to measure contraceptive effectiveness came quite late. As a way of escaping the biases of the classic methodology based on the Pearl pregnancy rate, the single-decrement life table was applied by Potter to both follow-up and retrospective studies of contraceptive effectiveness.[10] Tietze, who contributed in many ways to this technique, took the next step of computing rates of IUD loss specific to different causes of termination, but these rates were not additive.[11] Shortly thereafter a procedure to make specific rates

[5] C. L. Chiang, "A Stochastic Study of the Life Table and Its Applications: III. The follow-up Study with the Consideration of Competing Risks," *Biometrics*, 17, March 1961, 57-78. See also C. L. Chiang, "On the Probability of Death from Specific Causes in the Presence of Competing Risks," *Proceedings of the Fourth Berkeley Symposium on Mathematical Statistics and Probability*, IV, Berkeley and Los Angeles: University of California Press, 1961, 169-80.

[6] A. S. Littell, "Estimation of the T-year Survival Rate from Follow-up Studies over a Limited Period of Time," *Human Biology*, 24, May 1952, 87-116.

[7] L. Elveback, "Estimation of Survivorship in Chronic Disease," *Journal of the American Statistical Association*, 53, June 1958, 420-40.

[8] A. W. Kimball, "Disease Incidence Estimation in Populations Subject to Multiple Causes of Death," *Bulletin de l'Institut International de Statistisque*, 36, 1958, 193-204.

[9] For a succinct review and useful bibliography, see M. C. Sheps, "Characteristics of a Ratio Used to Estimate Failure Rates: Occurrences per Person Year of Exposure," *Biometrics*, 22, June 1966, 310-12, 320-21.

[10] R. G. Potter, "Additional Measures of Use-Effectiveness of Contraception," *The Milbank Memorial Fund Quarterly*, 41, October 1963, Part I, 400-18, and "Application of Life Table Techniques to Measurement of Contraceptive Effectiveness," *Demography*, III, No. 2 (1966), 297-304.

[11] C. Tietze and S. Lewit, "Intra-Uterine Contraception: Effectiveness and Acceptability," in S. J. Segal et al. (eds.), *Intra-Uterine Contraception*, Amsterdam: Excerpta Medica International Congress, 1964, Series No. 86, pp. 98-110.

additive was devised, essentially on a collaborative basis, by Tietze and Potter. It was also found that both types of rates, additive and non-additive, belonged to a larger set of rates, associated with the multiple-decrement life table and treated in the literature cited above. Unfortunately this literature does not provide a life table model precisely matching the study design and measurements of a prospective study of contraceptors. Hence it has been necessary to develop such a model complete with standard errors.

C. BASIC CONCEPTS

To measure adequately the use-effectiveness of IUD, one needs to know for any given length of time since first insertion the proportion of women still retaining the device as well as the proportions losing it to specified causes. The analysis would be simple and straightforward if one knew when and under what circumstance all women in the sample who lost the device did so. Unfortunately, in any follow-up study of users of intrauterine devices, observation will be complete in this sense for only some of the women. Other women are lost to follow-up or observation is truncated by the end of the study, so that an important fraction of the sample must be coded as continuing users when last seen. To increase information and avoid bias one wants to use these incomplete histories as well as the more complete ones when estimating the retention and loss of IUD as a function of time from insertion.

A standard strategy in this kind of situation is to subdivide the time period into subintervals, with the latter measured from some meaningful point in time, and then to organize the data so that for each successive subinterval one knows the number of persons exposed to the risk of a specified event and the number of such events befalling them. One can then compute subinterval rates as well as their complements, the latter interpreted as probabilities of "surviving" the subinterval without the event occurring. Multiplying the first k probabilities of subinterval survival yields the probability of surviving to the end of the kth subinterval, and the complement of this last estimate yields the cumulative proportion expected to experience the event by the end of the period of k subintervals.

Applying this approach to the present problem, one subdivides the observation period of two and a half years into thirty monthly subintervals; the data on first segment length and terminal status are organized so that for each month (measured from time of first insertion) one has the number of women still retaining the device at the start of the month as well as the number of pregnancies, expulsions, removals, and withdrawals from observation that occur during the month. If one is interested in retention and loss of IUD relative to the combined risks of pregnancy, expulsion, and removal, one first calculates monthly rates of loss. The complements of these rates define the monthly probabilities of retaining the device. Multiplying together the first k of these monthly probabilities of retention yields the probability of retaining the device for k months, while the complement of this latter probability defines the cumulative proportion of acceptors expected to lose the device within k months after insertion.

The advantage of the technique is that each incomplete history is being used to contribute one month (or fraction thereof) of experience to every monthly rate it overlaps with.

The above approach has been called the "life table" or "actuarial" approach, to distinguish it from the "ad hoc" or "direct" approach.[12] With the latter method, to derive a probability of surviving a specified risk for k months, one would utilize only histories possibly observable k months or longer (i.e., acceptors coming under observation k months or more before end of the study) and one would have to exclude any case lost to follow-up earlier than k months after insertion. Obviously the direct approach is wasteful of information as well as being extremely awkward in computation, because the fraction of histories eligible for attention keeps shifting as the duration of k months is changed.

The multiple-decrement life table admits of many types of monthly and cumulative rates, only two of which are being used here. What will be called "net rates," following the terminology of Tietze, allow for the presence of competing risks. For example, a net cumulative rate of pregnancy allows for, and is slightly reduced by, some women expelling or removing the device before they have had a chance to become accidentally pregnant. It is a net frequency in the sense that it might have been higher except for the effects of competing risks.

Alternatively, if one wants to estimate what might have been the

[12] Berkson and Gage, *op.cit.*, pp. 270-86.

pregnancy rate in the absence of expulsions and removals, one is dealing with what Tietze calls a "gross" rate. In the absence of competing risks, all women remain exposed to the risk of pregnancy until it occurs. The maximum or gross frequency of pregnancy is being registered in the absence of competing risks.[13]

Net rates have the important property of being additive. The net rates of pregnancy, expulsion, and removal add up to exactly the rate of termination for the three reasons combined. Accordingly, net rates are entirely appropriate if one is describing what is happening in a single sample or if one is seeking information on which to base an extrapolation to durations longer than those actually observed.

However, a difficulty arises when one wishes to compare the pregnancy rates of two different samples. If the net cumulative pregnancy rate in sample B is significantly higher than that in sample A, it may be because the monthly risks of pregnancy are consistently higher in B than in A. It may also be because the competing risks of expulsion and removal are lower in sample B, so that women in this sample are exposed to the risk of pregnancy on average longer than those in A. Indeed, it is possible to have lower monthly rates of pregnancy in B but nevertheless a higher net cumulative rate if the competing risks loss in B are sufficiently lower than those in A. Thus, use of net rates for purposes of comparing levels of a specific risk in two samples does not always lead to simple interpretation.

Better fitted for this task is the gross cumulative rate. Predicated on the assumptions that there is only a single cause of device loss and that all competing risks are eliminated, a gross cumulative rate of pregnancy is a pure function of the monthly rates of pregnancy and formally independent of the level of competing risks. Hence, in the example above, given lower monthly rates of pregnancy in B than A, one can be assured that a lower gross cumulative rate will be calculated for B. In this fashion, gross rates produce sample comparisons of simpler meaning.

D. QUALIFICATION

It is well to point out two of the conditions necessary if the life table approach is to yield unbiased results. In the case of the single-

[13] What are being termed "net" and "gross" rates in this report, Neyman (*op.cit.*, p. 71) has called "crude" and "net" rates and Cornfield (*op.cit.*, p. 603) has called "mixed" and "pure" rates.

decrement life table, if women lost to follow-up are a selected group, so that those who remain under observation are also selected, then naturally the monthly rates based on the latter's experience are bound to be biased. This point is so obvious that it hardly needs stress.

It may not be so obvious that a similar possibility of bias exists when one passes from net to gross rates. If risks of pregnancy, expulsion, and removal as they vary among women are intercorrelated, then gross rates will be only partially effective in their appointed task of eliminating the effects of differing levels of competing risks in a comparison of a particular risk in two different samples. For example, suppose that risks of pregnancy, expulsion, and removal are positively intercorrelated. Suppose, further, that samples A and B are identical in their compositions of pregnancy risk, but that in sample B the incidence of expulsion and removals is much higher than in A. Because of the positive association among different risks, the higher frequencies of expulsion and removal in B would accelerate the screening out of pregnancy-prone women, so that at any time after first insertion, the women in B still wearing the device would be selected for low pregnancy risk to a greater extent and would therefore tend to generate lower monthly rates of pregnancy than the women in A. In this situation, use of gross rates would not wholly eliminate the effects of differing levels of competing risk on pregnancy rates, though doubtless it would eliminate most of the effect.

E. ASSUMPTIONS

As a last preliminary before going into procedural detail, it is useful to collect together and to comment briefly upon the various assumptions to be made. In the case of 650 uncoded first segments, basic information was missing because not even a single follow-up visit was achieved. Six assumptions may be listed:

1. With uncoded first segments excluded from analysis, the remaining first segments are each associated with a length and a terminal status. Length is measured in terms of ordinal months, defined more carefully in the next section. A terminal status reduces to one of the following mutually exclusive categories: pregnancy, device expelled, device removed, continuing user.[14]

[14] Naturally, in some cases it was not altogether clear which terminal status to assign a first segment. As far as possible, uncertainties of coding were resolved in

2. Events terminating segments or observations thereof are distributed uniformly over the month.
3. Uncoded first segments are unselected with respect to relevant risks and may be excluded without biasing results.
4. Cases lost to follow-up in the kth month are unselected relative to the subsample effectively observed during that month.
5. Risks of pregnancy, expulsion, and removal vary as a function of length of time since first insertion, but for a given duration are the same for all women still retaining the device.
6. Sample size is "adequate."

Assumption 1 summarizes the basic coding and its aims. Assumption 2, which is of course only an approximation, is useful for the computation of monthly rates. It means that women who terminate IUD or withdraw from observation during a given month may be thought of as contributing one-half month of exposure during that month. As made clear in the preceding section, assumptions 3 and 4 are necessary for unbiased net or gross monthly rates and assumption 5 is required as well for unbiased gross rates. Actually, a weaker assumption than 5 would serve this last purpose,[15] but assumption 5 is necessary as a basis for deriving the standard errors of monthly rates. It allows one to treat the loss of or failure to lose the IUD for a particular cause after a specified time from insertion as a binomial variate with the number of trials set equal to the adjusted number of exposure-months (defined later). Finally, assumption 6 is required for estimating the standard errors of cumulative rates. The argument used to derive these standard errors involves a series expansion and the ig-

conformity with the recommendations contained in C. Tietze, "Recommended Procedures for the Statistical Analysis of Clinical Data on Intra-Uterine Contraceptive Devices," July 1965, National Committee on Maternal Health, Inc., mimeographed.

[15] Unbiased gross rates are assured even if women vary in their risks of pregnancy, expulsion, and removal provided only that at any point in time the three sets of risks are independent. Given this independence for any duration from insertion, or given assumption 5, an important identity holds for gross cumulative rates. The product of the probabilities of retaining the device k months against the individual gross risks of pregnancy, expulsion, and removal equals the probability of retaining it k months against the three risks combined. For an algebraic proof, see Cornfield, *op.cit.*, pp. 604, 605.

noring of all moments of order greater than second. These neglected terms become smaller as sample size increases.

How unrealistic are assumptions 3 through 6? Concerning assumptions 3 and 4, most of the cases coded as "continuing users" represent women of whom observation was truncated by end of the study. There is little reason to suspect serious bias here, especially since no important differences in risks of pregnancy, expulsion, and removal were found to prevail amongst women classified by calendar date of first insertion.[16] Doubtless the uncoded first segments and cases lost to follow-up are selected, but encouragement to assume that the degree of selectivity is not great is drawn from the comparisons given in Appendix X-1. These show that such women match the total sample closely on most characteristics, including the crucial variables of age and parity at time of first insertion. Even when the differences between these cases with missing data and the total sample are significantly large, they do not affect the crucial differences between the total sample and the large part of the sample followed successfully according to the rules.

In the body of this report a number of differentials involving risks of pregnancy, expulsion, and removal were demonstrated. The very existence of these differentials proves that women do vary in their risks. Inherent in this variation is the possibility of intercorrelation among risks. The only real question is whether the magnitude of these correlations is large enough to distort seriously gross rates. Although the question cannot be answered with finality, indirect evidence casting doubt on the possibility of serious distortion was marshaled in a late section of Chapter X. Assumption 5, then, is certainly not valid, but may not lead to appreciably distorted gross rates or underestimated standard errors.

Finally, what represents an adequate sample size is hard to say. It differs from variable to variable and according to the criterion used. In deference to assumption 6, attention has been restricted to rates based on the first two years, or fraction thereof, of experience following insertion. More than two years after insertion, the number of sample women still under observation becomes sufficiently small so that not only do standard errors for monthly rates become large, but the basis of estimating these errors becomes open to question.

[16] See Chapter X, paragraph 9 of the section entitled "How Demographic and Social Characteristics Affect IUD Termination Rates."

F. A NUMERICAL ILLUSTRATION

1. NOTATION

Length of first segments is measured in terms of ordinal months; that is, it is known only that a segment ends in the first, second, third, etc. month following first insertion. If it ends during the first month—i.e., during monthly interval (0, 1)—it may be as long as 31 days. More generally, if it ends during the $(k+1)$th month—i.e., during monthly interval $(k, k+1)$—it may be as short as k months or as long as k months plus 31 days and averages approximately k months plus 15 days.

A convenient notation that will be used throughout is:

N_x = number of women retaining the device at the start of the monthly interval $(x, x+1)$—i.e., the $(x+1)$th ordinal month.
P_x = number of pregnancies during month $(x, x+1)$.
E_x = corresponding number of expulsions.
R_x = corresponding number of removals.
$T_x = P_x + E_x + R_x$ = total observed terminations during month $(x, x+1)$.
F_x = number of women lost to follow-up during month $(x, x+1)$.
C_x = number of continuing users last observed during month $(x, x+1)$.
$W_x = F_x + C_x$ = total women withdrawing from observation during month $(x, x+1)$.

The subscript x always denotes an integral number of months from time of first insertion. Note that $N_x = N_{x+1} + T_x + W_x$.

2. BASIC DATA

Table X-2a provides the basic information concerning the 6,645 first segments included in the analysis. (Not included in the analysis are the 650 uncoded first segments for which basic information is missing.) To keep the table to a manageable size, attention is confined to the 12-month period following insertion. Some 2,808 women lose the device or withdraw from observation after month 12 (second to last row of Table X-2a).

The segments involving known circumstance of loss are distributed by cause of termination and length in columns 2-4 of Table X-2a,

Table X-2a. First Segments, by Length and Terminal Status

Ordinal month x+1 (1)	Events occurring during ordinal month (x+1): Pregnancies P_x (2)	Expulsions E_x (3)	Removals R_x (4)	Lost to follow-up F_x (5)	Continuing users C_x (6)	Devices lost T_x (7)	With-drawals W_x (8)	All segments $T_x + W_x$ (9)
1	11	167	228	9	115	406	124	530
2	26	106	102	10	135	234	145	379
3	25	95	110	3	66	230	69	299
4	30	82	110	1	66	222	67	289
5	34	56	77	2	106	167	108	275
6	18	44	64	8	106	126	114	240
7	29	43	81	5	209	153	214	367
8	23	42	66	2	139	131	141	272
9	15	38	56	2	125	109	127	236
10	22	28	52	0	169	102	169	271
11	15	23	53	0	217	91	217	308
12	12	16	51	2	290	79	292	371
13 and over	114	86	340	10	2258	540	2268	2808
Total	374	826	1390	54	4001	2590	4055	6645

while the first segments of continuing users or women lost to follow-up are distributed by cause of withdrawal and length in columns 5 and 6. In column 7, P_x, E_x, and R_x values (from columns 2-4) are summed to give T_x values; in column 8, C_x and F_x frequencies are summed to give W_x values; and finally, in column 9, T_x and W_x frequencies are summed to give total number of segments having specified lengths.

3. COMBINED RISKS

Let q_x denote the conditional probability among women who retain the device at time x of losing it during the monthly interval $(x, x + 1)$. Then the probability of retaining it during that month against the combined risks of pregnancy, expulsion, or removal is $p_x = 1 - q_x$. The probability of retaining the device for t months is:

$$P_{0t} = p_0 x p_1 x \ldots x p_{t-1} = \prod_{x=0}^{t-1} p_x,$$

while the cumulative proportion expected to lose the device within t months is

$$Q_{0t} = 1 - P_{0t}.$$

The proportion of the original sample d_x losing it during the $(x + 1)$th month—i.e., monthly interval $(x, x + 1)$—is the first difference

$$d_x = P_{0x} - P_{0(x+1)} = Q_{0(x+1)} - Q_{0x}.$$

It is important to note that q_x is a conditional probability and not a central or m_x type of rate. An approximate estimate of q_x in terms of sample values is

$$\hat{q}_x = (P_x + E_x + R_x)/N_x^*,$$

$$\text{where } N_x^* = N_x - W_x/2.$$

The rationale for this approximate formula is as follows. Withdrawal from observation during month $(x, x+1)$—that is, during the $(x+1)$th ordinal month—is possibly concealing a loss only in the case of W_x women and does not affect the classification of the N_{x+1} women observed long enough to know that they continued wearing the device into the next month or the classification of the T_x women observed long enough to know the circumstance under which they lost the device during the $(x+1)$th month. From assumption 2 of the last section, it may be assumed that the W_x women average 0.5 month of exposure apiece during interval $(x, x+1)$, or $W_x/2$ months in all. From assumptions 3 and 4, it may be assumed that these women are not selected with respect to their risks of pregnancy, expulsion, or removal. Hence, had they remained under observation $W_x/2$ months longer, they would have been expected to contribute an additional $q_xW_x/2$ losses. Accordingly, under conditions of complete observation during month $(x, x+1)$, we would have N_x women at risk and an expected total of $T_x + q_xW_x/2$ devices lost. We require, then, an estimator of q_x such that the following equality holds:

$$\hat{q}_x = \frac{T_x + \hat{q}_x(W_x/2)}{N_x},$$

the solution of which is given by

$$\hat{q}_x = \frac{T_x}{N_x - W_x/2}.$$

From assumption 5 of the last section that all women share the same risks of loss, it follows that $\hat{q}_x$ behaves as a binomial variable. With N_x^* taken as the number of independent trials, its standard error is

$$\hat{s}_{\hat{q}_x} = \left(\frac{\hat{q}_x\hat{p}_x}{N_x^*}\right)^{1/2}.$$

The following approximate standard error for P_{0t} is derived in section G1:

$$\hat{s}_{P_{0t}} = \hat{P}_{0t} \left(\sum_{x=0}^{t-1} \frac{\hat{q}_x}{N^*_x \hat{p}_x} \right)^{1/2} .$$

The next two tables are designed for deriving the above statistics. In Table X-3a, N^*_x values are obtained. Entered into column 2 are values of $T_x + W_x$, the total number of segments ending during each ordinal month. By cumulating these values from the bottom, we obtain in column 3 the N_x values. In column 4, W_x values are repeated

Table X-3a. Derivation of the Adjusted Number of Women Exposed N^*_x[a]

Ordinal month x+1 (1)	All segments $T_x + W_x$ (2)	Women exposed at start of month N_x (3)	Withdrawals W_x (4)	$W_x/2$ (5)	Adjusted number of women exposed N^*_x (6)
1	530	6645	124	62.0	6583.0
2	379	6115	145	72.5	6042.5
3	299	5736	69	34.5	5701.5
4	289	5437	67	33.5	5403.5
5	275	5148	108	54.0	5094.0
6	240	4873	114	57.0	4816.0
7	367	4633	214	107.0	4526.0
8	272	4266	141	70.5	4195.5
9	236	3994	127	63.5	3930.5
10	271	3758	169	84.5	3673.5
11	308	3487	217	108.5	3378.5
12	371	3179	292	146.0	3033.0
13 and over	2808				

[a] Relevant to net rates and rates of device loss for all causes combined.

Table X-4a. Computation of Rates Pertaining to Retention and Loss of Device Relative to All Risks Combined

Ordinal month x+1 (1)	Devices lost T_x (2)	Adjusted number exposed N^*_x (3)	Monthly loss rate $\hat{q}_x$ (4)	Monthly retention rate $\hat{p}_x$ (5)	Cumulative retention rate $\hat{P}_{0(x+1)}$ (6)	Cumulative loss rate $\hat{Q}_{0(x+1)}$ (7)	Standard error of $\hat{P}_{0(x+1)}$ (8)
1	406	6583.0	.061674	.938326	.938326	.061674	.0030
2	234	6042.5	.038726	.961274	.901989	.098011	.0037
3	230	5701.5	.040340	.959660	.865602	.134398	.0042
4	222	5403.5	.041084	.958916	.830039	.169961	.0047
5	167	5094.0	.032784	.967216	.802828	.197172	.0050
6	126	4816.0	.026163	.973837	.781823	.218177	.0052
7	153	4526.0	.033805	.966195	.755394	.244606	.0054
8	131	4195.5	.031224	.968776	.731808	.268192	.0056
9	109	3930.5	.027732	.972268	.711513	.288487	.0058
10	102	3673.5	.027766	.972234	.691757	.308243	.0060
11	91	3378.5	.026935	.973065	.673125	.326875	.0061
12	79	3033.0	.026047	.973953	.655592	.344408	.0063

from the last table, halved in column 5, and the quotients then subtracted from N_x values in order to derive in column 6 the adjusted numbers N_x^* of women exposed.

In Table X-4a, columns 2 and 3 repeat T_x and N_x^* frequencies from the two earlier tables. In column 4, $\hat{q}_x$ values are obtained from T_x/N_x^* and complements taken in column 5 to yield $\hat{p}_x$ values. A cumulative product of entries of the previous column yields the probabilities $\hat{P}_{0(x+1)}$ in column 6, the complements of which give the $\hat{Q}_{0(x+1)}$ entries of column 7. First differences of the figures of column 6—putting $\hat{P}_{00} = 1$—determine the proportion of acceptors estimated to lose the device each successive month. The final column contains the standard errors of $\hat{P}_{0(x+1)}$—which of course apply equivalently to $\hat{Q}_{0(x+1)}$—on the basis of several steps carried out by the computer without intermediate output.

4. NET RATES

Considered next are monthly and cumulative rates of loss for a specific cause, given the presence of competing risks. Illustration is in terms of net rates of expulsion.

Let Q_{xe} denote the conditional probability of a woman who retains the device at time x expelling it during the monthly interval $(x, x+1)$, given pregnancy and removal as competing risks. An estimate of Q_{xe} in terms of sample values is given by

$$\hat{Q}_{xe} = \frac{E_x}{N_x^*} = \left(\frac{E_x}{T_x}\right) \hat{q}_x.$$

The rationale behind this estimate is analogous to that for $\hat{q}_x$. Withdrawal from observation during month $(x, x+1)$ is possibly concealing an expulsion only in the case of W_x women and does not affect the classification of the N_{x+1} women who continue wearing the device into the next month or the classification of the T_x women, for whom circumstance of loss during $(x,x+1)$ is known. The rest of the argument employed to derive an estimate of $\hat{q}_x$ immediately follows. For the standard error of $\hat{Q}_{xe}$ we have:

$$\hat{s}_{\hat{Q}_{xe}} = \left(\frac{\hat{Q}_{xe}(1-\hat{Q}_{xe})}{N_x^*}\right)^{1/2}.$$

The expected proportion of acceptors d_{xe} expelling during the monthly interval $(x, x+1)$ is a product of the proportion P_{0x} still retaining the device at time x against the combined risks of pregnancy, expulsion, and removal times the conditional probability Q_{xe} of expelling during the monthly interval $(x, x+1)$ if the device was in place at the start of the month. Substituting sample values,

$$\hat{d}_{xe} = \hat{P}_{0x}\hat{Q}_{xe}.$$

The cumulative proportion expelling by time t—i.e., by the end of ordinal month t—is simply the sum of expected proportions of acceptors expelling during ordinal month t and earlier months:

$$\hat{Q}_{0te} = \sum_{x=0}^{t-1} \hat{d}_{xe} = \sum_{x=0}^{t-1} \hat{P}_{0x}\hat{Q}_{xe}.$$

A standard error for $\hat{Q}_{0te}$, which has a rather complicated expression, is derived in section G2.

Table X-5a. Computation of Net Rates of Expulsion

Ordinal month $x+1$ (1)	Expulsions E_x (2)	Adjusted number exposed N^*_x (3)	Net monthly rate $\hat{Q}_{xe}$ (4)	Cumulative retention rate: at end of month $\hat{P}_{0(x+1)}$ (5)	Cumulative retention rate: at start of month (6)	Proportion expelling $\hat{d}_{xe}$ (7)	Cumulative net rate of expulsion $\hat{Q}_{0(x+1)e}$ (8)	Standard error of $\hat{Q}_{0(x+1)e}$ (9)
1	167	6583.0	.025368	.938326	1.000000	.025368	.025368	.0019
2	106	6042.5	.017542	.901989	.938326	.016460	.041829	.0025
3	95	5701.5	.016662	.865602	.901989	.015029	.056858	.0029
4	82	5403.5	.015175	.830039	.865602	.013136	.069994	.0032
5	56	5094.0	.010993	.802828	.830039	.009125	.079119	.0034
6	44	4816.0	.009136	.781823	.802828	.007335	.086454	.0035
7	43	4526.0	.009501	.755394	.781823	.007428	.093881	.0037
8	42	4195.5	.010011	.731808	.755394	.007562	.101443	.0038
9	38	3930.5	.009668	.711513	.731808	.007075	.108519	.0040
10	28	3673.5	.007622	.691757	.711513	.005423	.113942	.0041
11	23	3378.5	.006808	.673125	.691757	.004709	.118651	.0042
12	16	3033.0	.005275	.655592	.673125	.003551	.122202	.0043

Table X-5a furnishes the statistics relating to net rates of expulsion. Taken from Table X-2a, the numbers of expulsions E_x occurring during each ordinal month are entered into column 2. The adjusted numbers of women exposed N^*_x, from Table X-4a, are distributed in column 3. In column 4, the net rates of expulsion $\hat{Q}_{xe}$ are calculated by E_x/N^*_x. In column 5, the proportions $\hat{P}_{0(x+1)}$ are repeated from Table X-4a and then repeated again in column 6, but this time are shifted down one position and $\hat{P}_{00} = 1.0$ inserted into the position left empty at the top of column 6. In column 5, $\hat{P}_{0(x+1)}$ is interpreted as the expected proportion of acceptors still retaining at the end of the $(x+1)$th ordinal month; whereas in column 6, the same figure is interpreted as the expected proportion of acceptors retaining at the start of the $(x+2)$th month and for that reason is put in the row corresponding to ordinal month $(x+2)$. Entries of columns 4 and 6 are multiplied together in column 7 to give the proportions $\hat{d}_{xe}$ of acceptors expected to expel during months $(x, x+1)$. Cumulative addition of these values from the top in column 8 determines the cumulative proportions of acceptors $\hat{Q}_{0(x+1)e}$ expected to expel by the end of ordinal month $(x+1)$. Standard errors of these cumulative proportions are enumerated in column 9.

Two tables analogous to Table X-5a are necessary to derive statistics relating to net rates of pregnancy and removal.

Incidentally, given that

$$\hat{Q}_{xp} = \frac{P_x}{T_x}\hat{q}_x;\ \hat{Q}_{xe} = \frac{E_x}{T_x}\hat{q}_x;\ \text{and } \hat{Q}_{xr} = \frac{R_x}{T_x}\hat{q}_x,$$

it is easy to see that

$$\hat{Q}_{xp} + \hat{Q}_{xe} + \hat{Q}_{xr} = \hat{q}_x,$$

and hence that the three monthly net rates are additive. Further, for the cumulative net rates of pregnancy, expulsion, and removal at the end of t months:

$$\begin{aligned}\sum_{x=0}^{t-1} \hat{P}_{0x}\hat{Q}_{xp} + \sum_{x=0}^{t-1} \hat{P}_{0x}\hat{Q}_{xe} + \sum_{x=0}^{t-1} \hat{P}_{0x}\hat{Q}_{xr} &= \sum_{x=0}^{t-1} \hat{P}_{0x}(\hat{Q}_{xp} + \hat{Q}_{xe} + \hat{Q}_{xr}) \\ &= \sum_{x=0}^{t-1} \hat{P}_{0x}\hat{q}_x \\ &= \sum_{x=0}^{t-1} \hat{d}_x \\ &= \hat{Q}_{0t}.\end{aligned}$$

Hence the three cumulative net rates are also additive.

5. GROSS RATES

Consideration now turns to monthly and cumulative rates of loss for a specific cause when that cause is assumed to be the only one operating in the population. Illustration is again in terms of expulsions.

Let q_{xe} denote the conditional probability of a woman who retains the device at time x expelling it during the monthly interval $(x, x+1)$ in the absence of competing risks. Define $p_{xe} = 1 - q_{xe}$. An approximate estimate of q_{xe} in terms of sample values is

$$\hat{q}_{xe} = \frac{E_x}{N_{xe}^{**}},$$

$$\text{where } N_{xe}^{**} = N_x - (P_x + R_x + W_x)/2.$$

The reasoning is essentially the same as before, except that this time we assume that the P_x and R_x women who lose the device by pregnancy or removal during the monthly interval $(x, x+1)$ average 0.5 months of exposure apiece and that if these two causes were eliminated so that these women might have continued under observation during month $(x, x+1)$ one-half month longer on average, then they would have contributed $q_{xe}(P_x + R_x)/2$ more expulsions. We also assume as before that the W_x women withdrawing from observation during $(x, x+1)$ might have contributed $q_{xe}W_x/2$ expulsions had they remained under observation the entire month. Hence we want an estimator of q_{xe} satisfying the equality

$$\hat{q}_{xe} = \frac{E_x + \hat{q}_{xe}(W_x + P_x + R_x)/2}{N_x},$$

the solution of which is

$$\hat{q}_{xe} = \frac{E_x}{N_{xe}^{**}}.$$

The denominator N_x^{**} for a gross monthly rate varies, depending on which risk is assumed to be operating to the exclusion of others. Thus,

$$N_{xp}^{**} = N_x - (E_x + R_x + W_x)/2,$$

$$N_{xe}^{**} = N_x - (P_x + R_x + W_x)/2, \text{ and}$$

$$N_{xr}^{**} = N_x - (P_x + E_x + W_x)/2.$$

Table X-6a serves the purpose of deriving N_x^{**} values for the three sets of gross monthly rates. Its column headings are self-explanatory.

Once having the gross monthly rates of expulsion, the derivation of cumulative gross rates of expulsion follows exactly the principles by which the cumulative rates of device loss $\hat{Q}_{0t}$ for all reasons combined are derived from the monthly rates $\hat{q}_x$ and $\hat{p}_x$. An estimate of the probability of retaining a device for t months when expulsion is the

Table X-6a. Computation of Adjusted Numbers of Women Exposed with Reference to Gross Rates

Ordinal month x+1	$(E_x + R_x + W_x) \div 2$	$(P_x + R_x + W_x) \div 2$	$(P_x + E_x + W_x) \div 2$	$N^{**}_{xp} = N_x - (2)$	$N^{**}_{xe} = N_x - (3)$	$N^{**}_{xr} = N_x - (4)$
(1)	(2)	(3)	(4)	(5)	(6)	(7)
1	259.5	181.5	151.0	6385.5	6463.5	6494.0
2	176.5	136.5	138.5	5938.5	5978.5	5976.5
3	137.0	102.0	94.5	5599.0	5634.0	5641.5
4	129.5	103.5	89.5	5307.5	5333.5	5347.5
5	120.5	109.5	99.0	5027.5	5038.5	5049.0
6	111.0	98.0	88.0	4762.0	4775.0	4785.0
7	169.0	162.0	143.0	4464.0	4471.0	4490.0
8	124.5	115.0	103.0	4141.5	4151.0	4163.0
9	110.5	99.0	90.0	3883.5	3895.0	3904.0
10	124.5	121.5	109.5	3633.5	3636.5	3648.5
11	146.5	142.5	127.5	3340.5	3344.5	3359.5
12	179.5	177.5	160.0	2999.5	3001.5	3019.0

only risk operative is given by

$$\hat{p}_{0te} = \hat{p}_{0e} x \hat{p}_{1e} x \ldots x \hat{p}_{(t-1)e} = \prod_{x=0}^{t-1} \hat{p}_{xe}.$$

The cumulative gross rate of expulsion by end of month t is simply the complement

$$\hat{q}_{0te} = 1 - \hat{p}_{0te}.$$

A standard error for $\hat{p}_{0te}$ is

$$s_{\hat{p}_{0te}} = \hat{p}_{0te} \left(\sum_{x=0}^{t-1} \frac{\hat{q}_{xe}}{N^{**}_{xe} \hat{p}_{xe}} \right)^{1/2}.$$

Table X-7a. Computation of Gross Rates of Expulsion

Ordinal month x+1	Expulsions E_x	Adjusted number of women exposed N^{**}_{xe}	Gross monthly rate $\hat{q}_{xe}$	Monthly retention rate $\hat{p}_{xe}$	Cumulative retention rate $\hat{p}_{0(x+1)e}$	Cumulative gross expulsion rate $\hat{q}_{0(x+1)e}$	Standard error of $\hat{p}_{0(x+1)e}$
(1)	(2)	(3)	(4)	(5)	(6)	(7)	(8)
1	167	6463.5	.025837	.974163	.974163	.025837	.0020
2	106	5978.5	.017730	.982270	.956890	.043110	.0026
3	95	5634.0	.016862	.983138	.940755	.059245	.0030
4	82	5333.5	.015375	.984625	.926292	.073708	.0034
5	56	5038.5	.011114	.988886	.915997	.084003	.0036
6	44	4775.0	.009215	.990785	.907556	.092444	.0038
7	43	4471.0	.009618	.990382	.898828	.101172	.0040
8	42	4151.0	.010118	.989882	.889733	.110267	.0042
9	38	3895.0	.009756	.990244	.881053	.118947	.0044
10	28	3636.5	.007700	.992300	.874269	.125731	.0045
11	23	3344.5	.006877	.993123	.868257	.131743	.0046
12	16	3001.5	.005331	.994669	.863628	.136372	.0048

These computations are illustrated in Table X-7a. For each ordinal month, the number of expulsions E_x and adjusted numbers of women exposed N^{**}_{xe} are taken from Tables X-2a and X-6a and entered into columns 2 and 3. The division E_x/N^{**}_{xe} yields the gross monthly rates $\hat{q}_{xe}$ in column 4, the complements of which, $\hat{p}_{xe}$, appear in column 5. Cumulative products of the $\hat{p}_{xe}$, multiplying downward, give in column 6 the proportions $\hat{p}_{0(x+1)e}$ retaining the device against the gross risk of expulsion for $(x+1)$ months. Complements are taken in column 7 to derive cumulative proportions expelling in the absence of competing risks. Their standard errors are given in the last column.

Two additional tables of the same format are necessary to derive comparable data respecting gross rates of pregnancy and removals.

6. CONCLUDING REMARKS

Admittedly, computation is heavy and not ordinarily feasible without access to a computer. The above illustration has required eight tables, even though only three causes of device loss were distinguished. With six risks distinguished, the number of tables jumps to fifteen. Furthermore, attention has been restricted to gross and net rates. Yet the multiple-decrement life table admits of a variety of partial rates. For instance, one could seek to answer the question: what would be the cumulative pregnancy rate at the end of *k* months if expulsions occurred, but no removals?

G. STANDARD ERRORS

1. GROSS CUMULATIVE RATE

The derivations of the next two sections are adapted from a proof supplied by Mr. W. Kenneth Poole. The assistance of Professors B. G. Greenberg and N. L. Johnson is also gratefully acknowledged.

We start by deriving a standard error formula for a gross cumulative rate, namely p_{0te}, the probability of retaining the device for t months if expulsion were the only risk of loss operative in the population. We have

$$\hat{p}_{0te} = \hat{p}_{0e}\hat{p}_{1e} \ldots \hat{p}_{t-1,e}$$

$$= \prod_{i=0}^{t-1} \hat{p}_{ie}$$

$$= f(\hat{p}_{0e}, \ldots, \hat{p}_{t-1,e}).$$

We now use the estimation principle that if f is a function of n random variables $\hat{X}_1, \hat{X}_2, \ldots, \hat{X}_n$, then

$$Var\ (f) \doteq \sum_{i=1}^{n} \sum_{j=1}^{n} \left(\frac{\partial f}{\partial \hat{X}_i}\right)\left(\frac{\partial f}{\partial \hat{X}_j}\right) \Bigg|_{\hat{X}=\mu} Cov\ (\hat{X}_i \hat{X}_j)$$

where all partial derivatives $\partial f/\partial \hat{X}_i$ and $\partial f/\partial \hat{X}_j$ are to be evaluated at the expectations of the n random variables $\hat{X}_i$, i.e., at $\mu = (E(\hat{X}_1), E(\hat{X}_2), \ldots, E(\hat{X}_n))$.[17] In the present case, it is assumed that when $j \neq j'$, $\hat{p}_{je}$ and $\hat{p}_{j'e}$ may be taken as uncorrelated so that $Cov(\hat{p}_{je}\hat{p}_{j'e}) = 0$. Accordingly,

$$\begin{aligned} Var\ (\hat{p}_{0te}) &\doteq \sum_{i=0}^{t-1} \sum_{j=0}^{t-1} \left(\frac{\partial \hat{p}_{0te}}{\partial \hat{p}_{ie}}\right)\left(\frac{\partial \hat{p}_{0te}}{\partial \hat{p}_{je}}\right) Cov\ (\hat{p}_{ie}\hat{p}_{je}) \\ &\doteq \sum_{i=0}^{t-1} \left(\frac{\partial \hat{p}_{0te}}{\partial \hat{p}_{ie}}\right)^2 Var\ (\hat{p}_{ie}) \\ &= \sum_{i=0}^{t-1} \left(\frac{p_{0te}}{p_{ie}}\right)^2 \frac{p_{ie}(1 - p_{ie})}{N_i^{**}}. \end{aligned}$$

Since these expected values are unknown, we substitute sample values including

$$N_i^{**} = N_i - W_i/2 - (P_i + R_i)/2,$$

$$\hat{q}_{ie} = 1 - \hat{p}_{ie} = E_i/N_i^{**}.$$

Then

$$\begin{aligned} Var\ (\hat{p}_{0te}) &\doteq \sum_{i=0}^{t-1} \frac{\hat{p}_{0te}^2(1 - \hat{p}_{ie})}{\hat{p}_{ie}N_i^{**}} \\ &= \hat{p}_{0te}^2 \left\{\sum_{i=0}^{t-1} \frac{\hat{q}_{ie}}{\hat{p}_{ie}N_i^{**}}\right\}, \end{aligned}$$

which is the approximate formula originally derived by Greenwood by means of another approach.[18]

2. NET CUMULATIVE RATE

We now consider the standard error of a net cumulative rate, namely $\hat{Q}_{0te}$, the probability of losing the device to expulsion some-

[17] L. Kish briefly discusses this estimation principle and gives additional references: *Survey Sampling,* New York: John Wiley & Sons, 1965, p. 585.

[18] Major Greenwood, "A Report on the Natural Duration of Cancer," *Reports on Public Health and Medical Subjects,* No. 33, London: Ministry of Health, H.M.S.O., 1926, pp. 23–25.

time during the interval $(0, t)$ in the presence of the competing risks of pregnancy and removal.

From earlier results,

$$\begin{aligned}\hat{Q}_{0te} &= P_{00}\hat{Q}_{0e} + \hat{P}_{01}\hat{Q}_{1e} + \cdots + \hat{P}_{0,t-1}\hat{Q}_{t-1,e}\\ &= \hat{Q}_{0e} + \hat{p}_0\hat{Q}_{1e} + \hat{p}_0\hat{p}_1\hat{Q}_{2e} + \cdots + \hat{p}_0\hat{p}_1 \cdots \hat{p}_{t-2}\hat{Q}_{t-1,e}\\ &= \hat{Q}_{0e} + \sum_{i=1}^{t-1}\left(\prod_{j=0}^{i-1}\hat{p}_j\right)\hat{Q}_{ie}.\end{aligned}$$

Study of the last expression shows that $\hat{Q}_{0te}$ is a function of $(t)+(t-1) = 2t-1$ random variables, i.e.,

$$\begin{aligned}\hat{Q}_{0te} &= f(\hat{p}_0, \hat{p}_1, \ldots, \hat{p}_{t-2}, \hat{Q}_{0e}, \hat{Q}_{1e}, \ldots, \hat{Q}_{t-1,e})\\ &= f(\hat{X}_1, \hat{X}_2, \ldots, \hat{X}_{2t-1}).\end{aligned}$$

By our basic estimation principle we have

$$Var\ (\hat{Q}_{0te}) \doteq \sum_{i=1}^{2t-1}\sum_{j=1}^{2t-1}\left(\frac{\partial\hat{Q}_{0te}}{\partial\hat{X}_i}\right)\left(\frac{\partial\hat{Q}_{0te}}{\partial\hat{X}_j}\right)\Bigg|_{\hat{X}=\mu} Cov\ (\hat{X}_i\hat{X}_j).$$

It is assumed that if $j \neq j'$, then $\hat{p}_j$ and $\hat{p}_{j'}$, $\hat{Q}_{je}$ and $\hat{Q}_{j'e}$, and $\hat{p}_j$ and $\hat{Q}_{j'e}$ may be taken as having negligibly small covariances. Hence the above expression reduces to

$$\begin{aligned}Var\ (\hat{Q}_{0te}) \doteq &\sum_{j=0}^{t-2}\left(\frac{\partial\hat{Q}_{0te}}{\partial\hat{p}_j}\right)^2 Var\ (\hat{p}_j)\\ &+\sum_{j=0}^{t-1}\left(\frac{\partial\hat{Q}_{0te}}{\partial\hat{Q}_{je}}\right)^2 Var\ (\hat{Q}_{je})\\ &+2\sum_{j=0}^{t-2}\left(\frac{\partial\hat{Q}_{0te}}{\partial\hat{p}_j}\right)\left(\frac{\partial\hat{Q}_{0te}}{\partial\hat{Q}_{je}}\right) Cov\ (\hat{Q}_{je}\hat{p}_j).\end{aligned}$$

There are five types of terms to be evaluated and in each case we substitute sample values for unknown expected values.

$$Var\ (\hat{p}_j) \doteq \frac{\hat{p}_j(1-\hat{p}_j)}{N_j^*} \qquad j=0, 1, \ldots, t-2$$

$$Var\ (\hat{Q}_{je}) \doteq \frac{\hat{Q}_{je}(1-\hat{Q}_{je})}{N_j^*} \qquad j=0, 1, \ldots, t-1$$

$$Cov\ (\hat{p}_j\hat{Q}_{je}) \doteq \frac{-\hat{Q}_{je}\hat{p}_j}{N_j^*} \qquad j=0, 1, \ldots, t-2$$

$$\frac{\partial \hat{Q}_{0te}}{\partial \hat{p}_j} \doteq \sum_{i=j+1}^{t-1} \frac{\hat{P}_{oi}\hat{Q}_{ie}}{\hat{p}_j} \qquad j=0,1,\ldots,t-2$$

$$\frac{\partial \hat{Q}_{0te}}{\partial \hat{Q}_{je}} \doteq \prod_{i=0}^{j-1} \hat{p}_i \qquad j=1,2,\ldots,t-1$$

$$=1 \qquad j=0$$

H. A COMPARISON OF STANDARD ERRORS

The formulas described above are not the only ones that have been used for computing standard errors of cumulative rates of IUD termination. In 1965, Tietze proposed a simplified estimator of standard errors applicable both to net and gross rates.[19] Subsequently, Tietze developed a second set of formulas. He does not claim statistical rigor for these either, but they are an improvement over those of the first set inasmuch as they are designed to reflect the rapidly increasing instability of cumulative rates when so long a duration from insertion is considered that residual sample size becomes small.

For convenience, we may refer to the "Tietze I" and "Tietze II" formulas and will be comparing them with the "Poole" formulas, derivations for which were given in sections F and G of this appendix. Two criteria will be set forth as a basis for discussing these three sets of estimators. A comparison of standard errors relating to the total Taichung sample is given at the end.

1. CRITERIA OF JUDGMENT

Two criteria useful for judging merit are: (a) rigor from the standpoint of statistical theory; and (b) utility for the following three specific purposes:

(1) to test hypotheses regarding levels of k-month cumulative rates of IUD loss, and more particularly to test the significance of differences between pairs of k-month loss rates;

(2) to indicate how many months a particular life table analysis may be usefully extended before results commence to become so wobbly as to lose interest; and

(3) to estimate in advance the precision to be expected from k-month

[19] Tietze, "Recommended Procedures for the Statistical Analysis of Clinical Data on Intra-Uterine Contraceptive Devices."

cumulative rates, given simplifying assumptions about monthly rates of loss, loss to follow-up, and schedules of insertion.

2. POOLE FORMULAS

These estimators, which have been used in the analyses of the present monograph, may be recommended as the most rigorous of the three sets of formulas from the standpoint of statistical theory. Two important qualifications must be noted, however. First, the formulas are derived on the basis of large sample theory, and consequently in the case of small samples give only approximate standard errors that may tend toward underestimation. Secondly, the Poole formula pertaining to the standard errors of a cumulative net rate is unappealingly complex, even if practicable on an appropriately programmed computer. This complexity renders the Poole formulas virtually useless for purposes of estimating in advance sample sizes needed for specified levels of precision.

3. TIETZE I FORMULAS

To define Tietze's original set of formulas, we may use the notation of section F. The standard error squared of a gross cumulative *k*-month expulsion rate $\hat{q}_{0ke}$ is estimated by

$$\hat{q}_{0ke}(1 - \hat{q}_{0ke})/N/k, \text{ where } N = \sum_{x=0}^{k-1} N_{xe}^{**};$$

while the standard error squared of a net cumulative rate $\hat{Q}_{0ke}$ is given by

$$\hat{Q}_{0ke}(1 - \hat{Q}_{0ke})/N'/k, \text{ where } N' = \sum_{x=0}^{k-1} N_{x}^{*}.$$

The above two formulas are non-rigorous in the sense that they are not derived by any standard technique of estimation from mathematical statistics. As will be shown below, in application to the total Taichung sample of IUD acceptors, the standard errors generated by these formulas remain in good accord with those of the Poole estimators for durations of one year or less from insertion. However, at longer durations, when residual sample size has become small, it becomes obvious that the formulas are not properly sensitive to the rapidly increasing instability of cumulative rates.

The simplicity of the Tietze I formulas makes them the most convenient of the three for purposes of estimating the precision to be expected from a given study design. Here one is trying to predict the standard errors of hypothetical cumulative rates that might result if specified study designs were realized. The specification has to include assumptions about conditional monthly rates of IUD loss and monthly rates of loss to follow-up, as well as the monthly schedule of insertions relative to the cutoff date. In addition, unless k refers to a short duration, any predicted standard error would have to be adjusted upward to allow for the tendency of the Tietze I estimator to yield standard errors that are too small.

4. TIETZE II FORMULAS

To cope with the problem of insensitivity to rapidly dwindling sample size and yet to retain some semblance of simplicity, Tietze has recently proposed another set of formulas. The standard error squared of the gross cumulative k-month rate of expulsion $\hat{q}_{0ke}$ is estimated by

$$\sum_{x=0}^{k-1} \frac{\hat{d}'_{xe}(1-\hat{d}'_{xe})}{N^{**}_{xe}}, \text{ where } \hat{d}'_{xe} = \hat{p}_{0xe} - \hat{p}_{0(x+1)e}.$$

The standard error squared of the net cumulative k-month rate of expulsion $\hat{Q}_{0ke}$ is estimated by

$$\sum_{x=0}^{k-1} \frac{\hat{d}_{xe}(1-\hat{d}_{xe})}{N^{*}_{x}},$$

where $\hat{d}_{xe}$ is given in column 7 of Table X-5a.

It can be seen that the structure of the above formulas is such that when N^*_x (or N^{**}_{xe}) becomes small, then the terms $\hat{d}_{xe}(1-\hat{d}_{xe})/N$ can be large, so that the standard error for a cumulative rate should increase rapidly when residual sample size dwindles to small size. Furthermore, the terms $\hat{d}_{xe}(1-\hat{d}_{xe})/N$ will be larger, for given N, when the monthly proportions expelling $\hat{d}_{xe}$ are larger, which is reasonable. Nevertheless, theoretical rigor cannot be claimed for these formulas any more than for the Tietze I formulas.

5. RESULTS

Standard errors have been computed for the total Taichung sample using Poole, Tietze I, and Tietze II formulas for both net and gross cumulative rates taken at several different durations. This comparison has been repeated for each category of both a detailed and a coarse classification of reason for IUD termination. Results pertaining to losses for all causes (i.e., pregnancy, expulsion, and removal) are given in Table X-8a. Tables X-9a and X-10a furnish standard errors relating to a relatively infrequent cause of loss, namely pregnancy with status of device undetermined. Tables X-11a and X-12a illustrate standard errors respecting a common cause of IUD termination, all removals.

With the standard errors from the Poole formula taken as a standard of 100, those generated by the Tietze I formula remain within a range of essentially 90 to 110 for durations of one year or less and within a range of 85 to 115 for durations up to 2 years. At a duration of 30 months when residual sample size has declined to 20 to 25 women, however, the standard errors from the Tietze I formula are

Table X-8a. Cumulative Rates of IUD Termination for All Causes: Comparison of Standard Errors Computed by Poole, Tietze I, and Tietze II Estimators

Interval from first insertion (months)	N[a]	Standard errors			Relative standard errors		
		Poole P	Tietze I T_1	Tietze II T_2	Poole P	Tietze I T_1	Tietze II T_2
1	6583	.296	.296	.296	100	100	100
3	5702	.424	.436	.455	100	103	107
6	4816	.520	.551	.605	100	106	116
12	3033	.628	.693	.832	100	110	132
18	1671	.723	.800	1.058	100	111	146
24	789	.836	.886	1.333	100	106	159
30	22	3.213	.866	6.689	100	27	208
36	2	5.333	.878	11.990	100	16	225

[a] N = number of women exposed during last month of interval.

Table X-9a. Cumulative Gross Rates of Accidental Pregnancy with Device Status Undetermined: Comparison of Standard Errors Computed by Poole, Tietze I, and Tietze II Estimators

Interval from first insertion (months)	N[a]	Standard errors			Relative standard errors		
		Poole P	Tietze I T_1	Tietze II T_2	Poole P	Tietze I T_1	Tietze II T_2
1	6381	.022	.022	.022	100	100	100
3	5592	.075	.074	.075	100	99	100
6	4755	.115	.114	.116	100	99	101
12	2996	.186	.182	.188	100	98	101
18	1652	.286	.255	.286	100	89	100
24	778	.383	.321	.391	100	84	102
30	21	.828	.403	.846	100	49	102
36	2	.828	.441	.846	100	53	102

[a] N = number of women exposed during last month of interval.

Table X-10a. Cumulative Net Rates of Accidental Pregnancy with Device Status Undetermined: Comparison of Standard Errors Computed by Poole, Tietze I, and Tietze II Estimators

Interval from first insertion (months)	N[a/]	Standard errors			Relative standard errors		
		Poole P	Tietze I T_1	Tietze II T_2	Poole P	Tietze I T_1	Tietze II T_2
1	6583	.021	.021	.021	100	100	100
3	5702	.068	.070	.071	100	103	104
6	4816	.099	.105	.106	100	106	107
12	3033	.145	.161	.164	100	111	113
18	1671	.195	.216	.235	100	111	121
24	789	.240	.264	.305	100	110	127
30	22	.425	.321	.596	100	76	164
36	2	.425	.352	.596	100	83	140

a/ N = number of women exposed during last month of interval.

Table X-11a. Cumulative Gross Rates of Removals of All Types: Comparison of Standard Errors Computed by Poole, Tietze I, and Tietze II Estimators

Interval from first insertion (months)	N[a/]	Standard errors			Relative standard errors		
		Poole P	Tietze I T_1	Tietze II T_2	Poole P	Tietze I T_1	Tietze II T_2
1	6494	.228	.228	.228	100	100	100
3	5642	.323	.329	.334	100	102	103
6	4785	.414	.428	.445	100	103	107
12	3019	.557	.582	.643	100	104	115
18	1663	.702	.715	.859	100	102	122
24	785	.889	.838	1.151	100	94	129
30	22	4.313	.978	6.860	100	23	159
36	2	8.307	1.026	14.204	100	12	171

a/ N = number of women exposed during last month of interval.

Table X-12a. Cumulative Net Rates of Removals of All Types: Comparison of Standard Errors Computed by Poole, Tietze I, and Tietze II Estimators

Interval from first insertion (months)	N[a/]	Standard errors			Relative standard errors		
		Poole P	Tietze I T_1	Tietze II T_2	Poole P	Tietze I T_1	Tietze II T_2
1	6583	.225	.225	.225	100	100	100
3	5702	.313	.322	.326	100	103	104
6	4816	.391	.416	.430	100	106	110
12	3033	.502	.557	.604	100	111	120
18	1671	.606	.681	.788	100	112	130
24	789	.731	.798	1.029	100	109	141
30	22	2.937	.981	5.620	100	33	191
36	2	5.289	1.080	11.428	100	20	216

a/ N = number of women exposed during last month of interval.

usually only one-fourth to one-half the size of those generated by the Poole formula.

Both for net and gross rates, the standard errors estimated by the Tietze II formulas are always as large as or larger than those generated by the Poole formula. The difference grows with increasing length of time from insertion. There is also a tendency for discrepancies to be greater for net cumulative rates than for gross cumulative rates and greater for common causes of loss (illustrated by Tables X-8a, X-11a, and X-12a) than for infrequent causes (illustrated by Tables X-9a and X-10a).

The above comparisons are no more than illustrations and there is no guarantee that another set of data might not produce a quite different set of contrasts between results of the Tietze II and the Poole formulas. For instance, after the twenty-fourth month the Taichung sample tapers more rapidly than would be the case for most samples. Hence the rapidity with which discrepancies develop after the twenty-fourth month between Poole and Tietze I or Poole and Tietze II standard errors is accentuated.

For what they are worth, the above illustrations imply that given a cumulative rate based on a common cause of device loss and on a duration long enough so that at the end of it residual sample size is small, the Tietze II estimator will yield appreciably greater standard errors than the recommended Poole formula corresponding to it. However, in view of the latter's increasingly approximate nature as residual sample size becomes small, this conservatism is not necessarily undesirable.

Appendix X-3. Who Has the IUD Reinserted After a First Termination?

BY R. FREEDMAN AND T. H. SUN

This appendix analyzes some characteristics related to reinsertion in the Taichung IUD Medical Follow-Up study. It is based on data for 2,650 women in the Medical Follow-Up study who had a first termination reported by August 1965, after excluding the 641 cases who were either lost to follow-up or whose reasons for termination were not ascertained. For the remaining 2,650 terminated cases our question is: What factors are related to whether they had the IUD reinserted?

The factors considered in this analysis are as follows:

Demographic factors:

1. Age at first insertion.
2. Number of pregnancies prior to insertion.
3. Number of induced abortions prior to insertion.
4. Number of live births and stillbirths prior to insertion.
5. Open interval prior to insertion.
6. Outcome of unintended pregnancy in the first segment.
7. Termination of last pregnancy prior to insertion.

Socio-economic factors:

8. Education of wife.
9. Education of husband.
10. Occupation of husband.
11. District in which residing.

Clinical factors:

12. Type of device used at first insertion.
13. Date of first insertion.
14. Agent of removal of first IUD.
15. Type of termination of first segment.
16. Number of months of use in first segment.
17. Contraceptive experience prior to insertion.

The data are summarized in Table X-13a, and in the discussion to follow, references are made to the various sections in that table.

Table X-13a. Reinsertion Rate of IUD Acceptors Who Terminated the First Segment by Demographic, Socio-economic, and Clinical Factors

	Reinsertion rate of women who terminated first segment by:					
	All reasons		Involuntary expulsion		Voluntary removals or termination other than involuntary expulsion	
Characteristics	Number	Rate (%)	Number	Rate (%)	Number	Rate (%)
All cases	2650	28.6	839	65.2	1811	11.7
Age of women at first insertion						
13-24	519	28.9	191	62.3	328	9.5
25-29	968	29.4	328	64.3	640	11.6
30-34	731	29.4	212	69.3	519	13.1
35 and over	426	25.1	107	64.5	319	11.9
Not ascertained	6	*	1	*	5	*
Number of pregnancies prior to first insertion						
0-1	123	22.8	45	53.3	78	5.1
2	334	30.8	131	63.4	203	9.9
3	450	30.0	173	60.7	277	10.8
4	525	30.3	165	68.5	360	12.8
5-17	1217	27.3	325	68.3	892	12.3
Not ascertained	1	*	--	--	1	*
Number of induced abortions prior to first insertion						
0	2003	29.8	689	66.0	1314	10.8
1	420	27.9	112	61.6	308	15.6
2-8	226	19.0	38	60.5	188	10.6
Not ascertained	1	*	--	--	1	*
Number of live births and still births prior to first insertion						
0-1	146	21.2	52	50.0	94	5.3
2	430	29.1	158	60.8	272	10.7
3	592	29.7	208	63.9	384	11.2
4	555	31.5	164	75.6	391	13.0
5-17	922	26.9	256	65.2	666	12.2
Not ascertained	5	*	1	*	4	*
"Open pregnancy interval" prior to first insertion						
0-3 months	495	26.3	143	65.0	352	10.5
3-6 months	455	25.7	133	60.2	322	11.5
6-9 months	338	27.5	102	65.7	236	11.0
9-12 months	303	31.7	111	68.5	192	10.4
12 or more months	975	30.7	331	65.6	644	12.7
Not ascertained	84	27.4	19	*	65	13.9

Table X-13a (continued).

Characteristics	Reinsertion rate of women who terminated first segment by: All reasons		Involuntary expulsion		Voluntary removals or termination other than involuntary expulsion	
	Number	Rate (%)	Number	Rate (%)	Number	Rate (%)
Outcome of unintended pregnancy in the first segment in program						
No pregnancy	2247	30.3	839	65.2	1408	9.5
Live birth	32	9.4	--	--	32	9.4
Fetal loss other than induced abortion	42	19.1	--	--	42	19.1
Induced abortion	208	30.8	--	--	208	30.8
Still pregnant	109	--	--	--	109	--
Not ascertained	12	*	--	--	12	*
Termination of last pregnancy prior to insertion						
No pregnancy	4	*	1	*	3	*
Live birth, survived one month or more	2069	30.1	699	66.2	1370	11.6
Live birth, died within a month	17	*	6	*	11	*
Fetal loss other than induced abortion	81	26.0	23	60.9	58	12.1
Induced abortion	429	23.1	100	60.0	329	11.9
Not ascertained	50	26.0	10	*	40	15.0
Wife's education						
No formal education	794	31.7	265	72.1	529	11.5
Primary school	1302	28.2	408	64.2	894	11.7
Junior high school	298	22.8	83	53.0	215	11.2
Senior high school or more	236	29.2	80	60.0	156	13.5
Not ascertained	20	10.0	3	*	17	*
Husband's education						
None	239	32.6	89	74.2	150	8.0
Primary school	1237	29.8	400	65.3	837	12.9
Junior high school	327	25.7	100	64.0	227	8.8
Senior high school or more	804	27.2	241	62.2	563	12.3
Not ascertained	43	18.6	9	*	34	5.9
Occupation of husband						
None	16	*	7	*	9	*
Professional, managerial, officials and proprietor of shops, factories	179	23.5	45	44.4	134	16.4
Clerical and sales workers	872	28.7	273	64.5	599	12.4
Skilled, semi-skilled and farmers	1077	30.5	369	67.8	708	11.0
Security and special services	462	27.1	132	68.2	330	10.6
Not ascertained	44	20.5	13	*	31	6.5

Table X-13a (continued).

	Reinsertion rate of women who terminated first segment by:					
	All reasons		Involuntary expulsion		Voluntary removals or termination other than involuntary expulsion	
Characteristics	Number	Rate (%)	Number	Rate (%)	Number	Rate (%)
Areal location						
Taichung, urban	1266	26.2	369	62.9	897	11.0
Taichung, rural	568	26.8	169	69.2	399	8.8
Taichung, district not ascertained	57	35.1	15	*	42	23.8
Outside Taichung	759	33.6	286	65.7	473	14.2
Type of device at first insertion						
Loop 1	1766	27.1	532	65.4	1234	10.5
Loop 2, 3, 4	224	25.5	77	63.6	147	5.4
Coils and silk gut	660	33.8	230	65.2	430	17.0
Date of first insertion						
July 62-Jan. 63	152	32.2	43	58.1	109	22.0
Feb. 63-Nov. 63	1543	28.2	477	62.5	1066	12.9
Dec. 63-March 64	372	28.2	109	73.4	263	9.5
April 64-Dec. 64	583	29.0	210	68.6	373	6.7
Agent of removal of first IUD						
Expulsion or pregnancy	1238	50.2	837	65.1	401	19.2
M.C.H.I.[a]	1101	9.7	2	*	1099	9.6
Private practitioner	252	7.5	---	---	252	7.5
Patient	38	21.1	---	---	38	21.1
Not ascertained	21	9.5	---	---	21	9.5
Type of termination of first segment						
Unnoticed expulsion	248	63.7	} 839	65.2		
Noticed expulsion	591	65.8				
Medical reason relevant to IUD	941	9.3			} 1811	11.7
Physical reason non-relevant to IUD	191	11.5				
Other medical reason non-relevant to IUD	16	12.5				
Fear of cancer or objection by others	28	10.7				
Changed to other methods	25	12.0				
Request of patient and other non-medical reasons	14	42.9				
Menopause, divorce, separation, widowhood	15	---				
Want more children	177	6.2				
Pregnant, IUD in situ	297	20.9				
Pregnant, not ascertained as to IUD in situ	107	14.0				

[a]M.C.H.I. = Maternal Child Health Institute.

Table X-13a (continued).

	Reinsertion rate of women who terminated first segment by:					
	All reasons		Involuntary expulsion		Voluntary removals or termination other than involuntary expulsion	
Characteristics	Number	Rate (%)	Number	Rate (%)	Number	Rate (%)
Number of months of use, first segment						
0-3	870	38.5	368	71.7	502	14.1
3-6	515	27.2	182	58.8	333	9.9
6-12	665	25.1	190	65.3	475	9.1
12-24	492	20.3	81	58.0	411	12.9
24-37	48	16.7	5	*	43	11.6
Not ascertained	60	13.3	13	*	47	12.8
Contraceptive experience prior to first insertion						
None	1767	29.4	608	66.0	1159	10.3
Ota ring[b/]	221	24.9	61	45.9	160	16.9
Others only	575	28.2	144	71.5	431	13.7
Not ascertained	87	24.1	26	57.7	61	9.8

[b/] Using Ota ring with or without other methods.

* Rate for those categories which have base less than 20 were not calculated.

Of the 2,650 IUD acceptors who terminated the first segment, 29 per cent had had a reinsertion by the time of the last follow-up (before August 1965). Among the factors examined, types of termination of first segment is the one which seems to have the most important effect on reinsertion rate. The difference between those who terminated by involuntary expulsion and those who terminated for other reasons is especially significant: 65 per cent of the former but only 12 per cent of the latter had reinsertions (section 15 of Table X-13a). Variations in reinsertion rates by many of the other factors seem to be related to the difference in expulsion rates. For instance, those who had no experience of pregnancy or induced abortion, those who used loop 1, coil or silkworm gut, and those who terminated the first segment within three months have relatively high reinsertion rates, probably because they also had higher expulsion rates. In order to control for this influence, the 2,650 women were grouped into two categories: those who terminated by involuntary expulsion and those who had the device removed for other reasons such as medical, physical, or psychological considerations, unintended pregnancy, etc.

For all the other factors examined, the reinsertion rate is consistently higher in the involuntary expulsion group than in the other by a very large margin in every category. For the involuntary expulsion group, reinsertion rate is quite high in all strata—never lower than 44 per cent and as high as 75 per cent. For the other group it is relatively low in all strata, ranging from 5 to 31 per cent. This indicates the overriding importance of type of termination in determining whether there is a reinsertion.

In general, reinsertion rates following either expulsion or removals are highest for women who are most strongly motivated as indicated by such phenomena as stage of family growth reached, previous contraceptive history, or outcome of recent pregnancies. For example, reinsertion rates increase with increasing number of births or pregnancies (sections 2 and 4) prior to the first insertion, up to four pregnancies or live births. After that, reinsertion rates level off or decline slightly. It is significant that the reinsertion rates should increase up to four births or pregnancies, because that is the number desired by most of the respondents in the various surveys. A rather large majority of Taiwanese women want three or four children.

A small minority of women became pregnant after the insertion of an IUD (sometimes with the device in place, sometimes not; sometimes the pregnancy had actually begun before the insertion but was not diagnosed at the time of insertion). Among these women with unintended pregnancies, the manner in which the pregnancy ended was strongly associated with the reinsertion rate (section 6). Among 208 women who terminated such an "accidental" pregnancy with an induced abortion, 31 per cent afterwards had an IUD reinserted. Women who use an illegal procedure to terminate a pregnancy are obviously highly motivated, so it is significant that their reinsertion rate is three times the average for reinsertions following "voluntary removals." Among the small group of 42 women whose "accidental" pregnancy terminated in a fetal death reported as involuntary and not induced, the reinsertion rate is also high—about twice the average. We suspect that a significant number of these cases may have had induced abortions not reported as such.

The manner of termination of the last pregnancy *preceding* the first insertion shows significant influence on the reinsertion rate only for those with an involuntary expulsion (section 7). Among these cases, those who had a child surviving at least one month had the highest reinsertion rates. Presumably, these women had the high motivation which comes from additional family growth and a recent reminder that additional children are still likely. We expected those who ended the preceding pregnancy with an induced abortion to have a high reinsertion rate, as was the case where a pregnancy occurred after a first insertion. But this was not the case, and we have no ready explanation. We also do not have any explanation for the fact that there is no systematic association of reinsertion rates by outcome of previous pregnancy for those who terminated the first segment other than by an involuntary expulsion.

The type of IUD first inserted is related to reinsertion rates among those who had other than involuntary expulsion, presumably because in many instances the doctors recommended switching from the types initially used to types later proved to be more satisfactory. Most of the women having insertion in the first stages of the Taichung program had either loop 1 or the coil or silkworm gut. These types were later regarded as less suitable than the larger loops of sizes 2, 3 or 4, so it is not surprising that reinsertion rates are high for those who initially had the less preferred devices. Such women might switch from one type to another at the recommendation of their doctors, without any very serious complaint as grounds, or might be advised to do so when they came in with a complaint (sections 12 and 13). Those who had loops 2, 3, or 4 were more likely to discontinue for quite other reasons and were therefore less likely to have a reinsertion. In the case of involuntary expulsions, the reinsertion rate bears no significant relation to the type of device, because the cause of the removal had nothing to do with the doctor's view of what was the best type of device.

There has been considerable concern about possible rates of removals without reinsertions, either when the woman removes the device herself or when a private practitioner not in the program removes the device. In the first place, the data indicate that not many removals can be attributed to these sources. The proportion of all expulsions or removals attributable to various agents or causes is as follows for all cases and for those terminating for causes other than involuntary expulsion:

Percentage Distribution of Women by Agent of Removal

Agent or cause of removal or expulsion	*All causes terminating first segment*	*Causes other than involuntary expulsion*
Expulsion or pregnancy	47	22
MCHI Clinic	42	61
Private practitioners	9	14
Patient	1	2
Not ascertained	1	1
Total	100%	100%

Secondly, the small number of women who removed the device themselves had very high reinsertion rates, so they must have changed their minds.[1] It is also significant that the reinsertion rate was not much higher when the removal agent was the official MCHI clinic rather than the private practitioner, although the private practitioner in Taichung would probably have a financial incentive to suggest something other than a reinsertion within the program to the patient (section 14).

Reinsertion rates increase moderately with increasing age of wife to a maximum at age 30-34, with a decline for the oldest age group, 35-47 (section 1). The increase in the first three age groups makes sense, since advancing age means more pregnancies and births and therefore greater probability that the desired number of children has already been attained. Presumably this makes for higher motivation. We do not know why this increase should not extend into the oldest age group as well. One possibility is that a significant number of such older women may have turned to the more permanent protection of sterilization, a quite frequent choice among older urban women. We hope to be able to check up on this possibility with data from follow-up visits on this entire sample. Another possibility is that the lower fertility of women in this oldest age group would influence a signifi-

[1] Dr. J. Y. Peng, who directed the action phase of the Taichung study, suggests that in those cases where the woman herself removed the device it was usually partially expelled, so that it would be more appropriate to classify these terminations as due to involuntary expulsion rather than removal.

cant number toward risk-taking when confronted with the disturbing, if minor, side effects that the IUD sometimes brings.

Reinsertion rates are relatively high in both groups of women if the first segment was terminated within three months (section 16). The remaining characteristics, considered generally, yield results which are not consistent with our expectations and for which we do not have plausible explanations even after the fact. We hope to be able to understand some of these results more completely later, with additional data and cross-tabulations from the existing data. We would welcome, in the meantime, plausible suggestions from our readers.

The "open pregnancy interval" prior to the insertion is simply the number of months between the last pregnancy prior to the insertion and the date of the insertion. This variable has been shown to have a substantial relation to the initial insertion rate and to other measures relevant to fertility. We had expected that those with a long open interval would have a low reinsertion rate, both because the motivation of another pregnancy was less recent and because those with longer intervals were more likely to have been successful in avoiding additional pregnancies by the use of some birth control method, perhaps in combination with lower fecundity, which would also decrease motivation for reinsertion. If they had already succeeded in avoiding a pregnancy for a longer period of time, presumably they would have had one or more alternatives to reinsertion. The data do not support this idea at all. There is really no systematic variation in relation to this variable, either for the cases of involuntary expulsion or the other cases (section 5). There may be a basic relationship hidden by the fact that those with longer intervals are likely to be of higher parity, and this is associated with higher rather than lower reinsertion rates. We shall be checking this possibility in the crosss-tabulations.

We had supposed that those with induced abortions prior to the first insertion would be so highly motivated that they would have a high reinsertion rate. This is not the case. The reinsertion rate is highest among those with no previous abortions in the group of women with involuntary expulsions, and the rate goes down slightly further for those with more than one abortion (section 3). In retrospect, it is possible to rationalize this on the grounds that the more the previous experience with abortion, the greater the likelihood that the woman might turn back to this or other alternatives rather than having a reinsertion. We are unable to provide as facile an after-the-fact rationalization for the cases terminated for causes other than involuntary expulsion where reinsertion rates are about equal for those with no or several abortions but significantly higher for those with only one abortion.

Such measures of social status and modernization as education and occupation are related in conflicting ways to reinsertion rates, and it is clear that we must find some other intervening variables to reconcile these various results. Reinsertion rates among those with involuntary expulsions decrease with increasing educational levels for either the wife or the husband. This seems reasonable. Since the better-educated couples are known to have more effective access to alternate methods of family limitation, we expect them to respond to minor side effects more quickly by seeking an alternative. Also, it is likely that the better-educated would be less tolerant of discomfort (sections 8 and 9). This plausible explanation would be more persuasive if it also applied to the other group of women who had terminated for other reasons, but there is no consistent pattern for either the wife's or husband's education in those cases.

For the involuntary expulsions, the reinsertion rates by the occupation of husband follow patterns consistent with those just found for education. Reinsertion rates are higher among the lower status occupations where alternatives are likely to be less frequent. In the case of occupation, however, the removals add another puzzling problem, because the reinsertion rate increases, rather than decreases, with occupational status (section 10).

We had previously found that retention rates were highest among cases coming from outside Taichung, lowest in the cases from urban Taichung, and intermediate in the rural Taichung cases. When we consider all the cases together there are small reinsertion differentials in this direction, but separating the cases into the two types of termination produces mixed results, and it is difficult to explain the pattern that is produced (section 11).

Index

Index

Index